A HISTORICAL
COMMENTARY ON ASCONIUS

A HISTORICAL COMMENTARY ON ASCONIUS

B. A. MARSHALL

UNIVERSITY OF MISSOURI PRESS
COLUMBIA, 1985

Copyright © 1985 by The Curators of the University of Missouri
University of Missouri Press, Columbia, Missouri 65211
Printed and bound in the United States of America
All rights reserved

Library of Congress Cataloging in Publication Data

Marshall, Bruce A.
An historical commentary on Asconius.

Bibliography: p.
1. Asconius Pedianus, Quintus, 9 B.C.–76. Orationum
Ciceronis quinque enarratio. 2. Cicero, Marcus Tullius—
Criticism and interpretation. 3. Rome—History—Republic,
265–30 B.C.—Historiography. I. Title.
PA6284.A3M3 1984   875'.01   84–2231
ISBN 0–8262–0455–4

∞™ This paper meets the minimum requirements of
the American National Standard for Permanence of Paper
for Printed Library Materials, Z39.48, 1984.

PA
6284
.A3
M3
1985

CANISIUS COLLEGE LIBRARY
BUFFALO, N. Y.

For Martin Frederiksen

CONTENTS

Preface ix

Abbreviations xiii

Part I — Introduction

Section One: The Range of Asconius' Commentaries 1

Section Two: The Purpose of Asconius' Commentaries 26

Section Three: The Sources of Asconius' Commentaries 39

Section Four: The Reliability of Asconius 62

Part II - Commentary

The Commentary on the Speech *in Pisonem* 81

The Commentary on the Speech *pro Scauro* 119

The Commentary on the Speech *pro Milone* 159

The Commentary on the Speech *pro Cornelio* 214

The Commentary on the Speech *in toga candida* 281

Bibliography 319

Indices 334

  I. Names and Places
  II. Laws

PREFACE

This book began as a doctoral thesis submitted to the University of Oxford in 1978. Since then I have had the chance to revise the material, in an attempt to take into account some of the recent literature. In some ways the writing of a commentary is a bibliographical exercise, and I am conscious that because of other commitments (which have too long delayed me in getting on with this task) and because of the need to keep the length of the book down (which some will say is already too long), I have not covered all of the literature which has appeared since the thesis was submitted. In particular I have not been able to take much into account material which has appeared in the last two or three years; and in general there could be the criticism that there has been too much reliance on literature in English. Blame both of those shortcomings on the length of time it takes for published work to become available in Australia and the difficulty of access "down under" to European publications.

Even so, with the range of material available and continually appearing on the topics covered by Asconius' commentaries, it would be difficult to keep up. In general a commentary is out-of-date almost as soon as it appears, and it does not seem to me to be a serious fault if the bibliography is not absolutely up-to-the-minute. What I have tried to do is to give a range of references which will provide basic information or a standard view or a starting-point for examining some of the controversies for which Asconius is a source of evidence. It is hoped that these references will be representative of the various different interpretations of these controversies and that they are the sort which should be readily accessible to scholars and students. Commentaries should not attempt idiosyncratic or debatable interpretations: I have aimed to provide a summary of the problems and the standard discussions of them, before putting forward my own conclusions, or in some cases refusing to take sides where the evidence does not seem to lean decisively one way or the other.

Asconius' purpose in writing his commentaries was to explain passages in Cicero's speeches to his sons, not to write an historical treatise. But inevitably his material has come to provide us with historical evidence, and he has become an important historical source in his own right. Hence this book concentrates on the historical events covered by Asconius, and deals with textual problems only incidentally. Asconius' commentaries constitute a veritable mine of information not only on the Ciceronian period but on many other topics referred to by Cicero and explained by Asconius. Consequently the commentary has had to range rather widely in Roman republican history (and even into the early imperial period), and has had to deal with personalities and events which are not strictly mentioned by Asconius himself. This has contributed to the length. Moreover, the same subjects appear repeatedly in different sets of comments and in different contexts; this means that there is a good deal of repeated discussion which also contributes to the length. I have tried to cut down some of the repetition by cross-references, but it did seem to me useful on many occasions to repeat the discussion so that readers would have it in front of them rather than have to turn pages backwards and forwards constantly.

In view of the length, it was not feasible to include a text of Asconius, and so it will be necessary to keep an edition of the author at hand, as well as having many of Cicero's works available. This style of commentary is increasingly popular, and seems to cause few problems. As this book is most likely to be used by scholars working in the field of Roman republican history, or by postgraduate and senior undergraduate students with access to libraries, there should be no problem with access to the necessary texts. The lemmata in the commentary are based on Clark's *OCT* of Asconius, but there should be no difficulty in following the discussion using any one of the other editions.

A number of people and bodies deserve my sincere thanks for help and encouragement at various stages of this project. David Stockton, the supervisor of the original thesis, is to be thanked for his willingness to meet every request for advice and comment; Barbara Levick and Robin Seager, the examiners of the thesis, kindly made detailed written comments available to me to assist in its rewriting for publication; my friends, Erich Gruen and Allen Ward, urged me to keep going at the times when my own enthusiasm for the task was flagging. I am particularly grateful to Martin Frederiksen, my tutor at Worcester College, who encouraged me when I first approached him with the idea for the thesis and who continued to encourage me thereafter until his untimely death.

I am also grateful to Worcester College itself, not only because it provided me with the environment to pursue my studies, but also because it aided me materially with the award of Amphlett of Clent Bursaries which allowed me to continue my doctoral candidature. The University of New England granted me two periods of study leave to pursue my candidature, provided a part-time research assistant at one stage to help with the revision of the thesis for publication, and generously made available a considerable subsidy to assist with the present publication.

Finally, my wife Fern earns my warmest appreciation for tolerating so often my pre-occupation with Asconius over so many years.

Armidale (N.S.W., Australia) Bruce Marshall
June 1984

ABBREVIATIONS

1. The abbreviations used for ancient authors and their works are those found in Liddell, Scott and Jones, *A Greek-English Lexicon*, and Lewis and Short, *A Latin Dictionary*.

2. For periodicals, the system of abbreviations used in *L' Année Philologique* is generally followed, with some slight modifications which should be intelligible.

3. Throughout the book, references to Asconius are by page and line number of Clark's edition (Oxford, 1907) and appear simply in the form, e.g., 84.12. Other scholiasts on Cicero's speeches are referred to by page and line number of Stangl's edition (Vienna, 1912) - e.g. Schol. Bob. 119.2.
   Other editions of Asconius are referred to by the following special abbreviations:
   KS = A. Kiessling and R. Schoell, *Q. Asconii Pediani orationum Ciceronis quinque enarratio* (Berlin, 1875)
   St = T. Stangl, *Ciceronis orationum scholiastae* (Vienna, 1912)
   G   = C. Giarratano, *Q. Asconii Pediani commentarii* (Rome, 1920)

4. The following sigla are used for the manuscripts of Asconius:
   S = Pistoriensis, Forteguerri 37 (copied by Sozomeno)
   P = Matritensis 8514 (formerly X.81) (Poggio's own copy)
   M = Laurentianus LIV.5 (from the apograph of Bartolomeo de Montepulciano)
   P^2 = corrections in the margin of P.

5. Fragments of Cicero's speeches are taken from G. Puccioni, *M. Tulli Ciceronis orationum deperditarum fragmenta* (Milan, 1972), 2nd edn., using the abbreviation P.

6. The following particular works on Asconius are referred to simply by author's name and page number:
   C. Lichtenfeldt, *De Q. Asconii Pediani fontibus ac fide* (Breslau, 1888)
   J.N. Madvig, *De Q. Asconii Pediani et aliorum veterum interpretum in Ciceronis orationes commentariis disputatio critica* (Copenhagen, 1828)
   S.J.E. Rau, *Variarum lectionum liber ad Ciceronis orationes pertinens* (Leiden, 1834)

7. For standard works of reference, the usual practice of abbreviation by initials has been followed.

8. The following special abbreviations for modern works are used:

Badian, *FC* = E. Badian, *Foreign Clientelae (264-70 B.C.)* (Oxford, 1958)
Badian, *Studies* = E. Badian, *Studies in Greek and Roman History* (Oxford, 1964)
Brunt, *Manpower* = P.A. Brunt, *Italian Manpower 225 B.C. - A.D. 14* (Oxford, 1971)
Crawford, *RRC* = M.H. Crawford, *Roman Republican Coinage*, 2 vols (Cambridge, 1974)
Greenidge, *Legal Procedure* = A.H.J. Greenidge, *The Legal Procedure of Cicero's Time* (London, 1901)
Gruen, *Politics and Courts* = E.S. Gruen, *Roman Politics and the Criminal Courts, 149-78 B.C.* (Cambridge, Mass., 1968)
Gruen, *Last Generation* = E.S. Gruen, *The Last Generation of the Roman Republic* (Berkeley and Los Angeles, 1974)
Jones, *Criminal Courts* = A.H.M. Jones, *The Criminal Courts of the Roman Republic and Principate*, ed. J.A. Crook (Oxford, 1972)
Lintott, *Violence* = A.W. Lintott, *Violence in Republican Rome* (Oxford, 1968)
Mommsen, *Staatsrecht* = T. Mommsen, *Römisches Staatsrecht*, 3 vols (Leipzig, 1887)
Münzer, *RA* = F. Münzer, *Römische Adelsparteien und Adelsfamilien* (Stuttgart, 1920)
Platner-Ashby = S.B. Platner, *A Topographical Dictionary of Ancient Rome*, rev. T. Ashby (Oxford, 1929)
SB *Att.* = D.R. Shackleton Bailey, *Cicero's Letters to Atticus*, 7 vols (Cambridge, 1965-70)
SB *Fam.* = D.R. Shackleton Bailey, *Cicero: Epistulae ad Familiares*, 2 vols (Cambridge, 1977)
SB *QF* = D.R. Shackleton Bailey, *Cicero: Epistulae ad Quintum Fratrem et M. Brutum* (Cambridge, 1980)
Sumner, *Orators* = G.V. Sumner, *The Orators in Cicero's Brutus: Prosopography and Chronology* (Toronto, 1973)
TP = R.Y. Tyrrell and L.C. Purser, *The Correspondence of Cicero*, 3rd edn., 7 vols (London, 1904)
Wiseman, *New Men* = T.P. Wiseman, *New Men in the Roman Senate 139 B.C. - 14 A.D.* (Oxford, 1971)

PART I

INTRODUCTION

SECTION ONE

THE RANGE OF ASCONIUS' COMMENTARIES

In the text of Asconius' commentaries as we have it, there are only five speeches commented on. They occur in the order: *in Pisonem, pro Scauro, pro Milone, pro Cornelio,* and *in toga candida*. In chronological order they should be: *pro Cornelio* (delivered in 65), *in toga candida* (delivered just before the consular elections in 64), *in Pisonem* (delivered in early August 55), *pro Scauro* (delivered in September 54), and *pro Milone* (delivered in April 52). It is clear that the commentaries were originally arranged in chronological order, for in the comments on the *in Pisonem* (which now come first) at 9.18 Asconius writes . . . *iam supra dictum est,* when the reference is to one place in the *pro Cornelio* and four in the *in toga candida* (which in our text are placed after the comments on the *in Pisonem*).[1] It is difficult to see why the commentaries should have got out of order. Madvig suggests that there are two possible explanations.[2] One is that the person copying out the manuscript found at St. Gall by Poggio in 1416 found not one codex but several, and copied them out just as they came to hand; in regard to this possible explanation it should be noted that Poggio himself wrote that he had to copy the manuscript out *velociter*.[3] This would also help to explain why material other than Asconian was added to the copy (i.e. Pseudo-Asconius, and the other works contained with Asconius, Quintilian and Valerius Flaccus). The other explanation is that the first three speeches in the text of Asconius as we have it (which do follow in chronological order) had by some accident been placed between the two parts of the commentary on the speech *pro Cornelio*; it may be significant that the comments on the second speech *pro Cornelio* would occupy about a page of manuscript, and that in two of the three main manuscripts copied from the St. Gall exemplar (S and P) there is a separate heading *pro Cornelio* for the comments on the second 'speech', suggesting that the heading was there in the original.[4] It is easy to see how pages could have been wrongly inserted between *pro Cornelio* I and II, and how a copyist might have tried to restore them to some semblance of order. However, the simple explanation for the unusual order may be that the manuscript was copied out hurriedly.

---

[1] Cf. Stangl, n. ad loc. (= 16.22).
[2] Madvig, pp. 32-3; cf. Kiessling and Schoell, intro. pp. xxii-xxiii.
[3] In a letter to Guarini of Verona (quoted in Clark, intro. p. xii); there was a similar letter to John Corvinus of Arrezio (ibid.).
[4] It is a mistake to think of this as a commentary on the second 'speech'; for the nature of this second *pro Cornelio*, see the commentary ad loc. in Part II.

Introduction: Section One

Five is a surprisingly small number of speeches to be commented on, in view of the great number of Cicero's speeches which would have been available to Asconius, and a rather odd selection of speeches, if that is all he chose to comment on. Another surprise is the long time-gap between the two groups of speeches in the commentaries we have: the *pro Cornelio* and *in toga candida* were delivered in successive years in the middle 60's, then a gap of nine years to the *in Pisonem*, the first of the three other speeches commented on (which were all delivered in the space of three years). It is clear that Asconius must have written commentaries on more than the five speeches we have; indeed he would have had to have done so if he were to fulfil his aim of explaining the speeches of Cicero to his sons. What evidence is there for conjecturing that Asconius wrote comments on the other speeches of Cicero?

It would be as well to begin with the internal evidence of Asconius' commentaries themselves. This evidence falls into two categories, the first being straight-out references which indicate a speech or speeches he has commented on, and the second of the sort where he reminds his readers of a point he has already made, by various, almost formulaic, phrases but where we no longer have the point. With both categories it is possible to conjecture specific speeches to which he is referring.[5]

References of the first category:

(1) 6.3-8 (5.14-18 KS, 14.10-13 St, 8.5-9 G):
itaque idem Cicero in ea quoque quam habuit in Catilinam in senatu, † *ait ... octavus decimus dies esset postea quam factum [est] senatus consultum ut viderent consules ne quid res publica detrimenti caperet, dixit vicesimum diem habere [se] s.c. tamquam [in vagina reconditum].*
This refers to *Cat.* 1.4, and of course it may mean no more than that Asconius knew the speech. If he did write a commentary on the *First Catilinarian*, it is reasonable to suppose that he wrote commentaries on the other three.

(2) 10.4-6 (9.9-11 KS, 17.1-2 St, 12.6-8 G):
dictum est in dissuasione legis agrariae apud populum plateam esse Capuae quae Seplasia appellatur, in qua unguentarii negotiari sint soliti.
This refers to *leg. agr.* 2.94; again it could mean no more than Asconius knew the speech, and the piece of information is a

---

[5] The references in brackets are to the page and line numbers in the editions of Asconius by Kiessling and Schoell (= KS), by Stangl (= St), and by Giarratano (= G), included here to make it easier to consult those editions. The text quoted is that of Clark.

common one.[6] Madvig, p. 22 n. 4, followed by Kiessling and Schoell,[7] thinks that this reference indicates a commentary on the *de lege agraria*.

(3) 18.1-2 (16.3-4 KS, 22.3 St, 21.3-4 G):
hanc quoque orationem eisdem consulibus dixit quibus pro Vatinio . . .
That this passage of Asconius suggests a commentary on other speeches, cf. the similar phrasing of the following passage (4). Both Kiessling and Schoell, and Stangl take this to indicate that Asconius had written a commentary on the *pro Vatinio*. The *quoque* suggests that there were further speeches from the same year which Asconius had commented on; Kiessling and Schoell, arguing that it should be a speech which was delivered between the *pro Vatinio* and the *pro Scauro*, pick on the *pro Plancio*.[8] It at least we know to have been written up for publication,[9] and therefore available to Asconius. But other speeches, delivered earlier in the year but now all lost, could just as well be candidates: the speeches *de Reatinorum causa, pro C. Messio,* and *pro Druso*.[10]

---

[6] E.g. Cic. *Sest.* 19; Schol. Bob. 109.11 (on *post red. in sen.* 17).
[7] References to the views of Kiessling and Schoell on this and on subsequent passages of Asconius are to the list of cross-references on pp. xiv-xix of the introduction to their edition; the views of Stangl on the likely point of a cross-reference can be found in his notes ad loc.
[8] They accept the argument of Wunder that the *pro Plancio* was delivered at the end of August or beginning of September. Our only evidence is that it was delivered before Cicero wrote to his brother in September 54 (*Q.f.* 3.1.11), saying that he was writing up the *pro Scauro* and the *pro Plancio* (and he mentions them in that order, suggesting that the *pro Plancio* may have come after the *pro Scauro*). Moreover, we know that the *pro Scauro* was delivered early in September (18.3-4).
[9] Cic. *Q.f.* 3.1.11. Much of the discussion here is based on the assumption that the speeches we know Cicero to have delivered were written up for publication and therefore available to Asconius as possible subjects for a commentary. Certainly speeches which do not seem of much importance were written up (e.g. those mentioned in the next note). Cicero wrote few speeches out fully beforehand; he prepared drafts, which were later written up by Tiro and published as *commentarii* (Quint. 10.7.31). Some speeches appear to have been known only from the *commentarii*, or even only from a *principium* (Ascon. 87.11-12), which might suggest that some speeches were never fully written up. On the whole question, see P. Laurand, *Etudes sur le style des discours de Cicéron*, 2nd edn. (Paris, 1925) p. 4, and J. Humbert, *Les plaidoyers écrits et les plaidoiries réelles de Cicéron* (Paris, 1925) esp. pp. 1-4; they are more concerned with the differences between the published version and the actually delivered version of the speeches we still have.
[10] For the dates of delivery, see Cic. *Att.* 4.15.5, *Scaur.* 27 (*de Reatinorum causa*); *Att.* 4.15.9 (*pro Messio*); *Att.* 4.15.9, *Q.f.* 2.16.3 (*pro Druso*). We know that the latter two at least were published: the *pro Messio* was known to Seneca (*contr.* 7.4.8), and the *pro Druso*, as well as Calvus' speech for the prosecution, to Tacitus (*dial.* 20).

(4) 57.1-2 (50.4-5 KS, 47.4 St, 62.4-5 G):
hanc orationem dixit L. Cotta L. Torquato coss. post annum quam superiores.

This must refer to earlier speeches on which Asconius had commented, as all the existing commentaries are on speeches delivered after the *pro Cornelio*. The speeches known for the year before the *pro Cornelio* are: the *pro lege Manilia* (or *de imperio Cn. Pompeii*), the *pro Cluentio,* the *pro C. Fundanio,* and the *pro C. Manilio* delivered at a *contio,* and the lost speech *pro Q. Mucio*.[11] Kiessling and Schoell, omitting mention of the last, think it most likely that commentaries were written on the two Manilian speeches and on the *pro Cluentio*; as almost nothing is agreed about the *pro Fundanio*, they pass over it. The Manilian speeches are very likely candidates, not only because Asconius shows a great deal of knowledge of Manilius' activities in the already existing commentaries (which probably resulted from a detailed study of the Manilian speeches), but also because those speeches would have been relevant to an understanding of a crucial period in Cicero's career and of the highly important figure of Pompeius in the history of the late republic. Moreover, there are other hints that these speeches were commented on: see passages (5) — (8) below. The one reference we have in Asconius to the *pro Mucio* (86.15ff.) does not allow us to say one way or the other whether he wrote a commentary on it; the reference by Asconius to the speech really deals with another matter (Fenestella's view that Cicero defended Catilina) and could be inferred from the lemma of Cicero itself (or at best from the summaries of Cicero's speeches which Asconius says [87.12] he had read).

References of the second category:

Very frequently throughout his commentaries Asconius provides us with cross-references to points he has already made. The variety of phrases he uses for these cross-references can be seen from the examples listed below and from the list of cross-references to known comments in Addendum I; the commonest form is *diximus* . . ., either as a principal verb or in a subordinate clause such as *ut iam* (or *supra*) *diximus*,

---

[11] The *pro lege Manilia* and the *pro Cluentio* still exist; there are several fragments of the *pro Fundanio* (31-2 P), and one fragment of the *pro Manilio* (31 P). For the *pro Fundanio,* see *comm. pet.* 19; for the *pro Manilio,* see Plut. *Cic.* 9, and the commentary on 60.10-14 in Part II; and for the *pro Mucio,* see Ascon. 86.3-18.

The Range of the Commentaries 5

occasionally varied by *significavimus* or *ostendimus*, with the less common variation (*ut*) *puto vos reminisci*. With the exception of places where the passive *dictum est* is used, there are only five instances where the verb is not in the first person plural,[12] and in nearly all of those *puto* is used (45.4 — *vos meminisse non dubito;* 52.18 — *significasse iam puto nos;* 53.13 — *puto iam supra esse dictum;* 68.22 — *puto vos reminisci;* 78.23 — *ut puto* [*vos reminisci*]).

It is important to note that all of these cross-references refer backwards, with adverbs like *iam, supra, ante* and *modo* occurring commonly in the phrases, and the verb always in the past tense.[13] That will provide a valuable clue in tracking down a speech which Asconius might have commented on, for one will always have to look for a speech which was delivered earlier than the one in which a particular cross-reference occurs, remembering that the commentaries were arranged in chronological order.

A second consideration for tracking down speeches on which commentaries were possibly written exists in relation to these cross-references. With about half of them, it is possible to find the point which is being referred to either in earlier comments on the same speech or in existing comments on an earlier speech (see the list of cross-references to known comments in Addendum I). But with the other half, we no longer have the point to which Asconius is referring, and by looking for a speech in which such a point might have been made the subject of a comment by Asconius, it is reasonable to deduce that that was a speech on which Asconius was likely to have written a commentary.

The following is a list of cross-references which provide internal evidence of this second category. They have been listed beginning with (5) to follow on from the above list of evidence of the first category, and in chronological order because that is the way the commentaries were originally arranged and because it will help to make clearer the possible speech(es) which a cross-reference may be referring back to, since they always refer backwards:

---

[12] There are two other instances where the first person might have been used, 11.15 and 93.16; in both places there are textual corruptions. In the first case Clark prefers to read the singular, in the second Stangl prefers to read the singular, but in view of the corruption it might be better to read the plural because of Asconius' preference for it. Cf. the discussion of passage (15) below, and passage (w) in Addendum I.

[13] There is another type of cross-reference which refers both backwards and forwards (5.1-2, 27.17, 80.5-6, 84.5). But in all four cases these are references to statements made by Cicero earlier or later in the same speech as that on which the comment is made containing the cross-reference.

A. pro Cornelio

(5) 64.17-18 (57.6-7 KS, 52.8 St, 70.4-5 G):
   P. Sulpicium in tribunatu hanc eandem legem tulisse iam significavimus.

(6) 65.3-5 (57.15-16 KS, 52.15 St, 70.13-15 G):
   ...Manilius, sicut iam ostendimus,... legem eandem Compitalibus pertulit.

(7) 65.8 (57.20 KS, 52.19 St, 70.18 G):
   C. Attium Celsum significat, sicut iam ante dictum est.

(8) 65.16 (58.4 KS, 53.1 St, 71.5 G):
   dictum est iam supra de his legibus, ...
   These four passages obviously refer to earlier comments on the activities of C. Manilius during his tribunate. Passages (5), (6) and (8) in particular refer to his law on distributing freedmen more extensively through the tribes, and this law is likely to have been the subject of a fuller explanation in the *argumentum* to the comments on the *pro lege Manilia*.[14] Note that in the last of these passages Asconius goes on to mention the law giving Pompeius the Mithridatic command, in support of which Cicero delivered that speech. Manilius' tribunician activities will also have been dealt with in Cicero's speech on behalf of Manilius at a public meeting, in which he agreed to defend him;[15] it is most likely to a comment on that speech that Asconius is referring in passage (7). There is a comment on Manilius' law on freedmen at 45.12-15, but as that occurs in the commentary on a speech delivered after this one, it is not the point of Asconius' cross-references here.

(9) 66.19 (58.27 KS, 53.19 St, 72.7 G):
   hic est Cotta de quo iam saepe diximus, ...
   Apart from the reference to C. Cotta in the comment on the very next lemma, and another later in the speech (78.23-24), neither of which count as they occur after this cross-reference, there is only one other reference to C. Cotta (14.20, in the comments on the *in Pisonem*). That too cannot be the point of Asconius' cross-reference here, as that speech was delivered well after the *pro Cornelio*. Moreover, when Asconius uses *saepe* in a cross-

---

[14] This is the view of both Kiessling and Schoell, and Stangl.
[15] For the details of the events related to Cicero's agreement to defend Manilius, see the commentary on 60.10-14 in Part II. The one fragment of the speech *pro Manilio* which we have (Nonius p. 434. 24-25 M) is no help: see J.T. Ramsey, *Phoenix* 34 (1980) 332-6.

The Range of the Commentaries 7

reference, he does mean at least several times (cf. passage (k) in Addendum I). Stangl suggests the following places as possible passages which were commented on: *Verr.* 2.1.130 and 2.3.18, *Caec.* 97, *leg. agr.* 2.58. Kiessling and Schoell list the two possible sections of the *Verrines*, and suggest also the possibility that Asconius wrote a commentary on the *pro Oppio*, delivered in 67 (i.e. before the *pro Cornelio*) at a trial in which the prosecution was undertaken by the brother of C. Cotta (Quint. 5.13.20 and 30, 6.5.10).

(10) 68.22-69.1 (60.24-61.1 KS, 55.7 St, 75.1-2 G):
puto vos reminisci has esse leges Livias quas illis consulibus M. Livius Drusus tribunus plebis tulerit.
As the *pro Cornelio* is the earliest speech on which we have Asconius' comments, we should look for a speech delivered earlier, in which reference is made to the Livian laws. Both Kiessling and Schoell, and Stangl find it in *Cluent.* 153, delivered in the preceding year. This is a likely candidate, as there are other hints that it was commented on (passage (4) above), and it was relatively close in time; since Asconius wrote his comments in chronological order, he would not be asking his readers to think back too far.

B. in toga candida

There are no cross-references of this type.

C. in Pisonem

(11) 6.15-17 (6.5-7 KS, 14.19-20 St, 8.16-18 G):
diximus iam antea a Q. Metello Nepote tr. pl. Ciceronem consulatu abeuntem prohibitum esse contionari de rebus quas in eo magistratu gessit.
Stangl suggests that this could be a cross-reference to *Sull.* 31 (which mentions Metellus Nepos' opposition to Cicero), delivered six years before the *in Pisonem*. The *pro Sestio*, delivered in 56 (just a year before the *in Pisonem*), is regarded as a more likely candidate by Kiessling and Schoell; again the reader's memory would not have to be stretched too far, and there are references in that speech to Metellus Nepos' difference with Cicero at § § 11, 72 and 130. Cf. the comment of the Schol. Bob. on § 130 (= 139.4-6). However, there are fragments of a speech *contra contionem Q. Metelli*,[16] which is an even more

---

[16] 83-5 P (together with *testimonia*).

8   Introduction: Section One

likely candidate, since it would have dealt specifically with
Metellus Nepos' blocking of Cicero.

(12) 8.12-13 (7.22-23 KS, 15.27-28 St, 10.11-12 G):
*diximus L. Pisone A. Gabinio coss. P. Clodium tr. pl. quattuor
leges perniciosas populo Romano tulisse.*
The Clodian legislation is likely to have been mentioned
frequently by Cicero, especially in the speeches delivered soon
after his return from exile, but there is only one speech, the *pro
Sestio*, where the same four pieces of legislation as listed by
Asconius are given in close proximity (§ § 55-56). One
additional piece of legislation (the law giving Macedonia and
Syria as provincial commands to Piso and Gabinius) is
mentioned in the passage from the *pro Sestio*.

(13) 9.17-18 (8.24-25 KS, 16.22-23 St, 11.19-20 G):
*Catilinam lege repetundarum absolutum esse accusante P.
Clodio iam supra dictum est.*
We do have an existing point for this cross-reference in the
comments on the *pro Cornelio* and the *in toga candida* (see
below on passage (n) in Addendum I), but as that would require
the reader to remember back a long way (given that there would
be quite a number of intervening speeches on which Asconius
commented) and he seems not to have asked his readers to
remember back too far (cf. (10) and (11) above), and as it is a
point which Cicero is likely to have made often, perhaps this is a
reference to a more recent speech.

(14) 9.22-23 (9.4-5 KS, 16.27 St, 12.1-2 G):
*L. Lamiam a Gabinio consule edicto relegatum esse iam
diximus.*
A further indication that there was a commentary on the *pro
Sestio*, since the banishment of L. Lamia is mentioned in that
speech (§ 29). Cf. Schol. Bob. 129.5-7.

(15) 11.14-15 (10.17-18 KS, 17.25-26 St, 13.14-15 G):
*...Ap. Claudius, sicut iam saepe significavimus, tum fuit
praetor.*
The mss. read *significabitur*, which Manutius has emended to
significavimus; this seems a reasonable emendation, since
Asconius prefers the first person plural (cf. 88.25), except in
phrases using *puto* (see above on p. 5), and in fact uses it in a
cross-reference phrase in the very next line. There is a number of
references to Ap. Claudius in the *pro Sestio* (§ § 77-78, 85, 87
and 126); he was praetor in 57 and worked in the interests of his
brother against the activities of Sestius, who was working for

The Range of the Commentaries 9

Cicero's recall, and so likely to be dealt with a good deal in comments on the *pro Sestio*.

(16) 11.15-18 (10.19-21 KS, 17.26-28 St, 13.15-18 G):
duos tribunos de quibus ipsis quoque iam diximus... Sex. Atilium Serranum et Q. Numerium significat.
This cross-reference is presumably to be taken closely with the preceding one. It helps to confirm the *pro Sestio* as a likely candidate for comment, since there is a number of references to these two tribunes (§ §72, 82, 85, 87, 89 and 94). §87 is particularly relevant because it makes the point to which Cicero refers in the lemma on which Asconius is commenting here, that these two tribunes had been 'bought'.

(17) 15.13-15 (14.1-3 KS, 20.12-13 St, 17.20-22 G):
fuit autem, ut puto iam nos dixisse, Pupius Piso eisdem temporibus quibus Cicero, ...
Kiessling and Schoell, and Stangl regard this as referring to a comment on *Verr*. 2.1.37 or on *dom*. 35. Neither of these passages is appropriate to the point that Cicero makes (i.e. Piso's desire for a triumph), but then Asconius' comment on this occasion does not deal with it either; rather he identifies the man mentioned by Cicero and says something general about him. That could well be the sort of comment he made on the passage from the *Verrines* or the *de domo sua*. There is some argument for choosing a passage from the latter speech as the likely point of the cross-reference, as closer in time to the *in Pisonem* (and hence not so far back for his readers to remember).

D. pro Scauro

There are no cross-references of this type.

E. pro Milone

(18) 45.4-6 (39.19-21 KS, 39.11-13 St, 49.21-23 G):
illud vos meminisse non dubito per Q. Fufium illo quoque tempore quo de incesto P. Clodi actum est factum ne a senatu asperius decerneretur.
Stangl suggests that this could be a reference to a comment on *Flacc*. 13 (delivered seven years earlier in 59), for the Schol. Bob.'s comment on that section from the *pro Flacco* says that Cicero's mention of a recent law refers to a *lex iudiciaria* proposed either by P. Vatinius or by Q. Fufius Calenus, and that might have been the nature of Asconius' comment on the passage of the *pro Flacco*. Or it could be a reference to a comment on the lost speech *in Clodium et Curionem*, delivered

10   Introduction: Section One

in 61.[17] The introduction by the Schol. Bob. to his comments on that speech refers to the role played by Fufius in supporting Clodius in the Bona Dea scandal, which is the matter dealt with in Asconius' cross-reference here. Stangl also mentions passages of the *Philippics* in which Fufius is mentioned (8.16, 10.3, 11.15 and 12.1), but as those speeches came after the *pro Milone*, Asconius would not be referring to them.

(19) 45.22-23 (40.10-11 KS, 39.24 St, 50.15-16 G):
L. Cassius fuit, sicut iam saepe diximus, summae vir severitatis.
Stangl suggests four places which could be the point of this cross-reference: *Rosc. Am.* 84, *Verr.* 1.30, 2.3.137, *Cluent.* 107, and *Sest.* 103. Kiessling and Schoell mention all but the passages of the *Verrines*. The three earliest references all mention the honesty and uprightness of Cassius and/or his authorship of the phrase *cui bono* (which is the point of Asconius' comment here); the passage in the *pro Sestio* refers only to his law on secret ballot. As the section of the *pro Roscio Amerino* contains mention of the well known phrase *cui bono* (which Asconius also goes on to mention following this cross-reference here), that speech has a stronger case for being regarded as one which Asconius commented on. But the use of *saepe* ought to suggest that Asconius made the point in his comments on a number of speeches, so this cross-reference might be evidence that the other speeches too were commented on.

(20) 52.18-21 (46.20-23 KS, 44.14-17 St, 57.24-27 G):
significasse iam puto nos fuisse inter leges P. Clodi... eam quoque qua libertini... possent in rusticis quoque tribubus ... ferre [suffragium].
This is taken by Kiessling and Schoell, and Stangl to refer to a comment on the lost speech *de aere alieno Milonis,* usually taken to have been delivered in 53.[18] There is a passage in that speech (frag. 17 in Schol. Bob. 173.1) dealing with *suffragium*; the scholiast says in his comment on that passage that a law giving freedmen an equal vote had been put forward by Clodius. This looks to be the same sort of comment that Asconius would

---

[17] On the date of delivery, see Cic. *Att.* 1.16.1, and the *argumentum* in Schol. Bob. 85-86. Kiessling and Schoell agree that the reference is to the *in Clodium et Curionem*. W.C. McDermott, *AJP* 93 (1972) 407ff., argues that the title *in Clodium et Curionem* is an error, and that the speech was only *in Clodium* (the speech *in Curionem* being separate and written in 59 or 58 in reply to an attack by Curio; it was never published, but subsequently found and conflated with the speech *in Clodium*).
[18] W.W. How and A.C. Clark, *Cicero: Select Letters* (Oxford, 1926) Vol. II, p. 12.

have made on such a passage, and it suggests that the speech was one he commented on.

(21) 53.13-14 (47.12-13 KS, 45.1 St, 58.16-17 G):
puto iam supra esse dictum Milone ex familia fuisse Papia.
Kiessling and Schoell, and Stangl relate this also to a comment on the *de aere alieno Milonis.* That seems particularly likely when the cross-reference occurs in a discussion of the statement by Cicero that Milo had gone through three inheritances, and was therefore in debt.

So much for the internal evidence of Asconius. There is only one piece of direct external evidence which points to a speech not otherwise known to have been commented on. In a section discussing Cicero's age when he delivered the *pro Roscio Amerino*, Aulus Gellius mentions that Asconius had pointed out an error made by Fenestella in regard to Cicero's age.[19] Kiessling and Schoell suggest that such a comment by Asconius is most likely to have been made in the introduction to comments on the *pro Roscio;* they add that § § 1-3 of Gellius' chapter, which mention a similar error by Cornelius Nepos in the first book of his life of Cicero, are likely to have been taken closely from Asconius' *argumentum* to comments on the speech. It must be said that the passage in Gellius does look very much like the sort of comment Asconius would make, especially in his introductions; in that case, Cornelius Nepos should be added to the list of sources used by Asconius.

Indirect external evidence can perhaps be gained from the later scholiasts on Cicero's speeches. It is a reasonable assumption that the later scholiasts borrowed from Asconius, and if traces of his work can be detected in later commentaries, then it is a simple matter to deduce that he commented on the speeches which are the subject of commentaries by the later scholiasts. The Scholia Bobbiensia and Pseudo-Asconius are likely to be the most helpful; the commentaries of the other scholiasts are either too brief to be able to deduce that they were borrowed from Asconius, or they deal with speeches which on other evidence can be said to have been commented on by Asconius. It is necessary to find only a few examples of comments on a particular speech which look as though they come from Asconius in order to suggest that he wrote a commentary on that speech. In many cases, such traces will help to confirm the hints about particular speeches already gained from the internal evidence of Asconius himself and discussed above.

The Bobbio Scholia contained commentaries on the following speeches of Cicero: *pro Sulla* (delivered in 61), *in Clodium et Curionem*

---

[19] Gell. 15.28.1-4. See also B. Marshall, *Rhein. Mus.* 123 (1980) 352.

(61), *de rege Alexandrino* (56), *pro Flacco* (59), *post reditum in senatu* (57), *post reditum ad Quirites* (57), *pro Milone* (52), *pro Sestio* (56), *in Vatinium* (56), *pro Plancio* (54), *de aere alieno Milonis* (53?), and *pro Archia* (63). It can readily be seen that they are out of chronological order.[20] The sources for the Bobbio Scholia are quite mixed: Sallust's *Histories* were perhaps still directly used, and the principal source for historical comments is likely to have been Cicero himself, with information gathered simply from the context in the actual speech or easily traced elsewhere in his works.[21] But in other places, the type of information, and even the very style, shows that the information has been taken from Asconius, especially in the introductions to the speeches. There are passages where he is clearly not using Asconius, for if he had he would not have fallen into error. For example, in the comment on *Sest.* 30 (129.10-12), dealing with the *lex Licinia Mucia*, he misunderstood the meaning of the verb *redigere*, which he had seen in Cicero's *pro Cornelio* and Asconius' comment on it (67.15ff.), and made the law an expulsion act, whereas if he had checked Asconius he would have interpreted the verb correctly.[22]

The following passages of the Scholia Bobbiensia look like borrowings from Asconius (or at least show Asconian influence). They are arranged in the order of the speeches as they occur in the text, using the page and line numbers of Stangl's edition of the scholia on Cicero's speeches (Leipzig, 1912) (= St). The collection mainly results from Stangl's suggestions in his notes ad loc., but occasionally from suggestions by Hildebrandt in the notes ad loc. to his edition of the Scholia Bobbiensia (Leipzig, 1907), marked with the abbreviation H. The plain references are to the page and line numbers of Clark's edition.

A. pro Sulla

(1) 78.34-79.3 St. Hildebrandt (= 9.28-10.7 H) suggests that this is Asconian. It looks like typically Asconian research into laws on *ambitus* (cf. 69.11-13, 75.7-9, 75.24-76.2, 88.15-18).

(2) 80.13-16 St (on the insults cast by Catilina, Clodius and Antonius at Cicero's 'newness'). In a comment on the *in toga candida*, Asconius refers to speeches supposedly delivered by

---

[20] For discussion of what might have been the original order, see Stangl, n. ad loc. on 118.6. P. Hildebrandt, pp. xlii-xliii of the introduction to his edition of the Schol. Bob. (Leipzig, 1907), sees no rationale in the order of commentaries.
[21] E. Badian, *JRS* 63 (1973) 125.
[22] For a discussion of the Schol. Bob.'s error and Asconius' rightness, see the commentary on 67.22-23 in Part II. For similar differences from Asconius, see passage (25) below.

The Range of the Commentaries 13

Catilina and Antonius, criticising Cicero (93.24-94.3); the wording is similar to the scholiast's comment here (e.g. *novitas, contumelius*), except that Clodius is added. Perhaps this comment came from Asconius' commentary on the *pro Sulla*, though the Schol. Bob. could have got it from the comment on the *in toga candida*. Cf. 12.11-13 H.

(3) 82.11-12 St (on tribunician opposition to Cicero at the end of his consular year). The Schol. Bob. names L. Calpurnius Bestia or (more likely) Q. Metellus Nepos. The latter is named by Asconius in a comment on the *in Pisonem* (6.15-17), but as that comment is in the form of a cross-reference to a point we no longer have, the point could have been made in a comment on the *pro Sulla*, from which the Schol. Bob. has got his comment. Cf. the discussion of passage (11) above in the list of internal evidence from Asconius.

B. in Clodium et Curionem

(4) 84.17-22 St (cf. 20.17-22 H). This passage from the *argumentum* (*nam tres illis temporibus Curiones inlustri nomine extiterunt...*) is reminiscent of 74.11-12 (*duo fuerunt eo tempore Cn. Dolabellae...*); cf. 74.5-7 which identifies two of the three Curiones mentioned in the comment of the Schol. Bob.

(5) 85.32-34 St. The precise voting figures are reminiscent of Asconius. Badian thinks that this comment and the preceding one are so reminiscent of Asconius that the Schol. Bob. must have got much of his *argumentum* from a commentary on this speech by Asconius.[23] Stangl thinks the voting figures may have come from the *acta* via Asconius, but the trial took place in 61 when the *acta* were not yet available. The voting figures could have come from the speech itself (frags. 26 and 28 = 90.17-19 and 91.8 St; cf. Cic. *Att.* 1.16.5).

(6) 86.30-31 St. Schol. Bob. mentions *opiniones aliorum*, and Stangl suggests that Asconius may be one of the *alii*. Cf. too Asconius' use of *opinio* (e.g. 50.14), which may be a device for covering up when he has forgotten precisely who his source was.

(7) 87.1 St. The phrase *diximus in argumento* is very reminiscent of the type of cross-reference used by Asconius, who prefers to use the first person plural (see above, p. 5), whereas the Schol. Bob. prefers to use either the first person singular (e.g. 118.6-7,

---

[23] Art. cit. (n. 21) 130 n. 48.

14   Introduction: Section One

131.19, 132.17, 148.11-12, 156.20, 159.26, 167.23, 171.23 St) or the impersonal passive (e.g. 92.35, 127.6, 139.4, 146.14, 149.28, 168.2 St), and only occasionally the first person plural. The use of the first person plural here, together with the sort of information contained in the comment, might suggest that the comment has been lifted from Asconius in its entirety. In passing, it might be noticed that the format of the Schol. Bob.'s commentaries is the same as that of Asconius — *argumentum* followed by *enarratio* (which the Schol. Bob. calls *explanatio* at the three points where the heading occurs [86.6, 110.13, 175.21 St], all the other points where the heading could occur being in parts of the text which have been lost). This is in general a reason for believing that the Schol. Bob. took a lot of his material from Asconius.

(8)   89.24-28 St. Stangl thinks this may have come from the *acta* via Asconius, but the *acta* did not exist yet. However, it does read like an Asconian comment, with its list of prosecutor and assistants (cf. 18.19-19.7, 54.11ff.).

(9)   90.1-6 St. Stangl thinks this comment on the first Ap. Claudius to be called Pulcher comes from either Livy (cf. *per.* 19) or Asconius. The latter does show an interest in families and *cognomina* (e.g. 2.18-19, 12.11-20, 25.24-26.1 [on the same family as the Schol. Bob.'s comment], 74.11-12).

(10) 91.13-14 St (cf. 29.4-6 H). The verb *communicare* used to describe the *lex Aurelia iudiciaria* is also used of it by Asconius at 17.6 and 67.11-12, though those references occur in his comments on speeches other than the one on which this comment of the Schol. Bob. is made (i.e. the *in Pisonem* and *in toga candida* respectively).

C.   de rege Alexandrino

There is not sufficient of the commentary on this speech to draw any conclusions.

D.   pro Flacco

(11) 96.26-29 St (on the hostility between L. Piso and C. Gracchus). Perhaps this information was picked up from Cicero himself who frequently refers to the enmity between Piso and Gracchus (*Verr.* 2.3.195, 4.56, *Font.* 39, *off.* 2.75, *Brut.* 106), but Stangl may be right in thinking it comes from Asconius, who Badian thinks is more likely to have done the work of collecting the

The Range of the Commentaries   15

evidence.[24] Asconius elsewhere shows an interest in the *cognomen* Frugi used by the Calpurnii Pisones (2.17-19), which appears in the lemma and the comment of the Schol. Bob. here.

(12) 96.31-34 St. Stangl thinks that this perhaps comes from Sallust via Asconius. Note the characteristic *ut supra diximus* of Asconius.

E. post reditum in senatu (or **cum senatui gratias egit**)

There is not sufficient of the commentary on this speech to draw any conclusion.

F. post reditum ad Quirites (or **cum populo gratias egit**)

Likewise.

G. pro Milone

There is no need to establish borrowings from Asconius by the Schol. Bob., as this is one of the speeches we know Asconius to have written a commentary on. However, a few examples of borrowings will help to illustrate the general principle that the Schol. Bob. did borrow from Asconius.

(13) 115.1-2 St (cf. 66.15-17 H). Presumably taken from 33.4-5 and 42.16ff.

(14) 116.4-13 St (cf. 68.8-69.9 H). Presumably taken from 43.3-18.

H. pro Sestio

(15) 125.27 St (*ut plerique arbitrati sunt*). Stangl thinks that Asconius might be included among the *plerique*. For similar phrases used by the Schol. Bob., see 85.18 (*ita in libris adhuc feruntur*), 86.30-31 (passage (6) above), 124.2 (*aput quosdam*), 130.22-23 (passage (18) below), 142.17 and 22 (*ut quidam putant... alii vero existumaverunt*). The *argumentum* looks Asconian, with details of charge, prosecutors and defence counsel.

(16) 126.18-22 St. Stangl thinks this comes from Asconius, possibly originally from Livy who was used as a source by Asconius (cf. *per.* 84-85). It reads like an Asconian comment.

(17) 127.26-27 St. Note the characteristic *ut saepe iam diximus* of Asconius. The *saepe* refers to a comment on frag. 27 of the *in*

---

[24] Ibid. 126 n. 30.

Clodium et Curionem (= 90.32-91.7 St) and perhaps to a comment on *dom*. 92 (which may be evidence for a lost commentary on that speech). It cannot refer to frag. 2 of the *de aere alieno Milonis*, since that speech was delivered after the one in which this cross-reference occurs.

(18) 130.22-23 St (*quod ab aliis proditum est*). Stangl thinks that the *alii* might include Asconius.

(19) 134.2-6 St.
(20) 135.17-22 St.
(21) 139.22-28 St.

Stangl thinks that all of these passages are taken from Asconius, but there is no strong evidence other than that they read like Asconian comments.

I. in Vatinium

(22) 149.3-6 St.
(23) 149.24-25 St.

Stangl thinks these two passages are taken from Asconius, but there is no evidence other than that they read like Asconian comments.

J. pro Plancio

(24) 167.23-30 St. A similar judgment to the one passed on the five preceding passages should be made. This comment deals with the famous letter of Cicero to Pompeius about his consulship, which Cicero refers to at *Sull*. 67 (so the Schol. Bob. may have borrowed from Asconius' comment on that speech).

K. de aere alieno Milonis

(25) 172.14-15 St. This comment by the Schol. Bob. shows that he was not using Asconius for this piece of information: he is wrong about Clodius' physical presence in support of Catilina after the latter had left Rome, for Asconius in his comment on the *pro Milone* (50.14-17) says that it was only *opinio* which gave Clodius this role. That is not to say that Asconius did not write a commentary on the *de aere alieno Milonis* (for there are other hints that he did — passages (20) and (21) above in the list of internal evidence from Asconius). There are in the same commentary some places where the Schol. Bob. borrows from Asconius, and others where he does not follow him; e.g. in the comments on the *pro Milone* he borrows from Asconius (see passages (13) and (14) above), but at 117.6-7 St he is not sure about the role of Fufius Calenus (which Asconius gets right at 44.20-21 because he took it from the *acta*). Moreover he deals with a different range of lemmata, and often a wider range (to judge from their commentaries on the *pro Milone*), so the Schol. Bob. had to get his information elsewhere and could not always depend on Asconius.

The Range of the Commentaries 17

(26) 173.7-10 St (cf. 156.19-23 H). A fragment from the speech actually delivered by Cicero at the trial of Milo;[25] Asconius knew this version of the *pro Milone* too (42.2-4). The phrase used in the Schol. Bob.'s comment here (*opinio erat*) is reminiscent of Asconius (e.g. 50.14).

L. pro Archia

(27) 175.33ff. St. Badian thinks that the Schol. Bob.'s *argumentum* to this speech was not based on Asconius or any other commentator, since it is deduced, even partly paraphrased, from Cicero's own speech.[26] But there is at least this one comment from the *explanatio* which may reflect Asconian influence.

(28) 179.6-8 St. The Schol. Bob. mentions some interesting information about some verses of the tragic poet Accius, who is an author mentioned by Asconius (16.17-18). Elsewhere Asconius shows interest in other poets (e.g. 16.12-13, 25.12, 93.22).

Though the comments on the Verrine speeches by Pseudo-Asconius are mainly grammatical, there is some historical material.[27] For a work which is essentially a compilation, its value will vary according to the quality of the sources which the compiler has used; the largest part of the historical material is derived from the speeches of Cicero themselves or other works of Cicero, but some information seems to derive from lost commentaries of Asconius.[28] It needs only a few examples of comments where it can be deduced that Pseudo-Asconius borrowed from Asconius, to establish the likelihood that the latter wrote commentaries on the *Verrines*; the following examples are given,[29] again using the page and line numbers of Stangl's edition and numbering the passages from (29) to follow on from the list of borrowings by the Schol. Bob.

(29) 193.29-30 St (cf. 193.19-21) (on *div in Caec.* 24). Pseudo-Asconius records that M. Terentius Varro was prosecuted by the young Ap. Claudius Pulcher for extortion in Asia; it is only here that the name of Varro's prosecutor is given. In the rest of the comment, Pseudo-Asconius refers to the prosecutions of the two

---

[25] See also Quint. 9.2.54, and cf. Clark's note on §33 in his edition of the *pro Milone*.
[26] Art. cit. (n. 21) 128-9.
[27] For judgments on the triviality and worthlessness of Ps.-Asc., see Madvig, pp. 90, 111-2 and 134, and Clark, intro. p. xi; for a kinder assessment, see H.W. Benario, *Historia* 22 (1973) 70-1.
[28] Madvig, p. 112.
[29] Cf. the list in Benario, art. cit. (n. 27) 68-71.

18 Introduction: Section One

Dolabellae by Caesar and Scaurus, which he may well have got from Asconius (26.13-18, 74.11-12), even if wrongly because he linked the defendants and prosecutors incorrectly and reversed the results. It seems most likely that he got the identification of Ap. Claudius as Varro's prosecutor from Asconius.

(30) 203.17-18 St (on *div. in Caec.* 63). Pseudo-Asconius identifies the Cn. Pompeius, who contended with C. Iulius for the right to prosecute Albucius, as Strabo and the father of Pompeius Magnus..Nowhere is it expressly stated that the Cn. Pompeius who competed with C. Iulius Caesar (who was also called Strabo) was Pompeius' father (though it must have been, since he and Caesar Strabo were contemporaries), but in two places Asconius expressly says that Strabo was the father of Pompeius Magnus (3.7, 14.11). He may well have made the point again in a commentary on this section of the *divinatio in Caecilium*, which in turn has been borrowed by Pseudo-Asconius.

(31) 216.20-22 St (on *Verr.* 1.30, concerning the *leges Cassiae*). Asconius give the details of both laws quite clearly (45.22ff. and 78.5-16). In the first of these comments by Asconius (on the *pro Milone*) we have a cross-reference (*sicut iam saepe diximus*) which ought to mean more than the one other reference we have in an earlier set of comments (on the *pro Cornelio*) and which suggests therefore a comment on this section of the *First Verrine* (see above, passage (19) in the list of internal evidence from Asconius).

(32) 217.21-22 St (on *Verr.* 1.31, on the origin of the *ludi plebeii*). The discovery of two alternative occasions for the institution of these games (cf. Liv. 23.30.17) does not look like the work of Pseudo-Asconius; it is more like the occasional antiquarian interest of Asconius (cf. his interest in the *ludi Megalenses* at 69.19ff.).

(33) 219.10-13 St (on *Verr.* 1.38, concerning *lis aestimata*). See discussion of next passage.

(34) 239.25-240.4 St (on *Verr.* 2.1.61, on procedure in extortion cases). Both of these comments reveal considerable legal knowledge; the ultimate source for the knowledge of procedure must have been the *lex Acilia*.[30] 'Pseudo-Asconius records the possibility of a four-fold monetary penalty which is not stated in the law. Yet this is precisely the kind of information which Asconius is

---

[30] The relevant passage is quoted by Benario, ibid. 69-70 (=Riccobono, *FIRA*^{2} 96).

accustomed to furnish (for he often shows his knowledge of *acta* and *leges*). Our late commentator can hardly be expected to have consulted the text of a law more than five hundred years old; Asconius unquestionably did, added his own comments upon it, and handed the information down to posterity in a commentary now lost but available to later commentators.'[31]

(35) 255.11-13 St (on *Verr.* 2.1.155, concerning the Sullan law which forbade tribunes to seek further office). Sulla's diminution of the tribunician power is commonly referred to, but Asconius is one of the few sources for the knowledge that tribunes were prevented from seeking further office (66.23-67.5, 78.23-25). The action of Opimius in using his veto in defiance of Sulla's law about the tribunate, which Pseudo-Asconius is discussing, was associated with the bill of C. Cotta to remove the bar on tribunes seeking further office; Asconius' references to Sulla's law occur in the context of discussing Cotta's action. So the information in Pseudo-Asconius looks very Asconian. Moreover, Asconius did a lot of research into Cotta's bill; hence it is information likely to be remembered, and used in more places than the two comments we have.

To sum up: the following table gives a list of the speeches for which there are hints, either from references in Asconius himself or from borrowing in the later scholiasts, that he wrote commentaries. They are all, of course, conjectural; those marked with a question mark are even more conjectural than most.

In conclusion, it can be said that Asconius probably wrote on a very large number of Cicero's speeches,[32] including both public and forensic speeches (though the latter point was already obvious from the selection of commentaries we now have). It seems, moreover, that the commentaries were written within a relatively narrow period (A.D. 54-57).[33] It would clearly have taken Asconius much longer than that to do the necessary research on such a large number of speeches, and so one must assume that, although the commentaries were written in a short period of time, they were the products of a long-term interest in things Ciceronian.

---

[31] Ibid. 70.
[32] Madvig, p. 21, says that Asconius commented on all of Cicero's speeches; Kiessling and Schoell find hints of commentaries on sixteen speeches other than the five we know of.
[33] For the arguments in favour of that time of composition, see below, pp. 28-30.

Speech	Year of delivery	Very conjectural	Internal evidence (passage nos.)	Scholiasts' borrowings (passage nos.)
pro Roscio Amerino	80		19	(Gell. 15.28.4)
divinatio in Caecilium	70			29-30
in Verrem 1	70		19	31-33
in Verrem 2.1	70		9, 17	34-35
2.2	70			
2.3	70		9	
pro Caecina	69		9	
pro Oppio	67	?	9	
pro lege Manilia	66		4, 5-8	
pro Cluentio	66		4, 10, 19	
pro Fundanio	66	?	4	
pro Manilio	66		4, 5-8	
pro Mucio	66	?	4	
de lege agraria 2	63		2, 9	
in Catilinam 1	63		1	
contra contionem Q. Metelli	63		11	
pro Sulla	63		11	1-3
pro Archia	63			27-28
in Clodium et Curionem	61		18	4-10
pro Flacco	59		18	11-12
de domo sua	57	?	17	17
pro Sestio	56		11-12, 14-16, 19	15-21
in Vatinium	56			22-23
pro Vatinio	54		3	
de Reatinorum causa	54	?	3	
pro Messio	54	?	3	
pro Druso	54	?	3	
pro Plancio	54		3	24
de aere alieno Milonis	53?		20-21	25-26

The Range of the Commentaries

One further point can be made in passing about the range of comments. The selection of passages in any one commentary of Asconius seems not only capricious but also narrow (compared to the larger number of lemmata dealt with by the later scholiasts).[34] The narrowness of the selection may result from the commentary being pitched at a lower level, but it might also be thought that what we have in each commentary is only a selection of what Asconius originally wrote. But that does not seem the case for two reasons. One, if he wrote a large number of commentaries (as seems likely), he would not have had time to write more than he did on each speech. Second, there is only one cross-reference which could conceivably refer to another comment on the same speech where the comment may be thought no longer to exist — 53.13-14 (passage (21) in the list of internal evidence); all other cross-references, including those to earlier comments on the same speech, can be satisfactorily explained. And even with this one, there is the likelihood of a suitable point for the cross-reference. Given the frequency with which Asconius makes a cross-reference, often to an earlier comment on the same speech, if there were parts of individual commentaries that have been lost, we would have expected a larger number of inexplicable cross-references. But as there are not, one can only assume that each commentary as we have it is complete. Similarly, with the cross-references of the type which refer backwards and forwards to statements made by Cicero in the same speech;[35] the points of these references can all be found in the existing commentaries, whereas if parts of the commentaries were missing, we would expect to find some cross-references of this type for which the point no longer exists in Asconius' commentaries as we have them. The conclusion must be that they are complete in themselves.

---

[34] For example, with the *pro Milone* where a comparison is possible, Asconius comments on passages from only nineteen chapters, whereas the Schol. Bob. comments on lemmata from thirty chapters (and a good deal of his commentary is missing).
[35] See above, n. 13.

ADDENDUM I
CROSS-REFERENCES TO KNOWN COMMENTS

Notes: 1. The passages are arranged in the chronological order of the speeches.

2. Those entries marked with an asterisk do not appear on Kiessling and Schoell's list (intro., pp. xvi-xix) or in Stangl's notes ad loc.; the one passage marked with a plus sign is missed by Kiessling and Schoell.

1. **pro Cornelio**
   [As this is the first speech chronologically, all the identifiable cross-references are to comments earlier in the speech.]

*(a) 61.12 (54.1 KS, 50.1 St, 66.15 G): *sicut diximus* = 57.4 (50.7 KS, 47.6 St, 62.7 G).

*(b) 61.16 (54.4 KS, 50.4 St, 66.19 G): *quod ipsum quoque diximus* = 57.5 (50.8 KS, 47.6-7 St, 62.8 G).

(c) 72.23 (64.14 KS, 57.24 St, 78.22 G): *diximus iam in principio* = 58.3-5 and 59.1-3 (51.2-3 and 51.23-52.1 KS, 47.17 and 48.14-16 St, 63.2-5 and 64.2-5 G).

(d) 78.23 (69.31 KS, 61.20 St, 85.12 G): *ut puto [vos reminisci]* = 67.1-4 (59.5-7 KS, 53.23-24 St, 72.12-16 G). The supplement was put forward by Madvig, p. 72, on the basis of 68.22, and followed by Kiessling and Schoell; Clark, Stangl and Giarratano credit the supplement of them.

+(e) 79.21 (70.29 KS, 62.5-6 St, 86.17 G): *ut iam diximus* = 60.19-21 (53.10-12 KS, 49.18-19 St, 65.20-66.2 G).

2. **in toga candida**

(f) 87.19 (78.13 KS, 68.7 St, 95.7 G): *diximus et paulo ante* = 84.7-11 (75.3-7 KS, 65.16-19 St, 84.13-17 G).

(g) 88.18 (79.11 KS, 68.29 St, 96.8 G): *de quibus iam diximus* = 75.7-9 (66.21-24 KS, 59.8-10 St, 81.9-12 G). A cross-reference made to a comment on the *pro Cornelio*, but it was an earlier speech.

(h) 88.25 (79.17-18 KS, 68.34 St, 96.14-15 G): *quibus ... significavimus* = 84.12-14 (75.8-10 KS, 65.20-21 St, 91.18-20 G).

The Range of the Commentaries

(i) 89.6 (79.28 KS, 69.8 St, 96.25 G): *paulo ante diximus* = 85.3ff. (75.23ff. KS, 66.6ff. St, 92.11ff. G).

(j) 89.16 (80.8 KS, 69.16 St, 97.8 G): *diximus modo de hoc* = 85.3-6 and 89.6-12 (75.23-76.2 and 79.28-80.4 KS, 66.6-8 and 69.8-13 St, 92.11-14 and 96.25-97.4 G). There is also a comment on Catilina's trial *de repetundis* at 9.17-18, but as it occurs in the comments on the *in Pisonem*, a speech delivered well after the *in toga candida*, Asconius cannot be cross-referring to that.

(k) 92.8 (82.22 KS, 71.10 St, 100.5 G): *dictum est iam saepius* = 66.7-12, 85.10-13, 87.13-15, 89.6-12 (58.15-20, 76.6-9, 78.7-9, 79.28-80.4 KS, 53.10-13, 66.11-13, 68.3-4, 69.8-13 St, 71.16-72.2, 92.18-21, 95.1-3, 96.25-97.4 G). The first of the frequent cross-references is to a comment on the *pro Cornelio*; the others are references to earlier comments on the *in toga candida*.

(l) 93.4 (83.14 KS, 72.1 St, 101.3 G): *diximus iam supra* = 88.25-29 (79.20-22 KS, 69.2-3 St, 96.15-19 G).

(m) 93.15-16 (83.25 KS, 72.10-11 St, 101.15 G): *quem . . . dixi* = 92.22-23 (83.5-6 KS, 71.20-22 St, 100.19-21G). For the reading, see below on (w).

3. in Pisonem

(n) 9.18 (8.25 KS, 16.22-23 St, 11.20 G): *iam supra dictum est* = once in the comments on the *pro Cornelio*, and three or four times in the comments on the *in toga candida*. There is a long gap (almost ten years) between the speech in which this cross-reference is made, and the known comments in which the point of the cross-reference occurs. As there are likely to have been intervening speeches on which Asconius wrote commentaries, and as the point being discussed is likely to have been frequently mentioned by Cicero (since it involved his two greatest enemies), this cross-reference may more rightly belong to the second category of internal evidence for lost commentaries discussed above. The *supra* in this cross-reference confirms that the comments were arranged originally in chronological order (see above, p. 1, and Stangl, n. ad loc.).

(o) 14.10 (13.1 KS, 19.18 St, 16.16 G): *diximus* = 1.1-2 (1.2-3 KS, 11.2 St, 3.2-3 G).

4. pro Scauro

(p) 25.1 (22.5 KS, 26.21 St, 28.17 G): *de quo supra diximus* = 23.23 (21.6 KS, 25.31 St, 27.9 G).

(q) 25.15 (22.19 KS, 26.31 St, 29.7 G): *ut supra diximus* = 23.24 (21.7 KS, 25.32 St, 27.10 G).

(r) 27.1 (23.22 KS, 27.26 St, 30.19 G): *demonstrasse vobis meminisse me*. This is not a cross-reference of the normal type (as the use of the verb *demonstrare* shows; it is not a verb which occurs in the various types of phrases used for cross-reference). The point here is that Asconius had pointed the building out on an actual tour of Rome.

(s) 27.18 (24.12 KS, 28.11 St, 31.16 G): [*ut supra diximus*] = 23.5-7 (20.20-22 KS, 25.17-18 St, 26.17 G). There is a lacuna of about twelve to fifteen letters at this point in all three main mss., and the supplement *ut supra diximus* is given by Kiessling and Schoell, followed by Stangl and Giarratano (but not Clark). As Asconius, when he makes the same point twice, very frequently provides some sort of cross-reference, especially when it is made in the comments on the same speech, the supplement is likely to be correct.

5. **pro Milone**

(t) 42.9 (37.5 KS, 37.21 St, 47.5 G): *ut in causae expositione diximus* = 40.21-22 (35.23-24 KS, 36.26-27 St, 45.15-16 G).

(u) 42.17 (37.13 KS, 37.26-27 St, 47.12-13 G): *de quibus ... diximus* = 32.24ff. (28.24ff. KS, 31.29ff. St, 37.10ff. G).

(v) 46.10-11 (40.26-27 KS, 40.8 St, 51.8-9 G): *quem ... diximus* = 33.5-9 (29.2-6 KS, 32.4-7 St, 37.18-22 G).

*(w) 47.21 (42.7-8 KS, 41.5 St, 52.22-53.1 G): *de quo supra diximus* = 33.5-8 and 46.10-12 (29.2-4 and 40.26-28 KS, 32.4-6 and 40.8-10 St. 37.18-20 and 51.8-10 G). The mss. all read here ... *Clodius Sex. Clodium de quo supra diximus*, leaving out the principal verb; Hotoman first suggested *misit*, and he has been followed by Kiessling and Schoell, and Clark. It is easy to see how the ending *-mus* could have been mistaken for the beginning of the next word *mis-* and that word missed out. Stangl, however, prefers to read *dixi misit*; that would be an unusual use of the first person singular in one of these cross-references (the plural being almost always used with *dicere*).[36] There is only one other use of the singular *dixi* (93.16); perhaps it too should read *diximus*, for there is possibly some textual corruption there. The mss. all have *dicit* (wrongly reported as

---

[36] See above, n. 12.

The Range of the Commentaries 25

dixit by Clark), which is conceivably the correct reading, since Cicero himself could have made the point in a part of the speech which Asconius did not comment on and which has therefore been lost to us; there are instances where Asconius gives cross-references to points made by Cicero himself (e.g. 5.1-2, 27.17, 80.5-6, 84.5),[37] but it must be admitted that in these cases the cross-references are always to statements of Cicero on which Asconius comments. An argument in favour of reading *dixi* (or *diximus*) instead of *dicit* at 93.16 is that the clause looks like one of the formulae for Asconius' own cross-references. Cross-references to lemmata of Cicero always have an adverb like *postea, supra, iam* etc.

(x) 50.22 (44.30 KS, 43.9 St, 56.3 G): *diximus in argumento orationis huius* = 36.18-19 (32.1-2 KS, 34.10-11 St, 41.12-13 G).

(y) 52.11 (46.14 KS, 44.9 St, 57.18 G): *ut saepe diximus* = 40.21-25 and 42.9-11 (35.23-27 and 37.5-7 KS, 36.26-28 and 37.21-22 St, 45.15-18 and 47.5-7 G). Stangl, n. ad loc., suggests that this is possibly also a cross-reference to a comment on a lost speech, presumably because *saepe* ought to mean more than twice. But as Asconius' cross-references always refer backwards and as the event referred to in the cross-reference took place during the course of the trial at which the speech on which Asconius is commenting was delivered (Plancus' *contio* just before the final day of Milo's trial), there could not possibly have been a speech of Cicero earlier than the *pro Milone* in which the event could have been mentioned. This cross-reference then can only be to earlier comments on the same speech.

---

[37] See above, n. 13.

SECTION TWO

THE PURPOSE OF ASCONIUS' COMMENTARIES

Before looking at the question of the purpose of Asconius' writing of commentaries on Cicero's speeches, it would be as well to determine what few personal details we know about him, to provide the background against which to discuss the likely purpose. Very little is known of his life: we do not, for example, know whether he undertook a public career — if he did, it would have some relevance to the question of the purpose of his commentaries. He was a native of Patavium, as his reference to *Livius noster* at 77.4-5 shows; Quintilian says that he learnt from Asconius that Livy used the spelling *sibe* and *quase* (for *sibi* and *quasi*) and that Asconius adopted the precedent,[1] suggesting that he and Livy had something in common such as the same Italian origin. His *Patavinitas* is confirmed by several inscriptions from the town in which the *gens Asconia* is mentioned,[2] and by the evidence of Silius Italicus who writes of a young man named Pedianus who came from the area supposedly colonised by the Trojan Antenor (i.e. the northern Adriatic coast of Italy) and from among the people who rejoiced in the spring of Aponus (i.e. Patavium), and who had no rival either in battle or when he preferred the peaceful company of the Muses and the obscurity of a studious life.[3] These verses were no doubt composed as a mark of honour for Asconius and celebrated his scholarly pursuits. They may not have described Asconius himself, for Silius wrote his poem after his consulship in A.D. 68, and by that time Asconius was an old man; they were perhaps written about one of his sons, who would have been slightly younger contemporaries of Silius (who died c. A.D. 100 at the age of seventy-five).[4] Silius himself may have come from Patavium.[5] His verses suggest that Asconius was at least a *domi nobilis*.

Asconius seems to have been familiar with the geography and

---

[1] Quint. 1.7.24: *sibe et quase scriptum in multorum libris est, sed an hoc voluerint auctores nescio: T. Livium ita his usum ex Pediano comperi, qui et ipse eum sequebatur.* It should be added that there is no sign of this spelling in the writings of either author.
[2] *CIL* V.2820, 2829, 2848, 2899, 2937.
[3] Sil. Ital. *Pun.* 12.212-222.
[4] Madvig, p. 17; contra, Kiessling and Schoell, intro. p. v, note.
[5] D.J. Campbell, *CR* 50 (1936) 56-8, who accepts evidence that Asconius was one of the poet's names; the evidence is an inscription from a temple of Aphrodite in Asia where Silius was governor c. 77 (W.M. Calder, *CR* 49 [1935] 216-7; cf. now W.C. McDermott and A.E. Orentzel, *AJP* 98 [1977] 24). For further discussion of Asconius' origins, see J.T. Ramsey, *HSCP* 80 (1976) 312.

The Purpose of the Commentaries   27

buildings of Rome and its environs; he knew the history of the temple of Apollo (90.6ff.) and the location of the Regia (48.12-3) and sites in the suburbs of Rome (50.7-9), and he actually pointed out the house of Largus Caecina (which had formerly belonged to the Scauri) to his sons on a tour of Rome (27.1ff.). This suggests that Asconius either lived in Rome, or at least had spent some time there (possibly while receiving his finishing education).[6] It is possible that he undertook a public career; he was well known and held in honour, as the verses of Silius Italicus show, and the notice of Jerome (discussed below), which indicates that he was regarded as a *vir illustris* by Suetonius, since it was derived from his lost work *de viris illustribus* (though the honour he was held in may derive from his reputation as a scholar rather than as a public figure). He seems to have been preparing his sons for entry to the senate, since at 43.27-28 he says that their age requires him to explain a piece of senatorial procedure, and this may suggest that he was himself a member of the senate. Moreover it is known that at least one member of his *gens* attained membership of the senate and got as far as the praetorship,[7] while another was a local magistrate in Patavium.[8] If Asconius was himself a member of the senate, it would explain how he had access to public documents such as *acta* and *leges* to which he frequently refers.

A determination of Asconius' age, and therefore the period in which he wrote his commentaries, is relevant to the question of the purpose of his writing. There is a notice in Jerome, drawn from Suetonius' *de viris illustribus*, under the year of Abraham 2092 (= A.D. 76, the seventh year of Vespasian's rule[9]):

> *Q. Asconius Pedianus scriptor historicus clarus habetur, qui LXXIII aetatis suae anno captus luminibus, XII postea annis in summo omnium honore consenescit.*

It is not clear whether the notice refers to the year of his blindness or of his death. Madvig (p. 16), whose dates for Asconius most commentators follow, favours A.D. 76 as the year of his blindness, thus making A.D. 3

---

[6] Cf. below, p. 36, for discussion of where his sons were educated.
[7] From an undated inscription (*CIL* V.2820), we know of a Q. Asconius Gabinius Modestus, who was praetor, proconsul and prefect of the treasury of Saturn (*PIR* 1².1204).
[8] C. Asconius Sardus (*CIL* V.2829; *PIR* 1².1208). From the same inscription, we know of this man's sister, who married Augurinus and was made a priestess of the divine Domitilla (hence dating the inscription to the Flavian period); her husband may have been the consular T. Mustius Hostilius Fabricius Medulla Augurinus (*CIL* V.2822; van Rohden, *RE* 2 [1896] 1527; Groag, *PIR* 1².1209, says she was his mother).
[9] Equated to A.D. 75 by Schanz-Hosius, *Geschichte der römischen Literatur*[4] (Munich, 1935) 2.732. The reference to Suetonius is in Reifferscheid, p. 92.

the year of his birth and A.D. 88 the year of his death.[10] Clark (intro. p. vi) takes the notice to indicate the year of his death, thus having him born in 9 B.C. and going blind in A.D. 64,[11] but an argument against this is that it would make him blind about the time that he was writing his commentaries.[12] Benario follows Madvig's dates, adding the further argument that Jerome, when writing the obituary of an individual, does so by using a verb which indicates death, whereas the verb used in his notice about Asconius (*consenescit*) is not of that sort; it refers to a significant event in his old age.[13]

Quintilian's use of the past tense in the passage quoted in n. 1 above indicates that Asconius was dead by the time the *institutio oratoriae* was written, and it is generally agreed that it was written shortly before the death of Domitian (A.D. 96). It is not clear from this passage of Quintilian whether Asconius and Livy were personally acquainted with each other. As the great historian died in A.D. 17, any contact between them could only have been when Asconius was very young, if the birth date of A.D. 3 is accepted; or else we would have to accept an earlier birth date for Asconius (which is possible from other evidence to be discussed below). Kiessling and Schoell (pp. vi-vii) postulate that, as Livy died at Patavium, he spent his final years there and Asconius could have come into contact with him during his secondary schooling; he would have been about fourteen when Livy died, and soon after he would have assumed the *toga virilis* and gone off to Rome to finish his schooling (which would have been normal for the son of an Italian aristocratic family). But Asconius' observation about spelling need not have been made from personal acquaintance with Livy; it could have resulted from a scholarly interest in the writings of a fellow-townsman.

There are two pieces of internal evidence which relate to Asconius' age, and the period in which the commentaries were written. At 27.4-5 Asconius writes: *possidet eam [domum] nunc Largus Caecina qui consul fuit cum Claudio*.[14] It is argued that he would not have written *Claudio* if the emperor were still alive; he would have added *Augusto* or *Caesare* or *imperatore*. Hence it is conjectured that the comment was written after Claudius' death in A.D. 54.[15] It must also have been written

---

[10] Wissowa, *RE* 2 (1896) 1524; cf. Shanz-Hosius, op. cit. 2.732. Ramsey, art. cit. (n. 5) 311-2, thinks that Jerome's expressions do not make it an obituary or a landmark in Asconius' life, and therefore places his birth c. 1 B.C. and death c. A.D. 84.
[11] Cf. G.C. Richards, *OCD*^{2}, p. 130; W. Strzelecki, *Der kleine Pauly* 1 (1964) 635.
[12] Cf. Madvig, p. 9.
[13] H.W. Benario, *Historia* 22 (1973) 64-5.
[14] The mss. have *Longus* (or *Lognus*) *Cicin(n)a*; the correction to Largus Caecina by Lipsius on the basis of Dio 60.10.1 is obvious.
[15] Madvig, pp. 4-5; Kiessling and Schoell, intro. p. x; Schanz-Hosius, op. cit. (n. 9) 2.732; Stangl, n. ad loc. (= 27.28); Clark, intro. p. vi; Benario, art. cit. (n. 13) 65.

The Purpose of the Commentaries

before Caecina's death, for he was still alive (*nunc*) at the time it was written. It is possible to fix the date of his death: he was one of the Arval brothers, and in the acts of that brotherhood he is recorded as being present at the rites celebrated during the reigns of Gaius and Claudius from A.D. 38 onwards, but at the sacrifices for the *imperium* of Nero at the beginning of October A.D. 57 he is not recorded as being present;[16] hence it can be determined that he died before that date. This all suggests a date of composition for the commentaries between A.D. 54 and 57.

The second passage occurs at 90.6-7: *ne tamen erretis, quod his temporibus aedes Apollinis in Palatio fuit nobilissima*... The tense of the verb in the subordinate clause has caused problems, and several emendations have been put forward.[17] Kiessling and Schoell think that the tense should be retained (since it is the common reading of the three main manuscripts) and that it should indicate that the temple of Apollo built by Augustus had been destroyed by the great fire in A.D. 64 during Nero's rule. It would follow that the comments on the *in toga candida* must have been written after that date. There are difficulties with such an argument. If the argument from the second passage is correct, the two passages taken together would indicate that the commentaries were written over a period of more than seven years (i.e. from between A.D. 54-57 to after 64), but as they seem on the surface to have been written by Asconius for his sons at a particular stage in their education (see below), he could not have taken too long a time over their composition, else the sons would have passed that stage. Further, it has been argued above that the commentaries were written in the chronological order of the speeches delivered by Cicero; the commentary on the *in toga candida* ought therefore to come before the commentary on the *pro Scauro*, whereas Kiessling and Schoell's argument would place it well after. And a final point: there is no evidence that the temple of Apollo was destroyed in the fire during Nero's rule. So the argument for dating the commentary on the *in toga candida* after A.D. 64 is not strong, and we are left with the difficulty of the tense of the verb in the passage quoted above.

From the evidence of the first passage (which is more securely dated to between A.D. 54 and 57) some have argued that all the commentaries

---

[16] W. Henzen (ed.), *Acta fratrum Arvalium* (Berlin, 1874) pp. 44, 46, 47, 49, 50, 51 (Gaius), 54, 55, 59 (Claudius), 64 (Nero) = A. Pasoli (ed.) *Acta fratrum Arvalium* (Bologna, 1950) pp. 112, 113 (bis), 13, 14, 114 (bis), 115, 116 (additional references can be found on p. 13).

[17] *Est* by Wesenberg, *sit* by Manutius (followed by Stangl), and *stat* by Rau. The mss. reading *fuit* is retained by Kiessling and Schoell and by Clark. There is one other place (22.3) where the reading should be *est* and one of the mss. has *fuit* (S, while P and M have *sit*).

were written in this period.[18] It has been suggested in an earlier section that, because Asconius commented on a large number of speeches, it would have taken a longer time than that fairly narrow period to undertake the research and prepare the material necessary to compose the commentaries. On the other hand, they must have been written in a relatively short period if they were to be of any use to his sons (for whom he said he wrote them). The answer is probably that, although they were written in a short time, Asconius had been collecting the material for them for a long time; indeed they were probably the fruits of the scholarly pursuits for which Asconius achieved a reputation. The short period of actual composition, with a large number of speeches involved, probably explains the brief and somewhat capricious selection of passages dealt with in any one commentary.

At all accounts, it seems reasonable to suggest that the commentaries were written somewhere in the period of Nero's rule, and very likely in the early part of it. That helps to confirm the conclusion drawn about Asconius's age from the notice of Jerome, for in the early part of Nero's rule he would have been in his early to mid-fifties (rather than in his late sixties to seventies, if the notice relates to the year of his death), which appears likely for a man whose sons were relatively young.[19] At the time of composition his sons were in their late teens or early twenties, and if Asconius were in his fifties when he wrote the commentaries, the sons would have been born when he was in his thirties (which is what one would normally expect). The commentaries were the work of a man who expected that he still had some of his life to go, for Asconius says on a number of occasions that he still has some more research which he intends to do.[20] Those intentions are more suited to a man in his fifties, and are not the sort of statements made by an old man.[21]

A comment by Philargyrius (followed by the Berne scholiast) on Verg. *Ecl.* 3.105 says that Asconius had actually heard Vergil speaking about his poetry.[22] But if we believe the notice in Jerome about Asconius' dates, he was not even born when Vergil died. This comment by Philargyrius has led Scaliger to postulate two Asconii, one who was known to Vergil and Livy and another who was the *scriptor historicus* of Jerome's notice. But

---

[18] For the references, see n. 15.
[19] Benario, art. cit. (n. 13) 65.
[20] 7.26, 10.19, 48.5, 48.23, 53.15-16, 92.2-3.
[21] Kiessling and Schoell, intro. p. xi; Stangl, n. ad loc. (= 15.6); cf. Madvig, p. 8.
[22] Hagen, Vol. III, fasc. II, p. 70: *item Asconius Pedianus ait se audisse Vergilium dicentem in hoc loco se grammaticis crucem fixisse: quaesituros eos si quid studiosius occultaretur, dicit autem poeta Coelium Mantuanam.*

The Purpose of the Commentaries 31

this argument is firmly rejected by Madvig,[23] who thinks that Philargyrius has made an error, getting wrong information from some *librarius* or epitomator.

In Rome, Asconius had contact with a number of prominent and (at times) influential people. He knew the consul of 8 B.C., C. Asinius Gallus, for Servius in a comment on Verg. *Ecl.* 4.11 says that Asconius had heard Gallus declare that the *Fourth Eclogue* was written in his honour.[24] On one occasion we know of, Asconius was taken to a dinner party given by M. Gravius Apicius as a guest of Q. Iunius Blaesus, the consul of A.D. 28 with L. Antistius Vetus,[25] and uncle of Tiberius' adviser Seianus; the conversation at the dinner party, reported in the Suda,[26] was about old age, and Blaesus' father, who had been consul in A.D. 10 (Tac. *ann.* 3.72 and 74) and was now a *sexagenarius*, was also present. Those contacts give some indication of the cultured and scholarly circles within which Asconius moved.

There are indications that Asconius wrote other works.[27] Donatus' *Life of Vergil* mentions a *librum contra obtrectatores Vergilii*;[28] a work on Vergil is suggested by a comment of Probus;[29] and Servius' comment, mentioned above, about Asconius' conversation with Asinius Gallus shows his interest in Vergil, as does Philargyrius' comment discussed above. The report of the discussion at Apicius' dinner party could have been taken by the Suda from a work by Asconius, *de longaevorum laude*,

---

[23] Madvig, pp. 7-8.
[24] Thilo and Hagen, Vol. III, fasc. I, p. 46: *Asconius Pedianus a Gallo audisse se refert hanc eclogam in honorem eius factam.* For the rejection of Servius' allegation, see R. Syme, *CQ* 32 (1938) 39.
[25] On the identification of the Blaesus mentioned in the account of the dinner, see Madvig, pp. 12-4; Klebs, in Wissowa, *RE* 2 (1896) 1525; cf. Riba, *RE* 10.1 (1917) 967.
[26] Adler, pp. 287-8 (s.v.'Απίκιος Μάρκος) (= Aelian. frag. 110, according to Hercher, Vol. II, p. 240; cf. his notes on frag. 246 in *Bibliotheca Graecorum Scriptorum* [Paris, 1858] pp. 458-9).
[27] For a list, see Wissowa, loc. cit. (n. 10) 1524-5; Shanz-Hosius, op. cit (n. 9) 733.
[28] Reifferscheid, p. 66: *Asconius Pedianus libro quem contra Vergilii obtrectatores scripsit pauca admodum obiecta ei proponit eaque circa historiam fere et quod pleraque ab Homero sumpsisset, sed hoc ipsum crimen sic defenderet assuetum ait, Cur non illi quoque eadem furta temptarent? verum intellecturos facilius esse Herculi clavam quam Homero versum subripere.* Cf. id. p. 57: *vulgatum est consuesse eum et cum Plotia Hieria. sed Asconius Pedianus affirmat ipsam postea maiorem natu narrare solitam invitatum quidem a Vario ad communionem sui verum pertinacissime recusasse.*
[29] Hagen, Vol. III, fasc. II, p. 329: *nec mirandum quod infra se senem dicit cum certum sit eum, ut Asconius Pedianus dicit, XXVIII annos natum Bucolica edidisse.*

which may have taken the form of a *symposium*.[30] Pseudo-Acron (on Hor. *sat.* 1.2.41) refers to a *Life of Sallust* written by Asconius;[31] a study of that historian's life might explain why Asconius was able to include so much detail about Sallust's tribunician activity in the *argumentum* to the comments on the *pro Milone*. However, Kiessling and Schoell argue that the incident referred to by Pseudo-Acron (the apprehension of Sallust in adultery by Milo) is not mentioned by Asconius when he refers to the *inimicitia* between the two men at 37.18-20 in the comments on the *pro Milone* and that therefore the *vita Sallustii* must have been written after the commentaries on Cicero's speeches.[32] Another work, *de origine gentis Romanae*, which was thought in the 16th century to have been written by Asconius, has now been shown to have been falsely attributed.[33]

The picture of Asconius which emerges, then, is that of a cultivated gentleman, living in the Julio-Claudian and Flavian periods, probably involved in public affairs but devoting his leisure hours to study and, like a Varro or a Messalla or a Pollio, writing down the fruits of his researches into the antiquity, literature and history of Rome.

The commentaries on Cicero's speeches by Asconius were ostensibly written for his sons. They are addressed directly at 43.28, and the second person plural is used commonly throughout the work, most frequently in the alternative forms of cross-references discussed earlier (p. 5). To gain some idea of the purpose of the commentaries, it is important to fix the age of the sons; we do not know how many Asconius had, but they were presumably close in age, as the address to them in the plural shows that they were at a similar stage in their education and that the commentaries were designed to be used by them at that same stage. The address at 43.27-28 is the only passage which will help to fix their age; after quoting

---

[30] Asconius' interest in old age is revealed by Plin. *NH* 7.159: *Sammulam quoque CX annis vixisse auctor est Pedianus Asconius.* From the references in Pliny and the Suda, Hirzel, *Rhein. Mus.* 43 (1888) 314, argues that Asconius wrote a *symposium* in the Platonic style, concerning the benefits of exercise and its effect on prolonging life; cf. Wissowa, loc. cit (n. 10) 1525; Schanz-Hosius, op. cit. (n. 9) 733; Kiessling and Schoell, intro. p. viii; Clark, intro. p. viii.

[31] Keller, Vol. II, p. 21: *Sallustius enim Crispus in Faustae filiae Sulla adulterio deprehensus ab Annio Milone flagellis caesus esse dicitur, quem Asconius Pedianus in vita eius significat.* The incident is first mentioned by Varro (in Gell. 17.18).

[32] Kiessling and Schoell, intro. pp. ix-x; cf. Stangl, n. ad loc. (= 34.31). The admission by Asconius at 91.2-3, that he had not yet found the name of the woman with whom Catilina had committed adultery and of the girl produced by that affair whom Catilina subsequently married, shows either that he did not know his Sallust (for the name of the girl, Aurelia Orestilla, is revealed in Sall. *Cat.* 15.2) or that he forgot; in support of the first possibility, Stangl, n. ad loc. (= 71.5-6), argues that Asconius had not yet written his *vita Sallustii*.

[33] Madvig, pp. 22-3.

a part of *Mil.* 14, Asconius comments: *quid sit dividere sententiam ut enarrandum sit vestra aetas, filii, facit.* This suggests that they were not yet of an age to know senatorial procedure (as well as suggesting that they were being prepared for entry to the senate ultimately, which in turn might indicate that Asconius himself was a member of the senatorial class).[34] In the republican period, one would imagine that this sort of information would be given during the *tirocinium fori*, the period of practical training in public affairs by the attachment of a boy to an experienced public figure about the time he assumed the *toga virilis* (i.e. about the age of fifteen or sixteen). Under the empire, the need for this period of practical training would have been reduced and boys would have tended to stay on at school longer, though there were still examples of *tirocinium fori*,[35] and there was still an emphasis on rhetorical training as a basis for public affairs in the later stages of a boy's education, since there was still a need for advocates and the exercise of rhetorical skill. Entry to the senate in the late republican period was by the holding of the quaestorship which was usually attained about the age of thirty; under the early empire the age for the quaestorship had moved forward and entry to the senate could be gained about the age of twenty-five.[36] It could be thought, therefore, that Asconius' training of his sons in senatorial procedure would be given when they were in their early twenties. But the simple style of his commentaries suggests sons of a younger age than that;[37] moreover, they are likely to have been away from their father on military service during their early twenties, if they were interested in pursuing a public career (and some military service is suggested by the verses of Silius Italicus, if they were written in honour of a son of Asconius: see above, p. 26). Perhaps the sons should be thought of as in their late teens when they had assumed the *toga virilis*, moved into the third level of their education (the rhetorical school), and begun that practical training in public affairs which was usually associated with that age.

At the second level of a boy's education, the grammar school, literature was the main study, and this involved explanation of the

---

[34] M.T. Griffin, *Seneca: a Philosopher in Politics* (Oxford, 1976) p. 85 n. 2, argues from the use of *aetas* at 43.28 that Asconius' sons were being prepared for entry to the senate. She also points out the success of Italians from Patavium in securing office and entering the senate in the early part of Nero's reign.

[35] For example, Quintilian was attached to Cn. Domitius Afer, cos. 42 (Quint. 5.7.7). Cf. the comments of Plin. *ep.* 8.14.4-10 on the differences in preparation of young men for public life between earlier times and his own day. Augustus revived the practice of allowing adolescents to stand at the doors of the senate-house to learn procedure (Suet. *Aug.* 38.2).

[36] Discussion of evidence in Syme, *Tacitus* (Oxford, 1958) Vol. II, App. 17 (pp. 652-3).

[37] For the argument that the style suited the age of his sons, see Madvig, p. 78.

standard works.[38] It was mostly poetry which was elucidated by the *grammaticus*;[39] generally speaking, prose writers belonged to other (and higher) branches of study — the orators to rhetoric, and the philosophers to philosophy. The position of historical writers was anomalous: there was no teaching of history as a subject on its own, and there was no reading of historical texts in the schools, except for Sallust eventually.[40] The aims of literary study in the grammar school are put by Quintilian (1.4.2, cf. 1.9.1) as *recte loquendi scientia* and *poetarum enarratio*; the procedure by which these aims were achieved involved the rote learning of large amounts of text by the pupils, but it also involved what is called *praelectio* by the teacher.[41] In his lectures the teacher explained the passage of text under study word by word, dealing not only with linguistic and grammatical points, but also stylistic features and the various stories that occurred.[42] It is in this last area that historical information would have been given; Cicero says (*de or.* 1.187) that *historiarum cognitio* was part of the *enarratio*.

The teaching of the *grammaticus* was, however, apt to become a pedantic and self-satisfied display of erudition; his lectures tended to deal with out-of-the-way learning. Others would try to out-do his knowledge or to catch him out, and he could become angry if his ignorance was revealed.[43] In this situation, pupils would not be led to a true appreciation of the aesthetic worth of the texts they were studying. Perhaps it was to fill in the gaps left by such teaching, or to provide some simple material, that Asconius wrote the commentaries for his sons.

Cicero was not studied much, if at all, at the grammar school stage. By Asconius' time his speeches would have been studied in the rhetorical school (the next stage) but then only as a model for oratory and not as a subject for literary study. Quintilian (2.5.20) quotes Livy as saying that other authors should be studied only in so far as they resemble Cicero; this suggests that Cicero was read in schools by Livy's time, but presumably

---

[38] The following discussion is based mainly on H.I. Marrou, *A History of Education in Antiquity*, 3rd edn., trans. G. Lamb (London, 1956) pp. 255-91, and M.L. Clarke, *Higher Education in the Roman World* (London, 1971) chap. 2. They in turn base their views on Quintilian's *institutio oratoriae*, which is likely to reflect educational practice of the time when Asconius was writing.
[39] Marrou, pp. 251-2; Clarke, p. 21. The range of authors studied was standard and limited. On *grammatici* see A.D. Booth, *Hermes* 106 (1978) 117-25.
[40] Clarke, pp. 21-2.
[41] Marrou, p. 279, suggests that the *praelectio* preceded the reading aloud of the passage set for study, while Clarke, p. 23, says that it followed.
[42] For an example of the sorts of topics dealt with in a *praelectio*, see Quint. 1.8.13-17.
[43] Clarke, p. 24 (based on Gell. 4.1, 6.17, 18.4.2, 20.10; Aug. *de ord.* 2.12.37); cf. A. Gwynn, *Roman Education* (Oxford, 1926) pp. 198f. Asconius' frequent criticism of Fenestella shows something of the same attitude (see below, pp. 53-5).

The Purpose of the Commentaries

only for style or as a rhetorical model. As part of the preparation for rhetorical study, pupils in the grammar school were set simple rhetorical exercises called *progymnasmata*, which included comparison of orators. Cicero and Demosthenes were among the orators set for comparison in such exercises,[44] which again suggests that there was some reading of Cicero in the grammar schools, but again only as a rhetorical model. Quintilian attempted to get students at his school to read Ciceronian and other speeches as models, but the experiment failed because they preferred to use Quintilian's own speeches as models.[45] He remained convinced of the value of the study of Cicero's speeches, but it is clear that Cicero was not yet widely read in either the grammar or the rhetorical school.

At about the age of fifteen or sixteen (i.e. about the time that a boy assumed the *toga virilis*), he went on to the tertiary level of his education, the rhetorical school, and he remained there until about twenty, or even more.[46] In Quintilian's time the change of *toga* made little difference, and the average student would continue to be a schoolboy; Aulus Gellius tells us that he continued to study under a *grammaticus* when he was an *adulescens* (7.6.12, 20.6.1), and the lines of rhetorical training were becoming blurred between the grammar and the rhetorical school. This is evident in Quintilian's school where the pupils were divided into classes according to age and ability (2.2.14).

The main subject studied at this higher level was, of course, rhetoric.[47] The high ideal of Cicero was that the study of rhetoric should be based on the widest possible culture, with a solid philosophical training, as well as the study of law and history; in practice rhetoric became dry academic theory, and history was reduced to a list of *exempla*, memorable words and deeds, which an orator would find useful to remember so that he could bring them out on the right occasions (such as the work of Valerius Maximus which was already in existence by the time Asconius wrote).[48]

One can imagine, then, that Asconius' sons, in their late teenage years

---

[44] Quint. 10.5.2-3; Plin. *ep.* 7.9; Suet. *gramm.* 25.5; cf. Varr. *ling. Lat.* 5.96f.
[45] Quint. 2.5.2ff., cf. 1.4.3.
[46] Marrou, p. 265. Others suggest a slightly earlier leaving age: Gwynn, p. 196, about nineteen, and Clarke, p. 33, about eighteen.
[47] The importance of rhetoric as a school subject can be gathered from the endowment of chairs of rhetoric and teaching positions. For example, Vespasian established salaried chairs of both Greek and Latin rhetoric at Rome (Suet. *Vesp.* 18). Caesar offered citizenship to teachers of the liberal arts (Suet. *Iul.* 42.2), and during a grain shortage Augustus expelled all foreigners except teachers and physicians (Suet. *Aug.* 42.3).
[48] In general on the use of *exempla* in oratory, see E. Rawson, *JRS* 62 (1972) 31, and M.M. Sage, *Historia* 28 (1979) 206-10.

(or perhaps their early twenties), were still at rhetorical school, among other things studying Cicero's speeches as rhetorical models, and possibly still doing some *enarratio* in the style of the grammar school (as Aulus Gellius later seems to have done), but needing some *historiarum cognitio* to fill out their study of the Ciceronian speeches, which their father supplied for them out of his own scholarship and interest.[49] One should note that Asconius uses the heading *enarratio* for his comments (the term is used for one of the aims of literary study in the grammar school), and precedes it with an *argumentum* setting out the context of the speech; the whole thing is much what one imagines the *praelectio* of the *grammaticus* to have been (and perhaps Asconius used that format because it was the one he would have been familiar with from his own school-days and because he realised it would be most appropriate to the age and school-experience of his sons).

It is not clear whether the sons went to school in Rome or in Patavium. Madvig (pp. 18-9, cf. p. 77) argues that Asconius did not always live in Rome, but spent some time back in Padua, since otherwise he would not have made such a comment as *demonstrasse vobis memini me hanc domum* ... (27.1ff.) or *via Appia est prope urbem monumentum Basili qui locus latrociniis fuit perquam infamis* (50.7-8).[50] What this suggests to him is that Asconius had pointed these places out to his sons during a visit to Rome; he would not have made this sort of comment if they all lived in Rome. But, given the size of Rome and the likely need for someone to point out the sights even to a resident, these comments could well have been made by Asconius to his sons while living in Rome. Moreover, his acquaintance with prominent Roman figures, the contact with Quintilian, the attention he received (indicated by the notice in Jerome), the possibility that he was involved in public affairs, all suggest that he lived in Rome and that his commentaries were written there. If the sons were educated in Patavium, it might have been difficult to get hold of a well-qualified teacher, and the commentaries might have been written to fill in the gaps left by a poorly qualified one. But it is more likely that his sons received their final education at least in Rome, just as Asconius himself probably had (which is what one would expect in a family of *domi nobiles*).

Madvig (pp. 58-9) explains the interest during the early empire in

---

[49] Ramsey, art. cit (n. 5) 312, thinks that the need for a secondary work such as that of Asconius can be appreciated in view of the large number of provincials who were coming to Rome for their education; language presented no barrier to them, but republican history almost certainly did.

[50] Kiessling and Schoell, intro. p. viii; they think that he lived in Rome but it was possible that he returned to Patavium for some time, perhaps during the reign of Nero. Clark, intro. p. viii, says it is uncertain whether he lived in Rome or Patavium.

writing historical (as opposed to grammatical) commentaries on prose orations like those of Cicero as a desire to understand what the free republic was like, now that there had been a major change in the constitution. He summarises Asconius' work as that of a *scriptor historicus*.[51] But the scale of Asconius' commentaries does not reach as high as that, and the level at which they are pitched is relatively low; even the style is simple, being appropriate to the age of his sons. The sort of comment made at 15.3 (*credo vos ignorare*) or 9.10 (*profecto intellegitis*) or 12.11 (*fortasse quaeratis quem dicat Marcellum*) reveals something of the purpose of the commentaries — to identify persons or institutions from republican history which are used as historical *exempla* in Cicero's speeches. They are not far removed, therefore, from the sort of collection of *exempla* provided by Valerius Maximus, and necessary no doubt to supplement his sons' studies because history was not a subject taught in the schools. It should be remembered that Asconius' comments range over the whole period of republican history, and not just the period when Cicero delivered speeches; given that Asconius commented on more than the speeches we have, a good deal of Roman history would have been covered in his comments, and presumably a good knowledge of it secured by his sons via these comments.

The dedication of a work to a son, either on the subject of rhetoric or of scholarship generally, was a commonplace in Latin literature.[52] Cicero's *partitiones oratoriae* was written for his son;[53] the date of publication is uncertain, but it could not have been much before the late 50's when the young Quintus was in his mid-teens and about to begin his rhetorical training. Quintilian's *institutio oratoriae*, published just before Domitian's death but reflecting twenty years of his teaching experience (and hence revealing attitudes towards schooling not long after Asconius was writing), was dedicated to Marcellus Victorius in the hope that it would prove of service in the education of his son Geta.[54] The prologue of Aulus Gellius' *Noctes Atticae* states that his writings were intended as a recreation for his children when they had some respite from business affairs and could unbend and divert their minds (§ 1), though he hopes for a wider audience who might have the leisure to study his observations and expand their knowledge (§ 14). Most significant is the late fourth century

---

[51] Borrowing the term from the notice of Jerome: cf. Kiessling and Schoell, intro. p. viii.
[52] On the series of authors who write, or pretend to write, at the urgent request of their friends, relatives, or publishers, see T. Janson, 'Latin Prose Prefaces: Studies in Literary Conventions', *Acta Universitatis Stockholmiensis* 13 (1964) 27-32. In addition to the examples given, cf. the treatise on rhetoric dedicated to C. Herennius, which was dedicated to the latter and written at his insistence (*Auct. ad Herenn.* 1.1).
[53] Cic. *part. or.* 1.
[54] Quint. 1. pr. 6.

commentary on Vergil by Tiberius Claudius Donatus, dedicated to his son, as the very title shows; it was written, he says, so that the son might compare his comments with those of other commentators and thus arrive at a fuller understanding.[55] These dedications provide the parallel for Asconius' composition: the commentaries were intended to help in the education of his children. They were not perhaps intended, in the style of Gellius, to absorb some of their leisure hours, though they were most likely the product of Asconius' researches in his own leisure hours.

How then did they come to be published? Parents clearly took an interest in the education of their children. Quintilian says that he was asked by certain of his friends to write on the art of speaking, and he dedicated his work to help in the education of a friend's son; Pliny the younger was asked to choose a teacher for a friend's nephew (*ep.* 2.18.2); Aulus Gellius wrote for his children's benefit. Asconius' scholarly interests were widely known among his contemporaries: Quintilian and Silius Italicus knew of his scholarly pursuits, and Pliny the elder knew at least of his book on old age; his commentaries on Cicero's speeches were known to Quintilian (5.10.9), and must therefore have already been in circulation, probably during Asconius' lifetime. It is likely that friends of Asconius asked for a copy of the notes he had prepared for his sons, wishing to use them with their own sons, when they found out how useful they were. Asconius cannot have had a wider audience in mind when he first wrote the commentaries, for the comment *demonstrasse vos memini me* at 27.1 seems unnecessary for an audience whom Asconius had not personally conducted around Rome. It might be considered to be a literary device to provide realism, but if so it is the only attempt to provide it. The address to his sons is no mere literary device (like Quintilian's and Aulus Gellius' dedications) to introduce a polished literary composition; the simple style and note-like quality of Asconius' commentaries shows what they were intended to be. The commentaries were still in circulation when Aulus Gellius collected material for his *Noctes Atticae* (written about the late 140's), for he refers to the commentary on Cicero's *pro Roscio Amerino* (see above, p. 11); by that time, commentaries for use in schools had obviously become more widespread, and it was to that use that Asconius' commentaries are most likely to have been put.

---

[55] Donat. *interpretationes Vergilianae*, pp. 1-2 Georg: *haec, fili carissime, tui causa conscripsi, non ut sola perlegas, sed ut conlatione habita intellegas quid tibi ex illorum labore quidve ex paterno sequendum sit. non enim aut illi omnia conplexi sunt, ut res ipsa indicat, aut ego tanta conposui quae te possint ad pleni intellectus effectum conpetenter instruere.*

SECTION THREE

THE SOURCES OF ASCONIUS' COMMENTARIES

Asconius is perhaps unique not only because he nominates such a wide variety of sources (in relation to the comparatively short length of the work as we have it) but also because he frequently mentions not just the name of his source but the part of the work from which it comes (e.g. 13.13-14 — *Iulius Hyginus dicit in libro priore de viris claris*; 13.19 — *Varro quoque in libro III de vita populi Romani*; 48.25-26 — *apud Tironem libertum Ciceronis in libro IIII de vita eius*).[1]

Some comments on particular sources frequently used:

1. Cicero

It is clear that a great deal of Asconius' material was drawn from Cicero's works themselves, even beyond the small number of instances where he specifically nominates a particular work. The writings of Cicero which Asconius used included, of course, the speeches (or rather the published versions of them) which he must have known extensively because he commented on a large number of them (if not all), and also the rhetorical works, as well as the posthumously published *expositio consiliorum suorum*. In the case where the Ciceronian version is known to us through later writers whom Asconius could conceivably have consulted, it is reasonable to assume that he did not get the version from them, but direct from Cicero. He would, of course, have had to rely a great deal on what he could remember from his reading of Cicero (as with all the sources he used). It would not have been easy to look up or check a reference in a papyrus roll, even given that the book was available in one's own library or in that of a nearby friend. Hence Asconius is not always able to give a specific reference to the source of a piece of information, nor perhaps would he have been expected to do so.[2] It is necessary to bear in mind, when assessing the validity of Asconius's apparently scholarly use of references almost in the modern critical way, that for a scholar working in the conditions of the ancient period memory would have played a very important role in the use of references.

---

[1] For a list of authors to whom Asconius refers specifically by name, see Addendum II at the end of this Section.
[2] Cf. the comment of G.P. Goold, *HSCP* 74 (1970) 135-6, on Servius: an ancient commentator would not expect to have to document every statement he made, especially when there would have been other commentaries available at the time to fill in the gaps in his bibliography.

As happens with all ancient commentators (and perhaps some modern ones too), much of the information is gathered simply from the context in Cicero's actual speech, sometimes not going much beyond mere paraphrase.[3] For example, the information at 1.2-3 that the *in Pisonem* was delivered a few days before the games conducted by Pompeius is derived from §65 of the speech itself; the description at 16.12-13 of Philodemus and his poetry is taken from §70 of the *in Pisonem*; the comment at 31.4-8 that Milo was confident he had the support of the *boni*, and of the people through his hand-outs (which lost him three inheritances) is drawn, as Asconius actually admits by the phrase *Cicero significat*, from the speech itself (§§5 and 95);[4] the description at 27.5-6 of the four huge columns in the atrium of Scaurus' house is taken from §45 of the speech, frags. 1 (= Quint. 5.13.40) and n (= Cic. *or.* 223; Quint. 9.2.15).[5]

There are even verbal echoes in Asconius' direct borrowings from the speeches themselves: for example, at 30.18-20 Asconius writes

praeterea in eundem annum consulatum Milo, Clodius praeturam petebat, quam debilem futuram consule Milone intellegebat.

which echoes Cic. *Mil.* 25

occurrebat ei [sc. *Clodio*] *mancam ac debilem praeturam futuram suam consule Milone.*

The last example shows that Asconius uses information from sections of a speech on which he does not specifically comment. A further example of this can be found in the concluding remarks on the *pro Milone* at 54.3-6 when he discusses the testimony of M. Cato which he had heard from M. Favonius of Clodius' threat to Milo. This is drawn from *Mil.* 27, though there is no comment on that section in the *enarratio*.[6] Such borrowing is more likely to occur in the *argumentum* and the concluding remarks than in the actual commentary.

Of course, with the comments on the two lost speeches, the *pro Cornelio* and the *in toga candida*, it is much more difficult to determine where Asconius is simply borrowing from or parapharasing the speech

---

[3] Cf. E. Badian, *JRS* 63 (1973) 125 and 130 (on the Schol. Bob.).

[4] There are two further examples where Asconius admits to using Cicero's speech: 31.13 (on the date of the brawl between Clodius and Milo, = *Mil.* 27) and 7.25 (on Metellus Celer's blocking of an attempt to hold the Compitalician Games, = *Pis.* 8). Cf. the example of 54.3-6, drawn from *Mil.* 27, which is discussed below.

[5] For more examples of such borrowings, see C. Lichtenfeldt, *De Q. Asconii Pediani fontibus ac fide* (Breslau, 1888) pp. 5-12 (hereafter referred to by author's surname only).

[6] Again Asconius admits that he has taken it from Cicero (*Cicero nominaverat* . . .).

itself. A good deal of the information in the *argumentum* to the *pro Cornelio* (especially details about the disturbance of the original trial and about the ultimate hearing) must have come from Cicero's speech itself. The *acta* had not yet been instituted, so Asconius could not have got anything from that source; there were senatorial records, which would presumably have been used for the details of the various laws proposed by Cornelius and the counter-measure on bribery proposed by the consul Piso; and details of judicial proceedings (charge, prosecutor, list of jury, interrogation of witness etc.) seem to have been kept,[7] which would also have provided information. Another important source of information about the trial and its background would have been the speech of the prosecutor Cominius which Asconius had access to (61.23-62.2). This would have filled out the information which could be surmised from Cicero's speech, so that it is not clear whether Asconius is using Cicero alone (since his reply to Cominius' statements might alone have given the background) or a combination of Cicero and Cominius.[8]

The following points look as though they might have been derived from the speech itself: the character reference for Cornelius at 57.4 (cf. 61.14) was presumably given by Cicero, as well as the information that he was a former quaestor of Pompeius. The flight of the Cominii described at 60.2-5 is clearly dealt with in *Corn.* I, frags. 13-15 P (which are not taken from Asconius' lemmata, a further example of information taken from sections of the speech on which there is no specific comment); one can assume, therefore, that in the original speech there would have been a fuller description of the disturbance to the first attempt to prosecute Cornelius, for the *operarum duces* of 59.22 and 60.11 are also mentioned in frag. 17 P (again not taken from the lemmata in Asconius). The list of prosecution witnesses, the five *principes civitatis*, at 60.19-21 and 79.20-24 will have been taken from the speech itself; in two of the fragments of the speech (*Corn.* II, frags. 5 and 6 P) Q. Catulus is specifically addressed, so it is clear that the others would have been mentioned in the full speech if we had it.

With the *in toga candida*, in addition to the information which Asconius could deduce from the speech itself, he had the *expositio consiliorum suorum* to fill out his comments (see below). Lichtenfeldt,

---

[7] In speeches delivered before 59 (the year the *acta* were instituted) Cicero indicates that such information was kept: reception of the charge (*Cluent.* 86), list of jury (*Verr.* 2.1.157), interrogation of witnesses (*Cluent.* 62), sentence (*fam.* 8.8.3).

[8] Lichtenfeldt, p. 10; cf. the reconstruction of the prosecution speech, based on Cicero's answers to it, by K. Kumaniecki, *Med. Kon. Vlaamse Weten.* 32 (1970) 12-26.

following Koetschau,[9] believes that the following items are likely to have been drawn from the speech itself. The occasion of the speech (83.4-12: *itaque haec oratio contra solos Catilinam et Antonium est . . . quod, cum in dies licentia ambitus augeretur propter praecipuam Catilinae et Antoni audaciam, censuerat senatus ut lex ambitus aucta etiam cum poena ferretur; eique rei Q. Mucius Orestinus tr. pl. intercesserat . . . ante dies comitiorum paucos*) seems to be suggested by frags. 1, 6, 12 and 13 P, and by the fact that most of the speech as we have it is directed at Catilina and Antonius. The comment that Cicero was closely related to M. Marius Gratidianus (84.10-11) will presumably have come from the speech itself; Gratidianus is mentioned several times in the speech. The several references to Clodius' prosecution of Catilina for extortion during his governorship of Africa may have been drawn from the speech itself, but this is a little more doubtful. It is mentioned elsewhere in Cicero's speeches, and is the subject of a comment by Asconius on *Pis.* 23 (9.17-18), and Asconius may have got at least some of his information about it for his comments on the *in tog. cand.* from Fenestella, since his discussion of the prosecution occurs where he is disputing Fenestella's view that Cicero defended Catilina. Some information about it may also have been drawn from the *expositio*. Likewise the comments about Antonius' depredations in Achaea (84.13-14); they may have been drawn from the speech itself, since the lemma on which Asconius is commenting refers to the prosecution of Antonius for those activities, or perhaps from the *expositio*.

Asconius does not gather information only from the particular speech on which he is commenting; he gets it from elsewhere in Cicero's works. Obviously he used information from other speeches; examples of this can be found in the earlier analysis of cross-references (see above, pp. 2-11) which help to establish the number of speeches on which he commented. One or two examples where Asconius does not use one of the formulaic cross-references will help to demonstrate how he uses other speeches as a source of information for a comment on a particular speech. The account at 10.15-19 in the comments on the *in Pisonem* of the auction of Cicero's property and the destruction of his house will have been taken from *red. in sen.* 18, *dom.* 62 and 113, and *Sest.* 54. The mention at 46.21-25 in the comments on the *pro Milone* of the plot said to have been formed by Clodius against Pompeius in 58 owes something to *Sest.* 69 and 84-85, and perhaps to *aer. alien. Mil.* frags. 4 and 9 (= 170 and 172 St).

Lichtenfeldt argues that the details of the *lex Aurelia* given at 17.4-7 and 67.11-12 are taken from the numerous references to the proposal for that law in the Verrine speeches (*div. in Caec.* 8, *Verr.* 2.2.174-175,

---

[9] Lichtenfeldt, pp. 20-2.

2.3.224, 2.5.177-178); he notes that Asconius' first comment on the law occurs in the context of a discussion of the prosecution of Verres.[10] But against this suggestion, one should point out that the Verrine speeches were all delivered before the Aurelian law was passed, at least fictitiously, and in the Ciceronian speeches the proposal of Cotta was to hand the courts over entirely to the equites,[11] whereas the description in Asconius is that of the division of the courts between the three *ordines*, which was the later compromise proposal passed after the trial of Verres had been completed.

A special problem exists in relation to the use by Asconius of one of Cicero's speeches as a source — the version of the *pro Milone* said to have been the one actually delivered by Cicero (42.2-4). That raises the question whether shorthand was yet well enough developed to be able to take down a speech, and it also raises the more general question about the publication of Cicero's speeches — were they written up soon after delivery, sticking fairly closely to the delivered version, or were they written up, sometimes much later, substantially altered for political (or other) purposes?[12] There is not space to deal with those questions here, and it is likely that they cannot be answered. Asconius states that he used the delivered version, which is so perfectly composed that it can justly be regarded as the best of all his speeches. For an explanation of the historical references it would not matter much if the versions differed greatly,[13] and they would not affect the discussion of the background which Asconius drew from other (and more reliable) sources.

There are indications that Asconius derived information not only from other speeches but from Cicero's oratorical works also. He specifically mentions two of them, *de optimo genere oratorum* and *de orator* (the references being to §10, and 1.30 and 3.31 respectively). The comparison of C. Cotta and P. Sulpicius at 14.20-21 (where Asconius specifically names his source as the *de oratore*), the comparison of C. Cotta, P. Sulpicius and C. Iulius Caesar Strabo at 66.20, and the description of C. Caesar Strabo as a leading orator at 25.11-12, are taken from *de or.* 1.30, 2.98 and 3.31; similar information occurs at *Brut.* 177,

---

[10] Ibid. p. 16
[11] Evidence collected in B.A. Marshall, *Rhein. Mus.* 118 (1975) 139-46.
[12] Cf. the brief discussion above, p. 3 with n. 9, with references to the important discussions of Laurand and Humbert. For a brief statement of the view that Cicero's speeches were published quickly and with little alteration, see W.C. McDermott, *TAPA* 101 (1970) 327-31, and *Philologus* 116 (1972) 277-84.
[13] J.N. Settle, *TAPA* 94 (1963) 268-80, solves some of the problems of the 'other' *pro Milone* by arguing that it is a forgery (or at least 'non-Ciceronian') and that the version used by Asconius (which he accepts to be close to the delivered speech) is the only truly Ciceronian one. See further discussion in Part II, comm. ad loc.

183, 204 and 297. As Asconius nominates the *de oratore*, one might argue that he used only that work for his information on Cotta, Sulpicius and Caesar Strabo, but it is only in the *Brutus* that Caesar Strabo's composition of tragedies (which are referred to by Asconius) is mentioned, so it would seem he used that work as well. The description of Q. Mucius Scaevola at 67.21 as *orator et iuris consultus* is similar to both *de or.* 1.180 and *Brut.* 145, while that of M. Pupius Piso at 15.13-18 comes from *de or.* 1.104 and *Brut.* 236.

The *expositio consiliorum suorum*, begun by Cicero in 59 but not published until after his death,[14] was used by Asconius for the comments on the *in toga candida*. The great problem with using this as a source is that, for both Cicero and Asconius, the information in it was very much *post eventum*; Cicero in particular was very biassed in his composition of these memoirs.[15] The comment at 83.25 that Crassus was the author of the 'first Catilinarian conspiracy' seems to derive from the *expositio*, which Asconius has mentioned just a little before, as he uses the verb *arguit* to introduce the comment.[16] Brunt also thinks that the statement about the formation of a *coitio* by Catilina and Antonius with the support of Crassus and Caesar comes from the *expositio*.[17] Lichtenfeldt thinks that the comments about the wicked deeds of Antonius and Catilina were taken from the *expositio* (e.g. Antonius' depredations in Achaea and subsequent trial before Lucullus and expulsion from the senate [84.12-25], Catilina's victims in the Sullan proscriptions [84.4-11]),[18] though some of this could have come from the speech itself, especially in the case of Antonius whom Cicero would probably have treated more leniently in his memoirs begun a few years after they had shared the consulship, when they had made a deal over their consular provinces, and when he was soon to defend his former colleague on a charge of extortion. Lichtenfeldt also thinks that the details of Catilina's prosecution for *repetundae* come possibly from the *expositio*, but other possible sources for it have already been discussed (see above, p. 42). The list of competitors for the consulship he also thinks comes from the *expositio*; it contains names

---

[14] Cic. *Att.* 2.6.2; Dio 39.10.3.
[15] He says himself that they would be written in the style of Theopompus; and Dio says that they were too scandalous to be published until after Cicero's death. Cf. Marshall, *Latomus* 33 (1974) 804-13. For the view that Cicero's memoirs may not have been as unreliable as they are sometimes made out to be, see E. Rawson, *LCM* 7 (1982) 121-4.
[16] Cf. P.A. Brunt, *CR* 7 (1957) 193: Cicero would not have dared to make such an allegation against Crassus while he were still alive. The one statement we know to have been contained in the *expositio* is that Crassus was involved in the Catilinarian conspiracy (from Dio).
[17] Brunt, loc. cit. 195.
[18] Lichtenfeldt, p. 22.

which do not appear in Cic. *Att.* 1.1.2 (so Cicero contradicts himself, if the *expositio* is the source for Asconius' list), but it is possible that Asconius did not make use of Cicero's letters (see below).[19]

A central concern of the *expositio* must have been the Catilinarian conspiracy, including the so-called 'first conspiracy'; the two items known to have been included in the *expositio* (Asconius 83.21-22; Dio 39.10.3) both relate to the Catilinarian business. As Asconius is known to have used the *expositio*, it is likely that he got his information about the involvement of Catilina and Piso in the 'first conspiracy' (92.15-20, 93.10 and 15-17) from there, rather than from any other source such as Sallust (who may have got his information from the *expositio* anyway).[20] The comment at 91.27-92.3 that Catilina subsequently married the girl produced by his own adulterous liaison with a noble woman may have come from the *expositio*; the incident is mentioned in Plut. *Cic.* 10 (without naming the women involved), and Plutarch's biography of Cicero relied rather heavily on Cicero's περὶ ὑπατείας (which must have contained a good deal of the information also found in the *expositio*, the central part of which dealt with the period around Cicero's consulship, i.e. the Catilinarian disturbances).[21] Asconius may have got the incident from the Catilinarian speeches, on which it appears that he wrote a commentary (see above, p. 2), since it is referred to at *Cat* 1.14. It seems more likely that Asconius got it from Cicero rather than Sallust, for he admits that he has not yet found the names of the women involved, whereas if he had read up the incident in Sallust he would have found the name of at least one of them (Aurelia Orestilla: Sall. *Cat.* 15.2).[22] What is odd is that Asconius did not find the names in the speeches of Lucceius against Catilina which he mentions as a source for this particular incident in his comments on the *in toga candida* (92.1-2, cf. 91.11-13). Lucceius threw up this scandalous charge against Catilina in those speeches, and we would have expected him to have mentioned the ladies' names. This is presumably an instance where Asconius' memory has failed him, or he has been unable to check his source.

Another source of information for Asconius was the *commentarii causarum* of Cicero, collected and published by Tiro. These were sufficiently detailed to take the place of a speech which had not been published.[23] Their coverage of the speeches was so complete that

---

[19] For a list of passages which Stangl thinks come from the *expositio*, see his note on 64.7-19.
[20] Marshall, art. cit. (n. 15) 809-10.
[21] Cf. Stangl, n. ad loc. (= 71.3-4).
[22] R. Syme, *Sallust* (Berkeley and Los Angeles, 1964) pp. 84-5; cf. above, p.32 n. 32.
[23] J. Humbert, *Contribution à l'étude des sources d'Asconius dans ses relations des débats judiciaires* (Paris, 1925) p. 65 (hereafter referred to by author's surname only).

Asconius could confidently assert that Cicero did not deliver a speech in defence of Catilina on the *repetundae* charge in 65 (87.10-12), since it was not listed among them. It is reasonable to assume that Asconius consulted *commentarii* other than those of Cicero.[24]

It is clear, then, that a very great deal of Asconius' information is drawn from Cicero himself, and that his knowledge of the great orator's work must have resulted from what had been a particular interest and study of his for a long time. There are, however, instances where Asconius is critical of Cicero's evidence. For example, at 2.26-3.1 (cf. 4.8-9) Asconius points out (incorrectly) that Cicero is wrong in calling Placentia a *municipium*, arguing that it was a *colonia*. At 31.17 Asconius, using the more reliable *acta*, states that the brawl between Milo and Clodius near Bovillae took place at the ninth hour, whereas Cicero says it occurred at the eleventh hour (*Mil.* 29), though here Asconius does not specify his disagreement with Cicero. A further instance where Asconius' information differs from that of Cicero, though the disagreement is not specifically pointed out by Asconius, can be found at 41.14-21: Asconius concludes that the brawl which led to Clodius' death began by chance, whereas Cicero argues that Clodius had deliberately laid a trap for Milo.

Even when disagreeing with Cicero, Asconius cannot quite bring himself to say that the great orator is actually wrong. At 2.26 (on the status of Placentia) he admits that he has great hesitation in understanding why Cicero calls it a *municipium*. At 5.16-6.8 he justifies the incorrect figure of forty years given by Cicero for the interval from the killing of Saturninus to his consulship (it should be thirty-seven) as being a rounded figure (like the twenty days of *Cat.* 1.4, when it should have been eighteen). At 13.4-7 and 13.22-14.3, he justifies Cicero's wrongful claim that his was the first house built at public expense by saying that he was speaking in the manner of an orator rather than an historian. At 37.16-17 Asconius notes an omission by Cicero but it is not done in any critical way. At 48.4-7, in remarking upon an incident involving Clodius and Cicero which the latter refers to, Asconius says that he has not yet been able to find out the details of the incident, but it must have taken place because he cannot believe that Cicero would ever tell a lie! Another instance of Asconius' analysis of Cicero's rhetorical technique is given at 69.24-70.25 where he explains that the variant versions given by Cicero of the story about Scipio Africanus' reservation of seats for senators at public games are a mark of his oratorical skill because he has altered the story to suit his audience. At 76.21-22 he claims that the figure of sixteen results not from Cicero's error but a mistake by the copyists!

---

[24] Humbert, pp. 67 and 70.

Such, then, is Asconius' belief in the *merita viri auctoritas* (24.12-13) that he cannot bring himself to disbelieve what Cicero says. In only one place is he prepared to say that Cicero is wrong, and even then he is hesitant. It follows that he is prepared to accept Cicero's statements and judgments uncritically in the main. This is manifest, for example, in the occasional use of pejorative terms which obviously reflect Cicero's thinking on the subject: e.g. at 8.13 Clodius' laws are called *perniciosae*, at 37.25 Plancus is said to have acted *infestissime*, and at 45.13-14 Manilius' proposal on freedmen is called *perditissima*. This acceptance of Cicero's statements occasionally leads Asconius into error himself, or at least into unwarranted assumptions. For example, at 2.18-19 he says that Piso belonged to the family which was called Frugi; that is not so (see Part II, comm. ad loc.), but Asconius has been led to say it, possibly by the phrase *moribus nomen* in the lemma which produced this comment (since Piso was distantly connected with the branch of the Calpurnii which did bear the name Frugi), but more likely by *Sest.* 21 where Cicero writes of Piso . . . *erat eo nomine ut ingenerata familiae frugalitas videretur*, . . .[25] Again, Asconius has been misled by the frequent accusations made by Cicero of Clodius' Catilinarian sympathies (e.g. *Mil.* 37 and 55, *har. resp.* 4-5, *dom.* 72) and by the numerous allusions in the *pro Milone* to recent violent activities by Clodius in Etruria (§ § 26, 50, 75, 87, 98) into thinking that Clodius had joined Catilina in Etruria, when he fled to Faesulae.[26] An example of an unwarranted assumption by Asconius can be found at 3.20-23: Asconius concludes, from the frequent references of Cicero to the honours given him by *tota Italia* on his return from exile, that the honours accorded him by Placentia, to which he refers in the lemma, relate to that occasion, but we have no evidence that that is the point of Cicero's reference.[27]

The most glaring omission in Asconius' consultation of Cicero as a source is his apparent failure to refer to Cicero's letters, at least those to Atticus. The most obvious instance of this is the failure to refer to *Att.* 1.1.1 and 1.2.1 to settle simply the dispute with Fenestella whether Cicero defended Catilina or not in 65, instead of the lengthy argument based on probability which he gives us (85-87). Another instance can be found at 48.4-5: Asconius would not have said that he had not yet found the date of Clodius' attempt on Cicero's life referred to at *Mil.* 37, if he had known *Att.* 4.3.3 (which gives the date of 11th November 57).[28] To

---

[25] Lichtenfeldt, p. 13, is sympathetic towards Asconius for the way he has been misled here.
[26] Further on this 'error' by Asconius, see ibid. pp. 13-6.
[27] Stangl, n. ad loc. (= 13.1-2); Lichtenfeldt, p. 16, says that it is not an unwarranted conclusion.
[28] Stangl, n. ad loc. (= 41.12-13); cf. Lichtenfeldt, p. 24.

counteract the positive view that Asconius did not know the letters to Atticus at all, Lichtenfeldt has drawn up a list of passages of Asconius where the information could have been taken from a letter of Cicero to Atticus, but even he admits that it could have come from other sources,[29] and with the exception of the last incident in his list, all of them deal with such well known events that the information could have come from any number of sources. There is at least one instance where Asconius seems not to have known the letters *ad familiares*: at 92.2-3 he admits to not knowing the names of Catilina's mistress and wife, yet at *fam.* 8.7.2 one of them is named (though it must be admitted that the allusion there is not specific).[30]

On the other hand there are instances when it is hard to see where Asconius got his information from, if not from a letter of Cicero. For example, could he have known of Pompeius' coolness towards Scaurus just before the latter's prosecution in 54 (19.25-26) if he had not known *Q.f.* 3.8.3 or *Att.* 4.15.4? In the same comment, Asconius says that Pompeius was cool towards Scaurus because of Mucia's *impudicitia* (she had been divorced by Pompeius and subsequently married Scaurus); Plut. *Pomp.* 42.13 says that the reason for Pompeius' divorce of Mucia (her *impudicitia*) was given in Cicero's letters. The only difficulty with using this as evidence that Asconius got the information from the letters is that we do not have a letter which talks of Mucia's *impudicitia*, only one which says Pompeius' divorce of her was warmly approved (Cic. *Att.* 1.12.3). Stewart has convincingly argued that Asconius' mistake over the date of the death of Cicero's father can readily be explained by supposing that Asconius read the first letters of the collection to Atticus in the order in which we now have them (which is out of chronology); this explanation would mean that the letters had, of course, already been published and were available to Asconius.[31]

Asconius' failure to use *Att.* 1.1 and 1.2 to refute Fenestella has been taken to show that the letters to Atticus were not available to him and therefore had not yet been published.[32] The general consensus of opinion

---

[29] Ibid.

[30] Cf. Humbert, p. 63 n. For a list of further instances where we might have expected Asconius to use Cicero's letters, see SB *Att.* 1.63-8.

[31] R.S. Stewart, *TAPA* 93 (1962) 469 n. 17. On Asconius' mistake, see below, Part II, comm. on 82.10-11.

[32] Examples of those who hold this view include F. Bücheler, *Rhein. Mus.* 34 (1879) 352-5. The view of J. Carcopino, *Les secrets de la correspondance de Cicéron*, trans. E.O. Lorimer (London, 1951) Vol. I, pp. 19-37, that the letters were

The Sources of the Commentaries 49

is that they were published in the form in which we have them c. A.D. 60, mainly based on the argument from silence in Asconius and the citation of the letters by Seneca (*ep.* 97.5). But we have no basis for judging what documents Asconius would think it necessary to use for his commentaries, and it is only his reputation for accuracy (which is under question: see below, Section Four) which leads to the assumption that he would in every instance have referred to the letters if they were available. Nothing can be inferred from his silence in some instances either for or against any date of publication.[33] Some passages hint at his knowledge of the letters, as suggested above, while other passages point to his apparent ignorance of them, but this may well be explained in a number of ways (see below). It must have been known that the letters existed; Cicero himself contemplated a collection (*fam.* 16.17.1, *Att.* 16.5.5); Tiro, who edited and published other works of Cicero, would at least have collected the letters together;[34] and Cornelius Nepos knew of a collection of eleven volumes of letters to Atticus from Cicero's consulship to the end of his life (*vit. Att.* 16.2-4). Asconius must have known of the existence of the letters, so it is odd that he did not find some way to consult them. Perhaps it may have been thought that the letters would be of little value in understanding the speeches, or that the day-to-day chit-chat which they largely contained would not be worth the effort of reading for the small end-product likely to be derived (remembering that Asconius wrote his commentaries on a large number of speeches in a relatively short time). Perhaps access in his time might not have been easy, particularly if (as seems possible) the project of publication was underway at about the same time as he was writing his commentaries. The collection which Cornelius Nepos had seen was in the hands of Atticus, and he was able to see it only because he was a friend of Atticus; it remained presumably in the hands of Atticus' heirs, and so access might have been difficult, especially if Asconius did not write his commentaries in Rome (see above, p. 36). Perhaps because

---

published for propaganda purposes in the time of Octavianus, has now generally been discredited. For a review of the question, see A. Setaioli, *Symbolae Osloenses* 51 (1971) 105-20; he concludes that the argument *ex silentio Asconii* is not strong and that examination of correspondences, especially between Cicero's letters and Valerius Maximus, suggests availability at least (if not formal publication) before the time of Seneca.

[33] Ibid. 111. Cf. the statement of D. Nardo, *Il 'commentariolum petitionis': la propaganda elettorale nella 'ars' di Quinto Cicerone* (Padua, 1970) p. 36: *o quando Asconio scriveva il suo commento l'epistolario ciceroniano non era ancora stato pubblicato, o Asconio, per ragioni che ci sfuggono, non lo conosceva, o, conoscendolo, per motivi anche pii oscuri, non lo citava.*

[34] That might have been difficult, since Cicero apparently did not keep copies of some of his letters (*Att.* 16.5.5; cf. SB *Att.* 1.72).

Cornelius Nepos had had something to do with the collection, Asconius did not think it worth much, for it seems that he did not have a very high opinion of that author (see below, p. 58). Or perhaps he simply forgot what was in the letters at a number of points where their information was relevant.[35]

2. Livy

There are only two specific references to the use of Livy, one at 66.23 in regard to the law of Cotta about the lifting of the ban on tribunes seeking further office (not mentioned in the *periochae* or Iulius Obsequens) and the other at 77.4 on the original number of tribunes (cf. Liv. 2.33.2). We would perhaps have expected Asconius to have referred to Livy a good deal more, since his work covered the period and was of very great authority by Asconius' time. Moreover, Asconius came from the same Italian town as Livy and would have had a natural interest in the writings of a fellow-townsman.

It is likely that where an item of information is well known, Asconius does not bother to name his sources, or he writes as if there was general agreement: e.g. the information at 12.1-3 about L. Paullus would have been generally known, and likewise at 77.14-16 Asconius retails a piece of information which he believes to be very well known (*notissimum*). The use of phrases like *traditur* or *dicitur* (48.13, 84.4, 91.27),[36] or *manifestum est* (76.10, 87.25, 90.6), or *intellegitis* (9.10, 92.15) are instances where he assumes that the item is general knowledge, or where he is conflating a number of sources. Sometimes these general introductory phrases may cover Asconius' inability to remember specifically where he got his information from,[37] or perhaps the information is Livian. For example, *notum est* at 17.17 (on Opimius' destruction of Fregellae) could introduce a piece of information collated from a number of sources, but it may also come from Livy (cf. *per.* 60). Similarly, where Asconius gives *annales* as his source, he may in fact be using Livy: at 3.1ff. on the *colonia* at Placentia, he got some of his information from Livy (though not the date of the foundation) since he tries to make sense of the confused list of founders' names which is discussed by Livy (see Part II, comm. ad loc.). Because of the correspondence he sees between the *argumentum* to

---

[35] Cf. below, pp. 53 and 60, on the instances where he may have forgotten the name of his source.
[36] There is a lacuna at 84.4 for which Stangl reads *traditur* and Clark reads *dicitur*; Kiessling and Schoell, and Giarratano emend to *[significat] Catilinam*. On the possible source(s) for 91.27, see above, p. 45.
[37] The phrase *opinio fuerat* (or similar), used three times, also seems to indicate that he has forgotten the specific source: see below, p. 60.

the *pro Milone* and Dio's account of the background to Milo's trial in book 42 (which he takes to be Livian), Lichtenfeldt thinks that the *annales* referred to as a source at the beginning of the comments on that speech (30.4) mean Livy also.[38]

Unfortunately we do not always have the relevant books of Livy, but have to rely on the *periochae* or the so-called 'Livian' authors like Cassius Dio in order to make comparisons and conjecture whether pieces of Asconius' information have come from Livy. A good example of how this process can be applied is to be seen in the account of the trial of the Vestals in 115-113, given at 45.27-46.6; the affair is mentioned in Liv. *per.* 63 and Iul. Obs. 37 (so is clearly Livian) and by a number of 'Livian' sources (Val. Max. 3.7.9, 6.8.1; Dio 36, frag. 87; Oros. 5.15.20-22), and so it is a reasonable assumption that Asconius got it from Livy. There are dangers, however, in assuming that, say, Dio is a 'Livian' author; he himself says that he spent ten years collecting his material, reading (so he claimed) nearly every book on Roman history (and not just Livy), and another twelve years writing up his selection of it.[39] It is clear that Dio had read widely and did not always follow Livy.[40] Hence, Lichtenfeldt's view that, because Asconius and Dio agree on events leading up to Milo's trial, Livy is their common source and that much of the information in the *argumentum* to the *pro Milone* comes from Livy, needs to be treated cautiously.[41] Much of the material for that introduction Asconius clearly got from the *acta*, and it may be that Livy or Dio got it from that source too. Similarly, Lichtenfeldt is too anxious to credit Livy as the source for Asconius' picture of Livius Drusus' optimate sympathies (69.1-3); he invites comparison with *per.* 70-71 and other 'Livian' sources.[42] But that was the standard view of Livius Drusus, and Asconius may well have gained it from a number of sources.[43]

3. Sallust

There is only one specific reference by Asconius to the use of Sallust, at 66.23 in regard to the law of Cotta which removed the ban on tribunes seeking further office. This comes from the *historiae*, which obviously

---

[38] Lichtenfeldt, pp. 28-33.
[39] Dio 72.25.5; on the breadth of his reading, see frag. 1.2., and cf. 53.19.6. Cf. F. Millar, A *Study of Cassius Dio* (Oxford, 1964) pp. 32-3.
[40] Ibid. pp. 34-8.
[41] Cf. Humbert, p. 130.
[42] Lichtenfeldt, p. 42.
[43] Cf., e.g., Cicero's description of Livius Drusus at *dom.* 50. For further detailed examination of passages showing signs of being taken from Livy, see Lichtenfeldt, pp. 34-46.

contained an account of Cotta's consulship, since we have a speech of his from that year preserved in the fragments of the *historiae* (2.47.1-14 M) and since his law was part of the agitation for the restoration of the tribunician powers, a subject in which Sallust would have been most interested. As with Livy, so with Sallust we would have expected Asconius to make a great deal more use of his work, as he had become a popular historian by Asconius' time. And especially as he must have studied Sallust's writings closely for the biography he wrote of him (unless one accepts the argument of Kiessling and Schoell and of Stangl [see above, p. 32] that Asconius did not write the biography until after the commentaries on Cicero's speeches, since in them he does not appear to be fully familiar with Sallust's works).

Of the commentaries which we have, the one most likely to have made use of Sallust's *historiae* is that on the *pro Cornelio*, because it fits into the time span we know of for Sallust's work. The last datable fragments (5.2.19-27 M) belong to 67 and deal with Gabinius' legislation; that was also the year of Cornelius' tribunate when he committed the offence for which he was eventually tried in 65, and it is obvious that Sallust would have given an account of his tribunician activity too. Cicero's speech on behalf of Cornelius makes a number of references to Gabinius' tribunician activity, and Asconius no doubt used the *historiae* to understand the point of these references. The year 67 is hardly likely to have been Sallust's chosen terminus for the *historiae*,[44] and he may well have gone on to describe the events of 66 and 65, some of which (e.g. the tribunician legislation of Manilius, the disturbance of Manilius' and Cornelius' trials, the ultimate trial of Cornelius) would have fitted well with his view of the conflict between the people and the nobility. Thus, Asconius' view that Cornelius' tribunate was a confrontation between a *popularis* and the conservatives (e.g. 57.8, 58.1, 58.24-25, 60.19-21) is likely to have been taken from Sallust, especially in the *argumentum* where he could not rely solely on getting his ideas from Cicero's speech itself.

As the first thirty-seven chapters of Dio book 36, which deal with the events of these same years, show traces of Sallust, a comparison of Asconius with Dio can provide the basis for the assumption that certain information in Asconius is derived from Sallust.[45] Thus, their accounts of Gabinius' threat to dismiss L. Trebellius (72.10-21; Dio 36.30.1-2) are very similar, and could suggest a Sallustian origin; the comparison in Asconius' account with the action of Ti. Gracchus against M. Octavius would be in keeping with Sallust's *popularis* stance (cf. *Iug.* 16.2). There

---

[44] G.M. Paul, *OCD*², p. 947. Syme, op. cit. (n. 22) p. 178 (cf. *Entretiens Hardt* 4 [1956] 188), thinks that Sallust stopped short at 67 because of death.
[45] Lichtenfeldt, pp. 48-50.

The Sources of the Commentaries

are dangers, however, in comparing Asconius and Dio, for there are quite wide differences in their accounts of the tribunate of Cornelius.[46]

Lichtenfeldt also suggests, without argument, that Asconius' account of Piso's passing by force of his counter-proposal on bribery (75.24-76.2) comes from Sallust.[47] At 58.20-23 (the confrontation with the consul Piso at the assembly at which Cornelius read out his own proposal on *solutio*) a more direct comparison is possible: there is a fragment of Sallust (5.2.27 M: *manum in os intendens*) which is usually attributed to this confrontation, and which has verbal echoes in Asconius' account (... *eos qui sibi intentabant manus* ...).

For the comments on the *in toga candida*, we would have expected Asconius to make some use of Sallust's *Catilina* (though much of that work was derived from Cicero, and Asconius' normal method would have been to take his information directly from Cicero, especially the Catilinarian speeches, on which he probably wrote commentaries). There is one section which seems to derive from Sallust — the account at 92.15-25 of Cn. Piso's plot against senators, his mission to Spain and his death there, which is very similar to Sall. *Cat.* 18-19 (especially in the hints of Piso's enmity with Pompeius, which are explicit in Sallust and not found elsewhere).[48] That Asconius got this account from a source other than Cicero is suggested by the phrase *fuit enim opinion* with which he begins; if he had got it from Cicero, he would not have bothered with such a phrase but accepted it as fact. The use of this phrase suggests that he has forgotten the name of the specific source from which the account was derived.[49]

4. Fenestella

After the *acta* (referred to six times, though five of those occur in the comments on one speech, the *pro Milone*), Fenestella is the source most frequently referred to by Asconius. There are five times in all: 5.8-9 (on the name of Piso's father-in-law), 31.14 (disagreeing with his date for Milo's journey to Lanuvium), 66.24 (on C. Cotta's law on the tribunate), 85.13 and 86.16 (rejecting his view that Cicero defended Catilina in 65). It can be seen that, when Asconius refers to Fenestella, it is mostly to disagree with him. There is another instance where it is known that

---

[46] See below, Part II, comm. on 57-8.
[47] Lichtenfeldt, p. 53.
[48] No hint of enmity is found, for example, in Cicero or Dio; Lichtenfeldt, p. 55, thinks that the description of Piso's activities derives from Livy. There is one small difference between Sallust's and Asconius' account: Asconius says that Piso planned *caedem senatus*, while Sallust talks of the murder of consuls (adding *plerique senatores* for the second attempt).
[49] Cf. below, p. 60.

Asconius found fault with Fenestella, over the age of Cicero when he delivered the *pro Roscio Amerino*.[50]

There are two places where editors have suggested that the name of Fenestella should be inserted to fill a gap in the text. One is at 1.7, where the name of the author who claimed that the *in Pisonem* was delivered at the end of the consulship of L. Domitius Ahenobarbus and Ap. Claudius Pulcher (i.e. 54, when the date should be 55) is missing in the text; Fenestella has been suggested in the *editio princeps*,[51] on the grounds no doubt that this would fit with Asconius' known tendency to disagree with Fenestella. The other place is at 70.9-13 where something has been left out at the end of the passage quoted from *har. resp.* 24 dealing with the setting aside of special seats for senators by Scipio Africanus at the Megalesian Games in his second consulship in 194, and at the beginning of Asconius' comment where he says that an author (missing) also wrote that the seats were set aside by the consuls Africanus and Sempronius Longus, without mentioning the Megalesian Games but recording them simply as votive games. Madvig, followed by Kiessling and Schoell,[52] suggests that Fenestella is the missing author, again presumably on the grounds that this represents a typical disagreement of Asconius with Fenestella. Further, discussion of games and the origin of the reservation of special seats would have been the sort of thing on which Fenestella is likely to have written, since he is known to have had an antiquarian interest. A discussion of variations in Cicero's accounts is also likely to have been of interest to Fenestella, since the citations of him by Asconius and Aulus Gellius show him to have been regarded as a Ciceronian expert.[53]

There is another instance where Asconius gives a version different to that of Fenestella (though on this occasion he does not specify his disagreement). At 16.5-6 Asconius says that Pompeius was the first to put on an elephant fight, at the games held in the circus celebrating the opening of his theatre in 55, while according to Plin. *NH* 8.19 Fenestella records that the first elephant fight in the circus took place in a.u.c. 655 (99 B.C.) in the consulship of M. Antonius and A. Postumius at the games put on by the aedile C. Claudius Pulcher.

The frequency with which Asconius refers to Fenestella (at least once

---

[50] Gell. 15.28.4: *in qua re etiam Fenestellam errasse Pedianus Asconius animadvertit, quod eum scripserit sexto vicesimo aetatis anno pro Sex. Roscio dixisse.*
[51] Cf. Kiessling and Schoell, intro. p. xiii n. For other suggestions, see Part II, comm. ad loc.
[52] For their suggested emendation for the whole passage, see Part II, comm. ad. loc.
[53] Lichtenfeldt, p. 55.

in each commentary we have except the *Scauriana*) suggests that he was used a good deal more than for the sections where his name is actually mentioned.[54] Asconius puts him on a par with Sallust and Livy, in a statement which hints at extensive use of all three (66.23 ff.), and it has already been suggested that the latter two were likely to have been used far more extensively than the one or two specific references to them indicate. What is difficult to explain is Asconius' constant desire to disagree with Fenestella. We have seen in the case of Cicero that Asconius can be critical, but even then he tries to find excuses; in the case of Fenestella he seems to go out of his way to be critical.[55] It has been suggested earlier (p. 34) that scholars tried to outdo each other in learning or to find errors in each other's work.[56] Perhaps there was an almost donnish rivalry between Asconius and Fenestella which explains Asconius' constant criticism.[57]

5. The *acta*

The source most frequently referred to by Asconius is the *acta*, though five of the six times fall in the comments on one speech, the *pro Milone*. The *acta* could, of course, only be used as a source for two of the commentaries which we have, for only two of the speeches were delivered in the period after the institution of the *acta* in 59 (i.e. the *pro Scauro* delivered in 54, and the *pro Milone* delivered in 52). This is revealed in the minute details in the *argumentum* and the conclusion to the commentaries on those two speeches (e.g. incidents leading up to the trial, specific dates, details of associated court cases, actions of presiding magistrates and other officials) compared to the comments on, say, the *pro Cornelio*.[58] They are even exploited far more fully for the comments on the *pro Milone* (as the greater length of the *argumentum* shows) because of the greater interest that surrounded that case, both at the time and later.

Apart from the instances where Asconius tells us that he is using the *acta*, one has to be careful in saying that he has used them directly for the *argumenta* and conclusions, for it is possible that much of what he says has come from other sources (which we see reflected in Livy, Appian, Plutarch and Dio).[59] When Asconius tells us that he is using the *acta*, it is

---

[54] Ibid.
[55] Cf. Syme, *JRS* 37 (1947) 202, whose assessment of Asconius' criticism of Fenestella is milder.
[56] Cf., e.g., Pliny's pointing out of an error by Fenestella at *NH* 9.123.
[57] It is possible that their careers overlapped: one set of dates for Fenestella puts his death in A.D. 36. Not that Asconius would have been uncritical of Fenestella if he were dead. Further on Asconius' criticism of Fenestella, see Marshall, *Rhein. Mus.* 123 (1980) 349-54.
[58] Clark, *CR* 41 (1927) 75.
[59] Lichtenfeldt, pp. 68-9.

assumed that he is referring to the *acta diurna populi*.[60] The term *acta* was also loosely used for the accounts (sometimes called *commentarii*) given by individuals of events in Rome in letters to their friends, especially those overseas on official duty;[61] often such accounts would be based on the official *acta*, with personal observations added by the author.[62]

The *acta* were instituted by Caesar in his consulship in 59, according to Suet. *Iul.* 20.1 (*inito honore primus omnium instituit, ut tam senatus quam populi diurna acta confierent et publicarentur*). Contrary to the view of Hübner,[63] who thinks that the details of senatorial discussions and decisions (which had been kept prior to 59 as *commentarii senatus*,[64] and which were presumably a source used by Asconius for comments on speeches delivered earlier than 59) continued to be kept separate from the *acta populi*, Humbert argues that they were not entirely separate. According to Suet. *Aug.* 36 (cf. 5), Augustus decided that separate senatorial records should be kept (presumably for security reasons), which shows that up until the time of that decision the *acta senatus* had been published with the *acta populi* (or at least that senatorial proceedings found their way into the *acta*: cf. 44.13-15). Further, Asconius uniformly calls *acta* those documents from which he derives information as much about the senate as about the people.[65] The sorts of information which the *acta* contained can be judged from a letter of Caelius to Cicero (*fam.* 8.1.1: *senatus consulta, edicta, fabulae, rumores*) though some of this may result from Caelius' own remarks, added to the official *acta* (cf. the things he decides to leave out at *fam.* 8.11.4: *multa transi, in primis ludorum explosiones et funerum et ineptiarum ceterarum*). The *acta* contained day-by-day accounts (e.g. Cic. *Att.* 3.15.6, 6.2.6), though they were not necessarily produced every day. They were not 'published' in the modern sense, and so if one wanted a copy, one had to have it copied out; that is why it was possible for a person to add his own observations when writing out a copy for a correspondent. The *acta* were not brief summaries, as the amount of detail in the *argumentum* to the *pro Milone*, which is drawn from the *acta*, shows; *contiones* were not reported *in extenso*, though a reasonable amount of

---

[60] For the variety of names used, see Humbert, in C. Daremberg and E. Saglio (ed.), *Dictionaire des antiquités* (Paris, 1877) Vol. I, pp. 49-52; O. Seeck, *RE* 1 (1894) 290.
[61] E.g. Cic. *fam.* 8.1.1-2, 11.4, 12.23.2, 28.3; cf. Lichtenfeldt, pp. 59-60.
[62] Humbert, p. 25.
[63] E. Hübner, *Neuer Jahrbuch für classische Philologie*, Suppl. III (Leipzig, 1857-60) p. 594, followed by Lichtenfeldt, p. 59; cf. pp. 68-9 where he argues that information about senatorial activities only found its way into the *acta diurna populi* incidentally.
[64] Tac. *ann.* 15.74.
[65] Humbert, p. 56.

detail must have been given (cf. the report of the *contio* of T. Munatius Plancus at 40.21-25); details of judicial proceedings were given, including summaries of speeches.[66]

Asconius claims to have read all the *acta* relevant to the period of the trial of Milo (44.8-10: *sed ego... acta etiam totius illius temporis persecutus sum*), and it is reasonable to assume that he had looked at all the *acta* relevant to the other speeches he commented on (that is, those delivered after 59). As already mentioned, the *argumentum* and conclusion to the commentaries on the *pro Scauro* and the *pro Milone* are the places where Asconius would have consulted the *acta* most, and hence they reveal the sorts of things which the *acta* contained. In particular the details of other trials following the condemnation of Milo given at the end of the *Miloniana* derive from the *acta* (though such details of judicial proceedings seem to have been kept before Caesar's institution of the *acta*),[67] and the conclusion to the comments on the *pro Scauro* giving the list of *laudatores*, the count of votes and the investigation of the prosecutors for *calumnia* will also have come from the *acta*. One interesting small point emerges: the order of names for the defence counsel in the cases of Scaurus (20.16-18) and of Saufeius (55.3-4), which was presumably taken accurately from the *acta* and which showed the order in which they spoke, reveals that Cicero did not speak in the most important place (last), despite his claim in *orator* 130 that he always did.[68] At one point the *acta* are used (perhaps unknowingly by Asconius) to correct Cicero regarding the time of the affray between Clodius and Milo near Bovillae (see above, p. 46). Clearly the *acta* were to be preferred to the evidence of Cicero himself.

Some brief comments on other sources:

1. Tiro

The biography of Cicero by his freedman Tiro is named as a source once by Asconius (48.25-26), but there are two other places where Asconius may have drawn on it. At 5.9-11 (on Tullia's marriages and death) Asconius' comment is very similar to Plut. *Cic.* 41.7-8, for which Tiro is earlier named as a source (cf. ibid. 49.2); as both Asconius and Plutarch make the same mistake of leaving out Tullia's second marriage to Furius Crassipes, it looks as though they are using a common source.[69] Lichtenfeldt thinks that the comparison of M. Pupius Piso and Cicero at 15.13-21 is taken from Tiro, rather than Cic. *Brut.* 236, 240 and 310 (a

---

[66] A.W. Lintott, *JRS* 64 (1974) 69 n. 91 and 74; contra, Humbert, pp. 40 and 60.
[67] See above, n. 7.
[68] Humbert, pp. 101-10.
[69] For further discussion, see Part II, comm. ad loc.

common source for Asconius' comparison of republican orators: see above, p. 44), since there is more information about Piso than is given in the passages from the *Brutus*.

2. M. Aemilius Scaurus

The elder Scaurus wrote an autobiography (Cic. *Brut.* 112; Tac. *Agric.* 1.3; Val. Max. 4.4.11). Lichtenfeldt thinks that the following passages were taken from it: 21.3-12 (Scaurus' prosecution by Cn. Domitius Ahenobarbus), 21.18-24 (Caepio's prosecution of Scaurus), 22.8-20 (Varius' prosecution of Scaurus), 23.3-8 and 27.16-19 (Scaurus' undistinguished forebears).[70] It is not clear whether Asconius got them direct; Lichtenfeldt thinks that they came through an intermediary, most probably Hyginus, whose book *de claris viris* was known to Asconius and was very likely to contain that sort of information about a well known figure like Scaurus. If Asconius had got it direct from Scaurus' autobiography, we would have expected him to name the source.

3. Cornelius Nepos

It is surprising that Asconius appears not to have used Cornelius Nepos' biography of Cicero; perhaps he did in those commentaries on speeches which we no longer have. Nepos' biography, a fuller treatment than his other biographies (since there was more than one book: Gell. 15.28.2), was written after Cicero's death and may have been critical of the orator (or at least it bent the truth a little: Gell. ibid.).[71] That may explain why Asconius did not use it, for he could not bring himself to be critical of Cicero. Humbert thinks that Asconius did not have any confidence in an author who could be wrong by four years in giving the age of Cicero at the time of delivering a particular speech, and so did not use him as a source.[72] In the passage of Gellius which is the source for our knowledge of the existence of Nepos' biography of Cicero, Gellius points out that error; in the same passage he notes that Asconius pointed out a similar error. Perhaps it was Asconius who formulated the hostility to Nepos as a source (and Gellius got it from Asconius), and for that reason Asconius did not use his work (though we would have expected him to use it and point out his disagreement, as he did with Fenestella).

4. Asinius Pollio

A supporter of Caesar and Antonius, Pollio retired from politics after his consulship in 40 to devote himself to literature, in particular to the

---

[70] Lichtenfeldt, pp. 73-6.
[71] E. Jenkinson, in T.A. Dorey (ed.), *Latin Biography* (London, 1967) p. 1 with n. 7.
[72] Humbert, pp. 135-6; cf. p. 73 n. 3.

writing of history. His *historiae* began with events of the year 60 and the formation of the *amicitia* between Pompeius, Crassus and Caesar,[73] and traced the development of civil war, probably ending with the battle of Philippi in 42. He was used as a source by, among others, Appian (*BC* 2.82).[74] Humbert thinks that the comment at 35.25-26, that because of delays in holding the consular elections for 52 rumour was increasing that Pompeius ought to be made dictator, comes directly from Asinius Pollio.[75] A similar statement is found at App. *BC* 2.20, with hints at the republican dislike for such an assumption of power which would be typical of Pollio — and he is known to have been used as a source by Appian. The *annales* which Asconius says he used as a source for the background to the trial of Milo (30.4) may therefore include the history written by Asinius Pollio.

Humbert also thinks that information on the trial of C. Cato in the *argumentum* to the *pro Scauro* came from Asinius Pollio, since he began his public career with the prosecution of Cato who was defended by Scaurus.[76] But the only information Asconius gives is the date of the trial and the result, and this he could have got quite easily from the *acta* which he was clearly using for this period (19.4-5).

It remains to make one or two general comments about Asconius' methods. The most obvious point to make is that he must have worked a great deal from memory. There was the sheer physical difficulty of checking a reference in a *volumen*,[77] and one would need either to have a copy of the work in one's own library or to have access to it in the library of a friend nearby.[78] It is possible that Asconius worked from a collection of notes, as examples are known of ancient authors collecting notes, e.g. Pliny the elder and Aulus Gellius. But Pliny's practice of taking notes on everything he read is noted as a peculiarity,[79] and in the case of works like those of Pliny and Aulus Gellius the arrangement of their notes would have been easier, for they simply had to write down what they had collected, whereas Asconius had to have a specific piece of information (and that would require a complicated filing system worked out in advance). Asconius' interest in Cicero presumably extended over a long

---

[73] Hor. *carm.* 2.1.1-2 and 14.
[74] On Pollio as a source for Appian, see P.J. Cuff, *Historia* 16 (1967) esp. 186-8.
[75] Humbert, p. 114 n. 1; cf. Lichtenfeldt, pp. 56-7, who argues tortuously that it comes from Fenestella via Pollio, and Stangl, n. ad loc. (= 33.26-28).
[76] Sen. *contr.* 7.4.7. For the details of the trial, see Part II, comm. on 18.17.
[77] McDermott, art. cit. (n. 12) 335.
[78] For a recent discussion of library resources and availability, see A.J. Marshall, *Phoenix* 30 (1976) 252-64.
[79] Plin. *ep.* 3.5.10. On Plutarch's use of notes, and the need for an ancient writer to rely on memory, see A.W. Gomme, *HCT* 1.78-80; cf. J.R. Hamilton, *Plutarch, Alexander: a Commentary* (Oxford, 1969) pp. xliii-iv.

time, but he wrote his commentaries in a comparatively short time, and so, unless he had decided a reasonable time in advance that he was going to write a commentary, he would not have organised himself to prepare the sort of notes which would be needed if he was going to use notes rather than his memory as the basis for composing his commentaries. If he had worked from notes, we would have expected even more frequent specific references, rather than the general phrases which he uses from time to time.

Asconius was not writing a continuous narrative (except in the *argumentum*), so he could not work like other historians (who could write with one or two rolls open in front of them as the basis for their narrative).[80] This in itself would require Asconius to work a great deal from memory. There are some general phrases which could indicate either generally accepted information, or perhaps lack of memory about the specific source (see above, p. 50), but there is one particular phrase which Asconius seems to use almost certainly when he has forgotten the name of his source: *opinio fuit* (or *fuerat*). It is used three times: at 33.18 (where the information is given by Cicero himself at *Mil.* 62-63), at 50.14 (where Asconius does not appear to realise that he has derived a conclusion [wrongly] from several statements of Cicero: see above, p. 47), and 92.15 (where the information on Cn. Piso is taken from Sallust: see above, p. 53). In all of these cases, the sources ought to have been known to Asconius, but he does not name them, suggesting that for the moment he has forgotten specifically who they were, and in turn that he did normally work from memory.

The reliance of Asconius on memory might even suggest that the specific references were remembered rather than looked up. In preparing a fairly simple set of notes for his sons' schoolwork, Asconius might just be remembering from his wide reading that Valerius Antias said such and such, or that such and such was dealt with in the fourth book of Tiro's biography of Cicero (we have no way of checking that this sort of reference is accurate). The reliance on memory might also explain the rather capricious selection of passages from each speech for comment: Asconius chose to comment only on those passages where he could remember something which was relevant. He does not always explain the point of a lemma (e.g. at 15.3ff. he does not tell us the point of Piso's desire for a triumph; at 24.22ff. he says almost nothing about M. Antonius; at 78.1ff. he does not explain the *leges Porciae*), and this suggests that the lemma has triggered off something he can remember (rather than its real point) and that is why he chose to comment on it.

[80] On the basis of Tac. *ann.* 13.20, C.B.R. Pelling, *Introduction, Text and Commentary on Chapters 1-27 of Plutarch's Life of Caesar* (Oxford diss., 1974) p. 38, thinks that three is the maximum number of rolls an author could have had open in front of him at any one time.

The Sources of the Commentaries

ADDENDUM II
LIST OF AUTHORS SPECIFICALLY REFERRED TO BY NAME IN ASCONIUS

Author	Work	Clark	Stangl	KS	G
Accius		16.18	21.4	14.29	18.22
Acta		19.4	22.20	17.2	22.9
		31.13	31.2	27.12	35.17
		44.9	38.29	39.3	49.5
		44.13	39.3	39.7	49.9
		47.1	40.21	41.13	52.3
		49.7	42.5	43.19	54.14
Annales		3.1-2	12.14	2.24	5.2
		30.4	30.4	26.5	34.5
C. Antonius	*oratio in Ciceronem* (?)	93.24	72.17	84.4-5	101.23
Atticus	*annalis*	13.18	19.5	12.10-11	15.20
		77.4	60.15	68.17	83.11
Brutus	*oratio pro Milone*	41.11	37.4-5	36.11	46.5
Caesar	*orationes in Cn. Dolabellam*	26.14	27.18-19	23.12	30.9
		(cf.74.11-12)	(58.21-22)	(65.25-26)	(80.14)
Caesar Strabo	*tragoediae*	25.13	26.29	22.17	29.5
Calvus	*oratio in Ciceronem* (?)	93.22	72.15	84.2	101.21
Catilina	*commentarii causarum*	93.24	72.17	84.4-5	101.23
Cicero	*expositio consiliorum suorum*	87.11	67.25	78.5	94.26-27
	de optimo genere oratorum	83.22	65.7	74.20-21	91.2-3
	de orator	30.6	30.5	26.6-7	34.6-7
	oratio pro Milone vere habita	14.21	19.26	13.12	17.3
	oratio in Cornelium	42.2	37.16	36.27-28	46.22
Cominius	*annales*	61.24	50.9	54.13	67.4
Fenestella		5.9	13.23	4.20	7.8
		31.14	31.3	27.14	35.19
		66.24	53.22	59.4	72.12
		85.13	66.13	76.9	92.21
		86.16	67.9	77.10	94.4
Iulius Hyginus	*liber prior de viris claris*	13.13	19.1-2	12.6	15.16
Livy	*ab urbe condita*	66.23	53.22	59.3	72.11
		77.4	60.15	68.17	83.11
Lucceius	*orationes in Catilinam*	92.1-2	71.5	82.16-17	99.23-24
Philodemus		16.12	20.29	14.23	18.16
Piso	*invectiva in Ciceronem* (?)	1.13	11.10	1.14	3.12
Sallust	*historiae*	66.23	53.22	59.3	72.11
Scaurus	*oratio pro se* (?)	20.18	23.27	18.11	24.1
	oratio in Cn. Dolabellam (?)	26.17-18	27.21	23.15	30.12-13
Tiro	*liber quartus de vita Ciceronis*	48.26	41.28-29	43.10-11	54.5-6
Tuditanus		77.4	60.15	68.16-17	83.11
Valerius Antias		13.18	18.28	12.1	15.11
		69.21	55.17	61.22	75.17
Varro	*liber tertius de vita populi Romani*	13.19	19.5-6	12.11-12	15.14

SECTION FOUR

THE RELIABILITY OF ASCONIUS

Since the publication of Madvig's treatise on Asconius some 150 years ago, which fixed for modern scholars the commentator's reputation for accuracy and reliability, no one has made a full scale attempt to impugn that reputation. It is true that some of his slips have been pointed out here and there,[1] but these have been excused as being well below the average, and the otherwise sound and very useful information has outweighed the occasional errors and helped to keep Asconius' reputation intact. Madvig could find only a handful of errors, and all of these he excused or found solutions for.[2]

Part of the reason that Asconius has acquired a reputation for reliability is the apparently scholarly way he goes about his task — the frequent references to his sources, and the critical appraisal of his sources.[3] But we have already seen that his use of references may be derived a great deal from memory, and in many cases we have no way of checking whether the references are accurate. In some cases it seems he has forgotten specifically who his source was, and this throws some doubt on whether his memory is accurate when he does make specific references. There are two main sources of whom he is critical — Cicero and Fenestella. In the former case, he cannot bring himself to say that Cicero is actually wrong,[4] and in the latter case there may have been some sort of personal rivalry (which throws some doubt on the validity of the criticism).

The following is a list of 'errors' by Asconius, arranged in categories of ascending order of seriousness, which may be of some help in attempting to evaluate his reliability:[5]

---

[1] See, for example, the comments of R.G.M. Nisbet in his edition of Cicero's *in Pisonem* (Oxford, 1961) pp. 54-6, and the list of errors in W.C. McDermott, *Hermes* 97 (1969) 242 n. 2.

[2] Madvig, pp. 66-71. As an example, cf. his explanation for Asconius' mistake over the date of the death of Cicero's father (below, no. 59): Madvig blames *reprehendentes et librarii.* For his summing up of Asconius' reliability, see pp. 62, 76-7 and 81; cf. Lichtenfeldt, pp. 1-2.

[3] On the desire that more of Asconius had survived than of even Sallust and Livy, see Lichtenfeldt, p. 2, and cf. Madvig, p. 81 n. 9. For a more recent statement of belief in Asconius' accuracy and reliability, see M. Griffin, *JRS* 63 (1973) 201-3.

[4] See above, pp. 46-7.

[5] The errors are numbered continuously and within each category are arranged in the order of the commentaries as we currently have them. For a full examination of each error, see the appropriate comment ad. loc. in Part II.

The Reliability of Asconius

I. Errors where Asconius has got the praenominal initial wrong, or where there is a mistake in numerical calculation. Given that Asconius was working a great deal from memory, and bearing in mind that it would have been difficult to calculate intervals of years when the method of dating in common use was by consulships, we can easily see why Asconius made such errors. They could, of course, have resulted from manuscript errors and not have been the fault of Asconius at all. Some few instances where it is possible that there has been poor copying of manuscripts have been included. In any case, these errors are not in themselves serious.

(1) 7.14: *post sex deinde annos*

The mss. all give the number of years as *novem*; the emendation to *VI* was made by Rinkes, and has been followed by all the modern editors.

(2) 17.12-14: *L. Opimius eiectus patria est qui et post praeturam et consul maximis periculis rem publicam liberarat.*

Asconius' phrase *in praetura* (which is correct to describe Opimius' activities) seems to be in contradiction with the phrase in this part of the lemma, *post praeturam*. The incorrect copying could derive from Asconius himself, or could have intruded into the mss. tradition.

(3) 19.6-7: *subscripserunt Triario in Scaurum L. Marius L.f.*

The mss. give *Q.* here for Marius' *praenomen*, but on the basis of his father's name and the evidence of 29.6, it is usually emended to *L.*

(4) 28.7-8: *L. Volcacius, Q. Metellus Nepos*

The mss. read either *m. vol. quintus* (S) or *m. vol. Q.* (P) or *m. vol. volq.* (M), which Manutius has corrected and filled out to *L. Volcacius, Q.* All three mss. give *M.* (instead of *L.*) for the *praenomen* of Volcacius Tullus.

(5) 28.18: *et M'. Glabrio, sororis filius*

The simplest of copyists' errors has *M.* instead of *M'*.

(6) 28.19: *P. Lentulus, Lentuli Nigri flaminis filius*

The mss. have *P.* for the *praenomen* of this man. We know only of a Lucius as the son of L. Cornelius Lentulus Niger, the *flamen Martialis*.

(7) 29.4: *P. Triarius*

Here the mss. give *C.* for Triarius' *praenomen*, but at 18.19 they have (correctly) *P.*

(8)   31.10, 51.9-10: *T. Munatius*

In these two places the mss. give *L.* for Munatius Plancus' *praenomen* but elsewhere (37.18, 40.21-22, 42.16, 52.11) it is correctly given as *T.* Oddly at 32.26, 37.1, 42.9 and 44.14, the praenominal initial is left out altogether. There is no consistency in the way that T. Munatius Plancus is referred to (cf. simply *Plancus* at 37.25 and 38.5, [*T.*] *Munatius* at 40.21-22, as well as the full name), and so it is hard to say whether Asconius is at fault, or the copyists. Confusion between L and T would be easy in uncials, and the exemplar from which our mss. were copied is usually taken to have been ninth century (and therefore written in uncials).

(9)   45.11-12: *constantiam L. Domiti quam in quaestura praestitit*

The mss. here read *in praetura*. At the time of Manilius' tribunate, it can only be Domitius' quaestorship which is meant. It could have been a copyist's error which wrote *praetura* for *quaestura*, or Asconius could have forgotten what Domitius' office was.

(10)   53.14: *T. Annio*

The mss. give *C.* for Annius' *praenomen* here, when it should be *T.* Presumably a copyist's error.

(11)   59.17-18: *detulit nomen Publius, subscripsit Gaius*

The mss. all give *C.* as the *praenomen* for the *subscriptor*, but Cic. *Cluent.* 100 suggests that the two brothers were named Publius and Lucius. Presumably Cicero is more to be trusted, and Asconius guilty of a lapse of memory.

(12)   59.18, 60.5: *P. Cassius*

The praetor of 66 is probably to be identified with Cicero's competitor for the consulship (a *biennium* later), in which case his praenominal initial should be *L.* (cf. 82.7).

(13)   60.21, 79.20 (cf. 81.6): *Mam. Lepidus*

In the first case, two of the mss. give *L.* and the other gives *M.*; in the other two places the mss. all give *M.* The man referred to is either Mam. Aemilius Lepidus or M'. Aemilius Lepidus. Either way, the mistake could be due to a copyist.

(14)   64.19: *ante XXIII annos*

The mss. have *XVI* here; figures can be notoriously corrupt, but it is hard to see how one can get *XVI* out of *XXIII* (unless an *X* has dropped out and the final *III* seen as *VI*). Asconius shows elsewhere that he had difficulty with addition and subtraction.

(15) 76.28: *T. Veturio Cicurino*

The mss. have *L. Vetrurio* with a variety of confusions for the *cognomen*; from Liv. 2.28.1 the *praenomen* should be *T.*

(16) 81.7: *ante II de XL annos*

The mss. have *II et XL*; Manutius has suggested the emendation *II de XL* (which has been followed by all the modern editors) in order to get closer to the correct figure; even so it should be thirty-nine years, not thirty-eight, from the date of the speech to Cn. Domitius Ahenobarbus' tribunate. And the emendation produces a numerical formula unique in Asconius. Perhaps he did write *II et XL* (cf. the similar formulae at 28.25-26, 55.17 and 56.1) and simply made an arithmetic error.

II. Errors which can be attributed to a mistake in Asconius' sources. These all occur in his comments on the *in Pisonem*. While it is true that these errors are not the fault of Asconius himself, part of his reputation rests on his critical ability, and these errors show that he did not always exercise that ability. One error in particular (no. 18) we should not have expected, as it deals with an aspect of Cicero's own life.

(17) 3.15-16: *deduxerunt triumviri P. Cornelius Asina, P. Papirius Maso, [Cn. Pompeius], Cn. Cornelius Scipio*

Two of the mss. (P and M) include all four names, while the third (S) correctly omits Cn. Pompeius; only three names are needed since it was a triumviral commission. Polybius (3.40.9) says the commission was made up of C. Lutatius Catulus and two former praetors, while Livy (21.25.3-4) says that it was made up of Catulus, C. Servilius Geminus and M. Annius, but adds that in place of the latter two certain annalists have M'. Acilius and C. Herennius, and others have P. Cornelius Asina and C. Papirius Maso. Asconius has one of these variants, with Cn. Cornelius Scipio instead of Catulus; he seems to have got only one annalist's version, or perhaps a confusion from two or more. Perhaps his memory has again let him down.

(18) 5.9-11: *Cicero filiam post mortem Pisonis generi P. Lentulo collocavit, apud quem illa ex partu decessit.*

Asconius makes two mistakes here. The first is that, after the death of Piso, Tullia was married to Furius Crassipes, and then to P. Lentulus Dolabella. The clause beginning *apud quem* . . . could mean 'who was her husband when she died', but it might mean 'in whose house she died'. If the latter, then Asconius has made a second mistake, since Tullia died soon after childbirth, not in Dolabella's house, but in her father's. It is odd that Asconius made such errors in regard to events closely connected with the life of Cicero himself.

(19) 13.8-9: *nam [M'.] Valerio Maximo, ut Antias tradidit, inter alios honores domus quoque publice aedificata est in Palatio*

There is no evidence, apart from this comment, that M'. Valerius Maximus (dict. 494) was awarded a house at public expense. The mistake has most likely come from Valerius Antias, whose fabrication of stories connected with the Valerian family is well known.

III. Errors which are derived from Cicero himself. Though, as we have seen, Asconius points out mistakes made by Cicero, he always finds an excuse or explanation for what the orator has said (or is at least hesitant to say that he is wrong).[6] This belief in the authority of Cicero leads Asconius into uncritical acceptance of his statements and judgments. This category is similar to the previous one, but contains mistakes of a somewhat more serious nature, as far as Asconius' reputation is concerned, since they derive from the works of the man on which he is writing commentaries.

(20) 2.18-20: *tamen non puto vos ignorare hunc Pisonem ex ea familia esse quae Frugi appellata sit; et ideo dicit aspernari eum moribus nomen*

Piso, the consul of 58, was not a descendant of the branch of the family who bore the name Frugi, though he was distantly related to it. Asconius has been misled by such Ciceronian statements as [*Piso*] *erat eo nomine ut ingenerata familiae frugalitas videretur* (*Sest.* 21, cf. *Pis.* 53).

(21) 4.9-11: *avum autem maternum Pisonis primo Gallum fuisse ideo ait quod venisse eum in Italiam dicit trans Alpis*

Asconius here accepts Cicero's exaggeration that Calventius, Piso's maternal grandfather, had come from across the Alps. This is a good example of where Asconius has written a comment derived purely from the context of the passage.[7]

(22) 13.4-7 (cf. 13.22-14.3): *hoc Cicero oratorio more, non historico, videtur posuisse: nam multis aetatibus ante Ciceronem nulli id contigisse verum est, nemini vero umquam antea videamus ne parum caute dicat*

---

[6] See above, pp. 46-7.
[7] Cf. above, p. 40.

Instead of accepting that Cicero has spoken in an oratorical manner, Asconius proceeds to find an excuse for what Cicero has said.[8]

(23) 31.17: *occurrit ei circa horam nonam Clodius*

This passage is included, not as an example of an 'error' by Asconius, but as an instance where he has failed to point out his disagreement with Cicero.

(24) 53.15-16 (cf. 31.7-8): *tertium partrimonium videtur significare matris; aliud enim quod fuerit non inveni*

While Asconius is duly cautious about identifying the third *patrimonium*, there is the possibility that he may have accepted an exaggeration by Cicero. Tyrrell remarks that we never hear of anyone who used up, say, two or four inheritances on acts of extravagence,[9] and so the figure of three may have been invented by Cicero.

(25) 66.12-14, 83.18-25 (cf. 83.2-4), 92.15-20.

Asconius accepts uncritically the existence of the so-called 'first Catilinarian conspiracy', especially Cn. Piso's part in it. Yet he must have been aware of the heavy bias in, say, Cicero's secret memoirs, which he acknowledges as a source in the second of these passages. And he must have known the passage in the *pro Sulla* (on which he probably wrote a commentary) in which Cicero disclaims any knowledge of a conspiracy in 66 (though he might have made such a disclaimer in the interests of his client).[10] The claim by Cicero that a conspiracy existed, which had been instigated by Crassus and in which Catilina and Piso were involved, was a later fabrication.[11] Asconius should have recognised that, or should he? There is a tendency to think that Asconius was acting like a historian and exercising a critical faculty. But it is important to bear in mind that he was a commentator, explaining to his sons what Cicero was saying. We should not, therefore, expect him to be historically critical always, for that was not his primary intention.

IV. A group of passages where it is not clear that there is an error by Asconius, but where there is a great deal of controversy. Part of the

---

[8] Cf. above, pp. 46-7.

[9] Tyrrell, in A.C. Clark (ed.), *Cicero: pro Milone* (Oxford, 1895) p. 86. There is a reference to the wasting (?) of a fourth fortune, by Mamurra in Catull. 29.17-20 (cf. E. Badian, *Class. Phil.* 72 [1977] 320-2), but only one of the four fortunes cames as a *patrimonium*.

[10] Cic. *Sull.* 11-12.

[11] For a recent discussion, with bibliography to date, see B.A. Marshall, *Latomus* 33 (1974) 804-9, and *Class. Phil.* 72 (1977) 318-20.

reason for the controversy is often that Asconius, with his reputation for accuracy, makes a statement which contradicts other pieces of evidence. If it were to be accepted that Asconius' evidence is not always accurate, then some of these controversies would perhaps be more easily settled. A fuller discussion of the arguments surrounding these controversies will be found in the commentary on the particular passages in Part II.

(26) 3.17: *eamque coloniam LIII deductam esse invenimus*

One has to resort to a number of assumptions and calculations to make Asconius' total correct. Perhaps the reading in Asconius is wrong, or perhaps he has made an arithmetic error (as he sometimes does).

(27) 21.4-5: *iratus Scauro quod eum in augurum collegium non cooptaverat*

Asconius says Scaurus was an augur, and Suetonius (*Nero* 2.1) that he was a pontiff. Modern scholarship cannot decide who is right, but it would be unwise to use the argument that Asconius is generally more reliable than Suetonius.[12]

(28) 22.5-8: *non multo ante, Italico bello exorto, cum ob sociis negatam civitatem nobilitas in invidia esset, Q. Varius tr. pl. legem tulit ut quaereretur de iis quorum ope consiliove socii contra populum Romanum arma sumpsissent*

The explanation for the introduction of the law (that the nobles were disliked for rejecting Italian citizenship) is incongruous with the scope of the law (to attack those who sympathisd with the Italians), particularly when some of those very same nobles were prosecuted in the court set up by the law.[13] Unless, of course, Asconius is explaining, not the introduction of the law, but the cause of the war (in which case it is a simplistic explanation).

(29) 23.16-17: *is propter multa flagitia cum de exsilio arcessitus esset ut in carcere necaretur, venenum bibit*

Asconius' report that Tubulus was recalled from exile in order to be executed in prison but that he forestalled execution by committing suicide is puzzling. There must be something behind Asconius' comment, but at face value it seems to contain too many legal anomalies.

---

[12] As does Badian, *Arethusa* 1 (1968) 29-31.
[13] Badian, *Historia* 18 (1969) 460.

(30) 30.1-2 (cf. 40.25-41.1): *orationem hanc dixit Cn. Pompeio III cos. a.d. VI Id. April.*

If we accept the mss. reading *VI* for the date of the last day of the trial when Cicero delivered his speech, the trial of Milo ought to have extended over five days, 4th-8th April (since it began *prid. Non. April.* — 39.7). In Asconius' description of the trial, however, only four days can be accounted for.

(31) 88.5-6: *Q. Gallium, quem postea reum ambitus defendit, significare videtur.*

This comment suggests that Asconius dated Cicero's defence of Q. Gallius after the delivery of the *in toga candida* (i.e. after 64), whereas *comm. pet.* 19 suggests that the defence of Gallius was undertaken before 64.

V. Unwarranted conclusions or inferences which often result from Asconius' attempts to expand and 'explain' on the basis of his own background of knowledge about the Ciceronian period, or even on the basis of the context of the passage itself on which he is commenting. If we may adapt what has been said of another scholiast, there are occasions where 'the information given is gathered from the context in Cicero's actual speech' but 'what he saw was at times not what was there, and his expansions turned into plain fiction.'[14] The last statement might be going too far in the case of Asconius, but there are some instances where his filling out of what Cicero says has led him to draw some unwarranted conclusions.

(32) 3.20-23: *de se autem optime meritos Placentinos ait, quod illi quoque honoratissima decreta erga Ciceronem fecerunt certaveruntque in ea re cum tota Italia, cum de reditu eius actum est.*

Stangl (n. ad loc. = 13.1-2) suggests that it is an unwarranted conclusion on the part of Asconius to say that the services of Placentia towards Cicero, referred to by him in the lemma, related to the activities connected with Cicero's recall. We do not know what Placentia's services to Cicero were, and this comment looks more like a deduction from the text itself which Asconius has filled out.

---

[14] Badian, *JRS* 63 (1973) 125 and 130, referring to the Schol. Bob.

(33) 10.8-9: *quod eos a quibus ipse expulsus erat adiuvisset*

Asconius misses the point of what Cicero is saying: Cicero is not explaining why the people of Capua rejected Piso when he came to visit them; his point is that a 'Capuan consul' ought to have been welcome but the people of that city saw him for what he was and rejected him. Asconius has produced an unwarranted explanation in attempting to fill out Cicero's statement.

(34) 16.13: *cuius et poemata sunt lasciva*

Asconius has perhaps taken too seriously Cicero's view of the immoral effect of Philodemus' erotic poetry.

(35) 48.7ff.: *sed videtur mihi loqui de eo die*

Having confessed his inability to discover the date of the incident referred to in the lemma, Asconius proceeds to make a guess, but his guess is wrong.

(36) 50.12-13: *saepe obiecit Clodio Cicero socium eum coniurationis Catilinae fuisse; quam rem nunc quoque reticens ostendit.*

Asconius goes on to retail the *opinio* that Clodius had started out to join Catilina when he fled to the camp of Manlius in Etruria at the end of 63, but had changed his mind and returned to Rome. But, as Clark remarks in his note on § 55 of the *pro Milone*, 'it is more natural to refer these words [of Cicero] to the "forays" of Clodius in Etruria, cf. § § 26, 50, 74, 98, than with Asconius to see in them an allusion to the story that Clodius started to join the Catilinarians at Faesulae.' Asconius' error is all the more startling because Cicero does mention Clodius' activities in Etruria in a number of places in the speech; it demonstrates that, in filling out a comment on the basis of the speech itself or from his own understanding, Asconius does not remember information even from the very speech on which he is commenting. This error ought perhaps to be included in the next category, where Asconius himself is clearly wrong.

(37) 61.7-11: *qua vero arte et scientia orationis ita ut et dignitatem clarissimorum civium contra quos dicebat non violaret, et tamen auctoriate eorum laedi reum non pateretur, quantaque moderatione rem tam difficilem aliis tractaverit lectio ipsa declarabit*

Asconius virtually admits here that he has drawn his conclusion from a reading of the speech itself, but it is an unwarranted conclusion.

(38) 74.4-5: *supererat autem ex eis qui illa iudicia metuerant vigens tum maxime C. [Curio pater] Curionis adulescentis eius*

Badian rejects Asconius' identification of one of the men whom Cicero refers to anonymously as having escaped prosecution when the courts were suppressed during the Social War, as Curio the elder.[15] The name and occasion supplied by Asconius can only be conjecture, and not very plausible, since there would hardly be any point in an elaborate paralepsis of an incident which occurred twenty-five years earlier.

(39) 89.18-19: *ita ut senatorum urna damnaret, equitum et tribunorum absolveret*

Asconius implies only two groups of votes, putting the equites and *tribuni aerarii* together as one group (cf. Cic. *Font.* 36, *Cluent.* 121 and 130), but in any case, separate voting by the three orders was not introduced until 59. Asconius has been guilty of a laxity of expression, resulting from his assuming (wrongly on the basis of later practice) the voting pattern from the internal evidence of the speech.[16]

VI. The group containing the most serious category of 'errors', where Asconius has just plainly made a mistake for which no mitigation can be found.

(40) 2.5-6: *cum revocati essent ex provinciis Piso et Gabinius sententia Ciceronis quam dixerat de provinciis consularibus*

Asconius is wrong to say that both Piso and Gabinius were recalled as a result of Cicero's proposal. It could be argued that Asconius' error resulted from an over-simplification (cf. 1.14-15).

(41) 2.26-3.1: *magnopere me haesitare confiteor quid sit qua re Cicero Placentiam municipium esse dicat*

Asconius is wrong in accusing Cicero of having made a mistake; he is the one who has made the mistake.

(42) 8.12-13: *diximus L. Pisone A. Gabinio coss. P. Clodium tr. pl. quattuor leges perniciosas populo Romano tulisse*

Clodius proposed (and carried) more than four laws during his tribunate in 58.

---

[15] Badian, art. cit. (n. 13) 453-4.
[16] C. Macdonald, *CR* 7 (1957) 198; see further, Part II, comm. ad loc.

(43) 12.13-15: *hic autem Marcellus . . . naufragio ad ipsam Africam periit paulo ante coeptum bellum Punicum tertium.*

Asconius has erred in saying that Marcellus was drowned just before the start of the Third Punic War, since his death occcurred in the second year of that war. This is not a simple numerical error (such as nos. 1, 14 or 26), since the event is dated in relation to the beginning of the war.

(44) 23.2-3 and 5-7: *quae generis claritas etiam inertes homines ad summos honores provexit . . . nam neque pater neque avus neque etiam proavus — ut puto, propter tenues opes et nullam vitae industriam — honores adepti sunt.*

The second part of Asconius' explanation is a contradiction of the earlier statement that advancement even for *inertes patricii* was almost automatic. Moreover, Cicero says (*off.* 1.138) that Scaurus' father was distinguished (and Asconius would normally have accepted a Ciceronian comment). This part of the explanation is presumably mere supposition on the part of Asconius.

(45) 27.18-19: *paternus avus proavusque Scauri humiles atque obscuri*

At 23.5-7 Asconius writes that the family lacked political success for three generations before Scaurus the elder, while here he says that it was only for two generations.

(46) 32.24: *noti homines elisi sunt, inter quos C. Vibienus senator*

According to Cic. *Mil.* 37, C. Vibienus cannot have been alive at the beginning of 52 to be involved in the public scenes following Clodius' death.

(47) 43.12: *uxoris eius Corneliae*

On the assumption that the Lepidus referred to at 43.4 is M. Aemilius Lepidus (and not M'. Aemilius Lepidus[17]), there is a possibility that Asconius is mistaken over the name of Lepidus' wife.

(48) 48.20: *ludos Apollinares*

The games which were being conducted when the riots over food shortages took place should have been the *ludi Romani.*

---

[17] As proposed by G.V. Sumner, *JRS* 54 (1964) 43 n. 19.

The Reliability of Asconius

(49) 52.25-53.1: *significant id tempus quo P. Clodius, cum adhuc quaestor designatus esset, deprensus est*

Asconius is wrong on two counts here. First, he is wrong in associating the senate's attempts to keep Clodius under control with the proceedings to prosecute Clodius for his involvement in the Bona Dea affair; Cicero at this point is referring to the senate's inability to control Clodius in the middle 50's. The second error is to say that Clodius was quaestor-designate when he was censured by the senate and an enquiry was ordered into his sacrilege; he most likely became quaestor on the day after the offence was committed, and he was certainly not prosecuted for sacrilege until the middle of his quaestorian year.

(50) 66.8-9 (cf. 85.10-12 and 89.8-12): *Catilina... eodem illo tempore erat reus repetundarum*

At 85.10-12 Asconius clearly dates the prosecution of Catilina to 65. Elsewhere Asconius contradicts this dating: at 66.8-9, he says that Catilina was *reus repetundarum* at the time of the disturbance to Manilius' trial (i.e. the end of 66), and at 89.8-12 he says that Catilina was prevented from standing at the consular elections at the end of 66 because he was then being prosecuted for provincial extortion. At best he is guilty of inconsistency or loose writing in dating the prosecution.

(51) 66.21-67.10

In commenting on the first of these two lemmata relating to laws proposed by C. Aurelius Cotta, Asconius merely assumes that they were laws relating to minor matters which were abrogated almost immediately on the initiative of Cotta himself, and he goes on to say that there is mention of only one law in the sources which was passed by Cotta, the one relating to the tribunate. Yet in the very next lemma which he quotes, there is mention of a law of Cotta dealing with *iudicia privata*, which lasted at least until the next year when it was abrogated by Cotta's brother Marcus. And Asconius seems not to know of another law relating to censorial leases, which is mentioned in a speech of Cicero (*Verr.* 2.3.19) and which he ought therefore to have known of.

(52) 68.6: *quod post triennium exortum est*

Asconius has miscalculated here, since the Italian War broke out late in 91, four years after the passing of the *lex Licinia Mucia*.

(53) 69.3-4: *postea eo licentiae est progressus ut nullum in his morem servaret*

Asconius' reason for the failure of Drusus is not accurate, or at least it may have been oversimplified to suit the level of his readers. It is true that

Drusus did not have the full support of his political associates for the franchise proposal, but they did not entirely abandon him because he had lost his self-restraint and moderation in these matters.

(54) 69.6: *decretum est enim contra auspicia esse latas*

Cicero (*dom.* 41) says that the Livian laws were declared invalid because they were passed contrary to the *lex Caecilia Didia*. That law said nothing about the relation of auspices to the passing of laws.[18] If Cicero is right about the law which Drusus' laws were said to have contravened, then Asconius is wrong to say that they were invalidated because they were found to have been passed contrary to the auspices.

(55) 74.1-3: *nanctus iustitii occasionem senatus decrevit ne iudicia, dum tumultus Italicus esset, exercerentur*

There is a conflict between the evidence of Cicero and of Asconius over which courts were suspended, and when. Whatever the solution, Asconius has been guilty of some misunderstanding about the suspension of the Varian and other courts.

(56) 75.7-9: *alterum L. Cotta, alterum L. Torquatus, qui cum haec Cicero dicebat coss. erant, ambitus damnarant*

Asconius clearly identifies one of the prosecutors of the consuls-elect for 65 as L. Torquatus, yet Cicero (*Sull.* 49-50, *fin.* 2.62) plainly states that it was the son of Torquatus who undertook the prosecution.

(57) 77.6-8: *nomina duorum qui primi creati sunt haec traduntur: L. Sicinius L. f. Velutus, L. Albinius C.f. Paterculus.*

Asconius seems to imply that there was agreement in the tradition about the names of the first two tribunes, which in turn suggests that the three sources nominated a little before this also agreed with each other. But we know that Livy (2.33.2) at least gives a different list. Asconius has not given the right emphasis to Livy's account of the procedure for co-option either.[19]

(58) 79.8: *secundo anno belli Italici*

The calculation is not strictly accurate, since the war had broken out in 91 and Asconius is commenting on an event in 89, i.e. the third year of the war. He is not good at arithmetic (see nos. 1, 14, 26, 43 and 52).

---

[18] Cf. Cic. *Att.* 2.9.1, where in a list of laws relating to the procedure for making proposals, observance of auspices is given separately from the *lex Caecilia Didia*.
[19] See Part II, comm. ad loc.

(59) 79.15ff.

Asconius has misunderstood the nature of the second speech *pro Cornelio*, taking it to be part of the defence, whereas it was mostly a literary adaptation of the interrogation of the witnesses.

(60) 82.10-11: *atque in petitione patrem amisit*

According to Cic. *Att.* 1.6.2, Cicero's father died in 68; Asconius says here he died in 64. In view of the inaccuracy of Asconius on other occasions (especially when he is calculating dates), it is more likely that he has made an error.

(61) 92.20-22: *Piso . . . missus a senatu per honorem legationis*

Asconius' terminology is incorrect here: Piso was not sent as a *legatus* but as *quaestor pro praetore*.

It is this accumulation of errors or possible errors, loose writing, and over-simplifications which, it is suggested, should lead us to lower our estimation of the worth of Asconius. It is true that some sixty-one 'errors', many of them minor or insignificant, is not a bad average in ninety-four pages of an Oxford Classical Text; many Roman historians would have a worse average. But the cumulative effect of the list of errors is to cast doubt on his hitherto highly regarded accuracy and to require much of his commentary to be treated with more caution. It is not just that he makes mistakes with the names of prosecutors or with the date of a man's death; he does not at times understand his sources properly, or he makes mistakes in historical judgment. His judgment is not necessarily better than ours; he tries 'to interpret words as he found them in the light of his researches into the Ciceronian period' but he is just as liable as we are to forget that the evidence available to him was limited and far from complete.[20]

Part of Asconius' reputation rests on the way he goes about his task, almost like a modern scholar: he cites his references, he is critical of his sources, and he admits where he is ignorant or has not completed his research.[21] As for the citing of references, it has been suggested earlier that they may have been remembered rather than looked up and checked; in a set of notes written quickly, Asconius may just have relied on his memory to comment that Tuditanus said such and such, or that such and such was said in the first book of Iulius Hyginus' *de claris viris*. In the end

---

[20] Badian, art. cit. (n. 13) 453-4.
[21] 7.26, 10.19, 48.5, 48.23, 53.15-16, 92.2-3.

we have no way of checking the accuracy of such references. And of course he does not nominate his sources all the time.[22]

His criticism of sources is mainly confined to two authors, Cicero and Fenestella. In the case of his main source, Cicero himself, he does on occasion make a criticism but then tones it down in some way; in general, however, he accepts uncritically whatever Cicero says and is consequently misled by him sometimes. In the case of Fenestella, Asconius follows a fairly normal pattern in mentioning him by name only when he wishes to disagree (except for one instance [5.8-9] where he accepts a statement by Fenestella); the frequency with which Fenestella is cited shows that he was a major source for Asconius, and that therefore he probably took a lot from Fenestella without criticism.

Of course, Asconius does not himself claim that he is aiming to give accurate historical information or to sort out historical truth.[23] It is only moderns, who seek to use every available piece of evidence (whether it was designed to be historical evidence or not), who invest Asconius with a reputation for historical accuracy. Jerome called him a *scriptor historicus*; Asconius would perhaps have been baffled by such a description. His purpose was simply to explain to his sons what Cicero meant by certain statements he made. Though he did it on occasion (but always with some reservation), he was not bound to point out in a historically critical way the inaccuracy of what was being said (e.g. he accepts unquestioningly Cicero's view of the involvement of Cn. Piso and Clodius in the Catilinarian conspiracies) or in making any comment to treat the matter under consideration in terms of its historical accuracy. He did not view his work as history.

This is not to say that he would not have tried to be accurate within the limits of what he was trying to do and what his memory would allow. It must be remembered that he probably wrote quickly, that he relied a great deal on memory, and that the work was pitched at a certain level and for a certain purpose (i.e. he wrote to help his sons with their rhetorical education).

This accumulation of mistakes does not invalidate a great deal of the information which Asconius gives; he is not the sort of person to make up graphic and plausible details as some others did.[24] As has been said earlier about the apparently capricious selection of passages for

---

[22] Perhaps he did check references, but only in those cases where the relevant book was readily available to him (such as in his own library, or one near at hand). Even so, it would require an act of memory to know what and where to check.
[23] Note where he is concerned only with recording tradition (e.g. 13.8-22, 76.28-77.8).
[24] Badian, art. cit. (n. 13) 454.

discussion, Asconius chooses to comment on those passages where he has something sensible and relevant to say, the choice being dictated probably by what he could remember from his long (and no doubt intelligent) researches into the Ciceronian period. The corollary to this is that he obviously chose not to make a comment on those passages where he could not remember anything relevant to say or where he knew he had not yet done enough research,[25] rather than to give a false or vague comment (though he did occasionally succumb to the temptation of simply filling out what the author had said, which amounted to not much more than mere paraphrase: see category III above).

As he did not view his work as history, we should perhaps not apply too strictly the rules of historical criticism to his commentaries. On the other hand, the collection of errors should lead us to question the over-generous conclusions about his reliability which were referred to at the beginning of this section, and to be more cautious in accepting too quickly what he says.

---

[25] See the list in n. 21.

PART II
COMMENTARY

THE COMMENTARY ON THE SPEECH IN PISONEM

[Note: Reference is made to the edition of the *in Pisonem* by R.G.M. Nisbet (Oxford, 1961) by the abbreviation Nisbet, with the appropriate page number.]

1.1-2: *haec oratio dicta est Cn. Pompeio Magno II M. Crasso II coss.*

Asconius states clearly that the *in Pisonem* was delivered in the second consulship of Pompeius and Crassus, a few days before the lavish games celebrating the opening of Pompeius' theatre; he rejects a counter-view that the speech was the last delivered by Cicero in the following year. As Nisbet points out (App. VIII, p. 199), 'there can be no doubt that the *in Pisonem* in its original form was delivered in 55 B.C.' He chooses somewhere between July and September, but it is possible to pin-point the time of delivery more accurately than that.

Asconius' statement of the time of delivery (a few days before Pompeius' games) seems to be confirmed by Cicero's own comment in the speech: *instant post hominum memoriam apparatissimi magnificentissimique ludi, quales non modo numquam fuerunt sed ne quo modo fieri quidem posthac possint possum ullo pacto suspicari* (§65). That the games held by Pompeius were extremely lavish, see Cic. *fam.* 7.1, *off.* 2.57; Plin. *NH* 8.20 and 53; Plut. *Pomp.* 52.5; Dio 39.38.1-6. Although in §65 Cicero does not mention the promoter of the games, it would seem that he was referring to those of Pompeius celebrating the opening of his theatre in 55. Associated with the theatre was a temple of Venus Victrix (Plin. *NH* 8.20; Gell. 10.1.1ff.; Tert. *spect.* 10); this temple was apparently built on top of the theatre in such a way that the rows of seats appeared to be the steps leading up to the temple.

In the *fasti Amiternini* (*CIL* 1^2.244; *Inscr. Ital.* 13.2.191), there is the following entry for 12th August:

> HERCVLI INVICTO AD CIRCVM
> MAXIM VENERI VICTRICI
> HON VIRTVT FELICITATI
> IN THEATRO MARMOREO

A similar entry is found in the *fasti Allifani* (*CIL* 1^2.217; *Inscr. Ital.* 13.2.191), though the location has been lost from the inscription in both cases. The theatre of Pompeius, being the first permanent one and made of stone, became known as the *theatrum marmoreum* (so Mommsen, commenting on these two *fasti* in *CIL* 1^2.324, and Platner-Ashby, p. 515). So, in the mention of Venus Victrix in these inscriptions, what we have looks like the date for the dedication by Pompeius in 55 of his theatre and temple of Venus Victrix (so Drumann-Groebe, 4.529; Platner-Ashby, pp. 515-6, 555; C. Koch, *RE* 8A 1.164; J.A. Hanson, *Roman Theatre-Temples* [Princeton, 1959] pp. 43 and 52-3).

If, then, we have a date of 12th August for the dedication of Pompeius' theatre and temple of Venus Victrix, and possibly also a temple of Hercules, the lavish games must have taken place at the same time. We know that the games went on for some days — the beast shows for at least five days (Cic. *fam* 7.1.3; Dio 39.38.2). The mention by Cicero of approaching games in §65, and Asconius' comment that the speech was delivered a few days before these games indicate that Cicero's speech attacking Piso was delivered early in August 55.

For a fuller discussion of the date of delivery of the *in Pisonem*, see B.A. Marshall, *CQ* 25 (1975) 88-93, and cf. *Antichthon* 8 (1974) 80-4.

1.7: .... *quidem*

Though the three main mss. normally vary on the length of lacunae, they all agree on the length of the lacuna here, four or five spaces. Three suggestions have been put forward for the identity of the missing authority. Kiessling and Schoell print Tiro in the text, and argue for it in their introduction (pp. xii-xiii), while suggesting Nepos as an alternative. J.P. Hildebrandt, *de scholiis Ciceronis Bobiensibus* (Berlin, 1894) p. 15 n. 3, also proposes Nepos. Stangl (n. ad loc.) says that the proposal of Tiro is based on the subscription written in the margin in one of the mss. of the second speech of Cicero's *de lege agraria*: *Statilius Maximus rursus emendavi ad Tyronem* . . . by which (supposedly) he means that this is evidence for Tiro's editing of Cicero's speeches (cf. F.W. Hall, *A Companion to Classical Texts* [Oxford, 1913: repr. 1968] p. 61; for the full text of the subscription, see A.C. Clark, praef. to Vol. III of Cicero's orations [Oxford, 1909] p. ix). We do have other evidence of Tiro's editing of Cicero's speeches (Gell. 1.7.1, 13.21.15-16 [referring only to *Verr.* 2.2 and 5]), as well as his editing of *commentarii* for cases for which Cicero did not write out speeches in full (Quint. 10.7.31): for a discussion, see W.C. McDermott, *Historia* 21 (1972) 277-80, and J.E.G. Zetzel, *HSCP* 77 (1973) 230-3. The knowledge that Tiro edited the speeches is not as relevant to the problem of filling the lacuna as the knowledge that he wrote a life of Cicero: the date at which Cicero delivered a speech is more likely to come from a biography than from a text of the speech. As we know that Tiro· wrote a biography of Cicero (for the evidence, see McDermott, art. cit. 282-5) and as the one reference that Asconius makes to Tiro is to his life of Cicero (48.25-26), his name looks the most likely candidate to fill the lacuna. A strong argument against having Tiro as the missing author is that he would hardly have got the date for the delivery of a Ciceronian speech wrong.

In Pisonem

Stangl says that the suggestion of Nepos is based on Gell. 15.28.1-5, which refers to an error of Nepos, even greater than that of Fenestella, on the age of Cicero when he delivered the *pro Roscio Amerino*, but it seems that this reference argues as much for Fenestella: it is put forward in the *editio princeps* (Venice, 1477), by Poeth, *de Fenestella* (in Stangl, ad loc.), by Lichtenfeldt, p. 56, and by H. Peter, *HRF*, praef. xxiv (cf. *HRR* 1.24 and 2.112). Lichtenfeldt rejects Nepos because he is not mentioned elsewhere by Asconius, and Tiro because he is mentioned only rarely (in fact, once: 48.25), and he proposes Fenestella because he is often mentioned and frequently criticised (two out of the four times Asconius mentions him; cf. Gell. 15.28.4, and above on pp. 53-5). The strongest argument against Fenestella is the number of spaces in the lacuna.

1.7-8: *posuit hanc inter eas orationes . . . ultimam*

Cicero (*Q.f.* 3.1.11, September 54) mentions an *oratio Calventi Mari* (for Cicero's use of Calventius as a nick-name for Piso, derived from his Gallic maternal grandfather, see *red. in sen.* 13, *prov. cons.* 7, *Pis.* 14). Perhaps this has been mistaken for the speech which Cicero delivered against Piso in 55, and someone (see preceding comment) has taken it to claim that Cicero's attack on Piso was the last speech he made in 54. The letter is referring, however, to Piso's published reply to Cicero's invective, which was also the published form of the speech delivered in the senate early in August 55 (on the date of the original delivery, see above on 1.1-2.). It is likely that Cicero rewrote his speech for publication at the end of 55 or beginning of 54; if the latter, it may also help to explain why someone thought it had been delivered in that year.

1.12-15: *deinde magis quidem naturale . . . post anni intervallum*

Piso published a speech, presumably towards the end of the year 54 (mentioned by Cicero in *Q.f.* 3.1.11, written in September 54), which was probably a reply to the published form of Cicero's invective; as it was published a year after the actual exchange between Piso and Cicero, it was probably its appearance which led the certain authority into thinking that Cicero's speech was delivered late in 54 (see preceding comment). This published speech of Piso has been taken by some to be the invective against Cicero included in the works of Sallust (R. Reitzenstein, *Hermes* 33 [1898] 87-101, and E. Schwartz, ibid. 101-8; for an examination of their view, see F. Schöll, *Rhein. Mus.* 57 [1902] 159-63). Syme tentatively suggests (*JRS* 37 [1947] 201) that the pseudo-Sallust invective is the work of an Augustan stylist writing a reply to Cicero in the character of Piso. For a brief examination of the question, see Nisbet, App. VII, and for a brief review of some of the literature, see E. Frankel, *JRS* 41 (1951) 192. Wiseman (*JRS* 56 [1966] 114-5) suggests that in return for dropping his attack on the Campanian land law Cicero was given a free hand to attack Piso, and that the latter's slow return from his province was due to his unwillingness to face the attack.

2.5-6: *revocati essent . . . sententia Ciceronis quam dixerat de provinciis consularibus*

E.G. Hardy (*CR* 31 [1917] 11-5) suggests that Asconius is mistaken in saying that Piso was recalled from his governorship of Macedonia by the *sententia* Cicero expressed in his speech *de provinciis consularibus*. In the debate on the consular provinces in the middle of 56 there were several proposals put forward before Cicero spoke:

1. that the two Gauls should be assigned to the consuls about to be elected (Cicero rejects this as uncompromising: *prov. cons.* 17)

2. that Transalpine Gaul and Syria be assigned (Cicero rejects this on the grounds that Caesar will not be able to complete his military project when he has achieved so much success, and that this proposal will leave Piso undisturbed; Cicero also accuses the proposer of moral cowardice for not suggesting Cisalpine Gaul, and thereby attacking the *lex Vatinia* by which Caesar was given that province and which some regarded as unconstitutional: § § 36-38)

3. that Cisalpine Gaul and Syria be assigned (Cicero says the proposer has thus allowed for Caesar's military aims in Transalpine Gaul and will respect the *lex Vatinia* by fixing the date at which the consul of 55 assigned to Cisalpine Gaul could take over in 54 [i.e. 1st March], but Cicero objects that this will create a constitutional anomaly, since whichever consul of 55 received the province would have a period of two months at the beginning of 54 in which he could not exercise his assigned *imperium*, and that this proposal also will leave Piso undisturbed: § § 37-38)

4. that Syria and Macedonia be assigned (this proposal was put forward by P. Servilius Vatia Isauricus: §1).

It was the proposal of Servilius Isauricus which Cicero followed (§17), adding a clause that the provinces of Syria and Macedonia be made praetorian for the following year 55. This clause meant that, while Syria and Macedonia would be allocated to the consuls of 55 to be taken up at the beginning of 54, the senate could assign praetors from the current year to those provinces and so effectively remove Piso and Gabinius from the beginning of 55. Under the *lex Sempronia* decisions on consular provinces could not be vetoed, but Cicero feared that it would be possible to veto the clause making Syria and Macedonia praetorian provinces. If that happened, at least Syria and Macedonia should be made the provinces for the consuls about to be elected, for in that way Piso and Gabinius would be removed at the beginning of 54.

In Pisonem 85

The outcome of the debate was a decision not in the form that Cicero had proposed (hence Hardy's claim that Asconius is wrong): only Syria was made a consular province for 54 (Caesar's provinces were left intact; the other consular province is not known — Spain is usually suggested) and only Macedonia was made a praetorian province for 55 (Cic. *Pis.* 88: *quid debilitatio atque abiectio animi tui, Macedonia praetoria nuntiata, cum tu non solum, quod tibi succederetur, sed quod Gabinio non succederetur, exsanguis et mortuus concidisti?*). Hardy is perhaps too harsh on Asconius, who was probably only over-simplifying (cf. 1.14-15: *qua revocatus erat ex provincia*).

2.18-19: *hunc Pisonem ex ea familia esse quae Frugi apellata sit*

Piso was not a descendant of the branch of the family which bore the name Piso Frugi: as Syme points out (*JRS* 46 [1956] 21), neither he nor his son bore the name Frugi. But he was distantly related to the Frugi branch of the Calpurnii Pisones, for Cicero often says of C. Calpurnius Piso Frugi that he was a *propinquus* of Piso (*Pis.* 12, *red. in sen.* 17, 38, *Sest.* 68). The connection was distant: Nisbet (p. 71 on *Pis.* 12) conjectures that the consul of 133, C. Piso's great-grandfather, and the consul of 148, L. Piso's great-grandfather, may have been cousins; the former had the name Frugi, and the latter Caesoninus, so the separation of the two branches goes back as far as then. For a conjectural family-tree, see Drumann-Groebe, 2.48, and Sumner, *Orators*, p. 146.

The point of Cicero's phrase *moribus nomen* is that the name 'Piso' itself has an air of *frugalitas*, because of its association with 'Frugi' (Nisbet, p. 53); cf. Cic. *Sest.* 21: *[Piso] erat eo nomine ut ingenerata familiae frugalitas videretur*, and *Pis.* 53. In view of that first passage and the frequent references to L. Piso's relationship to C. Piso, we can see how Asconius has fallen into the error of thinking Piso belonged to the family which had the name Frugi. It may not even be an error — he may mean it to be taken in the same way as Cicero's phrase is to be taken.

2.26-3.1: *magnopere me haesitare... Placentiam municipium esse dicat*

Asconius is wrong here in accusing Cicero of having made a mistake: he has made an error himself. Placentia was founded in 218 as one of a pair of Latin colonies with Cremona, on either side of the Po (Polyb. 3.40.3-5; Liv. *per.* 20; Vell. 1.14.8; Tac. *hist.* 3.34). On the republican practice of planting colonies in pairs, see E.T. Salmon, *Roman Colonization under the Republic* (London, 1969) p. 53, cf. n. 63. Some 6000 colonists were sent to each site, including 200 equites (Ascon. 3.13-14), which implies that Roman citizens were included in these Latin colonies (see below on 3.19-20). Eventually, because of losses of numbers as a result of incursions by the local inhabitants, it was refounded in 190 on a site about fifteen miles to the east (T. Frank, *JRS* 9 [1919] 202-7; U. Ewins, *PBSR* 20 [1952] 55), when 6000 new colonists were sent to it and Cremona. Placentia was, however, a *municipium* by Cicero's time, for as a holder of Latin status it would have become a *municipium* either under the *lex Iulia* of 90 or (less likely) the *lex Pompeia* of 89 (Ewins, *PBSR* 23 [1955] 77; Brunt, *Manpower,* p. 168, and N. Criniti, *L'epigrafe di Asculum di Gn. Pompeo Strabone* [Milan, 1970] p. 40, prefer the *lex Iulia*). An inscription from Placentia, referring to a *quattuorvir,* a regular sign of municipal status (Cic. *Att.* 5.2.3; A.N. Sherwin-White, *The Roman Citizenship*, 2nd edn. [Oxford, 1973] p. 63), seems to indicate that it was a *municipium* at some stage (*CIL* 11.1217, with note ibid. p. 242). Asconius is confused rather than mistaken, for it is probable that by his day Placentia had reverted to the status of *colonia* (Salmon, op. cit. pp. 138 and 162), a status which was highly prized in imperial times (Gell. 16.13.3 and 9), and which could be conferred on cities which had not even been formally colonised. The change in status probably came in the triumviral period or early principate (Salmon, op. cit. p. 162; for Octavianus/Augustus' colonial activity, see *RG* 15.3, 28.1-2).

3.3: *Pridie Kal. Iun.*

On the 'birthday' of a colony, see Salmon, op. cit. p. 26 and n. 31.

3.11-12: *ut petendo magistratus civitatem Romanam adipiscerentur*

For the early Latin colonies (probably because they contained some Roman citizens who voluntarily gave up their citizenship and assumed Latin status), the *ius migrationis* was a way of acquiring Roman citizenship. However, in 187, in response to Latin protests about the number of Latins who were being allowed to move to Rome, the senate restricted the Latin right to migrate to Rome freely by requiring a Latin to leave a son of adult age behind in his community, and at the same time it expelled 12,000 Latins who had moved to Rome recently (Liv. 39.3.4-6). In 177, again at the request of the Latins, the senate expelled Latins who had acquired citizenship by migrating since the measures of 187 (Liv. 41.8.6-12; cf. Cic. *Brut.* 170, and Douglas, ad loc.). The *ius migrationis* had disappeared, by the time of the Gracchi (according to Ewins, *PBSR* 20 [1952] 54 n. 1, 'for the benefit of the colonies themselves, to prevent the reduction of their manpower.') or by the time of the Social War (according to Sherwin-White, op. cit. pp. 111-2), and another path emerged — the acquisition of Roman citizenship by the holding of a local magistracy. On the date of the change, see G. Tibiletti, *Rendiconti dell' Istituto Lombardo* 66 (1953) 54-60, esp. 58; Brunt, *JRS* 55 (1965) 90-1; Salmon, op. cit. p. 118; Sherwin-White, op. cit. pp. 215-6.

3.13-14: *novi coloni deducti sunt, in quibus equites ducenti*

Salmon points out (op. cit. p. 67) that Asconius' use of *novi coloni* and his singling out of equites is reminiscent of the manner in which Livy describes foundations after the Second Punic War. It could be that Asconius has confused the first and second foundation of Placentia, and that may account for some of the puzzles examined in the next two comments. The number of colonists would help the confusion as it is the same figure — 6000 (though on the first occasion, it was 6000 for each of the colonies at Placentia and Cremona, and on the second occasion 6000 between the two of them). Equites were encouraged to go out with colonies to provide the governing class in the new organisation (Salmon, loc. cit.).

3.16: *P. Cornelius Asina, P. Papirius Maso, [Cn. Pompeius,] Cn. Cornelius Scipio*

Two of the mss. (P and M) include these four names, while the third (S) omits Cn. Pompeius. Clearly, P and M are wrong in including four names, since it was a triumviral commission: the one to go is Cn. Pompeius, since no Pompeii are known before the second century, and, as Stangl suggests (= 12.24), its inclusion is probably derived from the mention of Cn. Pompeius at 3.7. The name Cn. Cornelius Scipio is doubtful too. There is considerable confusion over the composition of the triumviral commission to found Placentia. Polybius (3.40.9) says it was made up of C. Lutatius (Catulus) and two former praetors, while Livy (21.25.3) says that it was made up of Catulus, C. Servilius (Geminus) and M. Annius. Livy adds the comment that there is no doubt about Lutatius' name but that, instead of Servilius and Annius, certain annalists have M'. Acilius and C. Herennius, and others have P. Cornelius Asina and C. Papirius Maso (§4). Polybius says that the commissioners, after arranging to parley with the Boii who had attacked the new colony while it was being organised, were treacherously imprisoned by them (3.40.10), while Livy says it is uncertain whether it was the commissioners or the envoys sent to complain to the Boii who were maltreated by them (21.25.5). Broughton, *MRR* 1.241 n. 12, seems to accept Livy's group of C. Lutatius Catulus, C. Servilius Geminus and M. Annius. He notes that Livy and Polybius agree on Catulus; he argues that Servilius had held curule office (Livy 30.19.9, cf. 27.21.10) and thus qualifies as one of Polybius' ex-praetors, and that his involvement is confirmed by his long detention as a prisoner of the Boii (A. Aymard, *REA* 45 [1943] 201; F.W. Walbank, *A Historical Commentary on Polybius*, 1.375), though this does not indicate whether he was a commissioner or an envoy. Whether, or when, M. Annius was a praetor is not known: it is the mention of him in this passage of Livy, combined with Polybius' comment about ex-praetors, that Broughton uses to say he must have been a praetor before 218. Münzer (*RE* 18.3.1063; *RA*, p. 112) on the other hand says that C. Papirius Maso probably held a praetorship before 218 and so qualified for membership of the commission.

The first two names in Asconius' list agree with one of the variations noted by Livy in the annalists, except that Asconius has P., and Livy C. Papirius Maso. Münzer (*RE* 18.3.1063, cf. 1065) says that the two men are the same and that the *praenomen* should be C., asserting that the copyist of Asconius has made a mistake by writing the initial letter of Papirius. If they are two distinct persons, we know nothing of the career of P. Papirius Maso (Broughton, *MRR* 1.242 n. 12), whereas we do know of a C. Papirius Maso who was *decemvir sacrorum* in 213 (Liv. 25.2.1, clearly distinguished by filiation from his cousin of the same name). Nor, if Asconius' inclusion of Cn. Cornelius Scipio is correct, do we know anything of his career. Münzer (*RE* 4.1487) suggests that the inclusion of P. Cornelius Scipio Asina is a doublet from Coelius Antipater on this man's father, Cn. Cornelius Scipio Asina, who went to the Carthaginian camp as an envoy in 260 and was treacherously captured during a conference (for the references, see *MRR* 1.205). Why Coelius Antipater is chosen he does not say; the suggestion of a doublet is rejected by Walbank, loc. cit. The son was not captured by the Boii, for he was present in Rome in 216 as *interrex* (Liv. 22.34.1) and in 211 (ibid. 26.8.2), and he is not mentioned as a captive with Servilius Germinus in 209 (ibid. 27.21.10) nor as released with Lutatius and Servilius Geminus in 203 (ibid. 30.19.7-9). As a man who had held the consulship in 221 he would not qualify as one of the two ex-praetors accompanying Catulus in Polybius' version. Asconius might well have picked up this man's name which had found its way into the annalists as a doublet, for he says that he got his information from the annals (3.1-2); it may also help to explain the inclusion of the name Cn. Cornelius Scipio (i.e. the father's name) in the list.

The somewhat negative conclusion to be drawn from the confusion seems to be that it is likely that in 218 there was more than one commission, since colonies were to be founded at two places, and in addition there were embassies to the Boii. The names of all these groups have been mixed up by the annalists whom Livy and Asconius used. Both Livy and Asconius claim to have got their information from annalists; though Asconius makes use of Livy (66.23, 77.4), he does not seem to have used him here, as he makes no mention of the confusion which Livy had seen. For an attempt to vindicate Livy's accuracy in using official information and annalistic sources for colonial activity, see P.L. MacKendrick, *Athenaeum* 32 (1954) 236ff.

3.17: *eamque coloniam LIII . . . deductam esse*

In the mss. there is a lacuna of three plus, five or eight letter spaces after *LIII*; O. Hirschfeld (in Stangl, n. ad. loc. = 12.25) wants to read *LIII annis post civitate R. donatam esse*, but that is too long for the letter spaces available and we have no evidence for the year in which the colony received the Roman citizenship. E. Bormann, *CIL* 11. p. 242, sees no reason for a lacuna after *LIII*, since the sentence makes good sense as it stands, and like most others he takes it to mean that Placentia was the fifty-third colony sent out by the Romans. Salmon (op. cit. p. 67) says that the figure is so high that it is universally recognised to include citizen or so-called Roman colonies as well as Latin ones. Mommsen (*Geschichte der römischen Münzwesens* [Berlin, 1860] p. 860) pointed out the apparent error in Asconius' calculation, suggesting that by 218 thirty-four Latin and eleven Roman colonies had been founded, a total of forty-five, which is probably too high (according to Salmon, loc. cit.). E. Kornemann (*RE* 4.516, s.v. 'Coloniae') merely notes Asconius' comment that Placentia was the fifty-third colony. Both Kornemann and Salmon agree in omitting from any calculation the joint-colonies founded by the Romans and the Latin League prior to 338, except those which retained the Latin status after the settlement of the Latin War in that year (seven altogether); following Liv. 27.9.7, they agree on a total of thirty Latin colonies down to 218. Salmon argues that Asconius' total can be made to come out right by assuming that the second *deductio* of Placentia was the fifty-third act of colonisation, and that Asconius has confused it with the first *deductio* of Placentia. This involves a further assumption, that groups of new colonists officially sent to a site were reckoned as new colonies and not just enlargements of existing ones, and that of the five colonies which received new groups of settlers between 218 and 190 (i.e. between the two *deductiones* of Placentia) there were only three official settlements (Cosa did not receive a triumviral commission and Placentia and Cremona were jointly resettled by one *deductio*). Salmon's calculation can best be represented in tabular form (op. cit. p. 68)

Latin colonies, 338 to 218	30
Roman colonies, 338 to 218	10
New Latin colonies, 218 to 190	2
New Roman colonies, 218 to 190	8
Refounded Latin colonies, 218 to 190	3
	53

That Asconius could have confused the first and second settlement of Placentia is suggested by his use of the phrase *novi coloni* (see above on 3.13-14): what would be the point of *novi* in referring to the initial settlement? Salmon misses a point in his own favour: he suggests that Asconius seems to be thinking of the first *deductio* because he lists as the founding commissioners those appointed for the first settlement. But, as suggested above (on 3.16), only one of the triumvirs on Asconius' list has a strong case for inclusion in the first commission, and this indicates that Asconius' information is quite uncertain.

There is one difficulty with Salmon's calculation. There may have been eleven Roman colonies down to 218, for Labici, which he includes in his list of joint-colonies of Rome and the Latin League, is included by Kornemann in his list of Roman colonies, on the basis of Liv. 4.47.7 (which talks of 1500 colonists being sent *ab urbe*). It was founded in 418, which does put it in the period of joint colonial activity, and the size of its contingent is considerably larger than the normal figure for a Roman colony (300: see Salmon, op. cit. p. 71).

There may be other ways of justifying Asconius' figure without going beyond 218. It is not necessary to exclude from the total those colonies founded by Rome and the Latin League prior to 338 because they were not founded exclusively by Rome: Rome no doubt took the initiative and tradition would have given her the credit (cf. Salmon. op. cit. p. 41). It should be noted that Livy calls the thirty Latin colonies existing in 218 *coloniae populi Romani*, no doubt because they contained some Romans, implying that the Romans thought of them in this way because they had taken the initiative. We can get a total of forty-seven colonies if we add together the thirty Latin colonies between 338 and 218, the ten Roman colonies founded down to 218, and seven joint-colonies founded before 338 (Salmon lists fourteen, but seven of these retained Latin status in 338 and are included in the thirty Latin colonies). That gives a total only six short of Asconius' figure, and Salmon admits that there may have been more joint-colonies which we do not know of (op. cit. p. 42). If we use one of Salmon's assumptions, that resettlements counted and apply it to the reorganisation of status for the seven joint colonies which remained Latin after 338, then we can get much closer to Asconius' total: fourteen joint-colonies, thirty Latin colonies and ten Roman colonies giving a total of fifty-four foundations down to 218. If we use Kornemann's list, we can do even better: he has twelve joint-colonies (he excludes Fidenae, which Salmon includes), thirty Latin colonies, and eleven Roman colonies (for he includes Labici, which Salmon includes as a joint-colony). Total: fifty-three.

3.19-20: *ut Quiritium aliae, aliae Latinorum essent*

Although Asconius is right in the technical distinction between the two types of colonies, it was not as clear as all that. There were Romans who voluntarily gave up their Roman citizenship and adopted Latin status in order to take part in Latin colonies, and there must have been Latins and even Italians who participated in Roman colonies, particularly at times when the Roman government found it difficult to find the manpower to fill its projected colonies (e.g. in the period after the Second Punic war: see Salmon, op. cit. pp. 98ff.). Livy describes the thirty Latin colonies still existing in 218 as *coloniae populi Romani* (27.9.10; cf. Cic. *Caec.* 98). Sherwin-White (op. cit. p. 99) goes so far as to say that this was because 'the greater part of the manpower of the Latin colonies was drawn from the body of the Roman citizens.'

4.10-11: *quod venisse eum in Italiam dicit trans Alpis*

Asconius includes here a statement by Cicero which probably occurred in the context of the passage quoted in the lemma but which is not actually included in the lemma — that Piso's maternal grandfather Calventius had come into Italy from across the Alps. This is clearly an exaggeration, for we subsequently learn from Cicero that Calventius was an Insubrian (§ 53, and frag. xv in Nisbet's edn.), from a Gallic tribe which lived north of the Po. It is true that the Insubres had come across the Alps originally, in one of the Celtic migrations c. 400 B.C.: the Romans thought they had used the north-western passes (e.g. Liv. 5.34.8-9), but archaeological evidence shows they used the central Alpine passes (T.G.E. Powell, *The Celts*, pp. 21-2). But that was a long time before Calventius lived. Cicero played a lot on Piso's Gallic extraction, not only in this speech (§ § 14 [Caesoninus Semiplacentinus Calventius], 34, 53, 62, 67 [with a pun on *gallus*]) but elsewhere (*red. in sen.* 13, 15, *prov. cons.* 7, *Sest.* 21, *Q.f.* 3.1.11). This is a case where Asconius has made a comment purely from the context of the passage, and as a result has been misled.

4.17: *C. Piso*

A reference to Cicero's son-in-law, C. Calpurnius Piso Frugi. He was distantly related to the consul of 58 (see above on 2.18-19), and Cicero often remarked in his speeches of this period that he was connected to the consul of 58 by his daughter's marriage to this C. Piso (e.g. *red. in sen.* 17, 38, *Sest.* 68). It seems best to take this rather corrupt sentence in the lemma either as a question, or as an ironic statement, as Nisbet does (p. 55). The second sentence makes better sense too if we read either *ei enim* (Clark) or *nam ei* (Ernesti), for the mss. *non enim* (SM) or *non ei* (P). C. Piso was betrothed to Tullia in 67 (Cic. *Att.* 1.3.3); as quaestor in 58 he negotiated with L. Piso (Cic. *Pis*. 13) and with Pompeius (Plut. *Cic.* 31.2) on Cicero's behalf in the troubled period before his exile, and worked energetically for his recall (Cic. *fam*. 14.2.2, *Sest.* 54, 68). Cicero thought highly of him, and refers to his *pietas* (*Sest.* 68, *Brut.* 272).

5.3: *Insuber quidam fuit, idem mercator et praeco*

In the *lex Iulia municipalis* (*CIL* 1.206, 11.94-96) there is a clause stating that those who were currently practising as auctioneers were forbidden to stand for any magistracy and so become members of the local senate; in this they were coupled with undertakers. If they were no longer practising that employment, they were eligible (see Brunt, *Manpower*, pp. 519-20, and SB, *Fam*. 2.383-4). It is to this provision that Cicero refers in a letter to Q. Lepta in January 45 (*fam*. 6.18.1). Cicero's statement is indicative of the dislike in which auctioneers were held: cf. Cic. *Quinct.* 11-12, and F. Hinard, *Latomus* 35 (1976) 730-1. Cicero here seems to be doubly implying that Calventius was not worthy of the marriage he secured, being a recently arrived Insubrian and an auctioneer.

5.9: *Rutilium Nudum*

The additional name *Atilium* in the mss. is rightly deleted. Very likely, this man is to be identified with P. Rutilius Nudus, one of the officers serving under M. Aurelius Cotta, the consul of 74, who received a command in Bithynia and the Propontis. This identification, based on Appian and Orosius, was first made by Th. Reinach, *Mithridate Eupator, roi de Pont* (Paris, 1890) p. 323 n. 1, and is followed by Münzer, *RE* 1A.1268 and *RA*, p. 323, by Broughton, *MRR* 2.105, by J. Bingen, *BCH* 78 (1954) 82-5, and by R. Syme, *Class. Phil.* 50 (1955) 137. On the question of his rank at the time, see E. Badian, *Gnomon* 33 (1961) 492-3; J. Briscoe, *CR* 24 (1974) 265, referring to D. van Berchem, *BCH* 87 (1963) 322-4, both accepting that he was quaestor.

5.9-11: *Cicero filiam post mortem Pisonis generi P. Lentulo collocavit, apud quem illa ex partu decessit*

Asconius makes two mistakes here: Tullia's first husband, C. Piso, died in 57, sometime before Cicero's return from exile; he was followed, not by Lentulus as Asconius says, but by Furius Crassipes, to whom Tullia was engaged on 4th April 56 (Cic. *Q.f.* 2.4.2, 5.1, *fam.* 1.7.11). It was in Crassipes' garden that Cicero had dinner with Crassus before the latter left for Syria in 55; in the letter describing the dinner Crassipes is called *gener (fam.* 1.9.20). *Gener* is sometimes used of a prospective son-in-law (e.g. Verg. *Aen.* 12.31 and 55) but always in the context of futurity; there is no indication in *fam.* 1.9.20, which describes an event at the end of 55, that Crassipes was still only engaged to Tullia, nor would we have expected the engagement to last nearly a year and a half. Hence Madvig's argument that Tullia never actually married Crassipes, in order to absolve Asconius of any error, will not stand up.

Tullia was divorced from Crassipes c. 51 and during Cicero's absence as governor of Cilicia she married P. Cornelius Dolabella, on her own initiative apparently, and not as a result of arrangement by Cicero (as Asconius says). Dolabella was himself recently divorced (*fam.* 8.6.1). The first Cicero knew of it was in a letter from Caelius written in June 50 (*fam.* 8.13.1, cf. 2.15.2); at the time Cicero was considering a marriage connection with Ti. Claudius Nero, who had visited him in Cilicia (*fam.* 13.64), or with Ser. Sulpicius Rufus the younger (*Att.* 5.4.1, 21.4, 6.1.10). Cicero was embarrassed, because at the time Dolabella was prosecuting Ap. Claudius Pulcher for *maiestas* and Cicero was writing compliments to Appius (*Att.* 6.6.1); he subsequently wrote to Appius to smooth the situation over (*fam.* 3.12). Dolabella had himself adopted by a P. Lentulus into a plebeian family so that he could stand for the tribunate, which he held in 47; hence he is referred to as P. Lentulus by Asconius. Appian (*BC* 2.129) has him born in 69, which would make him only nineteen when he married Tullia; although Cicero calls him a young man, he could not have been that young — even Caesar would not have let him hold the consulship at the age of twenty-five. Tullia was divorced from Dolabella late in 46 or early in 45: by the time of Tullia's confinement in January 45, Cicero was talking about getting the dowry back from Dolabella (Cic. *fam.* 6.18.5, to Q. Lepta, January 45). That indicates Asconius' second mistake: Tullia gave birth to this child, not at Lentulus' house, but at her father's house. In the same letter, Cicero mentions that he is detained in Rome by Tullia's confinement. Though ill, she was moved to Cicero's Tusculan villa, and it was there that she died.

One can perhaps see the source of Asconius' error: almost the same information is given in Plut. *Cic.* 41.7: γήμαντι δ' αὐτῷ μετ' οὐ πολὺν χρόνον ἡ θυγάτηρ ἀπέθανε τίκτουσα παρὰ Λέντλῳ· τούτῳ γὰρ ἐγαμήθη μετὰ τὴν Πείσωνος τοῦ προτέρου ἀνδρὸς τελευτήν. In the same chapter, Plutarch mentions a source — Tiro, and it may be that these errors were contained in Tiro's biography of Cicero which Asconius is known to have used. But it is hard to conceive of Tiro making such a mistake; perhaps Furius Crassipes has dropped out because he was not an important figure. For Asconius' error, see Y.G. Lepage, *LEC* 44 (1976) 245-6, following J. Carcopino, *Les secrets de la correspondance de Cicéron*, trans. E.O. Lorimer (London, 1951) 1.169 n. 2. Perhaps Asconius could have avoided the error if he had read the appropriate letters, but that raises again the question whether Asconius had access to the letters.

6.15: *Q. Metello Nepote tr. pl.*

Q. Caecilius Metellus Nepos, the son of Balearicus and grandson of Macedonicus (63.17-18), returned from service under Pompeius to secure election to the tribunate from December 63. He criticised Cicero's actions in regard to the Catilinarian conspirators and prevented him from delivering a speech when he laid down office at the end of the year, allowing him only to swear the oath that he had carried out his office faithfully (Cic. *Pis.* 6-7). As a political associate of Pompeius (who was married to his half-sister Mucia), Nepos attempted early in his tribunate to pass two measures in Pompeius' interests: one, to summon Pompeius to Italy to take command against Catilina, and the other, to allow Pompeius to be elected to the consulship *in absentia*. These proposals were vetoed by his colleague, M. Porcius Cato, who (it is said) sought election to the tribunate to oppose the designs of Nepos. In the confusion which followed, Nepos left Rome to rejoin Pompeius. On these matters, see C. Meier, *Athenaeum* 40 (1962) 103-25.

7.10: *senatus consulto collegia sublata sunt*

In the consulship in 64 of L. Iulius Caesar and C. Marcius Figulus (whom Cicero mentions in the sentence immediately preceding the lemma quoted by Asconius) a senatorial decree was passed suppressing the *collegia*. The view of A. Watson, *Law Making in the Later Roman Republic* (Oxford, 1974) p. 29, that the *s.c.* of 64 was formalised by a *lex*, is refuted by A.W. Lintott, *JRS* 65 (1975) 206. The decree meant effectively that the Compitalician Games could not be held as there were no masters of the guilds to conduct them. The mss. reading *Mario* for the second consul is clearly wrong (7.9): it is clear that Asconius meant *Marcio* from his comment *quos et ipse Cicero supra memoravit* (J.-M. Flambard, *MEFRA* 89 [1977] 118-9). On *collegia* in general, see below on 75.19.

7.14: *post VI deinde annos*

The mss. all give the number as *novem*: the emendation to *VI* was made by S.H. Rinkes, *Mnemosyne* 10 (1861) 207-9. Has Asconius made another mistake? It could be that some copyist has made a mistake in reading an original *VI* as *IX* and written it in full as *novem*: in this case the mistake must have already existed in the copy found at St. Gall, since all of our three main mss. have it. The universal practice for small cardinal numbers (i.e. those less than ten) in our mss. of Asconius is to write them in full (e.g. 8.13, 11.15, 39.23, 82.4), with the following exceptions (where they are written as numerals and where one would expect it):

(a) dates
(b) lists of votes in trials (e.g. 28.26, 53.20-22; but note 56.1-2 where the small numbers are written in full)
(c) in compound numbers (e.g. 39.12, 72.18), though occasionally the smaller numbers in the compound are written in full (39.21, 34.26), particularly in lists of juror's votes (28.25-26, 53.19, 55.17, 56.1)
(d) the unique instance *II de XL* (81.7).

If the usual practice was followed, *novem* was the form that would have been used in the exemplar copied by our three mss. (and not *VI* mistakenly seen as *IX* and written as *novem*; besides, all three would not have made the same mistake). It follows either that an error of this sort had found its way into the exemplar, or that Asconius had made a mistake. If we were to accept the figure nine, that would take us back to 67, but that is not possible on Asconius' own evidence, for he clearly nominates the consuls of 64 (despite the copyist's error with the name of C. Marcius) and later he implies (75.17-19) that the *collegia* were still active at the time of Cornelius' trial in 65. The attempt of Manutius, followed by Drumann (in Rinkes, loc. cit.), to keep the figure nine and emend the consuls to L. Caecilius and Q. Marcius (who held office in 68) will not hold up because Asconius would then have written *decem* not *novem*, and because he nominates the consuls whom Cicero has just mentioned and knew that the *collegia* were still active in 65.

With his knowledge of these events, it seems unlikely that Asconius made a mistake — perhaps a simple arithmetic error (it must have been difficult to calculate, when years were numbered by the names of consuls).

7.18: *facere [Kal. Ianuar.] praetextatum ludos Sex. Clodium*

The conjecture *Kal. Ianuar.* to fill the lacuna, suggested by Kiessling and Schoell, is a sensible one, based on Cicero's own words in the lemma. The name, Sex. Clodius, should be changed to Sex. Cloelius (the reading of P and M): see D.R. Shackleton Bailey, *CQ* n.s. 10 (1960) 41-2, and *Ciceroniana* n.s. 1 (1973) 1-6; contra, J.-M. Flambard, art. cit. 126-8. On *praetextatum*, see Nisbet, p. 66. Cloelius anticipated the law by holding the games three days before it was passed; it was passed on 4th January (C.C. Conrad, *Class. Phil.* 9 [1914] 78-82; contra, J.C. Rolfe, *Class. Phil.* 8 [1913] 82). Sex. Cloelius was a *scriba* (33.6) and so may have conducted the festival games as *magister scribarum* (A.W. Lintott, *G. & R.* 14 [1967] 163).

7.22: *L. Ninnius tr. pl.*

This tribune of 58, L. Ninnius Quadratus, attempted to support Cicero's cause throughout the year, and to propose a bill for his return from exile (references in *MRR* 2.196).

7.23: *Q. Metellus Celer, consul designatus*

Q. Caecilius Metellus Celer, consul in 60, was the brother of Nepos (see on 6.15, and below on 63.13-14). He opposed the interests of Pompeius during his consulship, the break in the link between these two Metelli and Pompeius being marked by the latter's divorce from their half-sister Mucia (E.S. Gruen, *Historia* 18 [1969] 77). Although Cicero says (see lemma) that Celer was able to prevent the games as a *privatus* (to contrast with Piso's lack of standing even as consul), the authority and prestige of a consul-designate was extensive: in this period, the consuls-designate spoke first in the senate (e.g. D. Iunius Silanus at the debate on the Catilinarian conspirators: Sall. *Cat.* 50.4; Plut. *Cic.* 20.3), and this position in the debating could be influential (J.P.V.D. Balsdon, *CQ* n.s. 10 [1960] 44). On the status of designated magistrates, see Mommsen, *Staatsrecht*, 1^3.590ff.

7.24: *magistros vicorum ludos Compitalicios facere prohibuerat*

The mss. have *magistri ludorum*: Nisbet, p. 66, is wrong in saying that, as the *collegia* had been suppressed and the *ludi* had been prohibited, *magistri ludorum* could not have existed in 61 (the year in which Celer was consul-designate). First, not all the *collegia* had been suppressed (75.17-19); perhaps only the *collegia Compitalia* had been suppressed (so J.V.A. Fine, *Class. Phil.* 27 [1931] 268) and effectively (though not necessarily expressly) this would mean that the *ludi Compitalicii* were brought to an end. Presumably the masters of those still in existence could have been called on to act as *magistri ludorum*. Second, the title *magistri ludorum* was presumably used for those persons responsible for running the games whoever they might be: the persons chosen by the tribune in 61 would have been called at the time by that title. The emendation, *magistri vicorum*, suggested by 7.13-14, is attractive since those in charge of the *ludi Compitalicii* are variously known as *magistri vicorum* and/or *pagorum*. This group had some sort of official existence (Liv. 34.7.2; *CIL* 6.1324, 2223-16), and they could have done the job in the attempted revival of the games in 61, in the absence of the *magistri collegiarum*. Cicero simply calls them *magistri*. On *magistri*, see Lintott, *Violence,* pp. 79-82, and *G. & R.* 14 (1967) 160-2, and on the relation between *magistri vicorum, magistri ludorum* and the *collegia*, see J.-M. Flambard, art. cit. 133-44.

7.26: *cuius tribuni nomen adhuc non inveni*

It is strange that Asconius was unable to discover the name of this tribune, particularly as it involved opposition to a man like Metellus Celer. As the Compitalician Games were held either at the very end of the year or at the very beginning (G. Wissowa, *RE* 4.791-2, s.v. 'Compitalia'), and as this incident occurred when Celer was consul-designate, the incident should be referred to late December 61 and involve one of the tribunes who entered office in December 61. Two only are known: L. Flavius and C. Herennius, and either could be the unknown tribune here, for they both came into conflict with Celer, Flavius over his proposal of a land bill in the interests of Pompeius, and Herennius over his proposal to transfer Clodius to plebeian status (references in *MRR* 2.184).

8.13: *quattuor leges perniciosas*

P. Clodius proposed and carried more than four laws during his tribunate in 58; Broughton, *MRR* 2.196, is able to list twelve separate proposals. Asconius probably has in mind here the four proposals put forward on 4th January; Dio 38.13.1-6 lists these four proposals as the first acts of Clodius' tribunate. *Triduo post* in the lemma implies three days after the Kalends of January: 4th January would have been the earliest possible date allowing for the necessary *trinum nundinum* following the tribunes' entry into office on 10th December: see Nisbet, p. 67, and cf. Lintott, *CQ* 18 (1968) 192, and A.K. Michels, *The Calendar of the Roman Republic* (Princeton, 1967) pp. 202-6. The four proposals which Asconius goes on

8.15-17: *frumentum populo quod antea senis aeris ac trientibus in singulos modios dabatur gratis daretur*

The figure of 6 1/3 asses per *modius* is confirmed by Cic. *Sest.* 55 (cf. Schol. Bob. 135.8-9): it is the same as the subsidised cost under the *lex Sempronia* of 123 (Liv. *per.* 60, though the figure here is an emendation). The subsidy on the cost of grain was abolished by Sulla, but restored by the *lex Aemilia* of the consul of 78, which set a limit of five *modii*, presumably per month, for each recipient (Gran. Lic. p. 34 F); this limit was retained under the *lex Terentia Cassia* of 73 (Sall. *hist.* 3.48.19 M), which mainly dealt with instructions on how the praetor was to requisition grain. Some 40,000 people received grain under this law, to judge from Cicero's statement (*Verr.* 2.3.72) that, after it was passed, 200,000 *modii* were about enough to satisfy the public distribution each month. During his tribunate in 62, M. Cato proposed a grain law: as the cost per *modius* prior to Clodius' law was 6 1/3 asses, this was presumably the subsidised cost fixed by Cato's law, since that was the last law dealing with such a matter. Cato's law meant an annual cost to the treasury of 7,500,000 drachmas (= 30 million HS: Plut. *Caes.* 8.4, cf. *Cat. Min.* 26.1); as this represents the difference between the actual cost (4 HS per *modius*) and the subsidised price (1 1/2 HS), there must have been about 200,000 recipients under Cato's law. Cicero says (*Sest.* 5) that Clodius' provision of free grain cost the state one-fifth of the *vectigalia*, about 17 million denarii (= 68 million HS), as the total state revenue was about 85 million drachmas at this time (Plut. *Pomp.* 45.4; T. Frank, *ESAR*, Vol. I, pp. 322-4). For calculations of the numbers receiving grain under the various laws, see Frank, loc. cit. pp. 328-30. R.J. Rowland, *ZPE* 21 (1976) 69-72, thinks that the price of 6 1/3 asses was a perquisite for the middle class, since the poor would not be able to afford even that price. On the grain laws in general, see C. Nicolet, *Le métier de citoyen dans la Rome républicaine* (Paris, 1976) pp. 250-79.

8.19: *legem Aeliam et Fufiam*

It is generally agreed that there were two laws, not one, but their relationship to each other is difficult to unravel. They were passed somewhere about 150. Asconius' discussion here (which is significant because it is not simply paraphrasing the lemma of Cicero) deals only with the *lex Aelia,* and it would seem from that discussion that the *lex Aelia* confirmed curule magistrates' right to proclaim *obnuntiatio* (i.e. to prevent the holding of legislative *comitia* by proclaiming beforehand that they would observe the heavens, *de caelo servare*). It is likely that it was this right which Clodius took away. The *lex Fufia* dealt most likely with a

98 Commentary

ban on the presentation of legislation between the announcement and the holding of the elections (Schol. Bob. on *Vat.* 23; cf. below on 63.18 on the *lex Caecilia Didia* of 98). Clodius' removal of this ban meant that legislation could in future be put forward on all *dies fasti* (Cic. *prov. cons.* 46). On the distinction between the two laws, see G.V. Sumner, *AJP* 84 (1963) 337-58, and in general on the two laws, see W.F. Macdonald, *JRS* 19 (1929) 164-79; S. Weinstock *JRS* 27 (1937) 215-22; J.P.V.D. Balsdon, *JRS* 47 (1957) 15-6; L.R. Taylor, *JRS* 52 (1962) 22-4; and A.E. Astin, *Latomus* 23 (1964) 421-45.

Despite Cicero's numerous statements that Clodius' law completely overthrew the *leges Aelia et Fufia*, it is clear that he only altered parts of them, for we have instances of persons being tried under the earlier laws (e.g. C. Porcius Cato was tried under the *lex Fufia* in 54 — Cic. *Att.* 4.16.5), and instances of *obnuntiatio* are found after 58 (for some examples, see Lintott, *Violence*, p. 147).

8.22-23: *de collegiis restituendis novisque instituendis*

For the suppression of the *collegia*, see 7.9-11, and for their restoration, see below on 75.17. That Clodius' purpose was to secure the support of the urban plebs by recruiting them through the *collegia*, see Lintott, *Violence*, p. 193, and J.-M. Flambard, *MEFRA* 89 (1977) 115-44.

8.24: *quartam ne quem censores in senatu legendo praeterirent*

Asconius has paraphrased Cicero's exaggeration here, in saying that the censorship was abolished by this law (cf. *Sest.* 55: . . . *ut censoria notio et gravissimum iudicium sanctissimi magistratus de re publica tolleretur*). As Asconius himself explains, the law stated that no one should be subject to censorial *notio* unless his case had been heard in person before both censors and both censors had agreed on the condemnation. Perhaps Clodius was led to propose this bill because of what had happened to his father in 86, when he was passed over in the list of senators by the censor of that year, L. Philippus (Cic. *dom.* 84).

9.14-15: *a Catilinae praevaricatore*

On Clodius' collusion, cf. Cic. *har. resp.* 42. E.S. Gruen (*Athenaeum* 49 [1971] 59-62) argues that Cicero has exaggerated the extent of Clodius' collusion in the prosecution of Catilina for provincial extortion in 65 (for it clearly suited his purposes to do so after his return from exile). Cicero's comment at the time, when he was thinking of defending Catilina (Cic. *Att.* 1.2.1: *iudices habemus quos volumus, summa accusatoris voluntate*) may mean no more than that Clodius was agreeable in the matter of the *reiectio* of jurors. Asconius is guarded in accepting the rumour of Clodius' collusion (87.13-15) and seems to have in mind only

In Pisonem 99

his agreement over the selection of jurors (see below on 85.12). Likewise he is guarded over the claim that Clodius was an ally of Catilina in the conspiracy of 63: see below on 50.12-14. For earlier relations between Clodius and Catilina, see below on 91.19.

9.22: *L. Lamiam a Gabinio consule edicto relegatum esse*

L. Aelius Lamia, a Roman knight, was relegated by Gabinius 200 miles from Rome (Cic. *red. in sen.* 12, *Sest.* 29, *Pis.* 64, *fam.* 11.16.2; Dio 38.16.4; Schol. Bob. 168.14). Lamia was probably the only *eques* banished; the plural *equites* is found at *Sest.* 35 and 52, *red. in sen.* 32, and *Pis.* 23, but it could well be rhetorical. *Relegatio* was milder than *exsilium*: the offender was sent out of Rome for a limited period of time and to a certain distance from the city, and he suffered no loss of political rights.

10.8-9: *quod eos a quibus ipse expulsus erat adiuvisset*

Asconius misses the point of Cicero's comment here: Cicero is not explaining why the people of Capua rejected Piso when he came to visit them — he is ironically contrasting what the consul of 58 thought of himself and his background with what others really thought of him. Asconius' explanation is an unwarranted conclusion (cf. a similarly unwarranted conclusion at 3.20-23). Cicero is wittily making two points: the choice of Seplasia, a street where the perfume trade was carried on (Cic. *leg. agr.* 2.94), to stand for Capua, is a play upon Piso's supposed effeminacy in using perfumes, though this was normally a charge which Cicero made against Piso's colleague Gabinius (cf. *Sest.* 19, *Pis.* 25). The second point is a play upon *Campanus consul*: as well as being consul at Rome in 58, Piso was also *duumvir* of the new colony at Capua, set up under Caesar's law in 59. He was, in a sense, a 'Capuan consul', and Cicero was no doubt thinking of the incident in 216, when the Capuans asked that one of the Roman consuls be a Capuan: the demand was contemptuously rejected, Capua rebelled and was crushed (Liv. 23.6.6; Cic. *leg. agr.* 2.93 and 95; cf. Sil. Ital. 11.123. For a similar play upon Piso's position, see Cic. *red. in sen.* 17, *dom.* 60). Cicero's point is that a 'Capuan consul' ought to be welcome in Capua, yet Piso was rejected.

The clause *ut dici audiebam* has been left out after *mehercule* in the quotation of the lemma by Asconius: on its significance, see Nisbet, p. 88.

10.19: *socrus Pisonis quae fuerit invenire non potui*

Asconius knew who Piso's father-in-law was — P. Rutilius Nudus (see above on 5.8-9). His explanation for being unable to discover who his mother-in-law was seems reasonable, if somewhat ingenuous: Nisbet, p. 90, holds it out as an interesting note for prosopographers.

11.9: *omnes magistratus*

As Cicero indicates, seven out of eight praetors and eight out of ten tribunes signed the proposal for Cicero's recall: for their names, see *red. in sen.* 19-23. Asconius identifies the three dissentients. Ap. Claudius Pulcher, praetor in 57, naturally opposed Cicero's recall, as he was Clodius' brother; he became consul in 54, and was reconciled to Cicero (Cic. *Mil.* 75) through the mediation of Pompeius (Quintil. 9.3.41); Cicero succeeded him as governor of Cilicia; he dedicated a book on augury, an art which he is said to have taken very seriously (Cic. *div.* 1.105), to Cicero (*fam.* 2.13.2, 3.4.1). Little is known of the two tribunes: Sex. Atilius Serranus Gavianus had been a quaestor in Africa c. 60 (*CIL* 1^2.2513), and was subsequently a *legatus* c. 55, possibly under Caesar (*MRR* 2.219).

12.2-3: *de Macedoniaque ultimum et Perse rege triumphavit*

L. Aemilius Paullus was consul in 182 for the first time, securing a command against the Ligurians which he carried on into the next year; for his victories, he was awarded a triumph (A. Degrassi, *Inscr. Ital.* 13.1.554). He served a second consulship in 168, gaining command of the war against Perseus in Macedonia; for his victory at Pydna he was given a second triumph. Cicero chooses him as the supreme example of a Roman general who won glory in Macedonia, to contrast with Piso's lack of success in the province where success was almost automatic (cf. § 96: *ex illo fonte et seminario triumphorum*). Cicero's claim that all governors with proconsular *imperium*, who had returned from Macedonia and who had not been convicted, had celebrated triumphs does not stand up: see Nisbet, p. 100. The most notable exception to Cicero's list of successful proconsular governors of Macedonia is L. Manlius Torquatus, cos. 65, who was governor of Macedonia in 64-63: he was not convicted on his return, but did not celebrate a triumph (Nisbet suggests it was perhaps because of the Catilinarian crisis). That Cicero forgot about him is surprising (and embarrassing), seeing that he was present in the senate during this debate (§ §47, 92): perhaps he made up for it in the laudatory remarks in §44.

12.5-6: *quod ibi rem non prospere gessit*

Asconius seems to accept Cicero's view of Piso's lack of success as a governor, for the use of the indicative here suggests this is Asconius' reason, not Cicero's: it further suggests that Asconius is not as unbiassed or impartial as some would like to think. Cicero (naturally) plays down Piso's success: for an assessment of his military campaigns, see Nisbet, pp. 176-80, and cf. Butler and Cary (ed.), *Cicero: de provinciis consularibus*, App. I, who are less generous in their assessment of Piso's governorship, while recognising Cicero's vituperations. Piso was hailed as *imperator* by his troops (§ 38): Cicero often refers to this title of his sneeringly (*har. resp.* 35, *prov. cons.* 7, 15, 38, *Pis.* 44, 53-55, 61, 70, 91, 97; the references in the first two speeches show that the title was gained by about the middle of 56). Piso is referred to as αὐτοκράτωρ in an inscription found at Samothrace (H. Bloch, *AJA* 44 [1940] 483-8). It must be admitted, however, that the title, though in theory only awarded for decisive victories, was often gained for trivial success, or even automatically for no success at all: cf. Cic. *Phil.* 14.11. Even Cicero himself claimed it for victories during his governorship of Cilicia.

12.12: *nepos M. Marcelli eius*

The grandfather of the man mentioned by Cicero, M. Claudius Marcellus, did attain the consulship five times, as Asconius goes on to say: in 222, 215 (*suffectus*), 214, 210 and 208. It was during his proconsulship in Sicily in 213-211, following his third consulship, that he besieged and captured Syracuse.

12.13-14: *hic autem Marcellus de quo Cicero dicit*

M. Claudius Marcellus, grandson of the above, held the praetorship in 169, going out to Spain during his year of office (Liv. 43.15.4) and remaining on *pro consule* in 168 (Liv. 45.4.1). He was elected to a consulship in 166, taking a command against the Alpine Gauls; for victories against them, he celebrated a triumph (Liv. *per.* 46; Degrassi, *Inscr. Ital.* 13.1.556f.). He secured a second consulship in 155, during which he suppressed an uprising by the Apuan Ligurians; for this he was awarded another triumph (ibid. 13.1.557). In 152 he held his third consulship: on the ways in which the legal difficulty of his candidature were overcome (i.e. the holding of a second consulship within ten years), see A.E. Astin, *Scipio Aemilianus* (Oxford, 1967) pp. 37-40. Marcellus took over the command in Nearer Spain from Q. Fulvius Nobilior, cos. 153, who had suffered serious reverses against the Celtiberi; his conciliatory attitude towards the Celtiberians and Lusitanians was disapproved of at Rome, and the war continued under Marcellus' command in 151 until he was replaced by L. Licinius Lucullus, the consul of that year. Astin (op. cit. p. 35) says that he celebrated a third triumph for victories in 151, but there is no evidence for this.

12.14-15: *naufragio ad ipsam Africam periit paulo ante coeptum bellum Punicum tertium*

It would appear from the context of the account of Marcellus' death in the summary of Livy (*per* 50; cf. *Oxyr. per.* 50) that he was drowned whilst on his way to Africa as a member of a three-man embassy to Masinissa in 148, the year in which Masinissa died and in which Scipio Aemilianus made arrangements for the division of his kingdom (Polyb. 36.16.10; Liv.

Oxyr. per. 50, and *per.* 50). This means that Asconius has erred in saying that Marcellus was drowned just before the start of the Third Punic War, for it happened in the second year of that war (for a discussion of the error, see *MRR* 1.462 n. 2). Appian's reference (*Lib.* 105) to an embassy sent by the senate to Masinissa in late 149 or early 148 which found the elderly king sick and dying seems to confirm that there was an embassy then to which Marcellus could have belonged. There were two embassies sent to Africa before the war began (and it could be these which have caused Asconius' confusion) but clearly Marcellus did not belong to either. The first was sent in 152 (Liv. *per.* 48; App. *Lib.* 69) when Marcellus was in Spain, and the second was sent in late 152 or early 151, when Marcellus may still have been in Spain. Even if he had returned, this second embassy does not appear to be the one to which Marcellus belonged, for Livy says it was made up of ten men (*per.* 48), whereas the one to which Marcellus belonged is described as a three-man embassy (Liv. *per.* 50). For the chronology and associated problems of the two embassies before the start of the war, see Astin, op. cit. pp. 270-2, and the literature cited there. On Marcellus' death by drowning, see Cic. *div.* 3.14, *fat.* 33.

12.16-17: *in monumentis avi sui ad Honoris et Virtutis*

The original part of this temple, near the porta Capena (Liv. 29.11.13), was built by Q. Fabius Maximus Verrucosus in 234, after his success against the Ligurians, and dedicated to Honos (Cic. *nat. deor.* 2.61) on 17th July (*fasti Antiates: Notizie degli Scavi di Antichita* (1921) pp. 102-3). M. Claudius Marcellus, the grandfather, vowed a temple to Honos and Virtus after the battle of Clastidium in 222 (Liv. 27.25.7, 29.11.13), and he renewed the vow after the capture of Syracuse (Val. Max. 1.1.8); he attempted to discharge the vow by rededicating the existing temple of Honos to both gods in 208, but this was forbidden by the pontiffs. Marcellus then restored the temple of Honos, and built a new part for Virtus, making it a double shrine, which was eventually dedicated by his son (cos. 196) in 205 (Liv. 25.40.1-3, 27.25.7-9, 29.11.13; Val. Max. 1.1.8; Plut. *Marc.* 28); it contained many of the treasures brought from Syracuse by the elder Marcellus (Cic. *Verr.* 2.4.121, *rep.* 1.21; Liv. 26.32.4). As well as placing in it statues of himself, his father and grandfather, the younger Marcellus probably decorated it with booty brought home from Spain in 151 which amounted to 600 talents (Strabo 3.4.13). For further discussion, see E. Samter, *RE* 8.2292-3, s.v. 'Honos', and Platner-Ashby, pp. 258-9.

13.8: *[M.] Valerio Maximo*

This ought not to be the M. Valerius Volusi f., cos. 505, who was awarded a house at public expense and whom Asconius mentions four lines later, since he did not have the *cognomen* Maximus. That name belonged to M'.

Valerius Volusi f. (and hence Kiessling and Schoell's addition of M. should be M'., if anything): he secured the name during his dictatorship in 404 (Cic. *Brut.* 54; Plut. *Pomp.* 13.11; Zon. 7.14). Even the ancient sources became confused: there is an *elogium* (Degrassi, *Inscr. Ital.* 13.3.78) which begins *M'. Valerius Volusi f. Maximus dictator, augur, prius quam ullum magistratum gereret dictator dictus est.* The *praenomen* M'. is also given in the *fasti triumphales,* the *fasti Capitolini,* and Dion. Hal. 6.39.2 (where he is called a brother of Publicola), while Liv. 3.30.5 (cf. 3.7.6, with Ogilvie's note) and Cic. *Brut.* 54, call him M. Münzer (*de gente Valeria* [diss., Berlin, 1891] pp. 18-25) identifies the man in the *elogium* with the consul of 505 (who, in his view, could have had the *cognomen* Maximus), but it is clear that there are two distinct persons, for the consul of 505, according to the tradition (Liv. 2.20.3), died at the battle of Lake Regillus in 496, while the man who became dictator was not appointed until 494 and, according to the *elogium,* had not held office before. Further, if the latter were a brother of Publicola, he would have to have had a different *praenomen* from the consul of 505 who was also a brother of Publicola. As Mommsen suggests, M. should be emended to M'. in Cicero and Livy (as it is most likely the simplest of copyist's errors): on the confusion, see Degrassi, *Inscr. Ital.* 13.3.78; *MRR* 1.14; R.M. Ogilvie, *A Commentary on Livy Books 1-5* (Oxford, 1965) pp. 306-7. A further source of confusion is that both men triumphed for victories against Sabines (Degrassi, *Inscr. Ital.* 13.1.535, 536). There is no evidence that M'. Valerius Maximus was awarded a house at public expense, though abundant evidence that M. Valerius Volusus was (see below on 13.12). Asconius seems to have in mind two separate examples: the use of *autem* at 13.12 implies that he has moved on to another example (rather than that he is continuing to speak of the same example, from the evidence of a different source), and the use of the *cognomen* Maximus in one case suggests that two different persons are intended. In view of the fact that, apart from this reference, there is no evidence that the dictator of 494 was awarded a house at public expense, it would seem that an error has crept in here. Either Valerius Antias (Asconius' source) has made the mistake (perhaps deliberately: Ogilvie, op. cit. p. 250, calls it 'presumably a Valerian variant to mitigate the suggestion that Valerii could even be suspected of *regnum*', in view of the popular suspicion of the original site of Publicola's house [see below on 13.14-15]); or Asconius has made the mistake; or he is talking of the same man in both cases and has mistakenly added the name Maximus, knowing that there was a brother with that name.

13.8: *ut Antias tradidit*

Velleius Paterculus (2.9.4) classes Valerius Antias (his *praenomen* is not known) as a contemporary of L. Cornelius Sisenna (died 67) and Q. Claudius Quadrigarius, which would suggest that his *floruit* was c. 80-60 (for rejection of other suggestions in favour of these dates, see Ogilvie, *Commentary on Livy*, p. 13; for a later, Caesarian, date, see J.D. Cloud, *LCM* 2 [1977] 225-7). He wrote a history of Rome in seventy-five books at least (frag. 62 P). His access to private records kept by the Valerian family allowed him to fill out the bald annalistic statements of public sources such as the *annales maximi*, compiled from the *tabula pontificum* by P. Mucius Scaevola shortly before 115, and the *senatus consulta* (for the sources available, see P.G. Walsh, *Livy: His Historical Aims and Methods* [Cambridge, 1961] pp. 110-1). It also led to the most striking single feature of his history — adulation of the Valerian family, especially noticeable in the first five books of Livy, for which Valerius Antias was a major source (Walsh, ibid. pp. 121-2; Ogilvie, op. cit. p. 14; contra, R.A. Laroche, *Historia* 26 [1977] 358-68). The passage we have here (which is recorded in Peter as frag. 17) is an example of this sort of exaggeration: the story, however, has not been used by Livy. For further on Valerius Antias, see H. Volkmann, *RE* 7A (1948) 2313-40, s.v. 'Valerius' no. 98. Asconius mentions him as a source again at 69.21.

13.11: *Varronem*

See below on 13.19. Varro is one of those who preserve the tradition that M. Valerius Volusus was awarded a house at public expense (see next comment).

13.12: *M. Valerio, quia Sabinos vicerat*

M. Valerius Volusus, cos. 505, was voted a site on the Palatine (ἐν τῷ κρατίστῳ, according to Dion. Hal. 5.39.4) and the costs of building a house at public expense as a reward for defeating the Sabines during his consulship (twice, according to Dion. Hal. 5.37.1-39.4; Plin. *NH* 36.112; Plut. *Popl.* 20.1-2). All the sources remark on the orientation of this house outwards, as an indication of the public esteem in which such heroes were held (Dion. Hal. 5.39.4; Ascon. 13.10-11; Plin. *NH* 36.112; Plut. *Popl.* 2). Dionysius gives the additional information that a bronze statue of a bull stood near the front doors of the house. For the possible confusion of this house with that of his brother, see below on 13.14-15.

13.13: *Iulius Hyginus*

C. Iulius Hyginus, a freedman of Augustus, was appointed librarian of the Palatine library established by Augustus in 28; he was born c. 60 and became a pupil of Alexander Polyhistor, and a teacher and friend of Ovid, whose poem *Tr.* 3.14 is usually described as being addressed to him. His scholarship was wide for he wrote on agriculture, history and archaeology, and religion, as well as preparing a commentary on Vergil. The work referred to here as *de viris claris* consisted of at least six books (Gell. 1.14.1): it is elsewhere called *de vita rebusque illustrium virorum* (so Peter, *HRR* 2.72 from Gell. loc. cit.). There is another work, the *exempla* (Gell. 10.18.7), which may be identified with the work on famous men (so C.J. Fordyce, *OCD*², p. 533). The fragments of his grammatical works and *testimonia* on his life and works are collected in G. Funaioli, *Grammaticae Romanae Fragmenta* (Teubner, 1907) pp. 525-37; see also Peter, *HRR* 2. ci-cvii.

13.14-15: *P. Valerio Volesi filio Publicolae aedium publice locum sub Veliis*

According to one version (Cic. *rep*. 2.53; Liv. 2.7.5-6 and 10-12; Dion. Hal. 5.19.1-2; Val. Max. 4.1.1), P. Valerius Publicola became the object of popular disfavour during his first consulship in 509 because, among other things, he was building (or had built) a house on the highest part of the Velia. He was thought to be aiming at *regnum*, and to placate the opposition, he moved his house from the top to the bottom of the Velia. In the references listed for this version, there is no mention of Publicola's house being built at public expense. In Plutarch's version (*Popl*. 10.3-4), Publicola pulled down his house on the top of the Velia, and out of admiration the people awarded him a site at the bottom of the Velia and had a house built for him: it is this version which Asconius has followed, getting it from Varro through Iulius Hyginus, though Asconius says that Publicola was given only the site for his house (cf. below, 13.24-25). Cicero also preserves this tradition at *har. resp*. 16 (*P. Valerio pro maximis in rem publicam beneficiis data domus est in Velia publice, at mihi in Palatio restituta*.), as does Pliny (*NH* 36.112). On the confusion of the various traditions, see O.L. Richmond, *JRS* 4 (1914) 208, and Platner-Ashby, p. 197.

13.15: *ubi nunc aedis Victoriae est*

According to Livy (2.7.12), this temple was built on a lower slope of the Velia towards the forum: in Livy (loc. cit.) and Plutarch (*Popl*. 10.4), it was a temple of Vica Pota, but this deity must have been identical with or closely related to Victoria, since that is the name Asconius uses (cf. Cic. *leg*. 2.28, where he says that Vica Pota is derived from *vincere* and *potiri*). It was dedicated on 5th January (*Notizie degli Scavi di Antichita* [1921] p. 84). On the temple and the derivation of the goddess's name, see Ogilvie, *Commentary*, pp. 251-2: he says that Livy does not imply that the shrine replaced the house of the Valerii, but that it survived although the house disappeared.

13.16-17: *Antiochi regis filio obsidi*

This man was the youngest son of king Antiochus III Magnus; he later became king as Antiochus IV Epiphanes. Following the defeat of his father at the battle of Magnesia (190), he was sent as one of the twenty hostages to Rome (App. *Syr.* 39), where he remained for some years. He succeeded to the throne in 175 on the murder of his brother, Seleucus IV Philopator, who had ruled since 187, despite the claims of the latter's son, Demetrius. Two years later, he secured the renewal of the treaty which had existed between his father and Rome, through the agency of the urban praetor of 173, A. Atilius Serranus, who was holding the office of praetor for the second time (Liv. 41.28.5), and who had been authorised by the senate to negotiate with Antiochus (Liv. 42.6.9-10). Livy mentions (ibid.) that he claimed to have received good treatment from the senate when he was a hostage at Rome, and that was presumably a reference to the provision of a house for him. This is the only reference to the house that we know of: C. Cichorius, *Untersuchungen zu Lucilius* (Zurich/Berlin, 1908, 1964 repr.) p. 10, is wrong in saying that the house was built for Demetrius, who was also a hostage at Rome from a little before 175 to c. 162 (Polyb. 31.11ff.) and who later ruled as Demetrius I Soter after the death of Epiphanes; Demetrius was the son of Seleucus, not Antiochus. On the length of Antiochus' stay in Rome as a hostage, see E.R. Bevan, *The House of Seleucus* (London, 1902) Vol. II, p. 124: he was exchanged for his brother's son, Demetrius, some time before 175, for App. *Syr.* 45 shows that, while on his way back to Syria before succeeding to the throne, he resided in Athens for long enough to have participated in Athenian public life. Further on Antiochus IV Epiphanes, see M. Wellmann, *RE* 1 (1894) 2470-6, s.v. 'Antiochos' no. 27, and O. Mørkholm, *Antiochus IV of Syria* (Copenhagen, 1966); on his eccentric and bohemian personality, see Polyb. 26.1 (from Athen.) and Liv. 41.20.

13.18: *Atticus in annali*

The *annalis* of T. Pomponius Atticus is referred to by name in Cic. *Att.* 12.23.2, and is probably the work referred to in Cic. *Brut.* 42 and 72. Asconius refers to Atticus as a source again at 77.4. The singular title *annalis* is unusual. The work was a history of Rome from its foundation: the last known reference is to an event in 155 (Cic. *Att.* 12.23.2, when the philosopher Carneades headed a delegation from Athens to Rome; cf. *acad.* 2.137). The work was published in 47 (R. Feger, *RE Suppl.* 8.520-1). See also A.E. Douglas, *AJP* 77 (1956) 380-1.

13.19: *Varro quoque in libro III de vita populi Romani*

M. Terentius Varro (116-27) not only wrote on a wide range of topics (we know the titles of fifty-five works, and that was not his total output), but he also undertook a public career, reaching the praetorship. He saw a good deal of service as a legate of Pompeius, first in Spain c. 76-71, then against the pirates in 67, and again in Spain (probably as *legatus pro praetore*, since Pompeius governed his *provincia* in absence) probably from 55-49. He also had links with Caesar, serving as one of the twenty commissioners set up by Caesar's agrarian law in 59; although he had fought on Pompeius' side in the civil war, he was pardoned by Caesar and given a special commission to collect a library (Suet. *Iul.* 44.2). His *de vita populi Romani*, a social history of the Roman people, written in four books, probably covered the period from the beginnings of Rome up to his own time (H. Dahlmann, *RE Suppl.* 6 [1935] 1243-6, s.v. 'Terentius' no. 84).

13.20: *Mutinae*

In Livy, the man's name is given as Muttines; he is called Myttones by Polybius (9.22.5) and Mutto by Iustin (18.4.3); and he appears on an inscription as Μάαρκος Ὀαλέριος ὁ Μοττόνης (W. Dittenberger, *Syll.*³ 585.87), obviously taking the *praenomen* and *gentilicium* from his commander in Sicily when he acquired Roman citizenship. Dittenberger, *Hermes* 15 (1880) 158-60, discusses the form of the name, arguing for Muttines and explaining the forms which appear in the mss. of Asconius. He turned up in Sicily in 211 in command of 3000 Numidian cavalry, which was part of a Carthaginian army landed after Marcellus' departure (Liv. 26.21.14-15); the Numidians were able to move about freely, ravaging the lands of Rome's allies (ibid.). In the following year, the Carthaginian army was stationed at Agrigentum under the command of Hanno, but much of its success was due to the Numidian cavalry under Muttines, who could not be shut off from Agrigentum by the Roman army under M. Valerius Laevinus (cos. 210) nor prevented from making raids. But Hanno, jealous of Muttines' success, tried to give command of the cavalry to his own son; Muttines then opened secret negotiations with Laevinus and eventually went over to the Roman side, helping them to capture the city (26.40.2-10). Subsequently Laevinus introduced Muttines and others who had helped him to conquer Sicily to the senate; according to Livy (27.5.7), Muttines was made a Roman citizen by a bill introduced in the assembly by the tribunes on the authority of the senate. There is no mention in Livy of a house being awarded to Muttines. He continued to serve under Laevinus in Sicily in 209, and later served under Scipio Asiaticus in Greece in 190 (Liv. 38.41.12). For his career, see V. Ehrenberg, *RE* 16 (1935) 1428-30, s.v. 'Myttones'.

14.2-3: *quod novum et huic primo et adhuc etiam soli contigit*

Asconius explains the differences between the grant of a house for Cicero and the awards of earlier houses in this way: either they were grants of a site or they were grants of a house to be built for the first time, whereas Cicero's was in fact to be rebuilt after it had been set on fire, destroyed and execrated. Cicero draws attention to the uniqueness of his grant in a different way at *har. resp.* 16 where he makes a similar claim to the one on which Asconius is commenting here: Cicero says ... *de mea domo,*

108   *Commentary*

quam senatus unam post hanc urbem constitutam ex aerario aedificandam ..., but goes on to say that what made it unique was that it was also absolved by the pontiffs, protected by magistrates and avenged by the courts. Cicero also mentions an earlier example in the house of P. Valerius (showing that he was not as incautious about such statements as Asconius [13.6-7] would lead us to believe), but points out that his house differed from that of Valerius because it was *restituta* (though, in a sense, one could say that Valerius' house was restored too, if one accepts Plutarch's version [see above on 13.14-15]; but then Cicero was speaking *oratorio more, non historico*, as Asconius [13.4] is well aware!). Asconius can be criticised for not being aware that Cicero knew of the difference between his grant and earlier grants, and so for claiming that Cicero has made too rash a statment: even if Asconius did not recall the passage in *har. resp.*, he should have been able to draw something from the *pontifices, consules, patres conscripti* which he quotes in the lemma.

14.11-12: *Pompeii pater bello Italico de Picentibus*

According to the triumphal *fasti*, Cn. Pompeius Strabo celebrated a triumph as consul for his victory over the Asculanian Picentes on 25th December 89 (Degrassi, *Inscr. Ital.* 13.1.85 and 563). As consul in 89, he had command against the Italians in the north, principally at the siege of Asculum, which he captured late in the year; he then took command in central Italy following the death of his colleague in the consulship, L. Porcius Cato.

14.12-13: *M. Crassi pater P. Crassus ante bellum Italicum de Hispanis triumphavit*

According to the triumphal *fasti*, P. Licinius Crassus celebrated a triumph as proconsul for his victory over the Lusitanians on 12th June 93 (Degrassi, *Inscr. Ital.* 13.1.85 and 563). He had held a proconsulship in Further Spain from 96-93, following his consulship in 97.

14.17: *eorum neuter*

The two men being discussed are C. Cotta (mentioned in the first sentence of the lemma) and L. Crassus (mentioned in the sentence in §62, immediately preceding the lemma here). Asconius could have made the point of his comment more immediately clear if he had included the preceding sentence.

14.20-21: *C. Cotta orator ille compar P. Sulpici qui est in dialogis Ciceronis de oratore scriptis*

C. Aurelius Cotta was consul in 75; he was a contemporary of P. Sulpicius (trib. 88), as Asconius says. Both received their oratorical

In Pisonem

training under L. Crassus and were members of a circle of brilliant young men, including M. Livius Drusus. They became the leading orators after the deaths of L. Crassus and M. Antonius (Cic. *Brut.* 183; for the sympathetic picture which Cicero gives of Sulpicius' political activities, see C.M. Chapman, *Acta Classica* 22 (1979) 61-72); it is these four figures who take part in the whole of the dialogue *de oratore*, with other figures appearing briefly in no more than two of the three books.

14.22-23: *cum decretus illi esset triumphus, mortuus est ante diem triumphi*

Cotta was given a proconsular command in Cisalpine Gaul; it is possible that he left for his province before the end of his year of office (J.P.V.D. Balsdon, *JRS* 29 [1939] 63). He remained in his province long enough to win a success which secured for him the award of a triumph, but he died before the triumph could be held (late 74 or early 73: see L.R. Taylor, *Class. Phil.* 36 [1941] 119; *MRR* 2.111).

14.24-25: *L. autem Crasso collega fuit Q. Scaevola pontifex*

L. Licinius Crassus and Q. Mucius Scaevola appear to have been political allies, since they shared all their offices, except the tribunate and censorship (Cic. *Verr.* 2.4.133, *Brut.* 160-161), and were connected by marriage, Crassus being married to Scaevola's cousin Mucia. The shared offices were the aedileship in 100, the praetorship by 98, and the consulship in 95; in addition Crassus was tribune in 107 and censor (with Cn. Domitius Ahenobarbus) in 92. The connection between the Mucii Scaevolae and the Licinii Crassi had begun in the previous generation, with the adoption of P. Licinius Crassus Dives Mucianus (cos. 131) and the support of this man and his brother P. Mucius Scaevola (cos. 133) for Ti. Gracchus' legislation. On the date of Crassus' marriage to Mucia, see Gruen, *Politics and Courts,* p. 114 n. 39.

15.2: *in decernendo triumpho*

Crassus was allotted the province of Cisalpine Gaul. That it was Cisalpine Gaul is suggested by Cic. *Pis.* 62 (where he is described as operating in the Alps) and *inv.* 2.111 (which says he operated *in citeriore Gallia*). Although Valerius Maximus (3.7.6: *cum ex consulatu provinciam Galliam obtineret . . .*) suggests he went to his province as proconsul, Cicero (*inv.* 2.111) says he went as consul: that he made his campaign and request for a triumph during his consular year is confirmed by the tense of *deposuerat*, if the interpretation given to that (see below on 15.5-6) is correct, and by the fact that Scaevola used his consular veto to block the award of a triumph (see below on 15.4). Crassus had merely suppressed bandits in Cisalpine Gaul, and Scaevola no doubt used the argument that a victory over these was hardly worthy of a triumph: for

Cicero's pun on Crassus' 'probing' for a triumph, see *Pis.* 62, and cf. Nisbet, ad loc.

15.3: *rei publicae magis quam collegae habere rationem*

In view of their political connection, it is hard to see why Scaevola blocked his colleague's request for a triumph. The reason given here is somewhat naive (though it may reflect what Scaevola said in public). Perhaps both Crassus and Scaevola retained a certain amount of political independence, despite their individual connection and common links with the Metellan faction, which occasionally led to disputes (see Badian, *Studies*, p. 43, and Gruen, *Politics and Courts*, pp. 114ff. and 198). If Scaevola had declined a province in his consular year (as is argued below), it is easier to understand why he would want to block Crassus' request for a triumph.

15.4: *ac ne fieret s.c. intercessit*

This looks like the imposition of a veto by a magistrate in office against a proposal put up by another magistrate for senatorial approval (Mommsen, *Staatsrecht* 1^3.282). This confirms that Scaevola had blocked Crassus' request for a triumph during their consular year. If Scaevola had taken a governorship in Asia following his consulship, and blocked Crassus' request on his return, one would have to ask what authority a returned proconsul would have to interpose a veto (and such an order of events does not fit with the pluperfect tense of *deposuerat*: see next comment).

15.4-6: *idem provinciam . . . deposuerat ne sumptui esset* †*oratio*†

Scaevola is known to have administered the province of Asia (Cic. *Att.* 6.1.15; Val Max. 8.15.6) and to have left it after only nine months (Cic. *Att.* 5.17.5), leaving one of his *legati*, P. Rutilius Rufus, in charge (Ps.-Ascon. 202.21 says he was quaestor: see *MRR* 2.8 and 9 n. 6). On those grounds, some have suggested that the province referred to here, following Scaevola's consulship, was Asia. But Balsdon has shown (*CR* 51 [1937] 8-10) that Asconius' phrase *deponere provinciam* means not that he had left his province (which would require some verb like *decedere*), but that he had refused to go out to a province at all. For the technical sense of *deponere provinciam*, cf. Cic. *fam.* 5.2.3, *Pis.* 5. Under the terms of the *lex Sempronia*, the consular provinces were known well in advance, and consuls-elect had the chance to reject the provinces allotted to them. In view of the probability that Scaevola did not go out to a province following his consulship, it is likely that Asia was the province he governed following his praetorship, which was held at the latest in 98 (so Balsdon, loc. cit. 9; Broughton, *MRR* 2.5 n. 2 and 7), and it would then follow that we do not know what province he rejected during his consulship. The description of it as one which led many good men astray could apply to almost any province! One objection to the view that he governed Asia in 97 is that it would leave a long gap between Rutilius' legateship and condemnation in 92 for provincial corruption, but Broughton (*MRR* 2.4 n. 2) sees similar gaps in other cases. Another objection (Münzer, *RE* 1A [1920] 1273-4, s.v. 'Rutilius' no. 34) is that Rutilius was a consular, and we would expect to find him as a legate on the staff of a consular, rather than a praetorian, governor: this is dismissed by Balsdon (loc. cit. 9) who says that his serving as a legate is surprising anyway, as he was almost a generation older than Scaevola. Balsdon misses the point that Scaevola was titled proconsul (*OGIS* 437, 439; Liv. *per.* 70), and it might not therefore have been so embarrassing for Rutilius to serve as a legate under him.

Balsdon's emendation of *ornatio* for the ms. *oro* is very attractive (loc. cit. 9; it was anticipated by J.S. Reid, *CR* 23 [1910] 21-2). According to Diod. 37.5.1, Scaevola paid all his expenses as governor of Asia out of his own pocket (perhaps that explains why he stayed only nine months!), and he would have been acting consistently if in 95 he refused a province on the grounds that he did not wish to involve the state in the expense of an *ornatio*. The objection that this noun is post-Augustan and rare is not a strong one. It is Asconius' word (if it is correct) and not Cicero's, and Asconius is himself post-Augustan; and clearly the noun could be derived from the verbal expression *ornare provinciam* which is very common. There is at least one other case where Asconius has formed a noun from a verb in a sense which is not common and not included in the lexicons (see below on 24.10-11). If this was the reason given by Scaevola, it would have been merely an excuse: a governor would have to be sent anyway, and the state would therefore be involved in the expense. Perhaps the real reason was that Scaevola, like Cicero later, did not like to be away from Rome: he had stayed only nine months in his earlier province.

Badian proposes the emendation *moratio*, but this is suggested to fit in with his view of the date of Scaevola's governorship, and of the meaning of *deponere provinciam* (*Athenaeum* 34 [1956] 104-23).

The tense of *deposuerat* makes better sense if we accept the view that Scaevola did not go out to a province at all following his consulship. If he had gone, he would not have returned till towards the end of 94, and in that case he would not have blocked the granting of the triumph to Crassus until he returned from his province, since the tense of *deponere* suggests that it preceded the action of *intercedere*. But by that time he and Crassus were no longer colleagues, whereas we are told that Scaevola rejected the claim of his *collega* (14.25 and 15.3; cf. Cic. *Pis.* 62). That seems to imply that Crassus had undertaken his campaign in Gaul during his term of office, and that he had returned at the end of the year to claim a triumph, which was then blocked by Scaevola. Prior to that blocking, Scaevola had rejected (pluperfect) his province: as the consular provinces were known well in advance, Scaevola had time between his appointment and the return of Crassus to reject the province allotted to him. For the view that Crassus operated against the Gauls while in office, see above on 15.2. For further confirmation that the blocking of Crassus' request by Scaevola took place in their consular year, since Scaevola could only interpose a veto while in office as consul, see above on 15.4. Of course the pluperfect might refer back several years to his praetorship: he might have rejected a province following that office, and gone out to Asia following his consulship. For further arguments in favour of a governorship of Asia following his praetorship, see *MRR Suppl.* p. 42, and for a return to the traditional view of a governorship in 94, see Badian, art. cit., and cf. *Historia* 11 (1962) 222. For a recent discussion of the date of Scaevola's governorship, see B.A. Marshall, *Athenaeum* 54 (1976) 117-30 (accepted by G.V. Sumner, *GRBS* 19 [1978] 147).

15.14-15: *Pupius Piso eisdem temporibus quibus Cicero*

The *Pupius* has been added as a correction of the mss. reading *P. Piso* by Manutius. The correction makes sense as the man clearly referred to here is M. Pupius Piso. His full name was M. Pupius Piso Frugi Calpurnianus: he was a member of the family of the Pisones Frugi, and had been adopted by M. Pupius (Cic. *dom.* 35), probably some time in the first quarter of the first century (A. Stein, *RE* 23.2 [1959] 1990). He was the brother of the praetor of 74 (R. Syme, *JRS* 50 [1960] 15).

15.15: *tanto aetate maior*

We do not know the date of his birth, so we cannot say how much older than Cicero he was. He held a quaestorship in 83 (*MRR* 2.63), which suggests that he was born c. 113 at the latest. His subsequent rise through the *cursus* makes it difficult to determine whether he held office at the minimum age: he failed at the aedilician elections in 75 (Cic. *off.* 2.58), secured a praetorship in 72 or 71 (*MRR* 2.117 and 121 n. 1), which would be consistent with a birth c. 113, but had to wait until 61 to secure the consulship, two years later than Cicero (15.18). This erratic success may indicate that he was not close to the minimum age when he secured office, and so would argue for a birth earlier than 113. Presumably he must have been some years older than Cicero (born 106) for Cicero's father to have entrusted his son to his care. On A.E. Douglas' theory for chronology in Cicero's *Brutus* (*AJP* 87 [1966] 290-304), Piso (mentioned in § 236) ought to be a close contemporary of M. Licinius Crassus (mentioned in § 233), who was born c. 115 or a little earlier (since he was over sixty when he left for the Parthian campaign in 55 — Plut. *Crass.* 17.2); he was an *aequalis* of Hortensius (§ 230), so a birth date of 114-3 is most likely (cf. Sumner, *Orators*, p. 127).

15.17: *multae erant litterae*

For Piso's philosophical and literary interest, see Douglas' note on Cic. *Brut.* 236: he was said by Cicero to be particularly learned in Greek philosophy and letters.

15.17-18: *orator quoque melior quam frequentior habitus est*

Piso's most famous case was his defence appearance in the trial of the Vestal virgins (Cic. *Brut.* 236), which is usually identified with the case in 73 (Cic. *Cat.* 3.9). For a discussion whether Catilina was involved in this trial, see below on 91.17ff. He must have established a reputation as a promising young orator by c. 90 for Cicero's father to have considered him a suitable tutor for his son. He is said not to have devoted himself fully to oratory, as being too strenuous for his health and because of his pedantic impatience with the loose and empty language which others found easier to put up with (Cic. *Brut.* 236: cf. the less kind character-sketch at *Att.* 1.13.2), and to have devoted himself to the pursuit of military glory: that seems to be true of his career after his praetorship, and may explain his infrequent appearances in court.

15.18-19: *biennio tamen serius quam Cicero consul fuit*

I.e. 61. He had secured the consulship with the support of Pompeius, who had written requesting a postponement of the consular elections in 62 to allow Piso time to return and stand (Plut. *Cat. Min.* 30.1; Dio 37.44.3). The consulship was a reward for Piso's service under Pompeius as *legatus pro praetore* from 67-62. He failed to get through the senate Pompeius' requests, but supported the cause of P. Clodius in the attempts to have the latter tried over the Bona Dea affair. This action brought him opposition from Cicero, who prevented him from securing Syria as his provincial command (Cic. *Att.* 1.16.8; cf. *prov. cons.* 36, and SB*Att.* 1.318). For his career, see A. Stein, *RE* 23.2 (1959) 1987-93; R. Syme, *C. & M.* 17 (1956) 130-1.

15.19-20: *triumphavit procos. de Hispania Q. Hortensio Q. Metello coss.*

Piso celebrated a triumph in 69 (in the consulship of Hortensius and Metellus) for a victory in Spain (Degrassi, *Inscr. Ital.* 13.1.565): Asconius is our only source for the year of his triumph. He served as governor of Spain following his praetorship in 72 or 71 (for the date, see *MRR* 2.117 and 121 n. 1), possibly as governor of both Nearer and Further Spain (P.B. Gimpera and P.A. Bleye, in R. Menéndez Pidal [ed.],

Historia de España, 2nd edn. [Madrid, 1955] Vol. II, p. 243). His request for a triumph on his return was opposed unsuccessfully by C. Calpurnius Piso.

16.5-6: *quibus ludis elephantorum pugnam primus omnium dedit in circo*

Cic. *fam.* 7.1.3; Sen. *brev. vit.* 13.6; Plin. *NH* 8.20-21; Plut. *Pomp.* 52.4; and Dio 39.38.2-3 all record that Pompeius used elephants in the beast-shows he put on to celebrate the opening of his theatre; Seneca and Dio say there were eighteen, while Pliny says there were seventeen or twenty. Seneca preserves the tradition that Pompeius was the first to use elephants in the circus, but Pliny (*NH* 8.19) preserves a variant, from Fenestella, which says that elephants were first used in games by the curule aedile, C. Claudius Pulcher, in the consulship of M. Antonius and A. Postumius Albinus in 99 (for the reputation of the lavishness of Pulcher's games, see references in *MRR* 2.1). This would be another instance of Asconius' disagreement with Fenestella (see above, p. 54), though he has not specified his disagreement here.

16.12: *Philodemum significat*

On Philodemus and his relationship with L. Piso, see Nisbet, App. III.

16.13: *cuius et poemata sunt lasciva*

Asconius has taken too seriously Cicero's suggestion (*Pis.* 68-72, cf. *red. in sen.* 14, and *Sest.* 23) that Philodemus' poetry is responsible for the immoral conduct of Piso's house. Cicero has clearly exaggerated, and the criticism of Philodemus himself is restrained. Cicero's real view of the philosopher can be found at *fin.* 2.119: *familiares nostros Sironem et Philodemum, cum optimos viros tum homines doctissimos.* He did write erotic poetry, but the genre was conventional, and he may have written much of it before he met Piso (Nisbet, p. 184), so he cannot really be charged with corrupting Piso. Asconius has fallen into the common trap of making a comment which merely paraphrases.

16.17-18: *hunc versum esse L. Acci poetae et dici a Thyeste Atreo*

See Nisbet, p. 150.

17.4: *legem iudiciariam*

Asconius mentions this law to set the background for the law proposed by Pompeius in 55, which is the one referred to in the lemma of Cicero quoted here. On *leges iudiciariae*, see M.T. Griffin, *CQ* n.s. 23 (1973) 108-21 (who argues that there were no *leges iudiciariae* covering the composition of the jury-courts in general until the Sullan period), and A.W. Lintott,

Zeitschrift der Savigny-Stiftung (Röm. Abt.) 98 (1982) 162-76 and 189-202. The law is referred to again at 67.11-13.

17.4: *ante aliquot annos*

In fact, fifteen years before in 70.

17.5-6: *tulit L. Aurelius Cotta praetor*

There are some unusual features about Cotta's proposing of this law. First, Cotta proposed it as praetor: one would have expected it to have been proposed either by a consul (e.g. in the same year the consuls, Pompeius and Crassus, had proposed the law restoring the full powers to the tribunate) or by a tribune (as concern for the conduct of senatorial juries was closely linked with agitation for the restoration of the tribunician rights: cf. the *contio* held by M. Lollius Palicanus and addressed by Pompeius in 71, at which he promised to restore the tribunes' rights and to do something about the jury-courts [Cic. *Verr.* 1.45; Sall. *hist.* 4.43 M; Ps.-Ascon. 220.10ff.], and the statement of Catulus [Cic. *Verr.* 1.44, cf. *div. in Caec.* 8] that there would have been less pressure for the restoration of the tribunician powers if there had not been so much disatisfaction with the senatorial juries). The bill was not officially promulgated until somewhere between 14th August and 19th September (i.e. between the first and second *actio* against Verres: Cic. *Verr.* 2.5.178), but it is clear that discussion of its terms had been going on for some time (Cic. *div. in Caec.* 8, *Verr.* 1.2), and that Cotta was the one leading these discussions (Cicero simply calls the proposer *praetor*: e.g. *Verr.* 2.3.223). That raises a second puzzle: the original form of the proposal was apparently to hand the jury-courts over entirely to the equites (Cic. *div. in Caec.* 8, *Verr.* 1.49, 2.2.174, 2.3.223, 2.5.177; cf. Liv. *per.* 97; Tac. *ann.* 11.22; Plut. *Pomp.* 22.3). Why did Cotta, *homo nobilissimus*, as Cicero calls him (*Verr.* 2.2.174) and presumably a man from the heart of the nobility (which is how his brother is described in Sall. *hist.* 3.48.8 M), propose to hand over control of the courts entirely to the equites, when we would have expected him to try and retain senatorial control? Why too did the proposal end up as a compromise solution? On these questions, see B.A. Marshall, *Rhein. Mus.* 118 (1975) 136-52, and cf. below on 67.11-12.

17.6-7: *communicata sunt iudicia senatui et equitibus Romanis et tribunis aerariis*

Though occasionally the jury-courts are loosely referred to as being divided between senators and equites (e.g. Cic. *Font.* 36, *Cluent.* 121, 130; Vell. Pat. 2.32.3; Liv. *per.* 97 even says they were handed over to the equites), it is clear that they were divided between these three groups (Cic. *Att.* 1.16.3, *Phil.* 1.20; Ascon. 17 and 67; Schol. Bob. 91.13-15; cf. the

116   *Commentary*

breakdown of votes at trials in Ascon. 28.25-27, 53.18-22, 55.5-7, 55.18-19). Discussion of the definition of the last two groups is extensive: there must, however, have been some point in distinguishing between them in the terms of the law, and hence it cannot be argued that both groups fall under the heading of that wider application of the term *equites*, the 'middle class'. On the evidence of Schol. Bob. 91.26, some have argued that the *tribuni aerarii* had a slightly lower census qualification than the equites (e.g. L.R. Taylor, *Party Politics in the Age of Caesar* [Berkeley, 1964] p. 201; Nicolet, *L'ordre équestre*, 1.598ff.), but others state that the equites and *tribuni aerarii* had the same census qualification (H. Hill, *The Roman Middle Class* [Oxford, 1952] pp. 156 and 212-4; M.I. Henderson, *JRS* 53 [1963] 63-4). For a recent summing up of the problem, see Jones, *Criminal Courts*, pp. 86-90, and cf. T.P. Wiseman, *Historia* 19 (1970) 71ff. The tribunate of the treasury was by now an obsolete military office. The *tribuni aerarii* were removed from the jury-courts by the *lex Iulia* of 46 (Suet. *Iul.* 41.2; Dio 43.25.1; cf. Cic. *Phil.* 1.19).

17.9-10: *amplissimo ex censu ex centuriis aliter atque antea lecti iudices*

From the evidence of Cic. *Phil.* 1.20 and [Sall.] *ep. ad Caes.* 3.3, this is usually taken to mean that Pompeius still retained the three *decuriae*, but chose the jurors from those with the highest incomes within each group, or at least imposed some sort of property qualification. This reduced the number on the *album iudicum*, drawn up annually by the *praetor urbanus*; with a smaller number of jurymen available, service on juries may now have been compulsory. Further on this *lex Pompeia*, and some of the problems associated with the composition of the jury-courts, see J.D. Denniston (ed.), *M. Tulli Ciceronis orationes Philippicae prima et secunda* (Oxford, 1926) App. II, esp. § § ii and iii; Greenidge, *Legal Procedure*, p. 448.

17.10: *aeque tamen ex illis tribus ordinibus*

That the three *ordines* continued to be equally represented on the juries under the *lex Pompeia* of 55 is borne out by the breakdown of the jury's votes in the trial of Scaurus in 54 (28.25-27): 22 senators, 23 equites, and 25 *tribuni aerarii* cast a vote. There may have been some who could not make up their minds, as the total of votes for condemnation or acquittal is only seventy, and the regular size for a jury seems to have been about seventy-five (Jones, op. cit. pp. 69-70). There was an alteration to the method of selecting the final jury-panel in the *lex Pompeia* of 52, which was brought in specifically for the trial of Milo for the murder of Clodius and which reduced the number of jurors to fifty-one (see below on 39.17ff.), but the principle of equal division between the *ordines* was

In Pisonem

retained, for in the breakdown of votes for two trials under this law mentioned by Asconius (53.19-22, 55.5-7), there were 18 senators, 17 equites and 16 *tribuni aerarii*.

17.17: *Opimium in praetura Fregellas cepisse*

L. Opimius was praetor in 125, and was in command of the forces sent to crush the rebellion at Fregellae; following the success of his campaign, the city was destroyed (references in *MRR* 1.510). For a fuller discussion of the revolt, see P. Conole, *Antichthon*, 15 (1981) 129-40. Asconius' phrase *in praetura* seems to be in contradiction with the phrase in the lemma, *post praeturam*; but the lemma has been carelessly copied from Cicero at some stage, for the mss. of the speech have *L. Opimius eiectus est e* (or *a*) *patria, is qui praetor et consul* ... Rau's conjecture *ex praetura* for Asconius is therefore unnecessary.

17.19: *in consulatu*

Opimius was elected to the consulship of 121 (*MRR* 1.520). He had stood for the consulship of 122, but had been beaten at the election by C. Fannius, who had had the support of C. Gracchus.

17.19-20: *Fulvium Flaccum consularem*

M. Fulvius Flaccus had been consul in 125, but had become a tribune in 122, acting as C. Gracchus' main supporter (*MRR* 1.517).

17.20: *C. Gracchum tribunicium*

C. Sempronius Gracchus had failed to be re-elected to a tribunate for 121, the year in which he and Flaccus ran up against Opimius' opposition. Flaccus too had no office in that year, hence Asconius refers to them as *consularis* and *tribunicius* respectively.

17.20-21: *oppressisse*

Opimius had secured election as an opponent of C. Gracchus' programme. In the disorders which resulted when Gracchus and Flaccus protested against the repeal of the *lex Rubria* (by which the colony at Carthage was to be set up), a *senatus consultum ultimum* was passed, and Opimius used it to crush Gracchus and his supporters (references in *MRR* 1.520). Velleius Paterculus (2.7.6) says that Opimius was motivated by a desire for personal revenge, rather than for the defence of the state, but he does not say what the personal feud was: perhaps it was the defeat of Opimius by Fannius for the consulship of 122. The stories told of his cruelty to the Gracchan supporters suggest some degree of personal animosity.

17.21: *ob quam invidiam postea iudicio circumventus est*

This refers to the trial of Opimius for treason under the Mamilian commission, set up as a *quaestio extraordinaria* by the tribune, C. Mamilius Limetanus, probably in the early months of 109. The crimes to be handled are specified in Sall. *Iug.* 40.1-2; the jury was composed of *Gracchani iudices*; and it is clear that the court would be harsh on those members of the nobility who were suspected of treasonable dealings with Jugurtha, since popular and equestrian feeling was united in running high against the nobility at this time. L. Opimius had headed the original senatorial embassy to Numidia in 116 to settle the rival claims of Jugurtha and Adherbal; although the settlement was reasonable, Opimius was suspected of taking bribes. As Asconius says, Opimius suffered in that trial as a result of earlier popular resentment: for a discussion of the real reason for Opimius' condemnation, and of the Mamilian commission in general, see Gruen, *Politics and Courts*, pp. 142-5. Opimius had been involved in an earlier trial, in 120, instigated before the people by a tribune of that year, P. Decius: it really dealt with the constitutional issue of the validity of the *s.c.u.* Gruen suggests that this attack on Opimius was not a revival of the Gracchan cause, but a personal vendetta by Decius (ibid. pp. 102-3).

THE COMMENTARY ON THE SPEECH *PRO SCAURO*

[Note: Reference is made to G. Bloch, 'M. Aemilius Scaurus: étude sur l'histoire des partis au VIIe siècle de Rome', in *Mélanges d'histoire ancienne* 25 (Paris, 1909), by the abbreviation Bloch, with the appropriate page number.]

18.1: *eisdem consulibus*

L. Domitius Ahenobarbus and Ap. Claudius Pulcher were consuls in 54.

18.2: *pro Vatinio*

P. Vatinius, the pro-Caesarian tribune of 59, had been successful in being elected to a praetorship for 55, mainly through the efforts of Pompeius and Crassus, who wished to keep Cato out of that office. In conducting his electoral campaign, Vatinius had employed gladiatorial shows in contravention of the *lex Tullia de ambitu*, but he was formally charged with *ambitus* under the *lex Licinia de sodaliciis* (which superseded previous *ambitus* laws and was passed between Vatinius' offence and formal prosecution in 54). Vatinius had entered office immediately on election, and so was immune from prosecution until 54; the prosecution was undertaken by C. Licinius Calvus (for fragments of his speech, see *ORF*^{2}, pp. 494-8, though it is not clear that all the fragments belong to this case, as Calvus had a running feud with Vatinius and is said to have prosecuted him a number of times). Though he had bitterly attacked Vatinius only two years earlier in relation to the trial of Sestius, and had supported Cato's candidature for the praetorship against Vatinius, Cicero was called upon to defend him at this trial, through pressure from Pompeius and Caesar who wished to protect one of their creatures (Cic. *fam.* 1.9.19). Vatinius was acquitted, as Cicero had predicted (*fam.* 5.9.1, *Q.f.* 2.16.3). For further details of the case, see E.S. Gruen, *HSCP* 71 (1966) 219-21.

18.6: *princeps senatus*

Scaurus was the most powerful political figure of his generation, dominating the senate for some twenty-five years. He is known to have been nominated or titled *princeps senatus* in the following years: 115 (Plin. *NH* 8.223), 112 (Sall. *Iug.* 25.4; cf. *MRR* 1.533 n. 2), 108 (presumably having been retained by the censors of that year: *MRR* 1.549), 100 (Cic. *Rab. perd.* 21, presumably having been reappointed by the censors of 102), and 90 (Ascon. 22.16-17). Between 100 and 90, it is assumed that he was reappointed as *princeps senatus* by the censors of 97 and 92 (so *MRR* 2.7 and 17). For other references to his position, cf. Cic. *Scaur.* 46, *de or.* 2.197; Val. Max. 4.4.11, 8.5.2; Plin. *NH* 36.116.

18.7: *vitricum habuit Sullam*

When Scaurus the elder died in 89, his wife, Caecilia Metella, the daughter of L. Caecilius Metellus Delmaticus (cos. 119, cens. 115(?) when Scaurus was first named *princeps senatus*), was married off to L. Cornelius Sulla, who thereby became the younger Scaurus' step-father. Scaurus' marriage to Metella may have been late in his life, after 102 according to Münzer, *RA*, pp. 280-1, followed by I. Shatzman, *Anc. Soc.* 5 (1974) 213; contra, Badian, *Studies*, p. 39, who puts it soon after his consulship; cf. Bloch, p. 22. On the part played by Sullan connections in the younger Scaurus' trial, see below on 19.16-17 and 28.7ff.

18.8: *abstinens fuit*

Cf. Cicero's claim that he was not avaricious (below, 26.22-23). Scaurus must have been one of the few Sullan connections to have avoided the accusation that he made money out of the proscriptions. He may, of course, have been too young to have taken part in the civil war: a praetorship in 56 and candidature for the consulship of 53 point to a birth date in the mid-90's, and hence to the possibility that he was only in his early teens during the civil war. On the extent of his inheritance from his father and mother, see Bloch, p. 20 with n. 3.

18.9: *ab hasta*

A spear was stuck in the ground at public auctions (originally as a sign of booty gained in battle or of magisterial authority): cf. Cic. *off.* 2.27 and 83.

18.9-10: *aedilitatem summa magnificentia gessit*

On the magnificence of Scaurus' aedilician games in 58, see Cic. *Sest* 116, *off.* 2.57; Val. Max 2.4.6-7; Plin. *NH* 8.64 and 96, 9.11, 34.36, 35.127, 36.50, 113-116 and 189; Schol. Bob. 135.29-30.

18.11: *ex praetura*

Scaurus was praetor in 56, in charge of the *quaestio de vi*, for he appears to have presided at the trial of Sestius (Cic. *Sest*. 101 and 116), and following his praetorship became governor of Sardinia, probably as proconsul (*CIL* 1^2.2.811).

18.13-14: *genus morum in eo paternum*

We know of no promagisterial command held by Scaurus' father (but cf. below on 19.12-13); as consul in 115 he campaigned against some Gallic and Ligurian tribesmen for which he celebrated a triumph (references in *MRR* 1.531). But it need not have been misconduct as governor of a province that Scaurus is said to have inherited from his father; there was certainly a widespread suspicion that the elder Scaurus had accepted bribes from Jugurtha (Sall. *Iug.* 29.3, 32.1, but cf. 15.4). Cf. the brief portrait of the elder Scaurus in Sall. *Iug.* 15.4; for an analysis of Sallust's picture of Scaurus as lacking in political principle, see A.R. Hands, *JRS* 49 (1959) 56-60.

18.15-16: *inter patronos causarum*

All that is known of Scaurus' oratory is his successful prosecution of Cn. Cornelius Dolabella (26.17-18, 74.12; Cic. *Verr.* 2.1.97; Ps.-Ascon. 194.6-7), his successful defence of C. Cato (mentioned here), and his speech in defence of himself in this case (20.18, 28.15-16). No comment is made on his ability. Cf. Malcovati, *ORF*[2], pp. 431-3.

18.17: *pro C. Catone*

C. Porcius Cato, as tribune in 56, supported Clodius, at the prompting of Crassus, in conflict with both Milo and Pompeius, and in particular he opposed Lentulus Spinther's claims (which Cicero supported) to the job of restoring Ptolemy Auletes (Cic. *fam.* 1.2.4, 5a.2, 5b.2, *Q.f.* 2.3.3-4). After the conference of Luca, he became reconciled to Pompeius and held up the consular elections in his and Crassus' interests (Liv. *per.* 105; Dio 39.27.3). In 54 he was prosecuted for his part in the turbulence involved in delaying the elections — once under the *lex Iunia Licinia* (a consular law of 62 requiring copies of all proposed legislation to be deposited in the *aerarium*: references in *MRR* 2.173), in which he was acquitted (Cic. *Att.* 4.16.5), and again under the *lex Fufia* (on this law, usually associated with the *lex Aelia*, see above on 8.19). The prosecutors, possibly at the second trial (SB *Att.* 2.208, cf. 201-2), were Asinius Pollio and C. Licinius Calvus (Sen. *contr.* 7.4.7); contra, J. Linderski in *Studi in onore di Edoardo Volterra* (Milan, 1969) Vol. II, pp. 296-8, who thinks that Asinius Pollio was prosecutor at the first trial and that Calvus spoke for the defence. Cato was acquitted at the second trial also, as Cicero had predicted (*Att.* 4.16.5), possibly through collusion (SB *Att.* 2.201-2); the date given by Cicero for his second acquittal (*Att.* 4.15.4: *a.d. III Non. Quint.*) brings it closely into line with Asconius' date for his acquittal, and it seems reasonable to assume that it was at the trial under the *lex Fufia* that Scaurus spoke in Cato's defence. The text of Cicero should be emended to *a.d. IIII* (as it usually is) on the basis of Asconius' date; though one of the mss. of Asconius (P) does have the reading *a.d. III*, the reading of the other two mss. is clearly correct in view of Asconius' later comment (19.5-6) that Cato was acquitted two days before 6th July.

18.18: *ad consulatus petitionem*

At the time of Scaurus' returning to stand for the consulship, it was

122   Commentary

thought that the elections for the consulship would soon be held (cf. 19.10-11); as it turned out, political manoeuvrings and scandals caused a string of postponements, and the elections were not held until July 53, a full year late (for the details, see Gruen, *Hommages à Renard* [Brussels, 1969] Vol. II, pp. 315-21). The candidates were two patricians, Scaurus and M. Valerius Messalla Rufus, and two plebeians, C. Memmius and Cn. Domitius Calvinus (Cic. *Att*. 4.16.6). The view of Cadoux (in *MRR Suppl*. p. 19) that the *lex Licinia* requiring that one of the consuls be plebeian had been repealed (or was obsolete) by the first century B.C. seems disproved by Cicero's comments at *Att*. 4.16.6 and *Scaur*. 34 (cf. SB *Att*. 2.202, and *MRR* 2.30 n. 3). Scaurus and Memmius were (initially, at any rate) supported by Pompeius and Caesar, and their rival candidates by enemies of Pompeius (Cic. *Att*. 4.15.7); eventually Messalla and Calvinus were elected.

18.19-20: *P. Valerio Triario*

Triarius was the son of the praetor of 78 (see next comment). He presumably had been approached to undertake the prosecution of Scaurus because of his inherited family connections with the Sardinians, whom his father had governed (cf. Cic. *Scaur*. 29). After failure in his prosecution of Scaurus on the charge of extortion (Cic. *Att*. 4.16.6, 17.5), Triarius undertook a prosecution of Scaurus again on a charge of electoral malpractice towards the end of the same year (Cic. *Att*. 4.17.5); App. *BC* 2.24 says this trial took place in 52 (accepted by Gruen, *Last Generation*, p. 348). This time, though Scaurus was again defended by Cicero, he was condemned and vanished into exile. There seems to have been a competition between Triarius and L. Iulius Caesar, son of the consul of 64, for the right to prosecute Scaurus on the *ambitus* charge (Cic. *Att*. 4.17.5), but it was Triarius who eventually undertook it apparently (*Q.f.* 3.2.3). On Triarius' friendly relations with Cato, see below on 19.21-25; Cicero was on friendly terms with the whole family, especially with Triarius' brother Gaius (*Att*. 12.28.3).

19.1-2: *filio eius qui ... L. Luculli fuerat*

Scaurus' prosecutor was the son of C. Valerius Triarius, who is usually taken to have been propraetor in Sardinia in 77 (*MRR* 2.91, wrongly given the *praenomen* L., but corrected in *Suppl*. p. 66) where he opposed the attempt of Lepidus to take refuge. On the basis of that governorship, he is usually assigned a praetorship in 78 (*MRR*. 2.86, again with the wrong *praenomen* subsequently corrected; cf. Wiseman, *New Men*, p. 269 nos. 458-9). His grant of citizenship to a Sardinian is mentioned in Cic. *Scaur*. 29. He served as a legate under Lucullus in the war against Mithridates from 73 to 67 (*MRR* 2.113, 120, 125, 130, 134, 141 and 148), mostly as a successful commander of the fleet of Lucullus in the Aegean and Black

Seas. His brother had been *quaestor urbanus* in 81. The family is not to be linked to the patrician Valerii; it may have originated from Fundi (Wiseman, loc. cit., based on *ILLRP* 604).

19.3: *postulatus [est]*

For a description of procedure in criminal trials, see Greenidge, *Legal Procedure*, pp. 459ff.

19.3-4: *M. Catonem praetorem repetundarum*

Having failed to secure election to a praetorship for 55 at the elections postponed to the beginning of that year, through the machinations of the 'first triumvirate' (Cic. *Q.f.* 2.7.3; Plut. *Cat. Min.* 42.1-5, *Pomp.* 52.2; Dio 39.32.1-3), Cato secured election to that office for the following year, and was obviously put in charge of the extortion court. The only other case we know over which he presided was that of Gabinius (Cic. *Q.f.* 3.1.15).

19.6: *subscripserunt*

An accuser could enlist *subscriptores* of his own choice (except that the court in a *divinatio* could assign one of the rejected accusers as *subscriptor* to his successful rival), usually up to the number of three. See Jones, *Criminal Courts*, pp. 63-4, and for a list of cases where the number of *subscriptores* is known, ibid. p. 129 n. 121.

19.6-7: *L. Marius L.f.*

Nothing else is known of this man (apart from what Asconius tells us here and at 29.3-6), unless he is to be identified with the quaestor of 50 who succeeded Sallustius (Cic. *fam.* 2.17.5; cf. Münzer, *RE* 14 [1930] 1810, 1817-8, s.v. 'Marius' nos. 4 and 20). He may have been the son (or at least the kinsman) of L. Marius, a tribune of 62, who co-operated with Cato, also tribune in that year (Val. Max. 2.8.1) and who in the next year served with Ser. Sulpicius Galba under C. Pomptinus in Gaul (Dio 37.48.1). Galba, as praetor in 54, eventually secured a triumph for Pomptinus. The mss. reading *Q.* for Marius' *praenomen* should be changed to *L.*

19.7: *[M.] et Q. Pacuvii fratres cognomine Claudii*

There is some dispute over the form of the *cognomen*. The mss. reading *Claudii* is accepted, e.g., by Stangl (cf. *Philologus* 69 [1910] 498), by Giarratano, and by Gruen, *Last Generation*, p. 333 n. 109 (who sees emendation as unnecessary and who wishes to use the mss. form to suggest that the Pacuvii were clients of Ap. Claudius: cf. E. Francken, *Mnemosyne* n.s. 11 [1883] 379). But others have questioned whether one can accept a *cognomen* Claudius (e.g. E. Courtney, *Philologus* 105 [1961] 154; D.R. Shackleton Bailey, *AJP* 96 [1975] 442; E. Rawson,

Historia 26 [1977] 348-9): for that reason Clark has printed *Claudi* (from Claudus), following Manutius (cf. *TLL* Onomasticon 481.12), while others have emended to *Caldi* (see Stangl's apparatus). It would be appropriate if the *cognomen* could be taken to connect these *subscriptores* with Ap. Claudius, consul in the year of this prosecution: his brother, C. Claudius Pulcher, currently governor of Asia, apparently desired the consulship of 53 but, as only one patrician could be elected, it was important to damage Scaurus' chances, or to eliminate him altogether by a conviction, hence Ap. Claudius promoted the prosecution (Cic. *Scaur.* 31-37; cf. Schol. Ambros. 275.15-23). C. Claudius withdrew his candidature, however, his command in Asia being prorogued into 53. Ap. Claudius did not lose interest in the case; he and his colleague in office, L. Domitius Ahenobarbus, concocted a scheme with two other candidates, Memmius and Calvinus, to secure their election and thus guarantee proconsular commands desired by themselves (Cic. *Att.* 4.17.2, cf. 15.7 and *Q.f.* 2.14 [15b].3), and so he pressed on with the prosecution of Scaurus to ruin his chances, and to promote those of Memmius and Calvinus.

19.8-9: *inquisitionis . . . dies tricenos*

In *repetundae* cases the prosecutor was allowed a longer period for the *inquisitio*; here, thirty days in each of Sardinia and Corsica. For the prosecution of Verres, Cicero was allowed 110 days (*Verr.* 2.1.30), though he used only half that allotment.

19.9: *neque profecti sunt ad inquirendum*

Asconius recognises the real reason: Scaurus' political opponents wanted to get the trial on before the consular elections (which were thought to be about to be held), for if Scaurus was successful at the elections, he would be immune from prosecution as consul-designate on any charge except electoral malpractice (D.R. Shackleton Bailey, *Phoenix* 24 [1970] 172-5; contra, E.J. Weinrib, *Phoenix* 22 [1968] 51ff., and 25 [1971] 145-50). In the defence speech, Cicero suggests other reasons for Triarius' failure to visit Sardinia to collect evidence (i.e. the Sardinians did not wish him to discover that the stories they told of Scaurus' misconduct were untrue: *Scaur.* 23-28), but privately he shows his awareness of the real reason (*Att.* 4.15.9: *fortasse accedent etiam consules designati; in quibus si Scaurus non fuerit, in hoc iudicio valde laborabit*).

19.12-13: *sicut pater eius fecisset*

It is difficult to find a prosecution of Scaurus' father which provides the sort of parallel suggested by Asconius here. He was prosecuted in association with an electoral campaign in 116 by P. Rutilius Rufus, a rival candidate at the consular elections in that year, but that was after Scaurus' success in securing the consulship for 115 (i.e. it was not brought on before the elections to hinder his candidature) and the case dealt with electoral malpractice (Cic. *Brut.* 113, *de or.* 2.280; cf. Tac. *ann.* 3.66, with Badian, *Studies*, pp. 106-7), a charge from which Scaurus would not be immune even if he were a designated magistrate. The prosecution of Scaurus by M. Iunius Brutus (Cic. *Font.* 38) has greater possibilities as the parallel. Two fragments of a speech delivered by Scaurus in his own defence *contra M. Brutum de pecuniis repetundis* survive (*ORF*^{2}, pp. 166-7). Charisius, in whose work the two brief fragments are quoted, specifically records it as a case of extortion, and that is confirmed by its association with three other well known cases in Cicero's reference to it in the *pro Fonteio*. Because it was an extortion trial, it is usually associated with Scaurus' only known command, that as consul in 115 against some Gallic and Ligurian tribesmen (for which he celebrated a triumph: Degrassi, *Inscr. Ital.* 13.1.84f. and 561), and therefore usually dated to 114 (Bloch, pp. 26-7, followed by Malcovati, *ORF*^{2}, p. 166, and Gruen, *Politics and Courts*, p. 125). There is no reason, however, not to associate the prosecution with a praetorian command. Unfortunately we do not know even the date of his praetorship, let alone whether he exercised a command during or after that office. The phrase *praetor adversus Iugurtham* in *vir. illus.* 72.4 should not be pressed too far; it is probably a mistake resulting from a compression of praetorship in one year, and criticism of Jugurtha in senatorial debates in a subsequent year (cf. Sall. *Cat.* 15.4f.; Sumner, *Orators*, p. 69). The latest possible date for his praetorship would have been 119, since he stood (unsuccessfully) for the consulship of 116; Sumner, loc. cit., argues convincingly for a praetorship in 119. If Asconius is right in suggesting a parallel between Scaurus and his father, we should look for a *repetundae* case resulting from a praetorian command and brought on for political reasons because of a bitterly fought consular election. The prosecution of Scaurus' father by Brutus might fit: it was a *repetundae* case, and it could just as easily have been brought on in 117 when the electoral contest was bitter (or even in 116 when Scaurus stood again and when the elections were even more bitterly contested). Brutus is described by Cicero as a professional *accusator* (*Brut.* 130, *Cluent.* 141, *off.* 2.50), so there is no problem in having him launch a prosecution earlier than the usual date given; nor is there any difficulty in having a gap between praetorian command (if Scaurus' praetorship was earlier than 119, a distinct possibility in view of his family's lack of success for three generations: see 23.5-8) and prosecution in 117 or 116 (for similar gaps in extortion cases, often for political reasons, see B.A. Marshall, *Athenaeum* 54 [1976] 122 n. 21). For further discussion of the parallel case, see Marshall, *AJP* 98 (1977) 417-9.

19.16: *fiduciam in paterni nominis dignitate*

For the standing of Scaurus' father, see above on 18.6 and cf. below,

20.20-21. For Cicero's appeal to the family name, see *Scaur.* 13, 45-47, and the fragments of the speech preserved in Ascon. 21.1-2, 21.14-17, 22.2-4, 22.22-26, and August. frag. a (in *OCT*). In mentioning in a letter written early in July 54 that Triarius had initiated the prosecution, Cicero says that the memory of Scaurus' father carried weight with the country voters (*Att.* 4.16.6; cf. Val. Max. 8.1.10).

19.16-17: *magnam in necessitudine Cn. Pompeii Magni*

As Asconius goes on to explain, Scaurus married Mucia Tertia after Pompeius had divorced her on his return from the East (Cic. *Att.* 1.12.3) and he had a son by this marriage who was therefore a *frater* of Pompeius' children. Pompeius' only known children from his five marriages are the two sons and a daughter he had by his third wife Mucia, to whom he was married for about twenty years (cf. Suet. *Iul.* 50). There was a further family connection, not mentioned by Asconius here, in that Pompeius' second wife Aemilia was Scaurus' sister; they were the children of the marriage of Scaurus the elder to Caecilia Metella and subsequently the step-children of Sulla (see above on 18.7). Aemilia was first married to M'. Acilius Glabrio (later cos. 67) but was divorced from him and married to Pompeius at the suggestion of Sulla, though pregnant to Glabrio at the time; she died in childbirth the same year (82), and Pompeius then married Mucia, also a Metellan connection (see below). There were not only family links; Scaurus had earlier served under Pompeius in Syria, remaining on there as proquaestor propraetor (*MRR* 2.163 and 168; cf. G.W. Bowersock, *JRS* 65 [1975] 182). A noticeable feature of this trial is the complex familial connections of Sullans and Pompeians among Scaurus' defence counsel (see below on 28.7ff.). Initially Pompeius seems to have supported Scaurus' candidature for the consulship, but by the end of July 54 seems to have begun to cool towards him (Cic. *Att.* 4.15.7; cf. Gruen, *Last Generation*, p. 148); in this trial he supported Scaurus by sending in a *laudatio* (28.7ff).

19.18-19: *Tertiam, Scaevolae filiam*

On Mucia, especially her relationship to Metellus Celer (cos. 60) and Metellus Nepos (cos. 57), see below on 63.13-14. Her father is usually taken to be the consul of 98, and the Tertia usually taken to denote that she was the third daughter of his marriage. On the use of numerals to indicate the order of birth of females, see H. Petersen, *TAPA* 93 (1962) 349-50, followed by W.C. McDermott, *Phoenix* 24 (1970) 40-3 (mainly on P. Clodius' sisters); T.W. Hillard, *Latomus* 32 (1973) 505-14 (also on Clodius' sisters) is more cautious.

19.19: *dimissam a Pompeio*

Mucia is said to have 'played around' during Pompeius' absence in the

Pro Scauro

East; he is said not to have believed the reports of her misconduct while he was away, but as soon as he landed in Italy he sent her a bill of divorce. According to Plut. *Pomp.* 42.7 he did not give a reason then or later, but Suet. *Iul.* 50 records the belief that Mucia was one of Caesar's 'conquests', and the story that Pompeius remarked a number of times that Caesar was his Aegisthus (that he gave a reason, cf. below, 20.1-2). The divorce took place towards the end of 62, for Cicero remarks on it in a letter written on 1st January 61, which suggests that it was recent (*Att.* 1.12.3).

19.21: *propter amicitiam*

This is the only reference we have to Flaminia (see Münzer, *RE* 6 [1909] 2503) and to the friendship which she and her son had with Servilia, stepsister of Cato and mother of Brutus. For a stemma showing the relationship between the last three, see Münzer, *RA*, p. 282; cf. Badian, *Studies*, pp. 40-3. Despite the friendly relations with Triarius, Cato is said to have conducted the trial with impartiality (20.5-6, cf. 29.1-4).

19.24-25: *maternam . . . auctoritatem*

Cf. the story that Cato did not proceed with his threat to prosecute D. Iunius Silanus for electoral corruption in 63 because he was married to Servilia (Plut. *Cat. Min.* 21.3-4), and the reaction of the women in Cato's family to his rejection of a marriage link with Pompeius (ibid. 30.3-8, *Pomp.* 44.2-4), and the claim that she could have a *senatus consultum* changed (Cic. *Att.* 14.11.1-3; cf. SB *Att.* 6.259). On Servilia's *auctoritas*, see Münzer, *RA*, p. 362, and D. Stockton, *Cicero: a Political Biography* (Oxford, 1971) p. 286.

20.2: *crimine impudicitiae*

Cf. above on 19.19.

20.4: *necessitudinis . . . liberos*

Cf. above on 19.16-17.

20.8: *frater ex eadem matre*

Faustus Cornelius Sulla was the son of the dictator's marriage to Caecilia Metella; her first marriage was to M. Aemilius Scaurus (cos. 115), and from that marriage there were two children, Scaurus and Aemilia (who was Pompeius' second wife): see above on 19.16-17. Faustus Sulla supported Scaurus at his trial (28.12-13); his sister Fausta was married to C. Memmius, the other candidate for the consulship who was being supported by Pompeius and Caesar, until a few months before the trial, and their son appeared on behalf of Scaurus (28.20-23).

20.10: *competitoribus Scauri*

I.e. Messalla and Calvinus. This is our only evidence that actual violence was involved in the competition for the consulship this year; otherwise we are told of scandalous deals and flagrant outlays of cash, so that finally all four candidates were charged with *ambitus*.

20.13: *sex patroni*

There was at this time no legal limit to the number of *patroni* that a defendant could brief; later a maximum was fixed. Before Scaurus' trial the number had rarely exceeded four, but he created a precedent by having six, which was followed by Milo (34.15-17). The number later rose sometimes to twelve (Greenidge, *Legal Procedure*, pp. 392 and 476). In addition to the large number of *patroni*, Scaurus spoke on his own behalf, nine consulars (including two of the *patroni*) sent in *laudationes* (28.7ff.), and another ten supporters were present to entreat the jury on behalf of the defendant. In all, twenty-three individuals supported Scaurus: for an analysis of the reasons for this large attendance, see below on 28.16-24.

20.15: *legem Iuliam*

Giarratano, n. ad loc., says that this was the judiciary law of Caesar passed in 46 (citing Cic. *Phil.* 1.20; Suet. *Iul.* 41; Dio 43.25.1; Gell. 14.2.1), but all we know of that law is that it dealt with the *decuriae* composing the jury-panels. Jones, *Criminal Courts*, p. 64, prefers a law of Augustus, presumably the judiciary law of 17 B.C., which regulated a wide range of matters associated with the courts (references in G. Rotondi, *Leges publicae populi romani* [Milan, 1912] pp. 448-50). In 52 Pompeius' judiciary laws are said to have restricted the number of *patroni* (see below on 36.10).

20.16: *hi sex*

Four of the *patroni* were at the top of the oratorical profession — Cicero, Hortensius, Calidius and Marcellus. The standing of the first two needs no description. Calidius was praetor in 57 (on the date see Sumner, *Orators*, pp. 147-8); he appeared in the case of Cicero's house (Quint. 10.1.23), and for Gabinius and Scaurus in 54 (Cic. *Q.f.* 3.2.1), and for Milo in 52 (34.17); he prosecuted Q. Gallius for *ambitus* (see below on 88.5) and was subsequently prosecuted for *ambitus* himself by the Gallii after failure at the consular elections for 51 (details in Gruen, *Last Generation*, pp. 269-70). On his oratorical strengths and weaknesses, see Cic. *Brut.* 274-278, and cf. *ORF*[2], pp. 433-8, and SB *Att.* 3.314. M. Claudius Marcellus was praetor no later than 54, and consul in 51; on his oratorical ability, see the brief statement in Cic. *Brut.* 248. The remarkable feature about P. Clodius' appearance, apart from his lengthy speech (Cic. *Scaur.* 37), is that he stood at the side of two of his most implacable enemies, Cicero and Milo (the latter also appeared on Scaurus' behalf — 28.21-22). Clodius also appeared on the same side as L. Cornelius Lentulus Niger (28.19) who had previously assisted in the prosecution of Clodius in 61 (Cic. *har. resp.* 37; Schol. Bob. 89.26). The other *patronus* of Scaurus, M. Valerius Messalla Niger, had a distinguished career (pr. by 64, cos. 61, *interrex* 55, cens. 55, *interrex* 53 and 52); he was not so much outstanding for oratorical ability as for hard work in his court appearances (Cic. *Brut.* 246).

20.19-20: *aedilitatis effusae memoria*

On Scaurus' aedilician games, see above on 18.9-10. In relation to this trial, Cicero says that Scaurus' aedileship was not ungratefully remembered (*Att.* 4.16.6).

21.3: *consul... cum [C.] Cassio*

Cn. Domitius Ahenobarbus and C. Cassius Longinus were consuls in 96.

21.4: *tribunus plebis*

On the date of Ahenobarbus' tribunate, see below on 80.18-19 and 81.7. One of his colleagues in that office was a distant relative of the man he shared the consulship with, L. Cassius Longinus: for a stemma of the Cassii Longini, see Sumner, *Orators*, p. 50, and for the links between them and the Domitii Ahenobarbi, see Gruen, *Politics and Courts*, p. 173. Both tribunes undertook prosecutions of Metellan connections. Apart from the prosecution mentioned here of Scaurus, who was the leader of the Metellan group, Ahenobarbus also prosecuted M. Iunius Silanus, a Metellan connection, for his failure against the Cimbri (see below on 80.20-22); Longinus sponsored a law expelling from the senate anyone whose *imperium* had been taken away by people, a measure chiefly directed at Q. Servilius Caepio, the most spectacular of the senatorial failures, and also a Metellan connection (see below on 78.11-16). In addition to taking advantage of popular dissatisfaction with senatorial commanders, these two tribunes seem to have been using factional rivalry in their legal proceedings.

21.4-5: *quod eum in augurum collegium non cooptaverat*

Suet. *Nero* 2.1 says that Ahenobarbus was angered by the pontiffs during his tribunate because they did not co-opt him to fill the place left vacant by the death of his father, and so he transferred the right of filling vacancies in the priestly colleges from co-option by the colleges themselves to popular election (cf. Cic. *leg. ag.* 2.17-19). The question is — who is right, Asconius or Suetonius, about the college to which Scaurus belonged?

R.M. Geer, *Class. Phil.* 24 (1929) 292-4, sees the accounts of the rejection of Ahenobarbus and the prosecution of Scaurus as closely linked, and argues that Scaurus was a pontiff (and so that it was the college of pontiffs who refused to co-opt Ahenobarbus, and that Asconius is wrong) for two reasons: one, that the charge brought against Scaurus by Ahenobarbus was one more naturally brought against a pontiff than an augur, since the pontifical college was concerned with the cult of the Penates at Lavinium (G. Wissowa, *Religion und Kultus der Römer* [Munich, 1912] p. 518), and two, that Ahenobarbus' grandfather was a pontiff (Liv. 42.28.13) and it was not unusual for son to succeed father in a priestly college (though we do not have evidence other than Suetonius for what college Ahenobarbus' father belonged to). L.R. Taylor, *AJP* 63 (1942) 409 n. 80, and W.C. McDermott, *Hermes* 97 (1969) 242 n. 2, accept Geer's arguments, and add that, according to a list of priests contained in *ILS* 9338, Scaurus was succeeded by a Cornelius Scipio Asiagenes at a time (88) when Sulla was already an augur and another Cornelius would probably have been excluded from that office (under the rule that no two people from the same *gens* could be members of the same college: Dio 39.17.1-2), which in turn suggests that Scipio Asiagenes succeeded Scaurus as pontiff (in *MRR* 1.562 n. 7; cf. B.W. Frier, *ANSMusN* 13 [1967] 111-8, and *Arethusa* 2 [1969] 187ff., using symbols on Sulla's coinage as evidence for his augurate earlier than 83).

E. Badian, *Arethusa* 1 (1968) 29-31, argues that Scaurus was an augur, countering Geer by saying that, although there is no evidence that the augural college was connected with the cult of the Penates, Scaurus may have had some individual connection with that cult, which would not contradict the possibility that he was an augur, or the charge may have had something to do with his consulship in 115 or censorship in 109, since higher magistrates conducted annual sacrifices to the Penates and to Vesta at Lavinium; that Asconius is generally more reliable than Suetonius, as the former shows by his careful research into the details of the voting at Scaurus' trial compared with the latter's confusion of Ahenobarbus with his father soon after the section referred to above; that, as we know Ahenobarbus was elected to a pontificate after the introduction of his law, it has to be supposed that another vacancy occurred in the college of pontiffs (if it had been from that body that Scaurus had secured his rejection); and that the argument that son often succeeded father in the same college is not strong, since we know that men tried to use their influence during their lifetime to get a son safely into another college (e.g. Cicero [*ad Brut.* 1.5.3] and Lentulus Spinther [Dio 39.17.1]). It may, however, be relevant to note that Scaurus' son became a member of the college of augurs. Badian also rejects the arguments based around Sulla's augurate, claiming that his coins do not show an augurate before 83 (cf. J.R. Fears, *Historia* 24 [1975] 597-8).

Frier, *Arethusa* 2 [1969] 190, is more cautious; for him the

Pro Scauro 131

contradiction between Asconius and Suetonius is still *sub iudice*. Sumner, *Orators*, pp. 98-100, accepts that Scaurus was an augur, and says that there is not necessarily a contradiction between Asconius and Suetonius, since the latter does not mention Scaurus; he tries to reconcile the two passages by postulating that Ahenobarbus was rejected by both the pontiffs and augurs in 104 (i.e. Suetonius indicates that Ahenobarbus was angry with the pontiffs for failing to co-opt him to his father's place as pontiff, and Asconius indicates that he was angry with Scaurus for failing to co-opt him to a vacant augurate) and that when subsequently the pontifex maximus, L. Caecilius Metellus Delmaticus, died in 103, he seized the opportunity to have himself elected to replace Delmaticus under the law he had introduced himself. This supposes three vacancies in the priestly colleges in the space of a year or two (when only two are known). As a further argument that Scaurus was an augur, Sumner says that Scaurus, who was inaugurated in 123 (*ILS* 9338), in accordance with the common practice whereby a deceased priest was replaced by a relative, may well have succeeded M. Aemilius Lepidus Porcina, who is last heard of as punished by the censors of 125 (*MRR* 1.510 and 511) and who was an augur.

The answer to the question whether Asconius is right or wrong remains uncertain. He is certainly capable of mistakes, and Badian's argument that he carefully researched the details of Scaurus' trial may not stand up under closer scrutiny (see below on 21.10 and 11). Either Asconius or Suetonius could be wrong, since it would obviously be a simple mistake to confuse one priestly college with another.

Sumner's argument (which is part of a longer argument in favour of dating Ahenobarbus' tribunate to 103 by spreading out over the years 104-3 the incidents mentioned here and at 80-81: see below on 80.18-19) tries to avoid the contradiction between Asconius and Suetonius by supposing one more vacancy in the priestly colleges than we know of (admittedly vacancies were common: on the high mortality of priests, see D.E. Hahm, *TAPA* 94 [1963] 75), but it would be simpler to have the incidents all take place in the one year and to date Ahenobarbus' tribunate to 104 (for which we have some evidence), to have only one vacancy in 104 (that of his father in the pontifical college), to have Scaurus as a pontiff secure his rejection from that college (i.e. Asconius has made a simple mistake), and to have Ahenobarbus then prosecute Scaurus and pass his law about election to the priestly colleges. The content of the *lex Domitia* is of no help in deciding the issue, as it provided for election to all four major priestly colleges.

An alternative is that Suetonius is wrong (and Velleius too about the date of Ahenobarbus' tribunate), and the following happened, all in 104: Ahenobarbus' father (an augur) died, but Scaurus secured the rejection of Ahenobarbus from the college of augurs; he retaliated by prosecuting

Scaurus and introducing the law about election to the priestly colleges; a vacancy occurred in the pontifical college (possibly due to the death of Delmaticus) to which Ahenobarbus was elected; soon after he was elected pontifex maximus. We do not know the date of Delmaticus' death; it is known only because Ahenobarbus was elected to replace him. The date of 103 is predicated on the notice in Liv. *per.* 67 about Ahenobarbus' election, combined with Velleius' date for his tribunate and law about the priestly colleges (but that date may be wrong). The position of pontifex maximus had been elective from at least the late third century B.C. (Taylor, *Class. Phil.* 37 [1942] 421-4) with the election, when required, held only once a year between the consular and praetorian elections (id. *AJP* 63 [1942] 388; cf. Cic. *ad. Brut.* 1.5.4, *fam.* 8.41). As Ahenobarbus' new law used the same electing body as for the position of pontifex maximus, it could well be that the vacancy in the pontifical college had to wait some months to be filled (and there would have been time for this suggested sequence of events to have taken place within one year) and that Ahenobarbus was then elected to fill it and the vacant position of pontifex maximus at the same time.

The last two paragraphs, of course, deal more with the question of the date of Ahenobarbus' tribunate. Even if all the incidents took place in one year, and not two as Sumner argues, that does not tell us which year — 104 or 103. There is any number of combinations which can be created by rearranging the sequence of events and conjecturing which author is right and which wrong, and which can be used to provide an answer to the augur/pontiff question and to the date of the tribunate.

21.5: *diem ei dixit apud populum*

There are other references to the trial (Cic. *reg. Deiot.* 31; Val. Max. 6.5.5; Plut. *inim. util.* 9 D with the roles of prosecutor and defendant reversed; Dio 27 frag. 92), but they are no help in solving the question of the date of Ahenobarbus' tribunate or the augur/pontiff question. They all refer to the story that, at the time of Ahenobarbus' prosecution of Scaurus, a slave of the latter came to Ahenobarbus offering to lay charges against his master, but Ahenobarbus refused to listen and ordered the slave to be arrested and returned to Scaurus. Plutarch and Valerius Maximus point to the *inimicitia* that existed between Scaurus and Ahenobarbus; in addition to personal reasons, factional rivalry may have played its part in this prosecution (see above on 21.4).

21.7-8: *sacra publica . . . quae Lavini fierent*

The pontifical college was concerned with the cult of the Penates at Lavinium (Wissowa, op. cit. p. 518), but if Scaurus was a pontiff, it is hard to see why he, and not the pontifex maximus, should have been personally blamed for any negligence of the cult (O. Seeck, *Rhein. Mus.* 56 [1913]

11). The higher magistrates too had certain responsibilities in connection with the cult; e.g. the consuls had to lead the procession to Lavinium (Wissowa, op. cit. pp. 527-8). So it may have been as censor or consul that Scaurus committed the offence, and not in his role as priest. Or again, if he were an augur, since the presence of an augur was normally required for the proper performance of any solemn ceremony, it is possible that on some occasion he had an official place in the proceedings, even if not in the ceremony, and that was the basis of the charge (Badian, *Arethusa* 1 [1968] 30 with n. 20), though the verb *fieri* at 21.9 suggests not a single incident but some general charge.

21.10-11: *a tribus tribubus . . . absolveretur*

Badian makes the point (art. cit. 30) that these figures reveal Asconius' careful research into the trial and the events surrounding it, and so his information on the priestly college to which Scaurus belonged is likely to be more trustworthy than the implication of Suetonius' evidence. It is not clear where Asconius would have been able to find information on tribal voting patterns in judicial assemblies; figures are also given for Ahenobarbus' prosecution of Silanus (two tribes, both named, voted for condemnation, and the rest for acquittal: 80.24-25), so some sort of record of figures must have been kept. But it is hard to see where totals for individual tribes would have been recorded; as a comparison, the separate tabulation of votes cast by the three *ordines* in the permanent courts was not made until 59 (see below on 28.25). There is no need to postulate detailed research by Asconius; the narrowness of Scaurus' acquittal, known and remarked on at the time, could have passed into fairly common knowledge and the comment on it could have been drawn by Asconius from his memory. Badian assumes (loc. cit.) that, in view of the closeness of the vote, Ahenobarbus must have had a sound case against Scaurus.

21.11: *pauca puncta*

Asconius' word for 'votes' here is (harmlessly) inaccurate. Prior to the introduction of secret ballot, each citizen delivered his vote orally to the *rogator* and a mark (*punctum*) was made with a sharp instrument by the *rogator* on a large wax tablet against the appropriate name or decision (Cic. *leg.* 3.33-34; E.S. Staveley, *Greek and Roman Voting and Elections* [London, 1972] p. 158). But after the introduction of secret voting, which began in 139 (see below on 78.5), the voter was issued with a ballot (*tabella*) which he marked himself. As Asconius is commenting on a trial before the people well after the introduction of secret ballot, he should not have used *puncta*. It is true that *punctum* continued to be used to mean 'vote' (e.g. Cic. *Mur.* 72, *Planc.* 54, *Tusc. disp.* 2.62), but only in regard to electoral votes, where the voter put a point against the name of the person he wished to vote for on a prepared ballot.

134   Commentary

21.16: *P. Rutilio damnato*

This suggests that Caepio's prosecution of Scaurus should be placed soon after Rutilius' condemnation, that is, in late 92 or 91, while the juries were still under the control of the equites before Livius Drusus' attempt to alter the composition of the juries (Gruen, *Politics and Courts*, p. 206), and during Drusus' tribunate (21.23-24).

21.18: *Q. Servilius Caepio*

Son of the consul of 106, who proposed the law which took away the exclusive equestrian control of the jury-courts and who went into exile following his condemnation for *maiestas* (for his failure against the northmen at Arausio in 105) in the court set up by Saturninus' law in 103 (sources in Greenidge and Clay[2], p. 78; cf. below on 78.14 and 79.8-9). Caepio and his law are to be distinguished from C. Servilius Glaucia, who also proposed a judiciary law (see below on 21.20); both laws are called *leges Serviliae*. There were links between the Servilii Caepiones and the Metellan group: Scaurus the elder, who was a member of the Metellan group, had once suffered bodily injury in defence of the elder Caepio, and Caepio the younger had married the sister of Livius Drusus, who in turn was married to Caepio's sister and who is shown to have had the backing of the Metelli during his tribunate in 91, since Scaurus was his chief adviser (on these links, see Badian, *Studies*, pp. 35-44). But Caepio the younger fell out with his Metellan connections; he broke with Livius Drusus, his friend and brother-in-law, in an obscure quarrel, and became the chief opponent of Drusus' tribunate; and he contracted an *inimicitia* with Scaurus, marked by the prosecution mentioned here and another under the *lex Varia* soon after (see 22.8-11). For further details and discussion, see Badian, loc. cit., and Gruen, *Historia* 15 (1966) 43-7.

21.18: *legationis Asiaticae*

The date and character of this *legatio* remain uncertain. As Caepio made it the basis of his prosecution, the latest possible date is 92 (not 93, as tentatively suggested by *MRR* 2.15 with n. 6, since the prosecution was in late 92 or 91), but the state of Scaurus' health in his latter years (cf. 22.10ff.) and the analogy with P. Rutilius Rufus (prosecuted in 92 for a legateship in Asia in 97: see above on 15.5-6) might suggest a date somewhat earlier. Val. Max. 3.7.8 says that Varius prosecuted Scaurus under his *lex de maiestate* for accepting a bribe from Mithridates during an Asian embassy (but he has clearly confused this prosecution with the subsequent one before the Varian commission, for he has got the prosecutor wrong and the cases heard under that law dealt with treason in relation to the Italian allies). Though the phrase *legatio Asiatica* and the analogy with Rutilius Rufus could suggest that Scaurus had once been on the staff of a governor of Asia, the evidence of Val. Max. suggests

Pro Scauro

membership of one of a number of embassies to Mithridates between 104 and 92, though this could leave a long gap between supposed offence and prosecution. Another, simpler, solution to the problem is put forward by M. Alexander, *TAPA* 111 (1981) 1-9: the phrase refers not to an embassy of which Scaurus was a member, but to the legateship of P. Rutilius in Asia under Q. Mucius Scaevola (the proximity of the phrase to the mention of Rutilius in the lemma could be said to make it grammatically clear), and that Caepio prosecuted Scaurus amid the general *invidia* stirred up by the case of Rutilius. For further discussion, see Bloch, pp. 30-3; Badian, *Athenaeum* 34 (1956) 120f. (who suggests 97-6 as the date); and Gruen, *Historia* 15 (1966) 56.

21.19-20: *reum fecit repetundarum*

Flor. 2.5.5 says that about this time Caepio singled out Scaurus and Philippus, the chief men of the nobility, and prosecuted them for *ambitus*. As L. Marcius Philippus became consul in 91, a charge of electoral malpractice seems acceptable; but there is no reason for a charge of *ambitus* in the case of Scaurus, and Florus could have in mind bribery during the *legatio Asiatica*. Cf. the account of the prosecution in Val. Max. 3.7.8 (preceding comment). Asconius' phrase *pecuniae captae* also suggests that the point of the charge was acceptance of bribes. The prosecution of Scaurus was supported by Cn. Cornelius Dolabella (26.9-11, 74.12). For further discussion of the trial, see Gruen, art. cit. 55-9.

21.20: *lege quam tulit Servilius Glaucia*

This law dealt with the re-establishment of equestrian control of the jury-courts in the *quaestio de rebus repetundis* after the *lex Servilia Caepionis* of 106, which took away full equestrian control. It was proposed by the tribune, C. Servilius Glaucia, either in 104 or 101: see J.P.V.D. Balsdon, *PBSR* 14 (1938) 102-6, and A.W. Lintott, *Zeitschrift der Savigny-Stiftung (Röm. Abt.)* 98 (1982) 189-91. In addition it effected two reforms in procedure: it provided for the recovery of funds not only from the immediate culprits but also from accomplices (Cic. *Rab. post.* 9), and introduced a compulsory adjournment (*comperendinatio* or *comperendinatus*) between *actio prima* and *actio secunda* (Cic. *Verr.* 2.1.26; Ps.-Ascon. 230-1). This law may also have provided for Latins who succeeded in a prosecution under it to receive Roman citizenship (Cic. *Balb.* 54, but cf. A.N. Sherwin-White, *JRS* 62 [1972] 92-7); but as Cicero describes the law making this provision as a very severe law promoted by the leading men of the state and the most responsible and prudent of citizens (words which he would hardly use of Glaucia and the populares), this provision may belong to the other *lex Servilia* (Jones, *Criminal Courts*, p. 53; cf. Badian, *CR* n.s. 4 [1954] 101-2; contra, B. Levick, *CR* n.s. 17 [1967] 256-8).

21.21-22: *Caepionem contra reum detulerit*

Scaurus countered Caepio's charge by launching a prosecution against him, presumably also on a charge of *repetundae* (though the basis of the charge is not known), and he arranged for Caepio's trial to be heard first. It is reasonably certain that Caepio's trial came to a result, since we have fragments of the speech delivered by Scaurus against Caepio which belong to the second *actio* (*ORF*², p. 167), and under the provision of *comperendinatio* (see preceding comment) the second *actio* closed the proceedings. Münzer, *RA*, p. 300, followed by *MRR* 2.24 n. 5, suggests that the charge against Caepio was *ambitus* for illegal canvassing for a praetorship of 91. This means that the trial would have to have taken place in 92, and in the December of that year, in view of the mention of the tribunate of Livius Drusus (i.e. after the latter had taken office). But the *actio secunda*, referred to in the fragments of Scaurus' speech, suggests a *repetundae* trial, since the arrangement of *comperendinatio* applied to *repetundae* trials. Further, we do not know the date of Caepio's praetorship. He must have held the office before the Social War, since he is included among the ex-curule magistrates serving as legates in that war; he could have been praetor in 92, since his quaestorship is to be dated to 103, rather than 100 (Badian, *Studies*, p. 35 with n. 9; Gruen, art. cit. 57 n. 151; cf. *MRR* 1.576).

21.23: *effecerit ut ille prior causam diceret*

It is not clear whether Scaurus' trial was ever brought to a conclusion. Gruen, art. cit. 57, suggests that the implication of this clause here is that Scaurus' case too came to trial, ending in an acquittal (like Caepio's, since both were about in subsequent years). Bloch, p. 30, argues, however, that Scaurus, having secured a delay by bringing the counter-charge against Caepio, urged Livius Drusus to reform the courts while his own case was pending, and that the case continued to be postponed until the death of Caepio when it was dropped. It is conceivable that such continued delay could be arranged in view of the changes to the composition of the jury-courts in the next few years and the suspension of the normal courts during the Social War (see below on 74.1-3).

21.24: *cohortatus sit ut iudicia commutaret*

On Drusus' programme as tribune in 91, which included a judiciary law, and the annulment of his legislation, see below on 69.1-5. Drusus' advisers, especially for the judiciary law, included Scaurus (see below on 69.2-3).

22.5: *Italico bello exorto*

On the outbreak of the Social War, see below on 68.1-5.

22.5-6: *cum ob sociis negatam civitatem . . . esset*

On the involvement of members of the nobility in the events which led up to the outbreak of the Social War, see below on 69.3-4 and 73.26-27. On the question whether the allies were really desirous of the citizenship, see below on 68.1.

22.6: *Q. Varius tr. pl.*

Varius was tribune in 90.

22.7-8: *legem tulit . . . sumpsissent*

Some of the *nobiles* who were prosecuted under the Varian law (for the list, see below on 73.26, and for the terms of the law, see Val. Max. 8.6.4 and App. *BC* 1.37) could hardly be guilty of assisting the Italian allies in their rebellion, since they seem to have had little sympathy with the allies' demand for citizenship (cf. above, 22.5-6) and to have supported measures directed against the allies, such as the *lex Licinia Mucia* of 95 (see below on 67.22-23). It is true that some, like Scaurus, had supported Livius Drusus' proposals (though not necessarily his proposal for Italian enfranchisement: see below on 69.3-4), but it is only in a negative way that they could be said to have caused the Italians to take up arms against Rome (i.e. their refusal to grant citizenship forced the Italians to rebel). The real motive for the early prosecutions under the Varian law seems to have been political: the opponents of Drusus used it to attack his supporters (cf. below on 73.26-27). For the subsequent developments in the use of the Varian court, and Varius' prosecution under his own law, see below on 74.1-3 and 79.9. On the apparent contradiction between the explanation for the introduction of the law and its subsequent operation, see Badian, *Historia* 18 (1969) 460. On the question whether the *lex Varia* set up a permanent or a special *quaestio*, see Gruen, *JRS* 55 (1965) 59-60, and R. Seager, *Historia* 16 (1967) 37-40.

22.9: *vetus inimicus Scauri*

That Caepio was an old enemy of Scaurus by 90 suggests a quarrel which goes back some time, probably to the mid-90's; it is probably connected with Caepio's falling out with the Metellan group (see above on 21.18). Caepio was one of the chief opponents of Drusus' tribunate, whereas Scaurus was one of Drusus' chief advisers.

22.11: *apud se*

The terminology used here is that of a trial *apud populum*; Varius as tribune required Scaurus to appear before himself, and Scaurus in his speech addresses the Quirites (22.18; cf. Val. Max. 3.7.8,). Yet the *lex Varia* set up a *quaestio*; Varius could not have been the president of that

138   Commentary

court and so we have an anomaly here regarding the prosecution of
Scaurus for inciting the allies to revolt. One theory is that Scaurus was put
on trial twice — once before the people at the instigation of Varius, and
subsequently before the Varian *quaestio*. But two trials on the same
charge would be absurd (after the charge had been dismissed the first
time), and Gruen's theory seems the most acceptable (art. cit. 62-3): the
incident described by Asconius here occurred at a *contio* summoned by
the tribune Varius, which was designed to arouse prejudice against
Scaurus for the forthcoming prosecution under the Varian law.

22.11: *anno LXXII*

Scaurus' birth-date would fall in 162-1. Sumner, *Orators*, p. 69, sees no
good reason for Kiessling and Schoell's change to *annorum*, though the
anno is a little unexpected.

22.12: *ex morbo*

Cf. Cic. *Rab. perd.* 21.

22.15: *accepto respondendi loco dixit*

A similar, but longer, statement is recorded in Val. Max. 3.7.8 (though he
has prosecutor and defendant around the wrong way, and associates
Scaurus' reply with the previous case relating to *repetundae*: see above on
21.18). For another version of Scaurus' speech, see *vir. ill.* 72.11, and for
the trial, see Cic. *Sest.* 101 and Quint. 5.12.10.

22.16: *Hispanus*

Varius seems to have had a variety of *cognomina* — Severus (in Val.
Max. 3.7.8), Sucronensis (in Val. Max. 3.7.8; Quint. 5.12.10; *vir. ill.*
72.11), and Hybrida (in Val. Max. 8.6.4). The latter was supposedly due
to doubts about the validity of his citizenship. The adjective used here by
Scaurus is a jibe at Varius' Spanish origins, manifest in his *cognomen*
Sucronensis (from the Spanish town of Sucro). That the account of this
trial came from Scaurus' autobiography, see Part I, p. 58.

22.16: *principem senatus*

See above on 18.6.

23.2-3: *quae generis claritas... provexit*

For the expectation of the patrician nobility that they would almost
automatically secure high office, note especially Cic. *Mur.* 15ff. and cf.
the comments of Catilina about the success of the unworthy Cicero in
beating him to a consulship in Sall. *Cat.* 31.7 and 35.3 (cf. below on 86.4-

5). But the majority of the fourteen patrician families still surviving from the fifty or so which existed in the early Republic were no longer in the forefront of the nobility (L.R. Taylor, *Party Politics in the Age of Caesar* [Berkeley, 1949] p. 26): e.g. Ser. Sulpicius Rufus, whose father was an eques and whose grandfather was not renowned for any outstanding deed, was annoyed at being defeated for the consulship by a man of less distinguished name, yet Cicero points out that his nobility had to be dug out of ancient records (*Mur.* 16; cf. M. Gelzer, *The Roman Nobility*, trans. R. Seager [Oxford, 1969] p. 32). And the example of Scaurus shows that promotion was not automatic.

23.6-7: *ut puto, propter tenues opes et nullam vitae industriam*

The first part of the explanation seems valid, for according to Val. Max. 4.4.11 (derived from the first book of Scaurus' own memoirs) Scaurus inherited only ten slaves and 35,000 HS, and according to the author of the *vir. illus.* 72.1 his father had had to become a charcoal seller because of poverty. Cf. I. Shatzman, *Senatorial Wealth and Roman Politics* (Brussels, 1975) pp. 263-4. The second part of the explanation is something of a contradiction with the statement at 23.2-3, that advancement even for *inertes patricii* was automatic. Cic. *off.* 1.138 says that Scaurus' father was distinguished. This part of the explanation for the family's lack of success is presumably mere supposition on the part of Asconius, perhaps from Cicero's speech itself (which at § § 45-46 concentrates on Scaurus' father and maternal grandfather). On Scaurus' family background, see Bloch, pp. 3-9.

23.7-8: *aeque ac novo homini*

Scaurus is compared to Q. Pompeius Rufus, a new man; both had the noble qualities of *animus* and *ingenium*, the one to achieve office and the other 'to revive the almost extinct memory of his family' (Cic. *Mur.* 16). Plut. *mor.* 318 C calls Scaurus a καινὸς ἄνθρωπος ἐκ ταπεινοῦ βίου καὶ ταπεινοτέρου γένους.

23.15: *L. hic Tubulus praetorius fuit*

L. Hostilius Tubulus was praetor in 142, and had been presiding officer of a *quaestio de sicariis*. On the question whether the *quaestio* was a permanent or a special one, see Gruen, *Politics and Courts*, pp. 29-30.

23.16-17: *is propter multa flagitia . . . venenum bibit*

Tubulus apparently accepted bribes in his conduct of the *quaestio de sicariis*, and he became a byword for iniquity and corruption (cf. 23.10-11 above, and Cic. *fin.* 2.54, 4.77, 5.62, *nat. deor.* 1.63 [= Lucil. 1312 M], 3.74, *Att.* 12.5b.3; Gell. 2.7.20). In the following year, he was prosecuted for bribery and corruption on the initiative of the tribune, P. Mucius Scaevola, who moved a *rogatio* to place the investigation in the hands of the senate, who in turn commissioned one of the consuls, Cn. Sevilius Caepio, to conduct the enquiry; anticipating the inevitable result, Tubulus went into exile. On the possible political implications of the trial, see Gruen, *Athenaeum* 43 (1965) 322-3. Asconius' report that he was recalled from exile in order to be killed in prison but forestalled his execution by taking poison is puzzling. No parallel can be found for the recall of an exile for a re-trial or to face a new charge, for Rome could have had no jurisdiction over an exile (Gruen, *Politics and Courts*, p. 30); hence the suggestion of Mommsen, *Strafrecht*, pp. 71 n. 1, 197 n. 2, 633 n. 4, that Tubulus was recalled to face a charge for an offence he had committed while in exile, is implausible. Moreover, it is hardly likely that Tubulus would answer a summons when he knew that it would involve imprisonment and execution. It is reasonable to assume that, as was customary, a decree of *aquae et ignis interdictio* was passed following Tubulus' voluntary exile, and as an exile he was forbidden to return on pain of death; if there is any truth in Asconius' report, it would be that Tubulus returned to Rome in defiance of the decree, was seized and sentenced to death, and took poison (Gruen, loc. cit.). But at face value, Asconius' statement contains too great a legal anomaly to be accepted, though there must be something behind his comment.

23.23: *hic Crassus fuit pater Crassi*

The lemma of Cicero, on which Asconius is here commenting, and the next lemma belong to the fragmentary beginning of Cicero's speech; and the lemma after that (24.21-23) occurs at the beginning of the text of the *pro Scauro* as we have it, where there is a discussion of honourable suicides. As the headings of the fragments given in some of the mss. of Asconius indicate that all three passages came close together and therefore in the context of that discussion, in identifying the Crassi mentioned we should look for honourable suicides. For the identifications, see Marshall, *Latomus* 35 (1976) 91-6.

23.24: *periit autem in dominatione L. Cinnae*

One version of the death of P. Crassus (cos. 97) is that he committed suicide during the Marian terror in 87 (Cic. *Sest.* 48, *de or.* 3.10; Liv. *per.* 80); this is the version consistently followed by Cicero. Others say that he was executed along with his elder son by Fimbria (Luc. 2.125; Plut. *Crass.* 4.1; Flor. 2.9.14; Aug. *civ. dei* 3.27); others merely list father and son among those killed in the Marian terror (Cic. *Tusc.* 5.55; Diod. Sic. 37.29.5; Schol. Gronov. 286.10); App. *BC* 1.72 has the version that Crassus killed his son to anticipate their pursuers and was himself killed by them. For a favourable re-assessment of Cinna's *dominatio*, see E.

Badian, *JRS* 52 (1962) 46-61 (= *Studies*, pp. 206-34), and C.M. Bulst, *Historia* 13 (1964) 307-37.

23.25: *alios principes optimatum*

For a list of some of those killed, see 25.4ff.

23.25-26: *collegam suum Cn. Octavium*

Octavius and Cinna were colleagues in the consulship of 87. For the references to Octavius' attempt to block Cinna's takeover of the state and his death, see *MRR* 2.46. The Crassus being discussed in this comment by Asconius had served as a legate under Octavius against Cinna.

24.1-20: *STATIM . . . sed quaesitum ab aliis est*

The modern editions of Asconius, beginning with Kiessling and Schoell, who are followed by Stangl and Clark, wrongly report that Madvig wishes to delete the whole of this section, including the lemma of Cicero; Giarratano puts both lemma and comment inside square brackets, but does not say on whose suggestion the passage should be deleted. However, Madvig, pp. 78-81, merely wishes to delete Asconius' comment; he is followed by Rau, pp. 102-3. His reasons for removing the comment are that, if accepted, it would be the sole example of a grammatical comment by Asconius, that the writer of the comment seems unaware that Cicero frequently uses a disjunctive without a following one (and Asconius knew his Cicero too well to make that mistake), and that we should have expected a comment on M'. Aquilius, since all the other persons mentioned in these three passages of Cicero (i.e. P. Crassus, Crassus *superior*, the Iulii and M. Antonius) received a comment from Asconius. It is reasonable to assume, however, that Asconius included the lemma here and made some sort of comment on it, otherwise the first two sentences of his comment on the next lemma (especially *quia ante mentionem fecit P. Crassi*) would be meaningless. Those sentences too imply that the nature of the comment might have been other than historical, for he has left the identification of the Crassus in this lemma until then. It should be noted that Asconius does not always comment on everything mentioned in a lemma; e.g. in the next comment he says very little about M. Antonius, and at 78.1ff. he does not explain the *leges Porciae*. For discussion whether this passage should be deleted, see Marshall, art. cit. 94-6.

24.2: *Crassi . . . superioris*

He is identified more fully by Asconius in his comment on the next lemma (25.3-4). He is *superior* in the sense of being earlier than the P. Crassus used as an example of an honourable suicide in the preceding lemma

(23.19-22); the use of an earlier Crassus as an example was no doubt suggested to Cicero by his phrase *eiusdem stirpis et nominis* in the preceding lemma. There is one version of the death of Crassus Mucianus which makes him an honourable suicide (and so a suitable example for the discussion of such suicides with which our text of the *pro Scauro* begins): after he was captured in battle with Aristonicus, in order to avoid disgrace he provoked his Thracian guard to kill him by poking him in the eye with a stick (Val. Max. 3.2.12; Front. *strat.* 4.5.16; Flor. 1.35.4-5; Oros. 5.10.1-3).

24.4: *M'. Aquilius*

Cicero is contrasting the behaviour of Crassus Mucianus with a M'. Aquilius who attained the same *honores*, but whose conduct was not honourable. The reference is to the consul of 129; he took over from M. Perperna, who succeeded Crassus Mucianus, in the command against Aristonicus, completing the mopping-up operations and organising the province of Asia. According to Flor. 1.34.7, Aquilius hastened the end of the war by the wicked conduct of poisoning the springs around some towns to secure their surrender, thus bringing shame on his victory and disgrace on Roman arms. Florus specifically draws the contrast with Mucianus' honourable conduct, suggesting that there was a traditional contrast between them which Cicero has here followed.

24.7: *coniunctio disiunctiva*

The combination *neque . . . neque* is not a disjunctive conjunction, but a co-ordinating conjunction (H.J. Roby, *Latin Grammar*, Part II, § 2216, compared with § 2235). Asconius (or whoever wrote this comment, if it is not genuine) is confused here: he becomes involved in explaining the absence of a second *neque*, when he should be concerned with the unusual combination *ac neque*.

24.10-11: *illam appositionem*

That this is an instance of the use of the word in the meaning 'addition' (overlooked in some lexicons), see Marshall, *Glotta* 53 (1975) 292-3.

24.15-16: *sic, inquam, . . . quaesitum ab aliis est*

Most editors place this fragment immediately before the fragment recorded at 23.19-22, i.e. just before the text of the *pro Scauro* as we have it begins.

24.23-24: *summo ingenio praeditus M. Antonius*

The lemma as quoted in Asconius has *ingenio*, while the ms. of Cicero has *imperio*. Either would suit: *ingenium* would describe Antonius' ability as

Pro Scauro

an orator, while *imperium* would refer to his command against pirates in Cilicia which he held as praetor in 102 and as *praetor pro consule* in 101-100 and for which he celebrated a triumph. It is clear that the M. Antonius referred to is the famous orator who was consul in 99 and censor in 97, since he was a contemporary of the 'other Crassus' (i.e. the consul of 97 who is referred to in the passage at 23.19ff.; cf. 25.1-4).

25.1: *hic alter Crassus*

Asconius makes it clear that in the lemma just quoted Cicero is returning to the example of the Crassus referred to in the passage at 23.19ff., and has used *alter* to avoid confusion with the Crassus mentioned in the passage at 24.2-4. This confirms that the Crassus mentioned in the earlier passage is the consul of 97, since he was a contemporary of two Iulii and a M. Antonius killed during the Marian terror.

25.3-4: *qui fuit pontifex maximus . . . ut occideretur*

P. Licinius Crassus Dives Mucianus was elected pontifex maximus on the death of P. Cornelius Scipio Nasica Serapio in 132 (Cic. *Phil.* 11.18; Liv. *per.* 59). As consul in 131, he desired the command against Aristonicus and, as pontifex maximus, he prevented his consular colleague, L. Valerius Flaccus, who was also *flamen Martialis*, from taking up the command, disregarding any religious restriction on himself. He paid the penalty for his *avaritia* with his death in the campaign (Justin. 36.4.8; cf. Liv. *per.* 59, and Vell. Pat. 2.4.1 — versions which have him killed in battle by Aristonicus, and not those which tell of an honourable death). Further on these events, see Marshall, *AJP* 95 (1974) 64-6, and above on 24.2 and 4.

25.5-6: *Lucius et consul et censor fuit*

L. Iulius Caesar was consul in 90 and censor in 89. As consul he had command generally in the south against the rebellious allies, where he was finally successful; he proposed the law granting citizenship to the Latins and Italians who had not taken up arms or who laid them down in good time (Vell. Pat. 2.16.4; App. *BC* 1.49). For the scope of the law, see A.N. Sherwin-White, *The Roman Citizenship*, 2nd edn. (Oxford, 1973) p. 148; contra, P.A. Brunt, *JRS* 55 (1965) 95. As censor, he and his colleague, P. Licinius Crassus, completed the *lustrum*, but without completing a census of the citizens (Cic. *Arch.* 11), so the new citizens were not enrolled in the thirty-five tribes. They did control the sale and prices of foreign wines and perfumes (Plin. *NH* 13.24, 14.95).

25.6: *Gaius aedilicius*

C. Iulius Caesar Strabo Vopiscus was aedile in 90.

25.6-8: *Gaius aedilicius . . . cum Sulpicio tr. fuerit*

P. Sulpicius, as Cic. *har. resp.* 43 shows, began his tribunate with the many ties he had with the optimates still intact, but within a short time he 'abruptly abandoned his former friends and political associates, sought to enact by force proposals to which they were strongly opposed, ended up as the ally of Marius, and died in Rome's first civil war, which his violent tactics had done much to precipitate' (T.N. Mitchell, *Class. Phil.* 70 [1975] 198). The reason for Sulpicius' volte-face has been the subject of debate, but it clearly had some link with his opposition to Caesar Stabo's attempt to stand for the consulship without having held the praetorship. Badian's view (*FC*, pp. 230-4, expanded in *Historia* 18 [1969] 481-90) is that in 89 Strabo was aiming at the consulship of 88 so as to secure the Mithridatic command, though his candidature was illegal, that Sulpicius began by defending the optimate cause in opposing Strabo's ambition but this drew him into association with Marius (who was contending with Strabo for the Mithridatic command) and that his alienation from the optimates was hastened by their refusal to proceed with the reform programme which had been evident in the tribunate of M. Livius Drusus, and which Sulpicius wished to continue. Gruen, *JRS* 55 (1965) 72, believes that Strabo was aiming in 88 for the consulship of 87 and that Sulpicius opposed him because he had already formed an alliance with Marius; he says that the reasons for Sulpicius' conversion are unfathomable, and that Cicero's statement that he opposed Strabo *ab optima causa* ought not to be pressed. Mitchell, art. cit. 198ff., argues convincingly that Strabo's candidature was not illegal (based on Cic. *Phil.* 11.11) and that he had been granted an exemption by the senate from the requirement of holding the praetorship; Sulpicius, in collaboration with a fellow-tribune, P. Antistius (Cic. *Brut.* 226-227), at first tried to block Strabo by arguing the legal case against accepting his candidature (cf. *iure* at 25.10), but this failed and in the continuance of the issue (which shows that Strabo continued to be a candidate [cf. *id agebat* at 25.8-9], and which in turn suggests that he did receive a senatorial exemption) Sulpicius and Strabo clashed violently; that Strabo received a senatorial exemption suggests that he had the backing of the optimates, and Sulpicius' opposition suggests that he had already begun to abandon the optimate cause, a process which was hastened when the rejection of his opposition was taken as an affront to his *dignitas*. The whole question hinges on the date of Strabo's candidature (see next comment).

25.9: *ut omissa praetura consul fieret*

The traditional view is that Strabo sought election in 88 for the consulship of 87. Diod. 37.2.12-13 is the relevant source: 'when the Marsic war was nearly over, the internal disputes that had earlier occurred in Rome were set in motion again, as many prominent men became rivals for the command against Mithridates in view of the rich prizes it offered. For C. Iulius and C. Marius ... were struggling against each other, and the people were divided in sentiment for one side or the other. Other disturbances took place as well. The consul Sulla, however, left Rome and joined the forces assembled around Nola.' Gruen, art. cit. 72, says that Diodorus is clear in placing the rivalry between Strabo and Marius for the Mithridatic command (which was connected with Strabo's candidature for the consulship) in Sulla's consulship, i.e. 88, that Sulpicius was used by Marius to block first Strabo and then Sulla, and that Sulpicius' conversion took place before his opposition to Strabo's candidature. Badian, *FC*, p. 231 and art. cit. 482-3, argues that Strabo made his bid for the consulship late in 89, just after Sulpicius had entered office; the only specific chronological reference in Diodorus is the near completion of the Social War (which he takes to refer to 89), and Sulla's consulship is placed after the rivalry of Strabo and Marius, and the 'other disturbances' (which he takes to refer to Sulpicius' activities); moreover, the consular elections in 89 would not have been held until December, as the sole surviving consul for that year, Cn. Pompeius Strabo, was in the field until November and unable to return to Rome to conduct the elections until the last weeks of the year, and with the elections delayed so long 'struggles for the consulship could be expected to be fierce.' The strongest argument against Badian's view is put by Lintott, *CQ* n.s. 21 (1971) 448-9, and Mitchell, art. cit. 201: it is difficult to see how the senate could have supported an irregular candidate (if Strabo tried to stand in 89) when there were already two 'good' candidates, Q. Pompeius Rufus and L. Cornelius Sulla, who were linked by *adfinitas* and who were particular favourites of the *boni*. For a further discussion of the date of Strabo's attempt to stand for the consulship (favouring Badian's arguments) and of the political background to his attempt, see B.R. Katz, *Rhein. Mus.* 120 (1977) 45-63, and A. Keaveney, *Latomus* 38 (1979) 451-60.

25.11-12: *idem inter primos temporis sui oratores*

For Strabo's oratorical standing, see Cic. *Brut.* 177, *de or.* 2.98; Vell. Pat. 2.9.2. He is said to have been comparable in standing to Sulpicius and C. Cotta at 66.20; cf. above on 14.20-21. Strabo had a reputation for humour (Cic. *de or.* 2.98). For a list of his speeches, see *ORF*[2], pp. 273-5.

25.12: *tragicus poeta bonus*

Of his tragedies, three titles and four lines survive (A. Klotz, *Scaenicorum Romanorum Fragmenta* [Munich, 1953] pp. 304-5). Cic. *de or.* 3.30 says that not even in his tragedies did he exclude wit and humour, and *Brut.* 177 says that they were marked by *lenitas*. Cf. Val. Max. 3.7.11.

146   Commentary

25.14-15: *et hi autem . . . sunt occisi*

The evidence for L. Iulius Caesar's death: Cic. *de or.* 3.9-10, *Tusc.* 5.55; Liv. *per.* 80; Val. Max. 9.2.2. For C. Iulius Caesar Strabo's death: Cic. *Brut.* 307, *de or.* 3.10, *Tusc.* 5.55; Liv. *per.* 80; Val. Max. 5.3.3; App. *BC* 1.72; he had fled to Tarquinium to escape the slaughter following Marius' return. For M. Antonius' death: Cic. *Brut.* 307, *de or.* 3.10, *Tusc.* 5.55, *Phil.* 1.34; Liv. *per.* 80; Val. Max. 8.9.2, 9.2.2; Vell. Pat. 2.22.3; Luc. 2.121-124; Plut. *Mar.* 44.1-7, *Ant.* 1.1; App. *BC* 1.72; Flor. 2.9.14; Dio 45.47; Schol. Gronov. 286.9; he too had fled and went into hiding until his whereabouts were betrayed by a slave who had been sent out to buy some wine. The only accomplice that is known in these three cases is P. Annius who delivered the *coup de grâce* to M. Antonius after he had pleaded for his life and successfully held off his other assailants by the power of his eloquence. In the case of P. Crassus, some versions record that the executioner was Fimbria (see above on 23.24).

25.24: *duae familiae Claudiae*

There were more than two *familiae* within the Claudian *gens*: in addition to the Marcelli and Pulchri, there were the Claudii Nerones and the Claudii Crassi among others. On the distinction between the plebeian Marcelli and the patrician Pulchri, see Cic. *de or.* 1.176.

26.2: *Cicero lusit in [C.] Claudium*

The initial for the *praenomen*, missing in the mss. of Asconius here and in the lemma at 25.20, is supplied from the text of Cicero. C. Claudius Pulcher (pr. 56), brother of Ap. Claudius Pulcher (cos. 54) and currently governor of Asia, originally intended to stand for the consulship of 53; that would mean that there would be more than one patrician candidate — himself, Scaurus and Messalla Rufus, but only one could be elected (see above on 18.18). Hence Ap. Claudius promoted the prosecution of Scaurus, in his brother's interests, to damage Scaurus' chances or to eliminate him altogether (see above on 19.7). Cicero jokingly hints that one way to overcome the bar of having only one patrician consul is to do what C. Claudius' other brother, Publius, had done — transfer to plebeian status.

26.2-3: *cum quo in gratiam non redierat*

There is plenty of evidence for Cicero's strained relationship with C. Claudius' brother Appius (see the discussion in Gruen, *Last Generation*, pp. 353-4, and cf. above on 5.9-11); and Cicero's enmity with the other brother Publius is obvious. Appius had supported the moves for Cicero's exile and opposed his recall; there had been at least a superficial reconciliation with Appius in 54 (the year of Scaurus' trial), but it must

Pro Scauro

not have included Gaius (who presumably followed his two brothers in his attitude to Cicero's exile).

26.3: *P. Clodi erat frater*

Ap. Claudius Pulcher (cos. 79) had three sons — Appius (cos. 54), Gaius (pr. 56) and Publius (tr. 58, aed. 56), and at least three daughters; on his death in 76 he left the family in rather straitened financial circumstances (references in T.W. Hillard, *Latomus* 32 [1973] 505-6). On the subsequent careers of the two elder sons, especially their prosecutions in 51 and 50, see Gruen, *Last Generation*, pp. 351-5.

26.4: *qui... transierat*

By a *lex curiata*, probably in early April 59, Clodius transferred to plebeian status, through adoption by a certain P. Fonteius, who was nearly half his age; the new son was emancipated immediately and Clodius continued to bear his old name. The *transitio* was aided by Caesar, who as pontifex maximus presided over meetings of the *comitia curiata* dealing with adoptions, and by Pompeius, who as augur assisted with the auspices. Clodius had already tried in the previous year to transfer to plebeian status, but his *adfinis* Metellus Celer, consul in that year, refused to recognise it. For the details of both moves, see M. Gelzer, *Caesar: Politician and Statesman*, 6th edn., trans. P. Needham (Oxford, 1968) p. 77. Clodius' aim was to secure the tribunate.

26.9-11: *paternus inimicus... subsignaverat*

The father of the Dolabella who is referred to here had been killed in the rioting of 100; the father was a half-brother or cousin of Saturninus (Oros. 5.17.10), and he took the latter's side. It was Scaurus (the father of the subject of this speech) who as *princeps senatus* proposed the *s.c.u.* authorising the magistrates to deal with Saturninus and his supporters, so it is easy to see why the son of one of the victims should inherit and pursue an *inimicitia* against Scaurus. The prosecution, in which the younger Dolabella assisted his *propinquus* Caepio, took place in 92 or 91 and was answered by Scaurus with a counter-prosecution (see above on 21.18ff.). The exact relationship between Caepio and Dolabella is not known. For this incident, see Badian, *PBSR* 33 (1965) 49, and Gruen, *AJP* 87 (1966) 389-92.

26.15: *duos eodem eo tempore fuisse*

The one referred to in the lemma, the praetor of 81, who was subsequently prosecuted by the younger Scaurus, was the son of the man killed in the rioting of 100. The other was consul in 81, as a reward for his service under Sulla; the consulship was followed by a governorship of

Macedonia, for which he received a triumph in 78 or 77 (Cic. *Pis.* 44). The two men were only distantly related; for an attempt to reconstruct the family-tree, see Badian, art. cit. 48-51, and cf. Gruen, art. cit. 386-94.

26.16-17: *alterum C. Caesar accusavit*

In 77 the young Caesar brought the consul of 81 to trial on a charge of *res repetundae*, presumably for his actions during his recent governorship of Macedonia (references in Gruen, art. cit. 387 n. 8). He was defended by Q. Hortensius and C. Aurelius Cotta, Caesar's kinsman, and acquitted. Taylor, *Class. Phil.* 36 (1941) 119, sees Caesar's aim in the prosecution as no more than following the well-established custom of young men who wished to secure political advancement (cf. Gruen, art. cit. 387).

26.17-18: *alterum M. Scaurus et accusavit et damnavit*

The date of this case is not clear: it presumably took place soon after Dolabella's return from the governorship of Cilicia, which he held in 80-79 following his praetorship in 81, for the charge was provincial extortion. No defence counsel is recorded: Ps.-Ascon. 194.1ff., in saying that Hortensius defended Dolabella against Scaurus, has probably confused the two cases (cf. 234.25-32). This Dolabella was convicted, on the testimony of one of his subordinate officers, C. Verres, who had shared in his commander's depredations but who shifted the blame onto Dolabella; he fled, leaving behind poverty for his family. For a speculative analysis of the political implications behind the two trials, see Gruen, art. cit. esp. 397-8, and B. Twyman, *ANRW* 1.1 (1972) 855-6.

27.1-2: *hanc domum in ea parte Palatii*

The house was situated at the foot of the Palatine towards the forum. Part of the site had previously been occupied by the house of Cn. Octavius, built prior to his securing of the consulship for 165. The younger Scaurus bought it, demolished the house and built a larger one for himself (Cic. *off.* 1.138). Clodius bought the house from Scaurus a few months before he was killed in 52 (32.24-25), and it subsequently belonged to C. Caecina Largus. According to Plin. *NH* 17.5-6, Largus owned the house which had formerly belonged to the orator L. Crassus; it is likely therefore that the house of Scaurus and the house of Crassus adjoined each other (Platner-Ashby, pp. 178 and 189; contra, F. Millar, *The Emperor in the Roman World* [London, 1977] p. 19). On the use of this comment for the date of composition, see Part I, pp. 28-9.

27.4-5: *qui consul fuit cum Claudio*

A.D. 42 (*PIR* 2^2.101).

27.5-6: *quattuor columnae marmoreae insigni magnitudine*

Of the 360 marble columns used by Scaurus in the temporary theatre erected during his aedileship (see next comment), some were taken to decorate the atrium of his new house. Asconius says there were four; Pliny does not say how many but says they were the largest of those used in his theatre and measured thirty-eight feet. They were made of Lucullean marble and of such great size that Scaurus had to give special guarantees against breakage of drains while they were being transported to the Palatine.

27.7: *usus erat iis aedilis*

For the magnificence of Scaurus' aedileship in 58, especially the scale and lavishness of the temporary theatre (which Plin. *NH* 36.5 says was used for 'barely a month'), see the references collected at 18.9-10.

27.16: *avum hunc Scauri maternum*

As Asconius goes on to explain (28.5-6), the L. Metellus referred to here is the man who rebuilt the temple of Castor and Pollux, identified as Delmaticus by Ps.-Ascon. 254.28-29 (the booty from his Dalmatian campaign being used in the rebuilding). It follows that Scaurus' father had married a daughter of L. Caecilius Metellus Delmaticus (cos. 119). Badian, *Studies*, p. 39, is wrong in following Bloch's suggestion that Scaurus married a daughter of L. Caecilius Metellus Diadematus who as censor in 115 had named him *princeps senatus* for the first time in his consulship, though there is confusion whether Diadematus or Delmaticus was censor in that year (*MRR* 1.532-3 n. 1; cf. above on 18.6).

27.17: *pontificem maximum*

L. Metellus became pontifex maximus on the death of P. Mucius Scaevola (cos. 133), sometime before December 114 (since he presided at the trial of the Vestals at that time: Ascon. 45.27ff.; Macrob. *sat.* 1.10.5), until his own death in 103 (see above on 21.4-5).

27.18: *paternus avus proavusque Scauri*

See above on 23.6-7; there Asconius says that the family lacked political success for three generations before Scaurus' father, while here he mentions only two generations, omitting (strangely) Scaurus' father.

28.5: *Castoris et Pollucis templum*

The booty gained by Metellus in his Dalmatian campaign, which he conducted following his consulship in 119 and for which he celebrated a triumph in 117 (Degrassi, *Inscr. Ital.* 13.1.82-3 and 560), securing the

150   Commentary

cognomen Delmaticus, was used to restore the temple (Cic. *Verr.* 2.1.154; Ps.-Ascon. 254.28-29).

28.7: *consulares novem*

The consulships were as follows: L. Calpurnius Piso Caesoninus (58); L. Volcacius Tullus (66) — his only recorded judicial involvement; Q. Caecilius Metellus Nepos (57); M. Perperna (92) — also his only recorded judicial advocacy, and by now an elderly statesman (who outlived all his contemporaries — Val. Max. 8.13.4; Plin. *NH* 7.156); L. Marcius Philippus (56) — his only recorded judicial advocacy; M. Tullius Cicero (63); Q. Hortensius Hortalus (69); P. Servilius Vatia Isauricus (79) — his only recorded judicial advocacy and by now an elderly man; and Cn. Pompeius Magnus (70 and 55).

28.10-11: *horum magna pars . . . aberant*

There is no evidence that any of these consulars was away from Rome on official business, except Pompeius who (as Asconius goes on to say) remained outside the city because he was proconsul (cf. 34.4). L. Piso had returned from his command in Macedonia about July 55 (see above on 1.1-2.). L. Volcacius is not known to have been away. Q. Metellus Nepos had become governor of Nearer Spain following his consulship, but as the two Spains had been assigned to Pompeius in 55, Metellus ought to have been back in Rome by the time of Scaurus' trial. M. Perperna was surely too old to have been sent anywhere. L. Philippus is not known to have taken a province following his consulship, but it is possible he was away. Cicero and Hortensius were among the defence counsel, and so clearly were present. P. Servilius Isauricus was censor in 55 and still in office in July 54 (Cic. *Att.* 4.17.7), i.e. at the time the charge was laid against Scaurus, so he too is likely to have been in Rome. Either Asconius is mistaken about the number who were absent, or he means simply that they were not present in court.

28.13: *frater eius*

See above on 20.8.

28.16-24

The list of those who appeared or spoke on Scaurus' behalf is heterogeneous; some can be shown to have family links with him, others to have demonstrated a political stance, especially towards Pompeius, which makes their appearance on the list natural. But others seem quite out of place.

1. M'. Acilius Glabrio, nephew of Scaurus, son of Scaurus' sister Aemilia by her first marriage to M'. Acilius Glabrio (cos. 67); she

was divorced in 82 at the suggestion of Sulla and married to Pompeius, though pregnant to Glabrio at the time (see above on 19.16-17).

2. Paulus presumably is L. Aemilius Paulus, later to be consul in 50; he was the son of M. Aemilius Lepidus, the rebellious anti-Sullan consul of 78 whose forces were defeated by Pompeius; his brother (the future triumvir) was married to a daughter of Servilia (who may have been behind the scenes in the prosecution of Scaurus — see below).

3. P. Lentulus (or perhaps L.: see below on 28.19) was the son of L. Cornelius Lentulus, installed as *flamen Martialis* during the pontificate of Metellus Pius from before c. 63 (Macrob. *sat.* 3.13.11) until his death in 56 or 55 (Cic. *Att.* 4.6.1; the latter date is accepted by SB *Att.* 2.235, following Taylor, *Class. Phil.* 44 [1949] 217-20). The father had supported other Cornelii Lentuli in the prosecution of Clodius for sacrilege in 61; the father and the son were named by Vettius in the affair of 59 which was supposed to be directed against Pompeius; the father had been praetor by 61 and stood against Pompeius' man Gabinius for the consulship of 58 (Cic. *Vat.* 25); the son was Gabinius' prosecutor for *maiestas*, though it was thought that the acquittal was due to the prosecutor's collusion (Cic. *Att.* 4.18.1, cf. *Q.f.* 3.4.1), which could indicate co-operation with Pompeian interests. In general, the Cornelii Lentuli had shifted from being Pompeius' most prominent patrician supporters in the 60's to opponents in the 50's (Gruen, *Historia* 18 [1969] 80-2). Note too that Lentulus now appeared on the same side as Clodius, whom his father had earlier prosecuted.

4. L. Aemilius Buca: not otherwise known, except that he belonged to the first of the colleges of moneyers increased to four by Caesar, which struck coinage in 44. One of the coins issued by Buca depicts Sulla, and others have associations with Venus (with whom Sulla can readily be connected). This suggests that Buca was commemorating a distant relationship with Sulla (Crawford, *RRC* 1.94 and 493); because his name was Aemilius it is natural to suppose such a connection via Scaurus' own family, which might explain his appearance on Scaurus' behalf.

5. C. Memmius was the son of Fausta (recently divorced from his father — see 28.22-23) and so the nephew of Faustus Sulla and distantly related to Scaurus. He was the son of C. Memmius, one of Scaurus' competitors for the consulship of 53, but both had (initially at any rate) the support of Pompeius and Caesar (see above on 18.18). For the intricate relationships, familial and political, between the Memmii, the Cornelii Sullae, Pompeius and

Commentary

Scaurus, see Wiseman, *CQ* 17 (1967) 167; Gruen, *Historia* 18 (1969) 76-7; Sumner, *Orators*, pp. 85ff. The Memmii were not always consistent in their support of Pompeius.

6. T. Annius Milo, a known supporter of Pompeius and now related to Scaurus through his recent marriage to Fausta.

7. C. Peducaeus: apart from the mention here, known only as being killed at Mutina in 43 fighting on the senatorial side (Pollio in Cic. *fam.* 10.33.4).

8. C. Cato, following opposition to Pompeius early in 56, had attached himself to Pompeius after the conference of Luca (Liv. *per.* 105; Dio 39.27.3). Cato had been acquitted at his own trial just a month before, when Scaurus had spoken in his defence (see above on 18.17).

9. M. Popillius Laenas Curtianus (if Madvig's emendation of the name is right) is otherwise unknown.

Some similarities in political attitude can be detected in those who appeared as defence counsel (listed at 20.16-18), but there are again some apparent contradictions:

10. P. Clodius Pulcher was the son of a Metella and therefore a cousin of the Metellus Nepos who sent in a *laudatio* for Scaurus. Following the conference of Luca, he had turned from attacking Pompeius to supporting him. Moreover, personal friction had developed between him and his brother, Ap. Claudius Pulcher (who was behind the prosecution of Scaurus), which might explain their appearance on opposite sides on this occasion (Cic. *Mil.* 75). A most obvious contradiction is that Clodius appeared on the same side as Cicero and Milo.

11. M. Claudius Marcellus, later to be consul in 51: there was no strong political connection, and he was probably serving on the defence solely because of his oratorical skill (see above on 20.16).

12. M. Calidius: there is some hint of Pompeian orientation in that he appeared for both Scaurus and Gabinius in 54.

13. M. Cicero, a consistent supporter of Pompeius: he had possible ties with the elder Scaurus (Cic. *Scaur.* in Ascon. 22.22-23; cf. *leg.* 3.36).

14. M. Valerius Messalla Niger: his sister was Sulla's fifth wife, married in his last years (Plut. *Sull.* 35.5-10). Messalla was *interrex* prior to the election of Pompeius and Crassus to the consulship for 55, and he was subsequently elected with P. Servilius Vatia Isauricus to the

censorship of 55 at elections conducted by those consuls; it is likely therefore that the censors who were still in office in July 54 were favourable to Pompeius.

15. Q. Hortensius from his youth had close links with the Metelli, with whom the Aemilii Scauri were closely connected. Hortensius later was politically associated with M. Cato (as manifest in a wife-swapping which even the Romans regarded as extraordinary and in which Hortensius persuaded M. Cato to give his wife Marcia up to him). It was thought that Cato would favour the prosecution side in the case of Scaurus (see above on 19.21), so Hortensius' appearance on the defence side might appear to be a contradiction, further so because he had marriage connections with the Servilii Caepiones (Münzer, *RA*, pp. 342-6) and Servilia was thought to have been behind the prosecution.

Among those who submitted *laudationes* there seem to be some even stranger appearances:

16. L. Calpurnius Piso: his grandfather had been defended by the elder Scaurus in an extortion trial (Cic. *de or.* 2.265). Piso had been elected to the consulship of 58 with the support of Pompeius (among others), but he was taking now the same side as Cicero who had bitterly attacked him in a speech delivered just twelve months before this trial.

17. L. Volcacius Tullus: there is little evidence of a strong political connection but it may be significant that, when rejecting Catilina's candidature as consul in 66, he consulted a *consilium publicum* which probably consisted of the conservatives who had earlier opposed the Pompeian tribunes, Gabinius, Cornelius and Manilius, and which contained Q. Caecilius Metellus Pius and Metellan supporters like Catulus, Hortensius and the Luculli (see below on 89.10), and that in early 56 he proposed that the commission to restore Ptolemy Auletes should be conferred on Pompeius (Cic. *fam.* 1.1.3, 2.1-2, 4.1).

18. Q. Caecilius Metellus Nepos: he had his early career under Pompeius but, although he had shown opposition to the 'first triumvirate' and supported Clodius in 57-6, he had not broken with Pompeius as sharply as his brother after Pompeius' divorce of their half-sister Mucia in 62 (see below on 63.13-14).

19. M. Perperna: he had served the Cinnan régime as censor in 86, and his son, after holding Sicily for the Marians in 82, went on to serve as a legate under Lepidus and Sertorius, both anti-Sullan (*MRR* 2.91, 95, 100, 105, 120).

20. L. Marcius Philippus was now the father-in-law of Hortensius, which might explain his appearance. His daughter's first marriage to Cato might have aligned him with the Servilii, but there were competing interests: his father, after serving the Cinnan régime as censor with M. Perperna in 86, opportunely moved to Sulla's side in the civil war and served as his legate in 82, and he also assisted Hortensius in the defence of Pompeius in 86. Interest in Sardinia might also have been involved in Philippus' appearance at Scaurus' trial, since his father's legateship had been served there.

M. Cicero and Q. Hortensius — see comments on nos. 13 and 15 above.

21. P. Servilius Vatia Isauricus the elder was the grandson of Metellus Macedonicus, was awarded a triumph in 88 at the instigation of Sulla following a successful praetorian command, and was intended for the consulship of 87, for which he was defeated by Cinna because of Sulla's unpopularity. He served successfully as a legate under Sulla in 82, and was Sulla's choice for the consulship of 79. He spoke in favour of the *lex Manilia* of 66 conferring the extensive Eastern command on Pompeius, and he held the censorship with Messalla in 55, which (as argued above) was likely to be favourable to Pompeius. Yet there were occasions when the elder Servilius had opposed Pompeius, especially in the early years of the 'triumvirate': in 59 he testified for the defence at the trial of L. Valerius Flaccus, which had been instigated by Pompeius, and in early 56 he proposed to keep the job of restoring Ptolemy Auletes from Pompeius completely by suggesting there be no restoration at all (Cic. *fam.* 1.1.3), and he verbally attacked Clodius following the latter's reconciliation with Pompeius after the conference of Luca (Cic. *har. resp.* 2). His son clearly went in the other direction, marrying the niece of Cato, supporting Cato in 59 (Cic. *Att.* 1.19.9, 2.1.10), in 56 (Cic. *Q.f.* 2.3.2) and again in 54 (the year of Scaurus' trial) when they were colleagues in the praetorship (Cic. *Att.* 4.15.9, 18.4); the occasion in 56 was a senate meeting following a trial of Milo at which Pompeius had appeared for the defence and been shouted off the rostra, and Servilius the younger had been one of a number of senators to criticise Pompeius. On the alienation of the Servilii from Pompeius, see Gruen, *Historia* 18 (1969) 84-5.

22. Cn. Pompeius Magnus began his career under Sulla and had close family connections with Scaurus (see above on 19.16-17). He was also supporting Scaurus and C. Memmius for the consulship.

23. Faustus Cornelius Sulla, son of Sulla himself. In addition to his family connections with Scaurus, Faustus Sulla was related to Pompeius through marriage to his daughter Pompeia. However,

Pro Scauro 155

other members of the Sullan family were aligned against Pompeius in 54: e.g. P. Cornelius Sulla, married to Pompeius' sister, attempted to prosecute his man Gabinius for *ambitus*, with the help of C. Memmius, Pompeius' nephew.

In all, some twenty-three persons supported Scaurus' defence, an extraordinarily large number, and many of them had Sullan connections. In view of that, E. Courtney, *Philologus* 105 (1961) 151-6, has argued that the case is 'a throw-back to the politics of twenty and thirty and more years ago and the prosecution of the feuds of the great houses', a struggle between Sullani and Mariani. On the prosecution side, he sees Marian connections centering around revenge for the treatment of M. Aemilius Lepidus, the rebellious consul of 78: one of the assisting prosecutors was L. Marius, whose name alone is significant and who may have had political connections with Cato (see above on 19.6-7), and Cato was related to Servilia. Courtney argues that Servilia's influence behind the scenes was important for the prosecution of Scaurus: she hated Pompeius for the murder of her first husband, M. Iunius Brutus, in suppressing the uprising of Lepidus; her father had been the bitter enemy and prosecutor of Scaurus the elder, and the homonym of her first husband had also prosecuted him; and she kept up the connection with Lepidus, who had been opposed by a number of Scaurus' supporters, by weaving a network of marriage connections with the family of Lepidus (for a stemma, see Courtney, loc. cit. 153).

However, such an explanation for the sides taken in the trial of Scaurus is anachronistic for, as Gruen, *Last Generation*, p. 335, points out, the impact of links from an earlier generation would have been softened. And there had developed complicated and conflicting interests which make Courtney's explanation untenable; some have already been pointed out on the defence side in the case of L. Aemilius Paulus (no. 2), Lentulus Niger (no. 3), C. Memmius (no. 5), P. Clodius (no. 10), L. Calpurnius Piso (no. 16), Q. Caecilius Metellus Nepos (no. 18), P. Servilius Vatia Isauricus (no. 21), and P. Cornelius Sulla (under no. 23). There were contradictions on the prosecution side too. The major one for Courtney's explanation, noted by him, is that the father of Triarius, the principal prosecutor, had fought against Lepidus. Ap. Claudius Pulcher, who was behind the prosecution, had turned to supporting Pompeius, who was on the defence side, following the conference of Luca which he attended; about this time his daughter was married to Pompeius' son (though the marriage is dated later by Gruen, *Historia* 18 [1969] 101-3); he came into conflict with the younger P. Servilius Vatia Isauricus, whose father was on the defence side, over the affair of C. Messius in 54 (details in Gruen, *Last Generation*, p. 316) and over the granting of a triumph to C. Pomptinus, also in 54 (see above on 19.6-7).

Ciaceri, *Cicerone e i suoi tempi* (Milan, 1930) 2.121-7, argues that

Caesar and Pompeius backed Ap. Claudius Pulcher in the prosecution of Scaurus, and that enemies of the 'triumvirate' supported Scaurus (though he does not know what to make of Clodius), but such a view is contradicted by the list of persons supporting the defence (many of whom had links with Pompeius — and Pompeius himself openly sent in a *laudatio* of Scaurus).

The views discussed above are all attempts to explain the trial of Scaurus in terms of political attitudes adopted by individuals. Gruen, *Last Generation*, pp. 334-17, in rejecting Courtney's interpretation, tries to find a more general reason for the appearance of what seems to be an assorted collection of persons. He takes the appearance of such a large number to show that the trial was exceptional and not typical. His view is that *ambitus* prosecutions, especially after elections, were common and regarded as 'fair play', but accusations on other charges, designed to remove a competitor even before the elections were held, would create a dangerous precedent in the aristocratic competition for office; it was fear of this precedent being created that induced the aristocracy to rally to Scaurus' support. It does seem reasonable to suppose that a large number of the aristocracy felt that Scaurus, an aristocrat of the bluest blood who could expect to secure a consulship and against whom his rivals were making scandalous contracts and laying thin charges, was being badly treated, and they perhaps feared that, if it could happen to someone like him, it could all the more easily happen to them.

Although the appearance of such a large number is exceptional, one cannot entirely agree with Gruen that the case is not typical. The view of Meier, *Res Publica Amissa* (Wiesbaden, 1966) p. 18, may be the most acceptable — that the trial of Scaurus demonstrates the basic unanimity of the senatorial aristocracy. The trial can be seen in one sense as non-political, with the appearance of a number of persons who at other times seem to be on opposite sides, but one can make too much of the apparent differences. And in another sense the trial is typically political, albeit an extreme example, in that the appearance of such a heterogeneous collection on the same side for the defence illustrates the normal (but sometimes conflicting) interplay of *amicitia, gratia, necessitudo* and *officium* which was central to the workings of political life at Rome. In essence, when there was no particular political axe to grind, Roman gentlemen preferred to appear for the defence.

28.19: *P. Lentulus*

Our only evidence for a second son of L. Cornelius Lentulus Niger, the *flamen Martialis*. We know of a son Lucius who was the prosecutor of Gabinius in 54 (Cic. *Att*. 4.18.1). At *Att*. 2.24.2 Cicero refers simply to *Lentulus, flaminis filius*; if there had been two sons, Cicero would hardly have omitted the *praenomen* here, and perhaps the *P.* in Asconius is

Pro Scauro 157

erroneous or corrupt (SB *Att.* 1.400; cf. Münzer, *RE* 4 [1900] 1375, s.v. 'Cornelius' no. 205). Manutius emended the *praenomen* to *L*. (accepted by Giarratano).

28.22: *ante paucos menses nupserat*

The date of the wedding is given as 18th November 55 in Cic. *Att.* 4.13.1 (i.e. nine months before). Fausta had a reputation for promiscuity (Macrob. *sat.* 2.29).

28.25: *sententias tulerunt*

According to the mss., 22 senators voted, 23 equites, and 25 *tribuni aerarii*, a total of 70 votes, of which only 8 were for condemnation (4 senators, 2 equites and 2 *tribuni aerarii*). Manutius emends the numbers voting to 24 senators, and 22 *tribuni aerarii* (cf. Rinkes, *Mnemosyne* 10 [1861] 213-4). The usual number for a jury seems to have been 75 (examples in Jones, *Criminal Courts*, p. 69; cf. Mommsen, *Strafrecht*, p. 218 n. 4), though smaller juries were used (e.g. the trial of Clodius in 61 where only 56 jurors voted: Cic. *Att.* 1.16.5 and 10, *in Clod. et Cur.* frags. 26 and 29 P). In the case of Gabinius for *maiestas* in 54, only 70 votes were recorded, 32 for condemnation (Cic. *Q.f.* 3.4.1). Jones, loc. cit., conjectures that the slightly smaller number of votes than the standard jury size in the trials of Scaurus and Gabinius was due to a few abstentions, but it may also have been due to rejection of jurors. A praetor of 59, Q. Fufius Calenus, passed a law that at *iudicia publica* the three *ordines* were to cast their votes separately (Dio 38.8.1), and so a separate tally was available (cf. C. Macdonald, *CR* 7 [1957] 198); prior to that only totals of votes cast for acquittal and for condemnation were available (e.g. the trial of Clodius mentioned above). In the case of trials *apud populum*, the number of tribal votes had been known from a much earlier period (e.g. the trial of Silanus in 104: below, 80.24-25).

29.1: *Cato praetor, [Cicero] cum vellet*

As the sentence stands in the mss., the sense is odd: Cato is said to give in to mob pressure to investigate the accusers for *calumnia*, when he wanted to anyway. To avoid this oddness, Mommsen, *Strafrecht*, p. 494 n. 7, would emend the *vellet* to *nollet*, while Clark would add *Cicero* as the subject of the *cum* clause. The *lex Acilia* required the praetor to ask the jury whether the accuser had been guilty of *praevaricatio* (*FIRA* 1.7.75); it is likely that under the judiciary laws of the late republic the praetor put the question of *calumnia* to the jury as well (Jones, *Criminal Courts*, p. 73).

29.4: *de calumnia*

At the time of the *nominis delatio*, the accuser swore an oath against

Commentary

calumnia. There was an oath against *praevaricatio* as well; the form laid down in the *lex Acilia*, probably the general rule, was that the accuser(s) 'will press this charge and will persevere in the accusation until sentence is given' (*Dig.* 48.2.7.1). On the oath against *calumnia* and the procedure to investigate it, see Greenidge, *Legal Procedure*, pp. 468-70.

29.7-8: *sine tunica . . . campestri . . . cinctus*

The *campestre* was a light apron, originally worn under the toga in place of the tunic, a custom retained by some old-fashioned people (hence by Cato: Plut. *Cat. Min.* 6.3 and 44.1); more commonly worn as the sole garment for exercise in the campus (hence its name). Cf. Hor. *ep.* 1.11.18, *ars poet.* 50. Lewis and Short, *Latin Dictionary*, s.v. 'campester' 2a, are wrong in supposing it to have been generally worn in hot weather to replace the tunic. As the trial took place in early September and the calendar was ahead of the seasons, it was still summer, and Cato may have appeared like this because of the heat (cf. *quia aestate agebatur*); but it seems to have been Cato's custom to dress like this. That there was a heatwave at the time of this trial is confirmed by Cic. *Q.f.* 2.16.1, 3.1.1.

29.10-11: *Romuli et Tati statuae . . . Camilli*

In a section dealing with the use of bronze for statuary, and in particular various styles in Roman statuary, Pliny groups these same three as examples of *togatae sine tunicis* (*NH* 34.23). This suggests a source common to Pliny and Asconius, perhaps Fenestella, who was known to have an antiquarian interest.

THE COMMENTARY ON THE SPEECH *PRO MILONE*

[Note: There is an excellent commentary by A.C. Clark on Asconius' commentary on the *pro Milone* in his edition of the speech (Oxford, 1895) pp. 94-118. These notes are intended to supplement Clark's commentary. References to the latter are by the abbreviation Clark, with the page number. Reference is also made to A.W. Lintott, 'Cicero and Milo', *JRS* 64 (1974) 62-78, by the abbreviation Lintott, with the appropriate page number, and to J.S. Ruebel, 'The Trial of Milo in 52 B.C.: A Chronological Study', *TAPA* 109 (1979) 231-49, by the abbreviation Ruebel, with the appropriate page number.]

30.1: *Cn. Pompeio III cos.*

52 B.C.; cf. 36.2-5

30.1-2: *a.d. VI Id. April.*

For a discussion of the date of the trial, see Clark, pp. 127-9, and Ruebel, pp. 245-7. The reading of the mss. here suggests the date of 8th April for the final day of Milo's trial (i.e. when the speeches were delivered). Elsewhere, the mss. give *a.d. II* or *III* for the *summus iudicii dies* (40.25-41.1), and they are usually emended to *VI* in the light of this earlier reading for the date. The date on which the trial began, 4th April, is supplied at 39.7: *prid. Non. April. reum adesse iusserunt.* Given that these dates are right, the trial should have extended over five days.

However, in Asconius' account of what actually happened, we can account for only four days. He says that on the first day there was a riot (40.1-6); then *per biduum* the interrogation of witnesses was conducted (40.11-12); and then *postero die, qui fuit iudicii summus* the *sortitio iudicum* and the speeches took place (40.25ff.). Towards the end of the third day, a *contio* was addressed by T. Munatius Plancus, who urged the people to turn up at the trial *postero die* and pressure the jury to condemn Milo (presumably meaning the last day of the trial). Elsewhere Asconius says that this *contio* was held on the day before the final day of the trial (42.10) and *post audita et obsignata testium verba* (52.11-15); and in § 3 of the speech Cicero calls it *hesterna contio* (i.e. it was held on the day before the delivery of the speeches).

Yet, when describing the law of Pompeius under which Milo was tried, Asconius seems to be saying that such a trial should last five days. He says that, under the terms of the law, the interrogation of witnesses should be held *per triduum*, then *quarta die adesse omnes in diem posterum iuberentur ac ... pilae ... aequarentur; dein rursus postero die* the

160 Commentary

sortitio of the jurors should take place and the final speeches be heard (39.15ff.).

A possible solution (which Clark and others have not allowed for) is that Asconius has simply been inconsistent (cf. Lintott, p. 73 n. 132). The dates may be correctly recorded, having presumably been taken from the *acta* (the main source used by Asconius for the introduction to the commentary on the speech); he is not likely to have been able to remember such precise information and so probably checked the dates in his source. But when he came to his account of the actual trial, he may have relied more on memory and been unaware that he covered only four days. For another example of inconsistency, cf. 23.5-6 with 27.18 (a discrepancy over the number of generations in which the Aemilii Scauri had not held office). Another solution, which would bring the account of the trial into line with the terms of the law, is that a *postero die* has fallen out of the account of Plancus' *contio* (Lintott, loc. cit.). This would be just as acceptable as Clark's deletion of *in posterum diem* at 39.18, which he suggests to suit his solution of dating the last day of the trial to *a.d. VII Id. April*.

30.4-6: ***ex oratione et annalibus . . . ex libro . . . de optimo genere oratorum***

The known references are *Mil.* 1-3 and *opt. gen. or.* 10. By *annalibus* Asconius may have Livy in mind: the Livian version is probably preserved in Dio 40.53.2-3 (cf. Liv. *per.* 107). He may also have in mind Pollio (see Part I, p. 59) and Fenestella (who was obviously a source for the introductory comments: 31.14).

30.8: ***P. Plautius Hypsaeus***

Hypsaeus had been a quaestor to Pompeius in the East (35.17-18) and been retained as proquaestor most likely (*MRR* 2.153, 163 and 181). The Plautii possessed long-standing affiliations with Pompeius (see Gruen, *Last Generation*, p. 108 n. 65); and now Pompeius, thwarted in the two previous consular elections, vigorously supported Hypsaeus (35.16-18), whose political loyalty had proved reliable. He was not elected, as political disturbances caused the elections to be cancelled; his career came to a swift end shortly after when he was prosecuted for bribery in 52 (cf. *largitione palam profusa* at 30.9-10) and found guilty, having been abandoned by Pompeius (Val. Max. 9.5.3; Plut. *Pomp.* 55.6).

30.8-9: ***Q. Metellus Scipio***

His full name, Q. Caecilius Metellus Pius Scipio Nasica, shows his pedigree: he was the son of P. Cornelius Scipio Nasica and Licinia, daughter of the great orator, L. Licinius Crassus, and grand-daughter of

Q. Mucius Scaevola; he was adopted by Metellus Pius, cos. 80 (Dio 40.51.3; cf. below on 74.16). His daughter was married first to P. Licinius Crassus, the son of the famous Crassus, and subsequently to Pompeius (see below on 31.9). For his career, with references to modern discussions of some of the problems, see I. Shatzman, *Senatorial Wealth and Roman Politics* (Brussels, 1975) p. 310. His pedigree was apparently not matched by his character: he was dull and lacking in ability (Cic. *Att.* 6.1.17), and fond of pornographic displays (Val. Max. 9.1.8).

30.9: *consulatum petierunt*

Milo had long calculated on a consulship; in 57 Pompeius had held out to him the hope of a consulship as a reward for their collaboration in the recall of Cicero (App. *BC* 2.16), but by November of 54, when Milo asked for encouragement, Pompeius promised him nothing (Cic. *Q.f.* 3.8.6; cf. App. *BC* 2.20); for a continuation of this attitude by Pompeius, see 35.16ff. and 38.1ff. The electoral campaign was conducted with bribery and increasing violence (for description and references, see Gruen, *Last Generation*, p. 152 with n. 132); the consuls of 53 were unable to conduct the elections and, like the preceding year, 52 opened without curule magistrates (see below, 30.20-31.3). The situation was resolved by the appointment of Pompeius as sole consul in March; he subsequently took Metellus Scipio as his colleague for the remainder of the year, probably about August (cf. *CIL* 1^2.2.993, which mentions them as colleagues on *Id. Sept.*).

30.9: *largitione*

As an example of the extent of one candidate's outlay, see the description of the costs of Milo's displays (31.6-8) and his distribution of 1000 asses to every man in the tribes after the killing of Clodius (33.20-21 and 35.15). All three consular candidates were eventually prosecuted for *ambitus*.

30.11-13: *Milo Ciceronis erat amicissimus ... operam tr. pl. dederat*

The general view is that, since Milo as tribune in 57 worked for Cicero's recall, it was in gratitude for that effort that Cicero continued to support Milo and finally defended him. Lintott, pp. 63-4, argues that in 57 Milo was working for Pompeius by organising gangs to counter the violence of Clodius and that he helped Cicero only indirectly, and that the friendship between Milo and Cicero developed later.

30.17: *Milo pro melioribus partibus stabat*

The assumption that Milo had the support of the *boni* (cf. 31.4-5: *cum*

162   *Commentary*

bonorum studiis, and 53.6-7) is perhaps drawn from the speech itself (cf. e.g. § § 3 and 95ff.), which continually contrasts Milo's actions with those of Clodius.

30.19: *praeturam petebat*

According to Cic. *Mil.* 24 and Schol. Bob. 172.32-34, Clodius stood for the praetorship of 53, but when the curule elections were so long delayed he decided to abandon his candidature since he would not have had enough time to use the office to stir up trouble, and to stand again in the following year. Badian, *Studies*, p. 150, thinks that Cicero's statement, composed after Clodius' death, is highly suspicious and a lawyer's trick (contra, Lintott, p. 66 n. 60).

30.19-20: *quam debilem futuram consule Milone intellegebat*

The clause is taken closely from § 25 of the speech itself.

31.6-7: *impensasque ludorum scaenicorum ac gladiatorii muneris maximas*

In November 54 (and still in December) Milo was planning *magnificentissimos ludos* which were to cost a million sesterces (Cic. *Q.f.* 3.8.6, 9.2). They had been held by July 53, since then Cicero wrote to Curio (*fam.* 2.6.3) that Milo had won the support of the man in the street by the magnificence of his public shows (cf. *Mil.* 95). Prior to these dramatic shows, Milo had put on a gladiatorial show (*Q.f.* 3.8.6), possibly during his praetorship and presumably *ex testamento* (otherwise he would have violated Cicero's law on bribery, passed in 63, which forbade the giving of gladiatorial shows during the two years that one was a candidate for office actually or prospectively, except on a day fixed beforehand by a will [Cic. *Vat.* 37, cf. *Sest.* 133]).

31.7-8: *in quas tria patrimonia effudisse eum Cicero significat*

The comment is taken from § 95 of the speech (see below on 53.13). The burden of debt which Milo incurred from his lavish displays was notorious. Early in 52 he was accused by Clodius in the senate with not having fully admitted his debts, and Cicero replied with the speech *de aere alieno Milonis*; then Milo admitted to debts of six million HS. When he went into exile, his debts totalled 70 million sesterces, according to Plin. *NH* 36.104. On the political consequences of falling too deeply into debt, see M.W. Frederiksen, *JRS* 56 (1966) 128-9. On the possibility that the number three is simply an invention of Cicero taken over uncritically by Asconius, see Part I, p. 67.

31.9: *Pompeius gener Scipionis*

The daughter of Scipio whom Pompeius married was Cornelia, recently widowed by the death of P. Crassus in the Parthian campaign. It was a good match for Pompeius, for it gave him attachment to the noblest families in Rome and she was apparently attractive, cultivated and unspoilt (Plut. *Pomp.* 55.1-2). It is difficult to date the marriage precisely; it took place most likely some time in 52. Plutarch puts it soon after Pompeius' appointment as sole consul; Asconius refers here to Metellus Scipio as Pompeius' father-in-law during the campaign for the consulship, but that may simply be sloppy writing, for there is no evidence that Pompeius supported Metellus Scipio's campaign in 53, only that of Hypsaeus (Gruen, *Last Generation*, p. 154 n. 142). The use of *gener* by Asconius here could imply that the marriage of Pompeius and Cornelia had already taken place, but *gener* can mean prospective son-in-law (*Dig.* 38.10.6.1; cf. Clark, p. 95).

31.10: *T. Munatius tribunus plebis*

Of the known tribunes for 52, three supported Clodius (T. Munatius Plancus Bursa, Q. Pompeius Rufus and C. Sallustius Crispus) and two supported Milo's cause (M. Caelius Rufus and Q. Manilius Cumanus). Immediately after his year of office, Plancus was prosecuted by Cicero under the Pompeian law *de vi* and went into exile (references in *MRR* 2.235). For his career, see Münzer, *RE* 16 (1935) 551-3, s.v. 'Munatius' no. 32; cf. Gruen, *Last Generation,* pp. 346-7.

31.10-11: *de patriciis convocandis qui interregem proderent*

The patrician members of the senate met in committee to select an *interrex*; a tribune could not veto the appointment made, but he could stop proceedings by preventing the senate from being called together (Mommsen, *Römische Forschungen*, 1.225).

31.12-13: *a. d. XIII Kal. Febr.*

This date, taken from the *acta* as Asconius goes on to say, would have been more accurate than Fenestella's. It agrees with the speech itself (§ § 27 and 98) and with other statements by Cicero (*Att.* 5.13.1: it was 560 days from the battle of Bovillae to 22nd July 51). For Asconius' disagreements with Fenestella, see Part I, pp. 53-5.

31.15-16: *Lanuvium, ex quo erat municipio et ubi tum dictator*

Lanuvium was twenty-eight kilometres south-east of Rome on the via Appia; when the Latin League was dissolved in 338, it was granted Roman citizenship, becoming a *municipium*, and its cult of Juno Sospes was officially adopted (Liv. 8.14.2). Other Latin towns where the chief magistrate was a single official termed a *dictator* included Caere, Tusculum and Nomentum. Note that in the peroration of the speech the possible grief of Milo's fellow-townsmen is not introduced to excite compassion, whereas in the case of Murena, who also came from Lanuvium, it is (Cic. *Mur.* 90; cf. Clark, p. 91).

31.16: *ad flaminem prodendum*

The *flamen* of Juno Sospes (or Sospita): see Cic. *nat. deor.* 1.82. Note the odd statement in App. *BC* 2.20 that Milo withdrew to Lanuvium not for this purpose, but because he despaired of securing the consulship due to Pompeius' playing him false.

31.16-17: *postera die*

Lintott, p. 68 n. 81, argues that, although Asconius states that the *flamen* was to be installed on the following day (i.e. 19th January), Cicero says explicitly in § 46 that the *flamen* had to be installed *illo ipso die*, a phrase which can refer to no other day than that of the journey. As this point is not entirely favourable to Milo (since it could suggest that he wished to be about on 18th rather than leave for Lanuvium on, say, 17th), Cicero's statement should be accepted (hence we have a mistake by Asconius). Clark, pp. 23-4 and 40, on the other hand, thinks that in § §27-28 and 45-46 Cicero is being deliberately ambiguous, and he accepts Asconius' statement that the *flamen* was to be installed on 19th; cf. Ruebel, p. 233.

31.17: *circa horam nonam*

On the morning of 18th January, Pompeius Rufus and Sallustius Crispus attacked Milo at a *contio* they had summoned (§45; 49.5-8). Milo left Rome for Lanuvium before this *contio* had finished (§27) and after a meeting of the senate had been dismissed, *post horam quartam*, according to Metellus Scipio (34.26-35.1). Cicero says (§29) that the fight between Clodius and Milo took place about the eleventh hour. Asconius' time of the ninth hour makes better sense. As the fight took place about nineteen kilometres from Rome, it is difficult to see how it could have started as late as the eleventh hour, if Clodius' body reached the city before the first hour of the night (32.18); and if, as Cicero seems to say (§ §45-46), it was necessary for Milo to appoint the *flamen* at Lanuvium on the same day that he set out from Rome, he would surely have been leaving things too late if he had only got as far as Bovillae by the eleventh hour. Asconius' time is likely to have been taken from the *acta* and therefore more accurate; it is confirmed also by the statement of the accusers quoted in Quintil. 6.3.49 (*quod Bovillas ante horam nonam devertisset*), which is not specifically rebutted by Cicero in his speech. Throughout the story Cicero tries to post-date Milo's movements, while the prosecution ante-dated them so as to suggest that Milo was loitering in Rome to effect the timing of his plan to ambush Clodius. Cicero boldly misstated the time of the affray partly to rebut the charge of loitering and

Pro Milone 165

partly to promote his claim in §49 that it was night-fall when Clodius left his villa (and so it was he who was planning the ambush). This difference over the time is an instance where Asconius has not pointed out his disagreement with Cicero (see Part I, p. 46).

31.18: *Bovillas . . . Aricia*

Clodius had left Rome on the previous day to address the local senators at Aricia, about twenty-one kilometres south of Rome on the Appian way (possibly as part of his electoral campaign). He returned by the Appian way on 18th January, stopping at his Alban villa, a little south-east of Bovillae. He also visited Pompeius' Alban villa at Alsium nearby some time late in the day (Cic. *Mil.* 54).

31.18-19: *Bonae Deae sacellum*

Cicero (*Mil.* 86) says that it stood on the estate of a young man, T. Sertius Gallus.

31.20: *servi XXX fere expediti*

The subsequent claim of Metellus Scipio that Clodius was accompanied by twenty-six slaves (34.26), eleven of whom were killed, while Milo travelled with more than 300 armed men, two only of whom were wounded (35.1 and 13), seems to be accepted by Asconius. Cicero (*Mil.* 53) vaguely implies that Clodius had a large number of men concealed in the terracing of his new villa.

31.23: *C. Causinius Schola*

A native of Interamna, according to Cic. *Mil.* 46; little is known of him apart from his friendship with Clodius (see Nicolet, *L'ordre équestre*, 2.834). He had earlier provided the alibi that Clodius was at Interamna at the time of the Bona Dea break-in (see below on 49.14). Wiseman, *New Men*, p. 37 n. 5, lists other friends of Clodius from a municipal origin, but Causinius Schola is the only one called *eques Romanus*.

31.24: *P. Pomponius, [C. Clodius]*

The *C. Clodius* was added by Manutius, presumably from Cic. *Mil.* 46 where a C. Clodius, *comes P. Clodii*, is associated with Causinius Schola in giving evidence about Clodius' movements on 18th January.

31.25: *Milo raeda vehebatur cum uxore Fausta*

Milo had married Fausta 'a few months' before the trial of Scaurus in September 54, following her divorce from C. Memmius (29.22-23); in fact the wedding took place in November 55. That Milo was travelling in a coach with his wife suggests that he was not deliberately planning to lay an ambush for Clodius (cf. Cic. *Mil.* 28 and 54).

31.26: *M. Fufio*

In his *OCT*, Clark accepts the usual amendment to *Fufio*, but in his edition of the *pro Milone* he sticks to the mss. reading *Fusio*. For his arguments for retaining the mss. reading, see p. 96 in his edition.

32.1: *gladiatores quoque*

On Milo's use of gladiators, cf. Cic. *Vat.* 40, *off.* 2.58; and in general on their use in armed entourages and in public violence, see Lintott, *Violence*, pp. 83-5.

32.2ff.

There are various details of the fight which are not found in Cicero (and therefore must have been found by Asconius in the *acta* or in the prosecution speeches) or which disagree with Cicero's account. The names of the two gladiators who were accompanying Milo, Eudamus and Birria, are not found in Cicero, nor the information that Birria wounded Clodius. According to Cic. *Mil.* 29, Milo was attacked simultaneously from the higher ground and from the front; Asconius says the fight broke out in the rear of Milo's column. Asconius gives the information that Clodius was carried wounded to a nearby inn and finished off there; this is not mentioned by Cicero (cf. 35.4-7). In general, Asconius' account is the more acceptable, having been based on a study of the evidence in the *acta diurna*, which would have contained verbatim reports of the speeches on both sides (Lintott, p. 69 with n. 91, argues from Tac. *dial.* 37.2 that reports of forensic speeches were contained in the *acta;* contra, J.N. Settle, *TAPA* 94 [1963] 277).

32.5: *rumpia*

See Clark's note, p. 96.

32.12: *M. Saufeius*

Little is known of this man, apart from his friendship with Milo and his subsequent prosecution for his part in the killing of Clodius (see below on 55.1ff.). He may have been connected with the notable family from Praeneste (see R. Syme, *Historia* 13 [1964] 121, and Nicolet, *L'ordre équestre,* 2.1012-3).

32.15: *Sex. Teidius*

Possibly a senator of quaestorian rank, to be identified with the lame man who in extreme old age joined Pompeius in Macedonia (P. Willems, *Le Sénat de la République Romaine* [Louvain, 1883] Vol. I, p. 500; Wiseman, *Latomus* 22 [1963] 90; Gruen, *Last Generation*, pp. 307 and 522). Plut. *Pomp.* 64.4 calls him Τίδιος Σέξτιος, but that could be an easy confusion of the name. For the orthography of the *gentilicium*, see *CIL* 1.1090.

32.18: *ante primam noctis horam*

See above on 31.17.

32.21: *uxor Clodi Fulvia*

Fulvia was the daughter of M. Fulvius Bambalio of Tusculum (whose *cognomen* was derived from his stuttering: Dio 45.47.4, 46.7.2) and Sempronia, the last daughter of the plebeian noble house of the Sempronii Tuditani. As both mother and father were at the end of a family line, Fulvia may well have been an heiress of some worth and a catch for a young *nobilis* of expensive habits and small income, like Clodius (C. Babcock, *AJP* 86 [1965] 5). The marriage took place somewhere between 62 and 60 probably; Clodius was certainly Fulvia's husband by 58 (Cic. *Phil.* 2.48). She is said to have nearly always accompanied her husband (Cic. *Mil.* 28 and 55), and it may be that she was exercising her own talents to further Clodius' ambitions (e.g. her ability to organise recruiting, seen in her activities on behalf of M. Antonius in 40, may have been used to organise the *collegia* which were used so much by Clodius in his political activity). Those talents of energy and determination were displayed in avenging her husband's death; she helped to maintain the anger of the Clodian supporters, and at the trial on the last day for the hearing of witnesses, she and her mother Sempronia stirred the bystanders deeply with their weeping (40.18-21). Fulvia was subsequently married to C. Scribonius Curio the younger and then to M. Antonius.

32.24: *noti homines*

A favorite phrase of Asconius: cf. 31.24, 32.2, 37.2, 59.21-22, 90.25. Cf. Clark, p. 96.

32.24: *noti homines elisi sunt, inter quos C. Vibienus senator*

According to Cic. *Mil.* 37, C. Vibienus died as a result of injuries received in a scuffle which occurred during the disturbances prior to Cicero's exile in 58. In that case, he could not have been alive at the beginning of 52 to be involved in the public scenes which followed Clodius' death, and Asconius would be guilty of a serious error, since his date for Vibienus' death is at variance with Cicero's in a commentary on the very speech of

Cicero which provides the evidence for Vibienus' death in 58. Cicero is to be preferred to Asconius (though the latter is accepted by *MRR* 2.498). On the assumption that Asconius would not be wrong, S.H. Rinkes, *Mnemosyne* 10 (1861) 216-7, suggests that the clause *inter quos... senator* is a gloss wrongly derived from Cic. *Mil.* 37 and that it should be deleted. He also suggests *visi* for *elisi*, which improves the meaning in Asconius. Clark accepts both suggestions, and deletes the clause; Giarratano accepts the *visi* and brackets the clause; Kiessling and Schoell, and Stangl note the two suggestions in their apparatuses. On the discrepancy between Cicero and Asconius, see Clark, p. 34, and H. Last, *CQ* 17 (1923) 97. On Vibienus in general, see Wiseman, *Mnemosyne* 16 [1963] 277-83.

32.25: *empta de M. Scauro in Palatio*

On the house, see above on 27.1-2. Clodius bought the house in late 53 at a cost of HS 14,800,000 (Plin. *NH* 36.103). Scaurus, who had got off a charge of *repetundae* in September 54 with the help of Cicero, Clodius and others, was subsequently found guilty of *ambitus* and went into exile (see above on 18.19-20); it is probable that the heavy debts incurred in his political expenditure combined with his conviction forced Scaurus to sell (Shatzman, op. cit. p. 291).

32.26: *frater L. Planci oratoris*

Probably connected with the Munatius of Tibur who was a legate (?) of Sulla in Chalcis (App. *Mith.* 34); the family presumably gained senatorial status under Sulla. L. Munatius Plancus had a variegated career (see Hanslik, *RE* 16 [1935] 545-51; Wiseman, *New Men*, pp. 242-3), culminating in a consulship in 42 and a censorship in 22. Regarding his oratory, Cic. *fam.* 10.3.3 refers to his *summa eloquentia*, and Jerome (on the year of Abraham 1992 = 25 B.C.) calls him *orator insignis* (possibly drawn from Suet. *rhet.* 6) His fine Latin style can be sampled at first hand in his surviving letters to Cicero.

32.27: *Sullae dictatoris ex filia nepos*

Cornelia, a daughter of Sulla's first marriage to Ilia, was married to the son of Q. Pompeius Rufus, Sulla's colleague in the consulship of 88. The tribune of 52 was one of the children of that marriage; his sister Pompeia was Caesar's second wife, divorced by him at the time of the Bona Dea scandal. Little else is known of this tribune, apart from his support of Clodius' cause in this year.

33.6: *Sex. Cloelio scriba*

That the form of the name should be *Cloelio* (and not the mss. *Clodio*),

Pro Milone 169

see above on 7.18. For Cicero's sneering references to his position as a *scriba*, see *dom.* 47, 83, 129, *har. resp.* 11, *Sest.* 133; for his possible connection with the *collegium scribarum*, see above on 7.18.

33.6: *in curiam*

The curia Hostilia, on the north side of the comitium in the forum; it was remodelled by Sulla and, after it was burnt down as Clodius' pyre, the task of rebuilding it was given to Sulla's son Faustus, who was Milo's brother-in-law (Dio 40.50.2-3). The blaze was extensive, for the pedestal of the ancient statue of the augur Attus Navius, which was near the steps of the curia (Liv. 1.36.5), was also burned (Plin. *NH* 34.21), as was the basilica Porcia (33.9). Clark, p. 97, thinks that the adjoining basilica Aemilia may have sustained damage in the fire, since it was subject to restoration in 50 by L. Aemilius Paullus. But it is not clear which basilica Paullus renovated, nor in which year: for a discussion, see Münzer, *Hermes* 40 (1905) 97; Platner-Ashby, p. 72; SB *Att.* 2.204-5. For the position of these various structures, see G. Lugli, *BCAR* 42 (1914) tav. ix-x.

33.7-8: *codicibus librariorum*

Not to be taken as 'books belonging to the booksellers' (and hence evidence that there were booksellers' shops in the forum near the curia), nor as the collection of laws and other documents formed by the secretaries of various senators which were left in the senate-house and which perished in the flames (Clark, p. 97). In this period *codex* means 'wooden tablet' and *librariorum* means 'clerk, copyist or scribe', so the phrase *codices librariorum* means 'scribes' notebooks', i.e. wooden (probably waxed) tablets, and the picture is that they were used with the other items mentioned, to provide fuel for the flames. It is appropriate that the mob who started the fire was under the leadership of Sex. Cloelius, himself a *scriba*. See N. Lewis, *BASP* 11 (1974) 49-51.

33.10: *M. Lepidi interregis*

Asconius (on §13 of the speech) says that Lepidus was appointed *interrex post biduum medium quam Clodius occisus erat*, taken by Clark, p. 97, to mean 21st January (following Mommsen, *Staatsrecht*, 1³.654 n. 4). However, it seems reasonable to accept Dio's evidence (40.49.5) that the senate met on the evening of 19th to appoint Lepidus and that he entered office the next day, 20th (Lintott, p. 70 n. 94; contra, Ruebel, pp. 235-6, who would have Lepidus' appointment begin on 19th). G.V. Sumner, *JRS* 54 (1964) 43 n. 19, thinks that the first *interrex* was M'. Lepidus (cos. 66) because of the name given for his wife (see below on 43.12).

33.10-11: *is enim magistratus curulis erat creatus*

In arguing in support of the case that there was a fundamental distinction

170   Commentary

in status between the *interrex* and the *magistratus populi* (the former being a true relic of the regal period and appointed only when the *patres* took back control of the state in the absence of the normalities of the *res publica*), E.S. Staveley, *Historia* 3 (1954/5) 196-7, explains this phrase as showing, not that the position of *interrex* was a curule magistracy, but merely that Lepidus was made a curule magistrate (aedile?) so that he could be appointed *interrex* (that being a normal qualification).

33.11: *absentis Milonis*

Milo's house was situated in the Cermalus; he had another, inherited from his adoptive father, on the clivus Capitolinus (Cic. *Mil.* 64). Both were apparently accustomed to withstand attacks (Cic. *Att.* 4.3.3; cf. *Mil.* 38). Milo had not returned to Rome following the killing of Clodius until the night of 19th January (33.19-20; cf. Cic. *Mil.* 61); he must not have returned to his own house, since he is said to have been absent when it was attacked and the attacks did not begin until 20th (cf. Dio 49.49.4).

33:13: *fasces ex luco Libitinae raptos*

See Clark, p. 98.

33.14: *hortos Cn. Pompeii*

Pompeius' garden villa was on the west of the Pincian hill, possibly stretching down into the campus Martius (Platner-Ashby, p. 270). It was outside the pomerium; since he had only proconsular *imperium*, Pompeius was careful to remain outside the pomerium (cf. 28.12 and 34.4). The senate held meetings in the portico attached to Pompeius' theatre so as to allow him to remain outside the city boundaries (52.3-4) and still be involved; cf. below on 36.19.

33.15: *clamitans eum modo consulem, modo dictatorem*

That Pompeius was deliberately engineering the situation so that he would be appointed dictator, see Cic. *Att.* 4.18.3; Plut. *Pomp.* 44.1-3; App. *BC* 2.20; Dio 40.45.5-46.1 and 49.5-50.3.

33.18: *in voluntarium exsilium*

Cf. Cic. *Mil.* 63.

33.20: *petebatque nihil deterritus consulatum*

Elsewhere (35.16-19, cf. 51.3ff.) Asconius reports that Milo asked Pompeius' advice about continuing his consular candidature, offering to withdraw if Pompeius should suggest it. Cf. App. *BC* 2.21; Dio 40.49. 4-5.

Pro Milone

33.21: *tributim in singulos milia assium dederat*

Cf. App. *BC* 2.22. The distribution amounted to 400 sesterces per man, and must have added enormously to the burden of Milo's debts. As Clark, p. 98, points out, a comparison can be gained from the distribution of only 300 sesterces per man under the term of Caesar's will.

33.22: *M. Caelius*

App. *BC* 2.22 has a curiously different version of the assembly summoned by Caelius. Cicero's evidence (*Mil.* 91) reveals that it was simply a *contio* that Caelius addressed. Caelius and Milo were linked by their shared hostility to Clodius; Caelius had been accused *de vi* by Clodius in 56, and by the *gens Clodia* on an unknown charge in 54 (Cic. *Q.f.* 2.12.2). Caelius continued to support Milo's cause (34.15, 36.13, 37.14, 55.4); when he broke with the Caesarians in 48 he sought and secured Milo's involvement (Caes. *BC* 3.21-22).

33.23: *ac [Cicero] ipse etiam causam egit*

Clarke includes *Cicero* in his *OCT* (accepting a reading which goes back to one of the Poggian-derived mss., *cod. soc. Columb.* B7), having left it out in his text of Asconius in his edition of the *pro Milone*. It is not included in the editions of Kiessling and Schoell, Stangl, and Giarratano; cf. Madvig, p. 50 n. 4. It is doubtful if Cicero did speak at this *contio*, in view of his silence at *Mil.* 91 about any role he played (Lintott, p. 70 n. 101), and so his name should not be included and the *ipse* should be taken to refer to Caelius.

34.2-3: *itaque primo factum erat s.c.*

Dio 40.49.5 says that the *s.c.u.* was passed on the evening of 19th January (the day after Clodius' death), but it is clear that it was passed later than that. Dio's statement is incompatible with the inactivity of Pompeius who was still in his *horti* on 22nd January doing nothing (51.3-7), and Asconius makes it clear that the *s.c.u.* was not passed until after a series of *interreges* (*alii ex aliis* — 33.25) who each held office for five days. It was most likely passed in the intercalary month, for it seems to be included in the series of events which Asconius says took place then (34.20-21: *haec agebantur mense intercalari*), but the tense of the phrase being considered here might suggest otherwise. Lintott, p. 71 n. 112, says that these events cannot all be fitted into the intercalary month and that the senate meeting at which Scipio spoke (c. 18th February) would then be out of order in Asconius' account (for the order of events in Asconius' account, see below on 34.21). The form of the *s.c.u.* is unusual; though it starts off with the usual formula, it goes on to name Pompeius specifically and to give him the right to collect troops in Italy (cf. Lintott, *Violence*, pp. 151-2).

172   Commentary

34.7-8: *postulaverunt apud eum familiam . . . exhibendam*

The two young men who initiated proceedings aginst Milo brought before Pompeius an *actio ad exhibendum*, 'an ordinary private law action, used *inter alia* as a preliminary to a noxal action against a master for damage done by his slaves' (Lintott, p. 71 with n. 109). Caelius did not question this procedure or use his veto on Milo's behalf, but himself demanded the slaves of some of the opponents. Theoretically the *interrex* handled litigation during his term of office (Cic. *fam.* 7.11.1; Mommsen, *Staatsrecht*, 1^3.660-1), so it is interesting that in this case the application was made to Pompeius. Perhaps this shows how widely the senate was already prepared to let him exercise powers as proconsul (Lintott, loc. cit.).

34.8-9: *duo adulescenti qui Appii Claudii ambo appellabantur*

These young men were the sons of C. Claudius Pulcher (pr. 56) and therefore nephews of Clodius and his elder brother Ap. Claudius Pulcher (cos. 54). Because neither of them bore the *praenomen* of their natural father, Clark, p. 99 (following Manutius), thinks that they had both been adopted by their uncle Appius, taking his *praenomen*. Wiseman's solution (*HSCP* 74 [1970] 207-21, followed by SB *Att.* 2.154) is that the younger of C. Claudius' sons was adopted by Appius, and consequently he changed his *praenomen* and his filiation, and that the other son was called Appius by his father, either because he used the *praenomen* of his own father (the consul of 79) or because there was another son, called Caius after his father in the usual way, who died young (requiring the second son to be given a different *praenomen*). One of the young men is subsequently called *maior* (39.11, 41.7), presumably the older brother; he is probably to be identified with the Ap. Claudius whose filiation we know as C.f. (Cic. *fam.* 11.22.1, dated to 43; cf. *Att.* 3.17.1). He became consul in 38. It is probably also this young man who is referred to in 58 as a possible prosecutor of Q. Cicero on his return from the governorship of Asia (Cic. *Att.* 3.17.1); despite this, and his role in prosecuting Milo, Cicero seems to have remained on good terms with him (*fam.* 11.22.1-2).

34.9-10: *C. Claudi, qui frater fuerat Clodi*

Clark, p. 99, thinks that the tense of *fuerat* implies that C. Claudius was dead; it may have been used simply because Clodius was now dead. On his return from a governorship in Asia (see above on 19.7), he was prosecuted for extortion, but the trial was apparently delayed until 51, when he was found guilty and went into exile; on the date of the trial, see Wiseman, *HSCP* 74 (1970) 207 (Claudius took no part in the prosecution of Milo, and so may have been in exile by then). The case carried on, since recovery of money due to the state was insisted on, and in the aftermath C. Claudius' younger son made some damaging revelations

Pro Milone 173

about his father's misconduct (Cic. *fam.* 5.8.2-4; Gruen, *Last Generation*, pp. 351-2; SB *Fam.* 1.389-401).

34.12-13: *duo Valerii, Nepos et Leo*

Two obscure personages: the first, P. Valerius Nepos, was the third accuser of Milo *de vi* (41.7), and the second, P. Valerius Leo, was a *subscriptor* in Milo's prosecution for *ambitus* (54.13-14).

34.11-15: *easdem Faustae et Milonis . . . et Q. Pompeii postulavit*

The reading of S and P is as follows: *easdem Faustae et Milonis familias postulaverunt duo Valerii Nepos (valerii nepotes* PM, *valerutiae potes* S) *et Leo et L. Herennius Balbus P. Clodi quoque familiam et comitum eius postulavit. eodem tempore Cecilius familiam Hypsaei et Q. Pompeii postulavit.* The reading of M deletes the words *et comitum* to *Cecilius familiam*, and is therefore of little use. The difficulty is where to punctuate. All the modern editions put a full stop after *Leo* and make *L. Herennius Balbus* the subject of the first *postulavit*, and emend *Cecilius* to *Caelius*, making it the subject of the second *postulavit*. However, L. Herennius Balbus is to be identified with one of the accusers of Caelius in 56 (Cic. *Cael.* 25), and hence is likely to have been a connection of the Claudian family (which was behind the prosecution of Caelius); he may have been related to the C. Herennius who attempted to secure Clodius' transfer to plebeian status in 60 (Cic. *Att.* 1.18.4, 19.5; Gruen, *Last Generation*, p. 307; cf. R.G. Austin, *Ciceronis pro M. Caelio oratio*, pp. 78 and 154). If he were a connection of Clodius, he would not have been likely to request Clodius' slaves for examination; hence it seems preferable to add him to the list of persons who requested Milo's slaves for examination and to put a full stop after his name (which is what M does). As Caelius (an obvious emendation for the mss. reading *Cecilius*) was supporting the cause of Milo, he is more likely to have requested the slaves of Clodius for examination, and it would make better sense to move the stop from after the first *postulavit* and place it after *Caelius*. He too may be the subject of the second *postulavit*, having requested for examination the slaves of Hypsaeus and Q. Pompeius who were both opponents of Milo, or else, as Clark, p. 99, suggests, the name has dropped out. The text would then read: *easdem Faustae et Milonis familias postulaverunt duo Valerii, Nepos et Leo, et L. Herennius Balbus. P. Clodi quoque familiam et comitum eius postulavit eodem tempore Caelius; [et or ...] familiam Hypsaei et Q. Pompeii postulavit.*

34.15-17: *adfuerunt Miloni*

Almost the same team as had spoken for Scaurus at his trial for extortion in 54 (see above on 20.16). Cato did not appear then, as he was praetor in charge of the court; it was thought he might not favour Scaurus (19.9ff.).

174   *Commentary*

On the attitude of Cato to Milo, see 53.24-54.7, and cf. Cic. *fam.* 15.4.12. Faustus Sulla had not spoken on Scaurus' behalf but had appeared among his supporters (28.21); he spoke up now on behalf of Milo who was his brother-in-law. This is not the same team who ultimately spoke for the defence at Milo's trial *de vi*; only Marcellus, Cicero and Milo are mentioned as participating for the defence there (40.4ff., 41.9). Cato served as one of the jurors at that trial (53.25).

34.17-18: *verba pauca Q. Hortensius dixit*

It seems that Hortensius successfully argued that the slaves concerned were now free men, for we hear no more of the application for examination. Asconius (35.14) says twelve slaves were manumitted; Milo cannot then have had as large an entourage as his opponents claimed (35.1), else there would presumably have been a number of slaves still available for examination. Hortensius continued to support Milo, for he spoke in favour of having him tried under the existing laws (44.16-17; Schol. Bob. 117.17-18).

34.21: *post diem tricesimum fere*

About 18th February (i.e. before the intercalary month started): for the relationship of this senate meeting and the date of the *s.c.u.* and the requests for examination of slaves, see above on 34.2-3. Asconius' account of events on this page is not strictly in sequence; for an analysis of events in the intercalary month, see Ruebel, pp. 239-40.

34.23: *contra Q. Caepionem*

The mss. here read *M. C[a]epionem*. Manutius would read *M. Ciceronem*; he is followed by Giarratano (on the basis of Cic. *Mil.* 12). Halm would read *M. Caelium*, which is possible since Caelius supported Milo's cause. It is difficult to see, however, how *Ciceronem* or *Caelium* could have been corrupted into *Caepionem*. Clark favours reading *Q. Caepionem*, a simple alteration, taking it to be a reference to M. Brutus (followed, most recently, by J. Geiger, *Anc. Soc.* 4 [1973] 149 n. 23, and Lintott, p. 71). Brutus did write a defence of Milo later, and so might have spoken on his behalf at this senate meeting, but there are arguments against this: he was then only a young man and is not known to have taken a role in public affairs at this time; he is not referred to simply as Q. Caepio, but at least in the form of Q. Caepio Brutus (cf. Cic. *Phil.* 10.25-26); Asconius elsewhere calls him M. Brutus (41.11) and is not likely to have used a different form here. Moreover, there is a chance that he was not in Rome at this time: he had been quaestor in 53 (*vir. illus.* 82.3-4) and had gone out to serve under his father-in-law Ap. Claudius Pulcher, the governor of Cilicia (who remained there until replaced by Cicero in 51). A fourth emendation is *M. Catonem*, put forward by Kiessling and Schoell (in the addenda) and by Stangl (on the basis of Cic. *fam.* 15.4.12); Cato supported the cause of Milo (34.17, 53.24ff.), and the corruption is palaeographically possible (e.g. the ninth century exemplar could have read *c[a]epionem* from an earlier *catonem* written in rustic capitals).

34.26: *cum sex ac XX servis*

See above on 31.20.

34.26-35.1: *post horam quartam, senatu misso*

See above on 31.17.

35.3: *tribus vulneribus*

Cic. *Mil.* 86 speaks of one wound only, and says nothing about Clodius being carried to a nearby tavern and Milo's assault on it. Presumably Asconius got these details from a report of Metellus Scipio's speech in the *acta* (Stangl, n. ad loc. = 33.6-19).

35.8: *parvolum filium*

Clodius had a son and a daughter by Fulvia; as the marriage took place probably between 62 and 60 (see above on 32.21), the boy can have been no more than about nine at this time. In correspondence between M. Antonius and Cicero in 44, the son of Clodius was called *puer* (Cic. *Att.* 14.13A and B); by then he was the stepson of Antonius, who was Fulvia's third husband, but he turned out to be a disappointment to his stepfather (Val. Max. 3.5.3).

35.13: *duos solos saucios factos esse*

Cicero states that Milo's coach-driver was killed (*Mil.* 29). He could have been a *libertus*, and so Metellus Scipio's allegation could have been literally true but misleading. Cicero's other vague statements about deaths among Milo's men should be treated with caution (Lintott, p. 69 n. 88).

35.14: *XII servos ... manu misisse*

Cf. *Dig.* 40.2.9: *iusta causa manumissionis est, si periculo vitae dominum servus liberaverit.*

35.16: *Milo misisse ad Cn. Pompeius*

Presumably this refers to the incident, dated to 22nd January (51.3-7), when Milo attempted to see Pompeius but was told through a neighbour not to approach him. It seems that Milo continued trying to see Pompeius, but the latter refused to admit him and kept to his gardens, even when granted powers by the *s.c.u.* Pompeius insisted that Milo be excluded from senate meetings (51.26-52.5, cf. 36.21-23); this was done, apparently, to create the impression that Pompeius was afraid of Milo (36.18-19, 50.22-23, 52.5-6).

35.17-18: *Hypsaeo summe studebat, quod fuerat eius quaestor*

See above on 30.8.

35.19: *Pompeius respondisse*

A typically non-commital answer from Pompeius; cf. e.g. Pompeius' refusal to say which of the proposals regarding the restoration of Ptolemy Auletes he wanted (Cic. *fam.* 1.1.3-4). And typically ungenerous, in view of Milo's past support; cf. the brutal reply to Hypsaeus' request for help when prosecuted later (see above on 30.8).

35.22: *C. Lucilium*

C. Lucilius Hirrus had been tribune in 53; he was a relative of Pompeius (Willems, *Sénat*, 1.520), and a further link with him is indicated by his support of the (unsuccessful) proposal of his colleague, M. Coelius Vinicianus, that Pompeius be made dictator (references in *MRR* 2.228). Despite Asconius' comment, his friendship with Cicero seems to be denied by his part in senatorial discussion of Cicero's request for *supplicationes* in 50 (Cael. in Cic. *fam.* 8.11.2; cf. *Q.f.* 3.6.4, and SB *Fam.* 1.386-7). For the rest of his career, see Münzer, *RE* 13 (1927) 1642-45, s.v. 'Lucilius' no. 25; Willems, loc. cit. For the incident which led Pompeius to use Lucilius and Cicero as intermediaries with Milo, see Cic. *Mil.* 65, and below on 51.7.

35.25-26: *Cn. [Pompeium] creari dictatorem oportere*

See above on 33.15.

36.1: *consulem sine collega*

For a discussion of Pompeius' appointment, with a list of ancient and modern references, see Gruen, *Last Generation*, pp. 153-5.

36.2-3: *M. Bibuli sententiam*

Plut. *Pomp.* 54.6, *Cat. Min.* 47.3-4; Dio 40.50.3-4. The proposal had the support of Cato.

36.3-4: *ab interrege Servio Sulpicio*

Ser. Sulpicius Rufus came at the end of a series of *interreges* (33.25). He

Pro Milone 177

was rewarded with a consulship the next year, having had to wait a long time since his praetorship in 65, and after failing in his attempt at the consulship for 62.

36.4: *V Kal. Mart. mense intercalario*

The intercalary month began either on the day after the Terminalia, which was celebrated on 23rd February, or on the second day after it (i.e. on 24th or 25th: Liv. 43.11.13, 45.44.3). There is argument whether in the year 52 the number of intercalated days was twenty-two or twenty-three (see M.T. Raepsaet-Charlier, *Historia* 23 [1974] 278-83), and on what day the intercalary month started. A.K. Michel's solution (*The Calendar of the Roman Republic* [Princeton, 1967] pp. 160-2, followed by Ruebel, p. 232 n. 4 and p. 246 n. 37) is that February always 'lost' five days when intercalation occurred (even though the intercalated month sometimes began on 25th), that the intercalary month always consisted of twenty-seven days (i.e. twenty-two intercalated days plus the five 'lost' days of Feburary), and that when it was necessary to intercalate twenty-three days, the intercalary month did not begin until 25th February, the 24th being a normal day. The intercalary month went through until the beginning of March, so that dates in the month were expressed by the sort of formula we have here. Clark, who believes (for other reasons) that only twenty-two days were intercalated in 52 and that the intercalated month consisted of twenty-seven days, dates Pompeius' appointment as sole consul to 24th of the intercalary month; this date is accepted by Ruebel, pp. 239-40. Lintott, p. 72 n. 112, though he believes that twenty-three days were intercalated in 52 (cf. *CQ* 18 [1968] 189, and SB *Att.* 3.212), accepts the view that there were twenty-seven days altogether in the intercalary month, but he is confused about the date of events at the end of the intercalary month (see next comment). If the intercalary month is to be regarded as having twenty-eight days, the date of Pomepius' appointment would be 25th of the intercalary month.

36.5: *post diem tertium*

Clark, p. 101, and Greenidge, *Legal Procedure*, p. 391, take this to mean 'on the fourth day', that is *prid. Kal. Mart.* (27th of the intercalary month, which they believe to have contained twenty-seven days). As the items which Asconius goes on to list here (36.7-9: the death of Clodius, the burning of the curia, and the attack on Lepidus' house) correspond to those discussed at the senate meeting which he elsewhere dates specifically to *prid. Kal. Mart.* (44.10), it is clear that he is referring to the same meeting in both places and that Clark's meaning for this phrase is correct. Linderski, *HSCP* 76 (1972) 196-7, and Lintott, p. 72, take the phrase to mean 'on the third day after', dating the senate meeting which considered the new laws to the 26th of the intercalary month and assigning

178   *Commentary*

the meeting described by Asconius at 44.10ff. to the 27th. This view is accepted by Ruebel, p. 240.

36.7: *alteram de vi*

Although there were laws in existence under which Milo could have been charged (*lex Cornelia de sicariis et veneficiis*, and *lex Plautia de vi;* cf. Clark, pp. 11-12 on Cic. *Mil.* 13), Pompeius obviously thought that additional legislation was needed, aimed directly at the events which had caused the recent chaos. His *lex de vi*, backed by a *senatus consultum*, instituted an *ad hoc* proceeding, and it included specific mention of Clodius' murder, the burning of the curia, and the attack on Lepidus' house. When the proposal was discussed in the senate, it was readily declared that the specific incidents were acts *contra rem publicam* (Cic. *Mil.* 12-13 and 31; 44.10-12), but there was hesitation about instituting an extraordinary *quaestio*. Hortensius moved that any trials connected with the incidents should be heard *extra ordinem*, but that they should be heard under the existing legislation (44.16-17; cf. Cic. *Mil.* 13). A senator, usually taken to be Fufius Calenus, called for Hortensius' motion to be divided: the first part was carried, and the second part was vetoed by the tribunes Plancus and Sallustius Crispus (on the two parts of Hortensius' motion, see below on 44.21-45.1). That left the way open for Pompeius to institute a *quaestio nova* by his *lex de vi*. It was not his aim to replace previously existing criminal law in this area, since it was left in force: e.g. Milo was prosecuted under the *lex Pompeia* and subsequently under the *lex Plautia de vi*, as were others (54.17-18, 55.10-11).

36.9: *alteram de ambitu*

Clark, p. 101, thinks that both the *lex de vi* and the *lex de ambitu* set up special *quaestiones*, but Gruen, *Last Generation*, pp. 236-7, thinks that the *lex de ambitu* set up a permanent court and was intended to be the operative statute on electoral bribery. In favour of the latter view, one could point to the fact that the law was made retroactive (App. *BC* 2.23; Plut. *Cat. Min.* 48.3) and that the law was still in operation in 51 in a case which had nothing to do with the events of 53 and 52 (M. Valerius Messalla: Cic. *fam.* 8.2.1, 4.1; Val. Max. 5.9.2). Again, Pompeius' law on *ambitus* did not entirely replace existing legislation; the *lex Licinia de sodaliciis* of 55, which had incorporated earlier legislation on electoral malpractice and added provisions on *sodalitates*, was still in operation, since Milo was prosecuted under both Pompeius' law and the *lex Licinia* (38.22-39.2, 54.9-11 and 14-15) and Messalla, after being acquitted in one trial (presumably under the *lex Licinia de sodaliciis*: Cael. in Cic. *fam.* 8.2.1, 4.1; SB *Fam.* 1.385 and 389), was eventually found guilty *de ambitu*. Messalla's case, incidentally, shows that the view of Greenidge, *Legal Procedure*, p. 392, that the validity of both *quaestiones* set up by

Pompeius' laws was to last probably only until the end of 52, is unacceptable; while the majority of the cases under Pompeius' laws were heard in 52, some of the cases *de vi* were not heard until early 51 (Gruen, *Last Generation*, pp. 343-9, esp. n. 172). Cic. *fam.* 7.2.3 shows that the new procedures were still in operation early in 51 (on the date of the letter, see SB *Fam.* 1.351). The *lex de ambitu* was regarded by later writers as very important in controlling electoral corruption (Plin. *pan.* 29.1; Tac. *dial.* 38).

36.9: *poena graviore*

According to Greenidge, *Legal Procedure*, p. 391, the new penalty presumably was *aquae et ignis interdictio*, but the penalty under the previous *lex de vi* was exile (Cic. *Sull.* 89, *Sest.* 146). Perhaps confiscation was now added to the penalty as indicated by the sale of Milo's goods (see below on 54.20-21). Of the previous laws on *ambitus*, the *lex Calpurnia* of 67 provided for expulsion from the senate, exclusion from further offices, and monetary fines (see below on 69.12-13), and the *lex Tullia* of 63 added an exile of ten years for persons found guilty (Dio 37.29.1).

36.10: *forma iudiciorum breviore*

Some of the details of new procedures are mentioned by Asconius; while the bulk of the information relates to the trial of Milo *de vi*, certain of the procedures are said by Asconius to relate to both *quaestiones*. There was to be a strict time limit on all speeches, and the proceedings were to be completed in five days. An album of jurors was drawn up by Pompeius himself (38.17-19); on the final day of the trial, eighty-one jurors were chosen by lot, twenty-seven from the three orders, and the prosecutor and defendant were each allowed five challenges in each order, leaving a final number of fifty-one to cast the verdict (39.20-27). For the *quaestio de vi* Pompeius provided for the immediate selection by popular vote of an ex-consul as presiding officer (38.14-17); *quaesitores* for the other courts were appointed in the usual way (see below on 39.5-6). Other procedures not mentioned by Asconius include: the number of *patroni* on either side was restricted (Dio 40.52.1; but cf. above on 20.15); written testimony from absent advocates and character witnesses was banned (Plut. *Pomp.* 55.5, *Cat. Min.* 48.4; Dio 40.52.2); rewards were offered to those who were successful in prosecutions for bribery or who turned state's evidence, namely immunity from prosecution for their own similar offences in the past (App. *BC* 2.24; Dio 40.52.3-4); a fixed day, determined in advance, was required for each trial (Cic. *Att.* 13.49.1).

What is not clear is whether the new rules were intended to apply to all the criminal *quaestiones*. Clark, p. 101, thinks it likely that the new regulations were peculiar to the two special *quaestiones* and passed away

180   Commentary

with them; he argues that Cicero's comment in 45 (*Att.* 13.49.1: *scis enim dies illorum iudiciorum praestitutos*) implies that the system was not still in force then. The view of Tac. *dial.* 38.2 and of Dio 40.52.3 is that the new rules applied to all the courts (Mommsen, *Staatsrecht*, 4.325; cf. Douglas on Cic. *Brut.* 243). The voting figures given by Asconius for the trial of Saufeius under the *lex Plautia de vi* (55.16-17) total fifty-one; this suggests that at least the procedure for selecting jurors was intended to be applied to other courts (but cf. below on 38.17).

36.18-19: *seu timere se simulabat*

Cf. 50.22-23 and 51.26-52.6. Fear of assassination seems to have been part of Pompeius' personality (cf. Cic. *Sest.* 69, *Mil.* 65-66, *Q.f.* 2.3.3-4; and below, 38.3-4, 46.20-26 and 51.12ff.).

36.19: *plerumque non domi suae sed in hortis manebat*

In the disturbed days following the murder of Clodius, Pompeius remained in his *horti* (33.14, 51.3-7, cf. 50.22-26); even when he was armed with the authority of the *s.c.u.* (passed towards the end of February or in the intercalary month) and before he was made sole consul, he appears to have remained in his villa. Senate meetings were held in Pompeius' theatre so that he could be involved (52.3-5; Dio 40.50.2). Even after he was made consul, he seems to have remained in the area of his villa (46.25-26). In the next sentence Asconius describes how Pompeius suddenly dismissed a meeting of the senate because he said he feared the arrival of Milo; that is reminiscent of the comment that, after Pompeius' return to his villa from the collection of troops, Milo alone was not to be admitted (52.4-5). It may be that, after Pompeius was made consul, the senate occasionally met in his villa (though the very next meeting of the senate is reported as being held on the Capitol: Cic. *Mil.* 66). The decision of Pompeius to remain in his garden was dictated not only by his fear of assassination but also by his need to remain outside the pomerium, at least while he was technically proconsul only (cf. above on 33.14).

36.23: *proximo senatu*

Cicero records this meeting as having been held in the temple of Jupiter on the Capitol and as being *frequentissimus* (Cic. *Mil.* 66). He does not name the senator who made the charge in his account, but the other details are the same. Since the curia had been burnt down, the senate was meeting on the Capitol, which it occasionally did (principally for the first meeting of the year when the consuls were installed).

36.23: *P. Cornificius*

Clark, pp. 101-2, following Willems, *Sénat*, 1.537, identifies him with the

L. Cornificius who was among the prosecutors of Milo in the subsidiary trial *de vi* (38.23 and 54.18). Syme, *Historia* 4 (1955) 60-1, says that there is no reason to make such an identification: L. Cornificius may well have been the man who prosecuted M. Brutus in absence in 43, served Octavianus as an admiral and rose to a consulship in 35 (cf. Gruen, *Last Generation*, p. 342 n. 153). The Cornificii came from Lanuvium, as did Milo (Syme, art. cit. 61; Wiseman, *New Men*, p. 227); the most respectable were Cicero's competitor for the consulship, Q. Cornificius (mentioned at 82.9), and his son of the same name (pr. c. 45).

36.23-24: *ferrum Milonem intra tunicam habere*

Cicero uses the usual phrase *cum telo esse* (*Mil.* 66, cf. *Cat.* 1.15, and 55.12-13); elsewhere he makes it clear that the carrying of a weapon was not an offence (*Mil.* 11). There was a clause in the later *leges Iuliae de vi* which made it an offence (*qui pubes cum telo in publico fuerit*: *Dig.* 48.6.3); though this clause is referred to *vis privata* (since the *leges Iuliae* aimed to separate *vis publica* and *privata*), it is likely that it was taken from earlier republican legislation, either the *lex Lutatia* or the *lex Plautia*. But in that case, the clause must have had some qualification, such as *contra rem publicam* (Lintott, *Violence*, p. 119; cf. below on 44.12), since carrying a weapon was not an offence (otherwise we could not explain the increasing appearance of armed gangs in Rome). Pliny records (*NH* 34.139) an edict of Pompeius, issued in the disturbed days following the death of Clodius, *ut ne quis in urbe cum telo esset*, but presumably he too was concerned to prevent acts of public violence. The existing law on violence included the specific offences of armed attack on the senate and violence against magistrates (Cic. *Cael.* 1) and the occupation of public places (cf. below on 55.12-13); it may have been thought that Milo was carrying a weapon either to attack some senators or even Pompeius himself, but it would be necessary to prove his intention (cf. the phrase *cum telo dolo malo*: *Dig.* 48.6.10). As Cicero points out (*Mil.* 11), it was still necessary at law to prove the intention of carrying a weapon. It would, of course, be difficult to separate intention from the act of carrying a weapon, and Milo's opponents were presumably hoping to discredit him (and separate him further from Pompeius?) by making the claim that he was armed (cf. 38.1-3).

37.2: *M. Aemilium Philemonem*

This freedman of the first *interrex* of 52, M. Aemilius Lepidus, was obviously a person of some position; in April 53 Cicero stayed at his villa in Ulubrae in the Pomptine district (*fam.* 7.18.3). Clark regards him as a credible witness and accepts his story (pp. xxii and 102). It should be noted, however, that Cicero made no attempt to refute this claim, nor the one following in Asconius' account, nor the earlier one about the killing of slaves in Clodius' villa (35.7-11), and Philemon was not subsequently included among the witnesses at Milo's trial. Asconius does not venture to say whether the claim was true or false. As the via Appia ran through the Pomptine district, it is conceivable that Philemon was on the road, going either to or from his villa, when the fight between Milo's and Clodius' gangs took place.

37.6: *in villa Milonis*

Milo had an estate at Ocriculum in Umbria (Cic. *Mil.* 64), but if there is any truth in this story, it is more likely that Philemon and his associates were detained at Lanuvium, where it is very probable that Milo had property, since it was much closer to the scene of the encounter.

37.9: *triumvirum capitalem*

The *tresviri capitales* were elected together with other minor officials by the *comitia tributa* under the presidency of the *praetor urbanus* (Mommsen, *Staatsrecht*, 2^3.584). The incident described by Asconius here took place sometime in March (between Pompeius' appointment as sole consul and the vote on his two promulgated laws). As the elections were held in descending order, J. Linderski, *HSCP* 76 (1972) 196-7, argues from the existence of a *triumvir capitalis* at this time that the other magistrates had already been elected (those requiring consular presidency under Pompeius himself). Lintott, p. 72 n. 116, objects that, if they had been held, we would have expected Asconius to comment on it, and that it would have been odd for Pompeius to have conducted the praetorian elections without first electing a fellow consul. The latter objection is not valid, since it seems that there was a specific stipulation that Pompeius should not take a colleague (if he wanted one) until two months had expired from his appointment (Plut. *Pomp.* 54.5); in that case he could presumably have conducted the praetorian elections himself in the meantime.

37.10: *Galatam Milonis servum*

This seems to be a different story from that about one of Milo's drunken slaves who is supposed to have stabbed the *sacrificulus* Licinius to prevent him revealing their plot against Pompeius (Cic. *Mil.* 65; below, 51.8ff.). That incident took place before Pompeius became sole consul, whereas the incident related to Galata took place after.

37.17: *quia ita compereram, putavi exponenda*

As both of the stories were put forward at *contiones* summoned by tribunes, it is likely that the details were recorded in the *acta* and that Asconius got them from that source, which he used extensively for the introduction to his comments on the speech. The fact that he says there was no mention of the allegations by Cicero suggests that he did not get them from prosecution speeches or interrogation of witnesses.

37.18: *C. Sallustius*

The first mention by Asconius of this tribune's part in supporting the cause of Clodius and Pompeius; for other occasions on which he was involved, see 49.6-8, 49.24-50.1, and 51.8-14. There is a specific incident recorded which may be the basis for enmity between Milo and Sallustius. Gellius 17.18 records the story, taken from Varro, that Sallustius was caught in adultery by Milo, beaten with thongs and allowed to escape only when he had paid a sum of money. It is usually taken that the lady concerned was Fausta, given her reputation, and that the incident was recent to the events of 52. For a discussion of the incident, see J.E.G. Whitehorne, *CW* 68 (1975) 425-30, who concludes that it was part of the opposition's propaganda (cf. Hor. *serm.* 1.2.47-59), particularly when it is remembered that Fausta was related to Pompeius Rufus, the likeminded colleague of Sallustius. He escaped prosecution for the use of violence when at the end of his term of office he was no longer immune, but was subsequently expelled from the senate; again a charge of immorality was involved, but the real reason is likely to have been political rather than moral. Interestingly, the censor responsible for his expulsion was Ap. Claudius Pulcher (Dio 40.63.4), a brother of Clodius, who ought to have been grateful to Sallustius for the side he took in 52.

38.5: *dicturum quoque diem Ciceroni Plancus*

It is difficult to see what charge Plancus could have brought against Cicero. Cicero reciprocated Plancus' hostile attitude toward him (37.25-38.1); in one letter (*fam.* 7.2.2-3) he rejoiced over Bursa's condemnation and says that he hated him even more than Clodius. Though he had once defended him (the occasion is unknown), Cicero undertook the prosecution (unusual for him) of Bursa for violence in the rioting which followed the death of Clodius, when at the end of his term of office he lost his immunity from prosecution. Clark, App. II, pp. 129-33, places the trial in May or June 52 on the basis of Dio 40.45.2 where Pompeius Rufus, one of Bursa's colleagues, is called tribune in the middle of 53. That is most likely a mistake on Dio's part, and the trial is better dated to December 52 or January 51; that is consistent with its mention in Cic. *fam.* 7.2 which on other grounds can be dated to early 51 (SB *Fam.* 1.351). Dio 40.55.4 says that Cicero prosecuted no better than he had defended Milo — unfairly, since the prosecution was successful despite the efforts of Pompeius on Bursa's behalf (*fam.* 7.2.2) which included sending in a *laudatio* when his own law expressly forbade it (Plut. *Cat. Min.* 48.4; Dio 40.55.1). Cicero seems to have believed that Milo had been vindicated by Bursa's conviction.

38.14: *perlata deinde lege Pompei*

A space of *trinum nundinum* was required between promulgation and vote on a proposal. Clark, p. 103, thinking that the promulgation took place on *prid. Kal. Mart.*, the day the senate discussed the proposals (see above on 36.5), says the laws were passed on either 16th or 23rd March; Lintott, p. 73, thinking that the formal promulgation did not take place till 1st March, says the laws were passed on 18th March. Linderski, *HSCP* 72 (1976) 197 n. 63, says it could have been earlier if Pompeius was exempted from observing the *trinum nundinum*, in which case Plancus' *contio* held on 1st March (44.13-14) could have been to discuss the proposed laws. Pompeius' laws were passed at the urging of the tribunes, Pompeius Rufus and Sallustius (49.25-50.1).

38.16-17: *creatusque est L. Domitius Ahenobarbus quaesitor*

Pompeius as consul probably presided over the assembly which elected Ahenobarbus as *quaesitor*. Cic. *Mil*. 22 implies that Ahenobarbus was Pompeius' nominee. Ahenobarbus had been quaestor in 67, when he opposed the activities of Manilius (45.11-19), praetor in 58, and consul in 54, when he had opposed the coalition of Pompeius, Crassus and Caesar. He was married to Cato's sister Porcia.

38.17: *album quoque iudicum*

Pompeius himself drew up the list (Dio. 40.52.1) from the three orders of the *lex Aurelia* (cf. Cic. *Mil.* 21); it was a smaller and more select body than the ordinary album, and numbered 360 in all (Cic. *Att*. 8.16.2; Vell. Pat. 2.76; Plut. *Pomp.* 55.4). It would seem that this select album was to be used only for cases under the Pompeian law *de vi* (*qui de ea re iudicarent*), since in a letter of October 51 Cicero mentions the senatorial *decuria* of 300 (which presupposes an album of 900 *iudices* for the ordinary courts: Mommsen, *Strafrecht*, p. 130). Yet the figure of Plutarch for Pompeius' album is given in relation to the trial of Scipio under Pompeius' law *de ambitu* (which, it has been argued above, was intended to set up a permanent court). Perhaps Plutarch was wrong or the smaller album was to be used for the courts set up by both of Pompeius' laws, and for the year 52 only while the larger album continued to be used for the already established courts (Nicolet, *L'ordre équestre*, 1.620-3; cf. Gruen, *Last Generation*, p. 238 n. 116). For the procedure by which the jury was reduced to its final number, see 39.17ff.

38.20-21: *a duobus Appiis Claudiis*

Cf. above on 34.8-9. Subsequently (39.10-12, 41.6-7, 54.8-9, cf. 54.8-12) only the elder of the two brothers is recorded as taking part.

38.22-23: *itemque de ambitu ab iisdem Appiis, et praeterea a C. [A]teio et L. Cornificio*

A *divinatio* took place (39.5) which resulted in favour of the Appii (54.11-12), though when the case actually came up only Appius the elder is mentioned as prosecutor with the assistance of P. Valerius Leo and Cn. Domitius. Manutius would add *de vi* after *praeterea*, because we subsequently learn (54.18) that L. Cornificius was one of the prosecutors of Milo on an additional charge under the *lex Plautia de vi*. The difficulty with such an addition is the intention of the *divinatio* which follows. Perhaps the explanation for Cornificius laying a charge under the *lex Plautia* is that, having failed to secure the job of prosecuting Milo under one law, he turned to another. For further discussion of amendments, see Clark, pp. 103-4. On the identification of L. Cornificius, see above on 36.23.

38.23: *C. [A]teio*

The mss. read *c. ceteio*: Jordan conjectures *Cetego* (referring to a person otherwise unknown), while Clark plausibly conjectures *Ateio*, referring to C. Ateius Capito. The latter as tribune in 55 had opposed the activities of Pompeius and Crassus, especially the *lex Trebonia* and the granting of the Syrian command to Crassus; he was later expelled from the senate by the censor Ap. Claudius Pulcher for falsifying the auspices. He was a warm and constant friend of Cicero (*Att.* 16.16C, written to Capito, and 13.29.3 and 6). He was probably related to the senator L. Ateius Capito (*fam.* 8.8.5) who was *subscriptor* to a charge against Gabinius in 54 (*Q.f.* 3.15); cf. SB *Att.* 2.218, *Fam.* 1.402.

38.23-39.1: *de sodaliciis etiam a P. Fulvio Nerato*

The law *de sodaliciis* was proposed by Crassus in his second consulship in 55. At *Flacc.* 46 Cicero calls a man named P. Fulvius Neratus *lectissimus vir*; otherwise he is unknown. Clark, p. 104, conjectures from 54.16 that his accusation was prompted by a desire to gain the *praemium legis*.

39.5-6: *quaesitore A. Torquato*

The *gentilicium* of this man is given at 54.10, making his full name A. Manlius Torquatus. He is most likely to be identified with the praetor of c. 70 (*MRR* 2.127 and 237; J.F. Mitchell, *Historia* 15 [1966] 26); he fought on the Pompeian side in the civil war and after the battle of Pharsalus remained in Athens where Cicero wrote to him *fam.* 6.1-4. It would appear that none of the courts under which Milo was prosecuted was presided over by a praetor of 52 in the regular course of duty. The list of known *quaesitores* for that year is as follows:

1. L. Domitius Ahenobarbus: specially elected from the *consulares* to preside over the trial of Milo under the *lex Pompeia de vi*.
2. A. Manlius Torquatus: a *praetorius* who presided over the trial of Milo under the *lex Pompeia de ambitu*.
3. M. Favonius: presided over the conviction of Milo, presumably in absence, under the *lex Licinia de sodaliciis*; he was not praetor until 49.
4. L. Fabius: presided over the conviction of Milo in absence under a law *de vi* (presumably the *lex Plautia*).
5. Considius: presided over the trial of Saufeius under the *lex Plautia de vi*.

The last is the only one who might be considered to have been a praetor of this year, since he is the only one clearly known to have presided over a trial organised under one of the older existing laws. However, it is not certain how regularly praetors conducted trials under the Plautian law. The fact that another *quaesitor* was used for another case under the same law (most likely) suggests that it was not a regular area of jurisdiction for one praetor (Mommsen, *Staatsrecht*, 2^3.584, says that the *quaestio de vi* was never presided over by a praetor). Clark, p. 117, argues that the case before L. Fabius cannot have been under the Plautian law, precisely because Considius is nominated as *quaesitor* for that court. This makes the assumption that there would only be one *quaesitor* for that court in any one year. Clark thinks that the court under which Milo was charged *de vi* was the *lex Cornelia de sicariis* but as the charge is specified as *vis* and as the *lex Plautia* was the operative law on that offence (apart from the *lex Pompeia* under which Milo had already been charged) it must be that law to which Asconius is referring (cf. Gruen, *Last Generation*, p. 343 n. 155). There is the further question whether the curule elections had been held yet (see above on 37.9): if they had not, Considius clearly cannot have been a praetor. That would also explain why *quaesitores* were used for some of these courts.

39.7: *prid. Non. April*.

4th April. For problems related to the dating of the trial, and in particular the discrepancy between the details of the law on this page and the actual account of the trial on 40-41, see above on 30.1-2.

39.12: *a Milone servos exhiberi*

The demand met with much the same ineffectual end as the earlier request (see above on 34.7-8). Presumably here the slaves were required as part of the interrogation of witnesses which occupied the first three days of the trial.

Pro Milone   187

39.17-18: *dicta eorum iudices consignarent*

On the basis of Caes. *BC* 3.14 that in the cases of those exiled under Pompeius' laws different benches of *iudices* heard the evidence from those who pronounced the sentence, Greenidge, *Legal Procedure*, pp. 394-5, has constructed the theory that the oral evidence was delivered before the *quaesitor* and a small *consilium*; on the third day a digest of the evidence was read over and approved by the *consilium* (this is what he takes the original mss. reading *confirmarent* to mean; cf. the sealing of testimony [52.11-12] and the next comment); on the fourth day the lots were prepared in the presence of all the *iudices* (the *omnes* of 39.18 implying that they had not all been present up until this time), and on the fifth day the final jury of eighty-one was chosen by lot and the verified digest of the evidence read out to them before they heard the final speeches from prosecution and defence; since Pompeius' album was a small one, the fifty-one required for any one case could only be empanelled for a single day. Clark, p. 105, counters by saying that Caesar's evidence is that of a hostile critic, and that Caesar talks only of those found guilty of *ambitus*, not of Milo's trial *de vi*; the suggestion that some of the jurors would be wanted for other cases would hardly apply to Milo's trial, since it is unlikely that any other legal business would have been conducted during it. It must be said that Asconius' account does suggest that the final panel of eighty-one was selected out of all the jurors (who presumably had heard the evidence up to the day of the drawing of lots); on the other hand it does seem wasteful to have the whole album of 360 jurors sitting for three days to hear the evidence. Discussion is complicated by the fact that we do not know the relationship between Pompeius' album and the normal album (see above on 38.17). Gruen's conclusion (*Last Generation*, p. 238 n. 116) seems the best: the exact relationship between the bench which sat for the first four days and the eighty-one selected on the last day is unclear, but the crucial point is that the final panel could not be known until the day the verdict was handed down (and so tampering with the jury was made more difficult).

39.18: *consignarent*

The mss. reading is *confirmarent*; on the basis of 52.11-12 (*post audita et obsignata testium verba*), Clark accepts Manutius' emendation to *consignarent*. Mommsen, *Strafrecht*, p. 422, accepting the mss. reading, thinks the phrase means that the *lex Pompeia* gave permission to the *iudices* to make statements on the case. This would be unusual, and would require exemption from the rule in the *lex Acilia* (line 39: *iudex nei quis disputet*). The remarks of Cicero at *Mil.* 55 to individual *iudices* seem to appeal to their memories and not to their testimony.

39.19-20: *pilae . . . aequarentur*

Cf. below on 71.8. The purpose of the examination of the lots was to see

188 Commentary

that they were all alike and that they contained the correct names (see Greenidge, *Legal Procedure*, p. 395 n. 2).

39.21: *sortitio iudicum fieret unius et LXXX*

It is usually assumed that there were twenty-seven from each of the three orders of the *lex Aurelia*, since Asconius says (39.25-26) that the accuser and the defendant were allowed to challenge five jurors *ex singulis ordinibus*, so that the final jury should have been made up of seventeen from each order. But the final count of votes (53.19-22) shows eighteen senators, seventeen equites and sixteen *tribuni aerarii*; a similar inequality is found in the trial of Saufeius *de vi* (55.5-7). A.W. Zumpt, *Criminalrecht*, 2.2.467, thinks that the numerals are corrupt and that the numbers in the three orders were equal; cf. Stangl, n.ad loc. (= 45.6).

40.1-2: *testis [C.] Causinius Schola*

For all that we know of this equestrian friend of Clodius, see above on 31.23 and cf. Cic. *Mil.* 46. Apart from the persons nominated below by Asconius, evidence was given by Q. Arrius (the former henchman of Crassus) and C. Clodius (see 31.24), both mentioned at Cic. *Mil.* 46.

40.7-8: *praesidium imploraverunt*

For the use of a guard to prevent disturbance to a trial, cf. the trial of Manilius in 65 (below, 60.10-14) and of Clodius for sacrilege in 61 (Cic. *Att.* 1.16.5).

40.9: *ad aerarium*

The aerarium was part of the temple of Saturn, in the south-east corner of the forum, reasonably close to the rostra; Pompeius would have had no trouble hearing and seeing the disturbance. Schol. Bob. 112.5 presumably infers from this detail (wrongly) that the trial was conducted in the temple of Saturn.

40.15: *coponem occisum*

In the earlier account (32.5-15) this detail is not mentioned.

40.16: *virgines . . . Albanae*

Clark, p. 106, conjectures that these were probably the Vestal virgins (cf. Manutius' emendation to *Vestales*), since Alba Longa was the ancient seat of the worship of Vesta. Another possibility is this: when the Romans destroyed Alba (Liv. 1.28ff.) most of the inhabitants were transported to Rome, but those who were not remained in neighbouring Bovillae where their descendants, known as Albani Longani Bovillenses, preserved

Pro Milone 189

Alban cults and memorials until imperial times (*ILS* 6188-9, cf. 2988 and Tac. *ann.* 2.41). It would be appropriate if evidence could be taken from priestesses of the locality where Clodius was actually murdered. There may also be some connection between this possibility and Cicero's appeal to Alban cults in § 85. In a passage immediately following (§ 86) Cicero refers to a chapel of the Bona Dea on the property where Clodius was (appropriately) first wounded. Clark reports Reid's suggestion (presumably based on this reference) that the *virgines Albanae* were priestesses of the Bona Dea.

40.18-19: *ultimae testimonium dixerunt*

Clark, p. 106, remarks that it is odd that two witnesses for the prosecution should have been heard last, and that Asconius does not mention here any evidence given for the defence. Cicero tells us that Cato's friend M. Favonius gave evidence about Clodius' threat to kill Milo (*Mil.* 44, cf. 26), but Asconius seems to say that the evidence about this threat was given by Cato from M. Favonius (54.3-6). For Sempronia and Fulvia, see above on 32.21.

40.22-23: *ut postero die frequens adesset*

For the discrepancy in the number of days taken for the trial caused by this account of Plancus' *contio*, see above on 30.1-2.

41.7: *M. Antonius*

There is no reason to doubt that this is the future triumvir (Clark, p. 106; Gruen, *Last Generation*, p. 339). That Cicero does not mention a prosecution of Milo among Antonius' misdeeds in the *Philippics* is not convincing, and no other M. Antonius is known for this period. Antonius was a close friend of Clodius in the early 50's; there had been a recent violent scuffle between them, but that may have been a temporary personal difference (Antonius was paying too much attention to Clodius' wife Fulvia: he was eventually to marry her — see above on 32.21). Cicero's reference to the scuffle (*Mil.* 40-41) would have special point if Antonius were one of the accusers.

41.9: *respondit his unus M. Cicero*

Under the law, three hours were allotted to the defence, and Cicero was given the task of speaking for the whole period. Though he did not speak with his usual *constantia* (which suggests that he lost the rhythm and impetus of his speech by digressing to deal with the interruptions and barracking of the Clodiani) and though Quintilian (4.3.17) calls the speech actually delivered and taken down an *oratiuncula*, 'the brevity of the written record [of the speech] is no reason to think that he gave up before his time ran out' (Lintott, p. 74), as Dio 40.54.2 says (see below on 42.1-2).

41.11: *quam formam M. Brutus secutus est*

On Brutus' published speech, see Quint. 3.6.93, 10.1.23, 10.5.20; Schol. Bob. 112.15-16; it was written as a rhetorical exercise. Cicero decided not to argue that the killing of Clodius was a service to the state. The rest of the discussion on pp. 41-2 of Asconius implies that Cicero's case in the delivered speech was fundamentally that of the rewritten speech.

41.14-15: *cum insidias Milonem Clodio fecisse posuissent accusatores*

The prosecution had to argue that Milo had criminal intent; in order to refute the prosecution's case, Cicero adopted the line that it was Clodius who laid the plot against Milo (*Mil.* 46ff.). For an analysis of the lines of argument and the reasons for adopting them, see Lintott, pp. 74-5; Gruen, *Last Generation*, p. 341.

41.21-22: *notum . . . erat utrumque mortem alteri saepe minatum esse*

Cic. *Att.* 4.3.5 (referring to events in 57), *Mil.* 25-26, 44, 52.

41.23: *maior quam Clodi familia*

On the size of the two entourages, see above on 31.20.

42.1-2: *itaque non ea qua solitus erat constantia dixit*

According to Dio 40.54.2 (cf. 46.7.2-3), Cicero was so overwhelmed by the sight of the troops that he did not deliver the speech he had prepared but was glad to retire after uttering a few inaudible words with difficulty. This story is no doubt the result of anti-Ciceronian bias in Dio's source. Plutarch (*Cic.* 35.2-4) has a similar story: Milo persuaded Cicero, knowing him to be a nervous starter, to be brought to the forum in a litter and to wait in it until the court convened, but even so Cicero was so put off by the sight of the troops that he could scarcely begin his speech and his voice faltered. These stories are obviously exaggerations; Cicero's nervousness is attributed to the sight of troops posted around the court, but he had already spent two days in court examining witnesses in the presence of the troops, and he had just spent two hours listening to the prosecution speeches under the same conditions. Moreover, he subsequently regarded the troops as having been posted there as much for his own protection (*fam.* 3.10.10), and in a letter of Balbus in 49 (in *Att.* 9.7B.2) it appears that Cicero had requested protection from Pompeius at

Pro Milone 191

the time of Milo's trial. As Asconius has just pointed out, it was the barracking of the Clodiani, rather than the sight of the troops, which put Cicero off. Cicero himself later believed that his performance on behalf of Milo had been forceful (*opt. gen. or.* 10), and his activities later in the year on behalf of Milonians and against Clodiani show that he had not been broken by Milo's condemnation. In general on Cicero's performance, see Settle, *TAPA* 94 (1963) 272-4.

42.2: *illa quoque excepta eius oratio*

On the grounds that shorthand had not been developed yet, Settle, art. cit. 274-80, argues that the 'other version' of the *pro Milone* was a forgery, either written by a Clodian to embarrass Cicero or as a later rhetorical exercise. The existence of the other version raises the whole question of the relationship between the delivered and the published version of a speech (see Part I, p. 3 with n. 9). Here we have the suggestion (if we believe Asconius) that there was little discrepancy between the two versions. An argument against Settle's idea of a forgery is the statement by Asconius, who had seen both versions, that they were much the same. What is likely is that the delivered version was taken down in some form (instances of such reporting are given in Settle, art. cit. nn. 20 and 21), reported (possibly in the *acta*) and passed into circulation in that way (Lintott, p. 74).

42.3: *scripsit vero hanc quam legimus*

The speech was presumably published before Cicero left for his governorship of Cilicia in the spring of 51. Clark, p. xxx, puts its publication between 1st August 52 and May of the following year (but does not say why he chooses August); Settle, art. cit. 273, thinks it may have been published soon after the trial when it might have been of some practical value in the continuing political struggles between Milonians and Clodians.

42.17: *in argumento huius orationis*

= 32.25-33.9. Cicero is referring not only to the *contio* addressed by Plancus and Pompeius Rufus which led to the burning of the senate-house but to the numerous *contiones* summoned by the pro-Clodian tribunes.

42.22: *rostra non eo loco quo nunc sunt*

The republican rostra were on the southern side of the comitium, and the curia was on the northern side. By Asconius' time, the rostra had been moved to the north-west end of the forum where Augustus had extended on the core of the rostra planned by Caesar. For description and discussion of republican and imperial rostra, see Platner-Ashby, pp. 450ff.

43.3: *post biduum medium*

On the date of Lepidus' appointment as *interrex*, see above on 33.10.

43.4-5: *non fuit autem moris*

On the responsibilities of the first appointed *interrex*, see Mommsen, *Staatsrecht*, 1^3.656ff.

43.10: *ex more quinque*

Mommsen, *Staatsrecht*, 1^3.656-7.

43.12: *uxoris eius Corneliae*

It is possible that Asconius is mistaken over the name of Lepidus' wife. By 50 at the latest, Lepidus was married to Iunia, the half-sister of Brutus; she was certainly of marriageable age by 52 (the date of the event referred to by Asconius), but there is no evidence that she was married to anyone before Lepidus. The only argument in favour of the possibility that between 52 and 50 Lepidus lost a first wife (Cornelia) and married a second (Iunia) is the character of his wife in 52, *cuius castitas* (Asconius says) *pro exemplo habita est.* Cicero's reference to Iunia in a private letter to Atticus written in February 50 (*Att.* 6.1.25) hardly fits someone who had exemplary *castitas* and might suggest that Lepidus had a different wife in 52, but such statements as that of Asconius are likely to have come from public utterances which may well be quite at variance with private reality (cf. Cic. *Cael.* 9, where Crassus' wife Tertulla is referred to as *castissima*, with Suet. *Caes.* 50 where she is listed among Caesar's 'conquests'). If Asconius is mistaken over the name, it is easy to find a possible source: Lepidus' son married a Cornelia and his nephew Paullus Aemilius Lepidus (cos. suff. 34) also married a Cornelia. For further discussion, see L. Hayne, *Latomus* 33 (1974) 76-9. Sumner, *JRS* 54 (1964) 43 n. 19, assuming that Asconius would not make a mistake about the name of a lady with a reputation for chastity, finds a way out of the difficulty by making the *interrex* M'. Aemilius Lepidus (cos. 66). But we have seen that Asconius is capable of such errors.

43.28: *vestra aetas, filii, facit*

For the relevance of this personal note to the purpose of the commentaries and the date of composition, see above Part I, p. 33.

44.1-2: *postulatur ut dividatur, id est de rebus singulis referatur*

On the procedure of *relationem* or *sententiam dividere*, see Cic. *fam.* 1.2.1; Sen. *ep.* 21.9, *vit. beat.* 3.2; Plin. *ep.* 8.14.6 and 15 (with the comments of Sherwin-White, ad loc.).

Pro Milone

44.10-11: *pridie Kal. Mart. s.c. esse factum*

Although Asconius says that the *acta* recorded nothing else being discussed in the senate that day other than the declaration that certain acts were *contra rem publicam*, it is clear from his report of Plancus' speech that more was discussed than that declaration, since the motion for a division presupposes a number of items for discussion. It is likely that the proposals for Pompeius' two new laws were discussed at the senate meeting on that day (see above on 36.5). The answer to the question, what was discussed at this meeting, is bound up with the question, what were the two parts of the motion subject to division (see below).

44.12: *contra rem p. factam*

By citing other instances of acts of *vis* which were associated with *contra rem publicam* declarations, Lintott argues (*Violence*, pp. 116-9; cf. art. cit. 72) that the declaration was made in order to facilitate a prosecution under the normal *quaestio de vi*. In this context it is informative that Asconius' account of Pompeius' law *de vi* (36.7-9) specifically includes the acts declared *contra rem publicam*. The success of the senate in making this declaration without veto placed a number of Pompeius' supporters in an awkward position (e.g. Plancus, who was ultimately tried *de vi* and condemned).

44.15-16: *haec dixit ad verbum*

The mss. read *Q.* (*q* S: *que* P¹ M: *Q.* P²) *Hortensium dixisse ... estimare* (*extimare* M). Clark emended the beginning to *cum Hortensius dixisset*, but saw that that would create a problem with *aestimare*. If it were left as an infinitive depending on *dixisset*, we would be asked to believe that Hortensius publicly said that he thought they would swallow a liberal dose of bitterness since he had given them a bit of sweetening. Those words are obviously what Munatius alleged that Hortensius thought. Hence Clark changed the infinitive to the subjunctive *existimaret*, but that gives a messy construction. Sumner, *Hermes* 93 (1965) 134-5, argues convincingly that one should not abandon the mss. reading lightly, and that the two infinitives *dixisse* and *aestimare* (or *existimare*) can be retained as *oratio obliqua* dependent upon the preceding *haec dixit*; the compiler of the *acta* has put what Munatius alleges Hortensius said and thought in the indirect form. The *oratio obliqua* must have been in the original, since Asconius says he is quoting verbatim. The passage should run thus:

> *Q. Hortensium dixisse ut extra ordinem quaereretur apud quaesitorem; existimare futurum ut ...*

44.21: *Fufium*

In view of Asconius' comment on the next page (45.4-6), this senator is usually identified as Q. Fufius Calenus. As praetor in 59 he had proposed the bill for the recording of jurors' votes by separate *ordines* (see above on 28.25), and as tribune in 61 he had vetoed a consular bill for a specially selected jury to hear the charge of sacrilege against Clodius, but was then persuaded by Hortensius to propose a special court with a normally selected jury (Cic. *Att.* 1.14.1 and 5-6, 16.1-2). Cicero does not name the senator who called for the division (§ 14: *postulante nescio quo*) and Schol. Bob. 117.6-7 is unsure of the identity (*sive Fufius Calenus sive alius* . . .). It may be that Munatius meant simply that a Fufius had been found, alluding to the similarity to the events of 61. In either case it would be appropriate for a Fufius to oppose Hortensius, since the latter had led the opposition to Fufius Calenus in 61 over the form of Clodius' trial.

44.21-45.1: *reliquae parti sententiae ego et Sallustius intercessimus*

Despite what Asconius goes on to say, he does not make clear what the senate wished to decree, since he does not say what the two parts of the divided motion actually were; he mentions only the part of Hortensius' motion that *extra ordinem quaereretur apud quaesitorem*. The majority opinion (e.g. Clark, pp. xxiv-xxv and 13-14; Lintott, p. 72) is that the two parts of the *sententia* were (i) that certain acts be declared *contra rem publicam*, and (ii) that Milo be tried under the existing laws, but *extra ordinem*. However, Schol. Bob. 117.14-15 writes: *nam duo conplectebatur, ut et veteribus legibus et extra ordinem quaereretur*. On the basis of this statement, Gruen, *Last Generation*, pp. 234-5 (cf. Mommsen, cited in Clark, p. 13), argues that the two parts were (i) that the prosecution be held *extra ordinem* and (ii) that it be conducted under the existing laws. Some support for this view comes from the speech itself (§ 14) where Cicero says: *quodsi per furiosum illum tr. pl. senatui quod sentiebat perficere licuisset, novam quaestionem nullam haberemus; decernebat enim ut veteribus legibus, tantum modo extra ordinem quaereretur. divisa sententia est postulante nescio quo . . .; sic reliqua auctoritas senatus empta intercessione sublata est.* However, Cicero does mention the *contra rem publicam* declaration just before this statement, and in the *argumentum* to the comments on the speech (115.2-3) the Schol. Bob. is aware of a senatorial decree that the murder on the Appian way was *contra rem publicam*. An argument against Gruen's view is the notice of Asconius that the only *s.c.* passed that day was the *contra rem publicam* declaration (which suggests that it was the part of the divided motion which was not vetoed). The effect of the veto on the second part of the motion (whichever of the two suggestions put forward it was) was to clear the way for Pompeius' institution of a *quaestio nova de vi* (and a *quaestio de ambitu*), despite some opposition from Caelius (36.13-15).

Pro Milone 195

45.4: *illud vos meminisse non dubito*

For the use of this phrase to help determine the range of Asconius' commentaries, see Part I, pp. 9-10.

45.11: *in quaestura*

The mss. read *praetura*, but if (as seems most likely) the subsequent description refers to the well-known tribunate of C. Manilius (entered in December 67) it cannot refer to Domitius' praetorship, which occurred in 58, but must refer to his quaestorship, held most probably in 67. Soon after entering office, Manilius brought forward a law *de libertinorum suffragiis*; it was carried on the day of the Compitalia, which we know from Dio 36.42.2 to have been 29th December, but then quashed by the senate (for the law and its annulment, see below on 65.35, and on the issue of voting rights in general for freedmen, see below on 52.18-19). Domitius had been vigorous in opposing this law of Manilius (cf. Schol. Bob. 119.14-17). If we were to retain the reading *praetura* and refer this account to events which were supposed to have taken place in 58, we would have either to conjecture that an otherwise unknown Manilius (or Manlius) proposed again the law which C. Manilius had brought forward in 67, or to assume that Manilius himself held a second tribunate in 58 and brought forward his proposal again. Both possibilities are unlikely. That it is a quaestorship of Domitius which is referred to is suggested by Cicero's phrase *iam ab adulescentia*: that is more appropriate to events of fifteen years before when Domitius would have been thirty-one, than to events of six years earlier when he was forty. Moreover, Domitius should have been consul in 55 *suo anno*; if he had been quaestor *suo anno*, it would have been in 67, and that seems to fit with opposition to Manilius at the end of that year. If it is Domitius' quaestorship which is meant, it is easy to see how the reading *praetura* has come from a copyist's confusion between the abbreviations q. and pr., or the error could have resulted because Asconius forgot what Domitius' office was at the time (see Part I, p. 64). On the confusion, see Badian, *Studies*, p. 143.

45.22: *L. Cassius*

See below on 78.5.

45.26: *cui bono*

Reference to Cassius' use of this phrase is made in Cic. *Rosc. Am.* 84, cf. *Verr.* 1.30, 2.3.137, *Cluent.* 197, and Val. Max, 3.7.9 (on Cassius' reputation for severity).

45.27-28: *quo tempore Sex. Peducaeus tribunus plebis*

The year 113: the date is confirmed by the fact that the orator L. Crassus was twenty-seven years old when he defended Licinia (Cic. *Brut.* 160).

45.28-46.3: *criminatus est . . . Marciam et Liciniam*

In 114, an omen appeared in which the maiden daughter of a Roman knight was struck by lightning; she was killed, her clothing rent, and her nakedness exposed, and the soothsayers interpreted this to mean that the Vestal virgins had violated their oaths. In December of 114, in a most spectacular case, no fewer than three Vestals, an Aemilia, a Licinia, and a Marcia, from the most distinguished families in Rome, together with their alleged paramours, were accused of *incestum* (Plut. *RQ* 83; Oros. 5.15.20-21). As was customary, the Vestals were first tried before the college of pontiffs; the result was that only Aemilia was condemned, while the other two were absolved. Exact dates are provided by Fenestella (in Macrob. 1.10.5-6): Aemilia was condemned *a.d. XV Kal. Ian.*, and Licinia pleaded her case *a.d. XIII Kal. Ian.* Public outrage was increased by the obvious cover-up, and at the beginning of 113 a tribune Sex. Peducaeus brought in a measure to censure the pontifex maximus and the whole college of pontiffs for a wrongful judgment and to set up a special commission under Cassius, who had a reputation for severity, to retry the case. All three Vestals were then condemned (references in *MRR* 1.536).

46.3-4: *populus hunc Cassium creavit qui . . . quaereret*

Gruen, *Politics and Courts*, pp. 127ff., thinks that, in addition to still existing widespread superstition which stirred emotions and outraged consciences, there were political considerations involved in this case, involving an attack on the Metelli. Cassius' behaviour as *quaesitor* was regarded as unjustifiably harsh (46.4-6), which may suggest that personal and political enmities were playing a part. Marcia may have been the grand-daughter of Q. Marcius Rex (pr. 144), and Aemilia a descendant of M. Aemilius Lepidus Porcina (pr. 143); those two men co-operated in 143 in a public works project involving the water-supply which was opposed by the *decemviri sacris faciundis*. Porcina was a political ally of Ap. Claudius Pulcher and an opponent of Scipio Aemilianus; as consul in 137 he opposed the *lex tabellaria* proposed by Cassius (who was then tribune) with the support of Scipio Aemilianus. The hostility continued when the censors, of whom Cassius was one, fined Porcina for excessive luxury (Vell. Pat. 2.10.1; Val. Max. 8.1.7). Licinia was a daughter of Gaius, most likely C. Licinius Crassus, who as tribune in 145 had put forward a proposal to change the method of appointment to the college of pontiffs from co-option to popular election; this proposal was thwarted through the efforts of C. Laelius and the Scipionic faction. Licinia was defended by her cousin, the great orator L. Crassus, who was by now a

Pro Milone

son-in-law of Q. Mucius Scaevola, a Metellan connection, but Crassus' defence was in vain and a blow to the Metelli. The pontifex maximus was L. Caecilius Metellus Delmaticus (cos. 119) who had recently succeeded P. Mucius Scaevola in that position; although he was not formally charged, the reversal of his decision on the Vestals would have been a damaging blow. Finally the young M. Antonius was charged, presumably as a paramour (see below); his co-operation with the Metelli can be seen later, and as a talented and promising *novus homo* who would have attracted the attention of the Metelli it may well be that this prosecution is further evidence for his connection with that group.

46.5: *praeterea complures alias*

The use of the feminine implies that other Vestals were condemned, but we have no evidence of that. One ms. (S) has *alios*, and although we have indications of the names of a number of paramours charged, there is no evidence for any of them being condemned, apart from the statement of Obsequens 37 that several Roman knights were punished along with the Vestals. M. Antonius was presumably charged as a paramour; Val. Max. 3.7.9 and 6.8.1 tells us that Antonius, recently elected quaestor, was on his way to Asia when he learnt of a charge of *incestum*, so he returned voluntarily to defend himself before the Cassian court. It is obvious that this charge was in connection with the affair of the Vestals (Gruen, *Rhein. Mus.* 111 [1968] 59-63). Antonius spoke in his own defence and was acquitted. Cicero reports that C. Scribonius Curio defended a Ser. Fulvius on a charge of *incestum* about this time (*Brut.* 122, *inv.* 1.80; cf. Schol. Bob. 85.18); the occasion and the outcome are not recorded, but a connection with the trial of the Vestals is possible (Gruen, *Politics and Courts*, pp. 129-30; cf. Münzer, *RE* 7 [1912] 248). A final possible paramour can be suggested: in some accounts it is said that a Roman eques corrupted Aemilia who in turn implicated the other two Vestals, and then he exposed all three through information laid by a slave (Oros. 5.15.22; Plut. *RQ* 83; Porph. on Hor. *sat.* 1.6.30). Orosius calls the man L. Veturius, while Plutarch calls him Βουτέτιος βάρβαρος, perhaps emended to Βάρρος on the basis of the name Barrus given by Porphyrio. The name L. Veturius Var(r)us is suggested by Nicolet (*L'ordre équestre*, 2.1074-5, cf. 1.529 n. 3); others suggest L. Betutius Barus, calling to mind the orator from Asculum whom Cicero (*Brut.* 169) calls the most eloquent of non-Roman orators (Gruen, op. cit. p. 130; Wiseman, *New Men*, p. 18). The involvement of the last man, together with the statement of Obsequens, has led to the view that the trials represented an attempt by the optimates to discredit the equites (e.g. Nicolet, op. cit. 1.529). Equites were not the only ones involved; several prominent members of the aristocracy were also involved.

46.10: *Sex. Clodius quem in argumento huius orationis*

For Clodius, read Cloelius (see above on 7.18). For his role in the

198   Commentary

cremation of P. Clodius' corpse and the burning of the senate-house, see 33.5-9.

46.20: *insidiata Pompeio*

The plot against Pompeius has already been mentioned, with most of the details given by Asconius here, at § 18 (cf. *Sest.* 69, *dom.* 67, *aer. al. Mil.* frags. 4 and 9 P; Plut. *Pomp.* 49.2). The date, 11th August 58, is alone provided by Asconius, and he presumably got it from the *acta*. For Pompeius' fear of assassination, see above on 36.18-19.

47.1: *Damione*

Otherwise unknown. During an attack by Clodius in November 57 (see below on 48.4-5), Cicero took refuge in the house of a Tettius Damio, but as that attack was launched by Clodius and as the Damio of the incident described by Asconius was working for Clodius, the latter can hardly be identified with the man who had protected Cicero on the former occasion.

47.2: *L. Novius tribunus plebis*

Tribune in the same year as Clodius (58); Asconius is our only source for this incident, when Novius imposed a veto on the cognisance taken by the other tribunes of an appeal by Clodius' freedman Damio relating to a supposed attempt on Pompeius' life. Novius is possibly to be identified with the Novius Niger who was in charge of a special commission to investigate Catilinarian conspirators (Suet. *Iul.* 17.1; Münzer, *RE* 17 [1937] 1216 and 1218, s.v. 'Novius' nos. 7 and 12), though it would be unusual to have as *quaesitor* in 62 a man of such low rank as one who did not become tribune until 58.

47.3: *[L.] Flavium praetorem*

The *L.* has been added by Kiessling and Schoell here and at 47.13, correctly, since L. Flavius is mentioned as praetor-designate in a letter of Cicero written towards the end of 59 (*Q.f.* 1.2.10-11). In view of Flavius' judgment against Damio in the interests of Pompeius in the incident being described here, and in view of his support of Pompeius' side in the dispute with Clodius (see below), he is probably to be identified with the tribune of 60 who proposed an agrarian law to provide land for Pompeius' veterans.

47.5-9

Clark inserts *si ab* after *et* at the beginning of this quotation from the *acta*, adds *-que* after *obsessus* at 47.7, and puts a comma at the end of that line. Sumner, *Hermes* 93 (1965) 135-6, has shown that the *ab* is unnecessary, and that the insertion of *si* and *-que* is gratuitous, for with a stop after *obsessus est* the quotation as given in the mss. makes good sense, even if awkwardly expressed.

47.10ff.

Asconius' account of this incident is the fullest. Cicero mentions the dispute between Pompeius and Clodius over the custody of Tigranes briefly at *dom.* 66 and *Att.* 3.8.3. Plut. *Pomp.* 48.6 says only that Clodius took Pompeius' prisoner Tigranes away from him. Schol. Bob. 118.24-119.3 concentrates on the details of the fight on the Appian way in which M. Papirius was killed. Dio 38.30.1-2 says that Clodius had taken a bribe to remove Tigranes from the house of Flavius and to let him go, with the result that there was a dispute with Pompeius and Gabinius which broke into a fight among their followers.

47.25: *M. Papirius*

Clodius' killing of Papirius is mentioned in § 18 of the speech, as well as in the lemma here from § 37. All that we know of him is revealed in Cicero's speech and Asconius' comments (cf. Nicolet, *L'ordre équestre*, 2.971). *IG* 12.2.88 refers to a *negotiator*, M. Papirius M.f. Celer, at Mytilene towards the end of the republican period.

48.4-5: *quo die periculum hoc adierit ... nusquam inveni*

There are some who make the incident described by Cicero refer to the attack on him by Clodius on 11th November 57, mentioned at *Att.* 4.3.3 as taking place while Cicero was going down the via sacra. Consequently they take Asconius' admission that he has not yet found the date to show that he did not know of Cicero's letters and that therefore they did not exist yet in a published form (see Part I, p. 47). However, the date of that attack hardly agrees with the *longo intervallo* (when Cicero has just been describing incidents from the year 58) or with the *nuper* (which ought to bring the attack closer to the time when the speech was delivered): see Clark, p. 35. On the other hand, Cicero immediately goes on to describe the attack on Milo's house, which looks like the one that took place on the day after the assault on Cicero described in the letter mentioned above, so that in the speech he may have had in mind the attack which occurred in 57. If that is the case, Asconius has made an intelligent, but wrong, guess, dating the attack to the previous year 53. He does get the location right — *nam in sacra via traditur commissa, in qua est regia*, which suggests he could remember an account of such an incident and which in turn suggests that he may have read it in the letters (but was unable to check it and so, as often, relied on his memory). Or, of course, it is an incident which could have been described in any number of sources (e.g. Tiro's biography), and which Asconius has remembered badly.

48.18: *L. Caecilius Rufus*

Half-brother to P. Cornelius Sulla, the consul-designate for 65 who was convicted of bribery; as tribune in 63 he proposed a bill to restore full civil rights to Sulla and P. Autronius Paetus, but it got no further than discussion in the senate (Cic. *Sull.* 62-66; cf. Dio 37.25.3). Caecilius also threatened to impose a veto on the agrarian bill of Servilius Rullus (Cic. *Sull.* 65). He was *praetor urbanus* (*CIL* 1^2.2.761) in 57; in view of Asconius' precise dating, the word *praetor* should clearly be added where the mss. have omitted it. He is listed by Cicero as one of the praetors who initiated public measures for his recall and as a man who was unofficially anxious to devote his wealth to assist Cicero at that time (*red. in sen.* 22). In 54 Caecilius assisted his relative P. Sulla, along with the latter's stepson C. Memmius and his son, in the prosecution of Gabinius *de ambitu*; Sulla got the job in a *divinatio* with L. Torquatus, the man who had secured his condemnation for bribery in 66 (Cic. *Q.f.* 3.3.2, *Att.* 4.18.3).

48.20: *ludos Apollinares*

A serious food shortage, with a consequent very high rise in prices, occurred about the middle of 57. In a letter written about 10th September 57 (*Att.* 4.1.6) Cicero reports on a speech he delivered at a meeting of the senate on the Capitol on 7th September (*dom.* 15-16), proposing to appoint Pompeius to a special command to solve the food problem; in the days just prior to that meeting, because of the very high price of grain, a crowd flocked first to the theatre and then to the senate. The riots extended over a couple of days; there was stone-throwing and an attack on the consul Metellus Nepos (ibid. 5-6, 12-13) at a senate meeting in the temple of Concord on 5th or 6th September, and crowds were even present at the senate meeting on the Capitol on 7th September, when they called on Cicero to make a proposal. Dio 39.9.2 gives the same story, that the entire populace rushed into the theatre which was being used for festivals and then to the Capitol where the senate was in session, threatening to use violence. It would seem that this is the same incident to which Asconius is referring, Caecilius being an obvious senator to be threatened. But at that time it would have been the *ludi Romani* which were being celebrated, and not the *ludi Apollinares*. The latter were conducted from 6th-13th July, while the *ludi Romani* ran from 4th-19th September (cf. below on 69.21-22). Asconius seems to be mistaken over the name of the games.

48.21: *annonae caritate*

The situation with the corn-supply led to the appointment of Pompeius to a five-year command: for the details see Cic. *Att.* 4.1.6-7, *Q.f.* 2.5.1, *dom.* 5-31 passim; Liv. *per.* 104; Plut. *Pomp* 49.5; Dio 39.9.2-3; Balsdon, *JRS* 47 (1957) 16-8.

48.23: *nusquam adhuc legi*

On Asconius' admissions of ignorance, see Part I, pp. 30 and 77. Clark, p. 35, thinks that, because Asconius was unsuccessful in identifying the occasion, it must have been an insignificant one.

48.24: *cum defenderet Milonem apud populum*

In 57 Milo as tribune endeavoured twice to prosecute Clodius (who was then a *privatus*) under the *lex Plautia de vi*, before he should become aedile and thus gain judicial immunity, but Milo's attempts were both blocked in the senate (for the details, see Clark, p. 37; Gruen, *Last Generation*, pp. 294-8). A third prosecution is talked of as impending in Cic. *har. resp.* 7 (delivered in May 56), but that could only mean that Milo, then a *privatus*, was threatening to prosecute Clodius, then a curule aedile. There were ancient precedents for this, but the practice had become obsolete (Clark, p. 37). In retaliation, when Milo became a *privatus* in 56, Clodius accused him of using violence. There were three separate hearings before the people — on 2nd, 6th and 17th February, with 7th May fixed for the casting of votes (Cic. *Q.f.* 2.3.1-2, 5.5). There is disagreement whether Clodius planned to prosecute Milo in a *iudicium populi* (e.g. Clark, p. 33; Lintott, *Violence*, pp. 96 and 218) or before the normal *quaestio de vi* (e.g. Gruen, op. cit. p. 298 n. 139). It was at the meeting on 6th February that Pompeius spoke on Milo's behalf; he got through his speech despite constant interruption from Clodius' rowdies (Cic. *Q.f.* 2.3.2, *fam.* 1.5B.1). The final trial never took place; the conference at Luca intervened, Clodius changed his political attitude towards Pompeius (who had been as much his target as Milo), and the proceedings seem to have been dropped.

48.25: *apud Tironem*

For Asconius' use of Tiro's biography of Cicero as a source, see Part I, pp. 57-8. On Tiro generally, see McDermott, *Historia* 21 (1972) 259-86.

49.5: *eo die quo Clodius occisus est*

On Cicero's deliberately ambiguous language about the date of the meeting in this section compared with § 27, see Clark, pp. 23-4 and 40-1. Asconius, who had the *acta* in front of him, knew that the meeting was held on 18th January, and his words imply that there was no meeting on 17th. So Cicero's attempt to suggest that Clodius abandoned an uproarious meeting on 17th and left Rome because he wanted to get ready to lay an ambush for Milo (§ 27) is misleading.

49.14: *Causinius*

Asconius is our only source for the information that it was Causinius

Schola who provided the alibi that Clodius was at Interamna at the time of the Bona Dea break-in. For his relationship with Clodius and his part in the trial, see above on 31.23 and 40.1-2.

50.7: *via Appia est prope urbem monumentum Basili*

Asconius is really commenting on the sentence in §49 which follows the lemma he has quoted. Cicero says that, if Milo was intending to lie in wait for Clodius near the city, he would have chosen to kill him at night *insidioso et pleno latronum in loco*. Asconius is suggesting that the monumentum Basili is such a spot; Cic. *Att.* 7.9.1 mentions that a friend of his, L. Quinctius, was robbed with violence there. TP, 1.159, commenting on the *bustum* where Catilina is said in *comm. pet.* 10 to have murdered M. Marius Gratidianus, take it to refer to the monumentum Basili on the basis of Asconius' description, but in some versions the murder of Gratidianus is placed near the tomb of the Lutatii (see below on 84.8-9).

50.12-13: *socium eum coniurationis Catilinae*

It is more natural to take Cicero's words to refer to the forays of Clodius into Etruria, which Cicero mentions a number of times in the speech (§ §26, 50, 74 and 98), than to see in them an allusion to the story that Clodius left Rome to join the Catilinarians at Faesulae in 63 (Clark, p. 48). This is an example of Asconius' (unsuccessful) attempt to expand Cicero's statement on the basis of his own knowledge, a trap into which it is easy for commentators to fall. For this error by Asconius, see Lichtenfeldt, pp. 13-16. The same error is made by Schol. Bob. 172.14 (presumably taken from Asconius).

50.14: *opinio*

Though there are numerous instances where Cicero compares Clodius' actions to those of Catilina (e.g. *Sest.* 28, *dom.* 72, *Pis.* 15-16), there is no report in our sources of Clodius ever leaving Rome to join the Catilinarians at Faesulae.

50.15: *Manli centurionis*

For Manlius' part in the Catilinarian conspiracy, see Sall. *Cat.* 24, 27-30, 33 and 36; Plut. *Cic.* 14.1-2; Dio 37.30.4-5. Sallust's account of Manlius' early actions suggests that initially he was independent and joined forces with Catilina only after the latter's final electoral defeat (Seager, *Historia* 22 [1973] 240-1; contra, Phillips, *Historia* 25 [1976] 443-4). Cic. *Cat.* 2.20 tells us that Manlius was a Sullan veteran, Plutarch that he had served with distinction under Sulla; it is Asconius and Dio who tell us that he was a former centurion.

51.1: *dixerat in contione*

Asconius obviously got the date of the *contio* (51.4-5: 23rd January) and the quotation from the *acta*.

51.7: *hominem propinquum*

In the earlier description of the incident, the name of the intermediary is given as C. Lucilius (see above on 35.22).

51.14-15: *Licinium quendam de plebe sacrificulum*

Cic. *Mil.* 65 refers to this story of Licinius (who is called there a *popa*). Cf. above on 37.10.

51.22: *Lucium quendam*

Otherwise unknown.

52.3-4: *senatus in porticu Pompeii haberetur*

Before he was made sole consul, Pompeius was technically proconsul and so unable to enter the pomerium. Even when armed with the authority of the *s.c.u.* he did not enter the city, and senate meetings were held in the portico of his theatre so as to allow him to attend (cf. above on 33.14). Even after Pompeius was made sole consul, he continued to stay mostly in the upper parts of his gardens, at least in the period up until the trial of Milo (cf. 50.24: *ante iudicium*), and it may be that the senate occasionally met even then in his villa (cf. above on 36.19).

52.11: *idem T. Munatius Plancus*

Asconius' identification does not seem to follow here. The lemma of Cicero is making the point that, if Milo had intended to use violence, Pompeius had the actual power and the force of precedent to get rid of him; that he did not do so proves that the claim about Milo is false. There is no reference to the exhortation of Munatius Plancus in the lemma, unless Asconius has in mind an expansion of the point made by Cicero in the sentence just prior to the lemma (that Pompeius was leaving the decision entirely up to the court) or a reference in the remainder of the sentence (which Asconius covers by a simple *et cetera*) to the *hesterna contio* (at which Plancus made his plea).

52.18-19: *inter leges P. Clodi quas ferre proposuerat*

This is one of what Cicero would have us believe was a bundle of pernicious proposals which Clodius was intending to put forward in the confident expectation that he would be elected to a praetorship (cf. *Mil.*

33); he was so confident of having them passed that he had them engraved in advance. The proposal he was planning was the oft-repeated one of distributing the freedmen equally in all the tribes: for a brief history of the voting rights of the freedmen, see Clark, p. 115, and S. Treggiari, *Roman Freedmen during the Late Republic* (Oxford, 1969) pp. 49-50 and 164-6, and cf. 45.12ff. and 64.11ff. The proposal is also mentioned by Cicero in the speech *de aere alieno Milonis*, frags. 17 and 18 P. Cic. *Mil.* 89 suggests a new twist with the proposal — that Clodius was intending to liberate other people's slaves and make them his own freedmen (cf. the story in Dio 39.23.2 that Clodius wanted slaves brought from Cyprus by Cato to be named Clodii). Cicero is exaggerating the extent of Clodius' proposals; though they had the power to submit proposals, praetors rarely did so. Some attribute the proposal to Clodius' tribunate in 58: see G. Rotondi, *Leges publicae populi romani*, p. 409.

52.25: *significat id tempus*

Asconius relates Cicero's comment only to the Bona Dea incident and the subsequent trial, but to judge from the list of Clodius' activities just given by Cicero in § 87 he has in mind more than that incident, and in particular Clodius' activities since his tribunate.

52.25-53.1: *quaestor designatus*

As a result of misunderstanding Cicero's term *privato*, Asconius wrongly assumes that Clodius was *quaestor designatus* when the *s.c.* censured him and the special *quaestio* was set up. He was probably *quaestor designatus* (and hence *privatus*) when he broke into the Bona Dea ceremony, since it seems to have been celebrated about 4th December (cf. Plut. *Cic.* 19.3) and the quaestors entered office on 5th December. But he was quaestor by the time the senate issued its decree of censure and the special court was set up, so it follows that, unless Cicero is using the term *privatus* to refer to a quaestor (cf. *Verr.* 1.37), he is using it literally, in which case he is referring to Clodius' conduct other than during this incident.

53.1-2: *cum intrasset eo ubi sacrificium . . . fiebat*

For the incident and the subsequent trial, including the intense debate over the form of the trial, see Gruen, *Last Generation*, pp. 248-9 and 273-6, and cf. above on 44.21.

53.6-7: *cum bonarum partium hominibus*

See above on 30.17.

Pro Milone

53.11-12: *tribus suis patrimoniis deleniret*

On Milo's lavish expenditure to secure popular favour, see 30.9, 31.5-8 and 33.21. On the possibility that the number three is an invention, see Part I, p. 67; it is only a guess that the third inheritance came from his mother.

53.13: *puto iam supra esse dictum*

Since the point of Asconius' comment is not the using up of three inheritances, but from whom the inheritances came, the cross-reference is not to a statement made in the introduction to the comments on this speech (31.7-8: *in quas tria patrimonia effudisse eum Cicero significat*), but more likely to a comment on the speech *de aere alieno Milonis*, which also dealt with the extent of Milo's debts and which would present an appropriate situation for a discussion of Milo's wasted inheritances (see Part I, p. 11).

53.13-14: *ex familia . . . avo suo materno*

Milo was by birth a Papius from Lanuvium; he inherited standing and (probably) property there from his natural father. The Papii came originally from Samnium; some reached the senate in the late republic, one at least of whom, L. Papius Celsus, came from Lanuvium (*MRR* 2.471-2 and 599; Shatzman, *Senatorial Wealth and Roman Politics*, p. 293). He was adopted by his maternal grandfather, T. Annius. Wiseman, *New Men*, pp. 58 and 213, argues that, since there is no answer to charges of ignoble birth in the *pro Milone* and since adoption was a favourite method used by noble families to avoid extinction, Milo was not a *novus homo* and T. Annius must have been descended from the family of the consuls of 153 and 128; Gruen, *Last Generation*, p. 174 n. 41, takes the absence of mention of a noble background by Cicero and Asconius to show that Milo did not have one (cf. Wiseman, *New Men*, p. 213; contra, Taylor, *Voting Districts*, p. 190). Milo inherited a house on the clivus Capitolinus from his adoptive father (see above on 33.11), while his estate at Ocriculum in Umbria may also have come from his adoptive father (note a C. Annius T.f. Milo at Assisium in Umbria: *CIL* 11.5448). Milo also had possessions in the Chersonese (Cic. *Att.* 6.1.19, 5.2).

53.22-23: *inscio Milone initio vulneratum esse Clodium*

This is in accord with Asconius' assessment that the affray at Bovillae arose accidentally: cf. 41.18-21.

53.25: *M. Catonis sententia*

On Cato's support for Milo, see above on 34.15-17. He had at the same time supported the proposal for the appointment of Pompeius as sole consul (see above on 36.2-3).

54.4: *audisse eum a M. Favonio*

For the conflict between Cicero and Asconius about the question, who actually gave evidence of this threat, see above on 40.18-19.

54.9: *opera maxime Appi Claudi*

Though at 38.20-21 both young men are recorded as initiating the prosecution of Milo, subsequently only the elder of the two is recorded as taking part. Similarly with the prosecution for *ambitus*, only the elder is mentioned at 54.11-12, but both had laid the charge (38.22).

54.10: *apud Manlium Torquatum*

On Torquatus, see above on 39.5-6.

54.12: *praemium lege*

The reward mentioned in two cases held between 69 and 66 (and hence under either the Sullan law or the Calpurnian law on *ambitus*) was that, if the prosecutor himself had been condemned for *ambitus* and his subsequent prosecution was successful, he was restored to full rights (Cic. *Cluent.* 98). Cf. the desire of P. Cornelius Sulla to secure the right to prosecute Gabinius for *ambitus* in 54 so as to regain access to *honores* from which he was barred forever after his own conviction for *ambitus* under the *lex Calpurnia* in 66 (Gruen, *Last Generation*, p. 323). Dio 40.52.3-4 gives the following complicated clause as part of the *lex Pompeia de ambitu*: if a person who had formerly been convicted of electoral malpractice secured the conviction of two men on charges similar to the one against himself, or even on slighter charges, or of one man on a greater charge, he received a pardon. Ap. Claudius is not known to have been convicted of *ambitus*, and he undertook the prosecution for family reasons (hence his rejection of the reward), so it is not likely that Asconius is referring to any pardon.

54.13-14: *P. Valerius Leo et Cn. Domitius Cn. f.*

On Valerius Leo, see above on 34.12-13. Domitius was perhaps a son of Cn. Domitius Calvinus, the consul of 53, who had moved towards Pompeius in 54 (Cic. *Q.f.* 3.4.1); hence a relative might have served Pompeius' interests in 52 (Gruen, *Last Generation*, p. 342 with n. 154; contra, Münzer, *RE* [1905] 1317, who takes him to have been an Ahenobarbus).

Pro Milone

Summary of cases described by Asconius on pp. 54-6

Ref.	Accused	Accusatores	Subscriptores	Defence	Quaesitor	Charge	Verdict	Votes
54.9-14 (cf. 38.22, 39.5-6)	Milo	Appii Claudii Pulchri	P. Valerius Leo Cn. Domitius Cn.f. (Calvinus?)	–	A. Manlius Torquatus	ambitus (lex Pompeia)	condemnation	–
54.14-16 (cf. 38.23-39.1)	Milo	P. Fulvius Neratus	–	–	M. Favonius	lex Licinia de sodaliciis	condemnation	–
54.17-18 (cf. 38.22-23, and 36.23)	Milo	L. Cornificius Q. Patulcius	–	–	L. Fabius	lex (Plautia?) de vi	condemnation	–
54.22-55.7	M. Saufeius	L. Cassius (Longinus?) L. Fulcinius C.f. C. Valerius	–	M. Tullius Cicero M. Caelius Rufus	–	lex Pompeia de vi	acquittal (26 to 25)	S.: 18 (10C, 8A) E.: 17 (9C, 8A) T.A.: 16 (6C, 10A)
55.10-19	M. Saufeius	C. Fidius Cn. Aponius Cn.f. M. Seius .... Sex.f.	–	M. Tullius Cicero M. Terentius Varro Gibba	C. (?) Considius	lex Plautia de vi	acquittal (32 to 19)	–
55.20-56.2	Sex. Cloelius	C. Caesennius Philo M. Alfidius	–	T. Flacconius	–	–	condemnation (46 to 5)	S.: 18 (16C, 2A) E.: 17 (14C, 3A) T.A.: 16 (16C)

54.15: *M. Favonium quaesitorem*

On his evidence at Milo's trial *de vi*, see above on 40.18-19 and 54.4. On his role as *quaesitor*, see above on 39.5-6; he did not become praetor till 49.

54.16: *P. Fulvio Nerato*

See above on 38.23-39.1.

54.17: *L. Fabium quaesitorem*

Otherwise unknown; on his role as *quaesitor*, see above on 39.5-6. Cf. Münzer, *RE* 6 (1909) 1746.

54.18: *de vi*

Clark, p. 117, argues that this trial of Milo was not under the *lex Plautia de vi*, but under the *lex Cornelia de sicariis*, since Considius is specifically named as the president of the Plautian court *de vi* (55.11), whereas the president of Milo's trial *de vi* was L. Fabius. However, this presupposes that in any one year there was only ever one *quaesitor* for the Plautian court, and this is by no means certain (cf. above on 39.5-6).

54.18: *L. Cornificius et Q. Patulcius*

On the identification of Cornificius, see above on 36.23; he had lost a *divinatio* with the Appii Claudii for the right to prosecute Milo *de ambitu* (see above on 38.22-23). Patulcius is otherwise unknown.

54.19: *in exsilium Massiliam*

Dio 40.54.3-4 records the remark made by Milo when he received a copy of the published version of Cicero's speech, that if the spoken one had been as good he would not now be eating the fine mullets of Massilia. Milo originally took no part in the civil war but he came out of exile in 48 at the request of M. Caelius to join the latter in an abortive insurrection against the Caesarians, which ended in the death of both of them (Caes. *BC* 3.20-22).

54.20-21: *bona eius propter aeris alieni magnitudinem semuncia venierunt*

Cicero was involved in the sale of Milo's property through the agency of Philotimus, a freedman of his wife Terentia. Because of complaints from Milo later about the deal (Cic. *Att.* 5.8.2-3), some have thought that Cicero profited unfairly from his former client's distress (e.g. J. Carcopino, *Les secrets de la correspondance de Cicéron* [Paris, 1947]

1.183-9; SB *Att.* 3.2.2, cf. *Cicero*, p. 98). Cicero claims that he proposed the formation of a syndicate to bid (successfully, as it turned out) for Milo's property in the interests of Milo himself (who had taken a number of slaves to Massilia with him) and of his wife Fausta, and to stop any sharp-dealing purchaser from getting hold of the property. Cicero's own complaints about Philotimus seem to have been that he embezzled some of the proceeds of the sale of Milo's property (in favour of his mistress Terentia, which may have been part of the growing friction between Cicero and his wife); see Cic. *Att.* 6.4.3, 5.2, and cf. A. Haury, *REL* 34 (1956) 179-90. It is not clear whether Milo's property had been confiscated and was up for sale as an additional penalty following condemnation (Carcopino, loc. cit.; Lintott, pp. 76-8) or whether it had been seized for sale by a praetor's edict in a private action brought by creditors (Shackleton Bailey, loc. cit.). Terminology suggests the former: *socius in bonis* is a term found only in the procedure of sale following confiscation, and it is used of Philotimus in Cic. *Att.* 5.8.2. Moreover, if it were a sale to satisfy creditors, they would hardly have allowed the goods to be sold *semuncia* (whether it means 'for a tiny sum' or literally 'for a twenty-fourth part'). If the process were sale after confiscation, then clearly that was the *poena gravior* of Pompeius' law *de vi* (36.9). The syndicate was fortunate to secure the property at a low price; this would work in Milo's favour, since pieces could be sold separately and some of the profit returned to him. This is probably what Cicero had in mind, but he had problems. He was concerned about payments to Milo's creditors (Cic. *Att.* 6.5.2) who still had to be satisfied by the new owners of Milo's property (i.e. the syndicate). Cicero could only have profited at the expense of Milo's creditors, and that he is not likely to have wished to do (cf. Cic. *Att.* 5.8.3: *statues ut ex fide, fama reque mea videbitur*). His concern about interest payments and Philotimus' cooking of the books perhaps shows that he was not trying to profit from Milo's distress, and the latter's complaints are likely to have been about the low return he was getting rather than Cicero's personal gain.

55.1: *M. Saufeius . . . qui dux fuerat*

Cf. below, 55.9-10 and 13. For his part in the killing of Clodius, see above, 32.11-12. The Saufeii were an old Praenestine family; one of them at least, C. Saufeius, an associate of Saturninus and quaestor in 99, became a Roman senator (Wiseman, *New Men*, p. 259), and another was a tribune who sponsored an agrarian law, presumably in 91 (since he is mentioned in the *elogium* of M. Livius Drusus: *CIL* 1^2.1.p.199; Syme, *Historia* 13 [1964] 121). An Ap. Saufeius (probably the same man who is called a *scriba* by Plin. *NH* 7.183, and noted as an example of sudden death) is recorded by Cic. *Att.* 6.1.10 as having helped him on a number of occasions, principally in regard to Bursa (presumably meaning Cicero's prosecution of Plancus Bursa *de vi* for his part in the riots associated with

Clodius' death). This Ap. Saufeius was the brother of Cicero's friend L. Saufeius, who was also a friend of Atticus (Nep. *Att.* 12.3). In view of Ap. Saufeius' likely opposition to a Clodian, he was presumably a relative of Milo's lieutenant M. Saufeius. On these Saufeii, see SB *Att.* 1.287 and 3.245.

55.2-3: *L. Cassius, L. Fulcinius C.f., C. Valerius*

Cassius is sometimes identified as L. Cassius Longinus, the brother of Caesar's assassin and tribune in 44 (cf. Cic. *Att.* 14.2.1, *fam.* 12.2.4, 7.1), and perhaps also as the *subscriptor* to the prosecution of Plancius in 54 (Cic. *Planc.* 58). The other two are otherwise unknown.

55.11: *Considium quaesitorem*

Since Considius presided over a court under one of the existing laws, he may have been praetor in this year, but it is not certain whether this was a regular praetorian court (see above on 39.5-6, and cf. Linderski, *HSCP* 76 [1972] 196 n. 59) or whether the curule elections for 52 had been held yet (see above on 37.9). If Considius were praetor in 52, and if Pompeius' law regarding provincial commands did not apply to the magistrates of that year, it would be possible to identify the *quaesitor* with either C. Considius Longus who was appointed governor of Africa c. 51 (Cic. *Lig.* 2; Schol. Bob. 291.6) or M. Considius Nonianus who was assigned to Cisalpine Gaul in succession to Caesar in 49. Some overcome the difficulty posed by Pompeius' law to postulate earlier dates for the praetorships of these two men, since neither is certain (Longus to 58 [Gruen, *Last Generation*, p. 512], and Nonianus to 54 [*MRR*, 2.222]). Clark, p. 117, makes the identification with Considius Longus; Willems, *Sénat*, 1.512, and Giarratano, n. ad loc., with Considius Nonianus. Mommsen identifies him with a C. Considius Nonianus who issued coinage c. 63 (Crawford, *RRC*, 1.448, dates his issues to 57, which would make him too young to be a praetor by 52).

55.11: *lege Plautia de vi*

This was the operative law on violence, at least from 63 onwards when the first case is mentioned (Sall. *Cat.* 31.4), but its relationship to the *lex Lutatia* is not clear. The consensus now seems to be that the *lex Lutatia* set up a permanent court to deal with persons engaged in *seditio* against the state, but since it was felt that there was a need to deal with acts of private violence, especially those which might affect the public interest, the *lex Plautia* was introduced to replace and extend the *lex Lutatia*. The most likely date for its introduction is 70, since there was a tribune Plotius in that year responsible for other legislation. For the various theories on the development of the law, see Lintott, *Violence*, pp. 107-24; Gruen, *Last Generation*, pp. 225-7; R.A. Bauman, *Labeo* 24 (1978) 60-74.

Pro Milone 211

55.12-13: *loca . . . occupasset et cum telo fuisset*

Obviously clauses in the *lex Plautia*; similar clauses can be found in subsequent legislation about violence. The phrase *cum telo* occurs in the *lex Iulia de vi publica* (*Dig.* 48.6.1.3 and 10; cf. above on 36.23-24). Statements in the jurists are of assistance in determining the word missing after *loca* (seven letter spaces in P, eleven letter spaces in M, no gap in S but a marginal note *spatium deficit unius dictionis*). The two main suggestions are *edita* (Mommsen, in Clark, n. ad loc.; Stangl, ad loc.; Giarratano, ad loc.) or *publica* (Mommsen, *Strafrecht*, p. 652, plus *armatis* [which would make it too long for the space]; Kiessling and Schoell, ad loc.). For *edita*, cf. Caes. *BC* 1.7.5: . . . *templis locisque editioribus occupatis* . . . For *publica*, cf. Paul. *sent.* 5.26.3: *templa, portas aliudve quid publicum armatis obsederit, cinxerit, clauserit, occupaverit,* and *Dig.* 47.22.2: . . . *qui hominibus armatis loca publica vel templa occupasse iudicati sunt.* For discussion of the supplement, see Lintott, *Violence*, pp. 114-5.

55.14: *C. Fidius, Cn. Aponius Cn. f., M. Seius . . . Sex.f.*

There is a gap (seven-eight letters in S and P, eleven letters in M) after Seius, perhaps a *cognomen*, or the name of a fourth *accusator*. The first two named are otherwise unknown. M. Seius is perhaps the eques and businessman (best known for his success in breeding peacocks and other birds for the table: Varr. *RR* 3.2.7-14, 6.3-6, and 10.1; cf. Plin. *NH* 10.52). He cultivated friendships with influential persons such as Ap. Claudius Pulcher (since the third book of Varro's *res rusticae*, in which M. Seius is named, has Ap. Claudius as the principal interlocutor), D. Iunius Brutus (Cic. *fam.* 11.7.1, but cf. SB *Fam.* 2.494), Terentius Varro, and Atticus (Cic. *Att.* 5.13.2, 12.11.1, *fam.* 9.7.1). A connection with Ap. Claudius might explain his prosecution of a supporter of Milo (Gruen, *Last Generation*, p. 343 n. 156). On Seius in general, see Münzer, *RE* 2A (1923) 1121-2; Nicolet, *L'ordre équestre*, 2.1016-7.

55.15: *M. Terentius Varro Gibba*

A young eques who was a pupil and admirer of Cicero (cf. *fam.* 13.10.1-4), he later became quaestor in 46 and tribune in 43 (see Nicolet, *L'ordre équestre*, 2.1034-5). He is to be distinguished from his famous namesake, the antiquarian scholar M. Terentius Varro; when Varro was proscribed in 43, Gibba who was tribune that year issued a statement making known his *agnomen*, taking every precaution not to be confused with the other (Dio 47.11.3-4).

55.20: *Sex. autem Clodius*

That the name should be Cloelius, see above on 7.18.

Commentary

55.21: *C. Caesennio Philone, M. Alfidio*

The first named is otherwise unknown. The second is identified by some (despite Suet. *Calig.* 23.2) with M. Aufidius Lurco, tribune in 61 and maternal grand-father of Augustus' wife Livia (Taylor, *Voting Districts*, pp. 188-9; *MRR Suppl.* 4; SB *Att.* 1.323). Wiseman, *Historia* 14 (1965) 334, rejects the identification with Aufidius Lurco and has an Alfidius as the brother of Alfidia, the mother of Livia. The question is discussed at length by Linderski, *Historia* 23 (1974) 463-80, with the conclusion that M. Alfidius and M. Aufidius Lurco are not to be identified, but that the former is the maternal grand-father of Livia.

55.22: *T. Flacconio*

Otherwise unknown.

56.3-4: *multi praeterea . . . damnati sunt*

The remainder of 52 and 51 is remarked on by the sources as a busy one for the courts (Cic. *fam.* 7.2.4, *Brut.* 243 and 324; App. *BC* 2.24; Plut. *Cat. Min.* 48.4-5; Dio 40.52.1, 55.1). The following are the known trials:

> [For the sake of completeness, all the trials of the period are given here, though not all of them will necessarily have arisen out of the disturbances of 52, and not all of them ended in a verdict of guilty, nor is it possible to tell whether those found guilty were condemned in their presence or absence.]

1. Q. Metellus Scipio, prosecuted *de ambitu* by C. Memmius; the charge was dropped when Scipio secured judicial immunity after being named by Pompeius as his colleague in the consulship (see above on 30.9).
2. P. Plautius Hypsaeus, prosecuted *de ambitu* and convicted, after being abandoned by Pompeius (see above on 30.8).
3. Q. Pompeius Rufus, prosecuted *de vi in* 51 at the end of his term of office by M. Caelius and convicted, despite appeals to his mother Cornelia, a daughter of Sulla (Val. Max. 4.2.7; Dio 40.55.3). He too received no support from Pompeius. G.V. Sumner, *AJAH* 2 (1977) 13-4, brings out the curious relations between Caelius and the Pompeii Rufi. In 62-1 Caelius had served as *contubernalis* on the staff of the governor of Africa, Q. Pompeius Rufus (pr. 63); the latter was subsequently called upon to give a character witness at Caelius' trial in 56. The nephew of this man, the tribune of 52, came into opposition with Caelius, his colleague in the tribunate, in the aftermath of the murder of Clodius (of whom he had been an extremely close friend): e.g. it was Caelius who demanded that the slaves of Q. Pompeius (and of Plautius Hypsaeus) be produced for questioning (34.14-15), and who, on the day after Pompeius had

joined Plancus in interrogating a *triumvir capitalis* for taking a slave of Milo's into custody, seized the slave and restored him to Milo (37.8-16). Despite all this, after Caelius had secured Rufus' condemnation *de vi*, and Rufus had gone to live in poverty at Bauli (Cic. *fam.* 8.1.5), Caelius is found acting on his behalf in a private suit against his mother Cornelia (Val. Max. 4.2.7).

4. T. Munatius Plancus Bursa, prosecuted *de vi* in 51 at the end of his term of office by Cicero himself (a rare appearance as *accusator*) and convicted. Pompeius tried to support Bursa by sending in a written *laudatio*, but this contravened his own law (see above on 36.10) and Cato, one of the jurors at the trial, brought that contradiction to the court's attention. The relatives of M. Saufeius were pleased at Cicero's attack on Bursa (*Att.* 6.1.10; cf. *fam.* 7.2.3). D.C. Earl, *Historia* 15 (1966) 310-1, thinks that Pompeius had made a bargain with the *boni* to sacrifice Rufus and Bursa in return for the condemnation of Milo.

5. M. Aemilius Scaurus, prosecuted under Pompeius' law *de ambitu* in 52; though supported by numerous defenders in 54, he was practically deserted now (even by his former patron Pompeius), but Cicero still came to his defence, unsuccessfully, since he was convicted and went into exile (Cic. *off.* 1.138; App. *BC* 2.24).

6. C. Memmius, prosecuted under Pompeius' law *de ambitu* and convicted; he tried to secure immunity by turning state's evidence and indicting Metellus Scipio (App. *BC* 2.24).

7. M. Valerius Messalla Rufus, prosecuted first under Pompeius' law *de ambitu*, defended by Q. Hortensius and M. Caelius, and acquitted, and subsequently under the *lex Licinia de sodaliciis*; this time he was convicted and exiled (see above on 36.9).

8. P. Sestius, prosecuted under a Pompeian law, possibly *de ambitu*, defended by Cicero, and acquitted (Cic. *Att.* 13.49.1, *fam.* 7.24.2). App. *BC* 2.24 records the conviction of a certain Σέξστος *de ambitu* (which confirms that the charge was electoral corruption) but he has got the verdict wrong (perhaps by confusion with the condemnation of Sex. Cloelius).

9. T. Fadius, condemned with no record of the charge (Cic. *fam.* 5.18.1-2). He was a former quaestor of Cicero; that his name does not include the *cognomen* Gallus, see Shackleton Bailey, *CR* n.s. 12 (1962) 195-6. The condemnation, by one vote, is ascribed by Cicero to a certain powerful figure (presumably Pompeius).

10. Servaeus, as tribune-elect for 50 prosecuted presumably *de ambitu* and condemned (Cael. in Cic. *fam.* 8.4.2). The vacancy created was filled by the younger Curio at a supplementary election.

THE COMMENTARY ON THE SPEECH *PRO CORNELIO*

[Note: Reference is made to the following articles by author's surname and appropriate page numbers only: M.T. Griffin, 'The Tribune C. Cornelius', *JRS* 63 (1973) 196-213; K. Kumaniecki, 'Les discours égarés de Cicéron pro Cornelio', *Med. Kon. Vlaam. Acad. Belg.* 32 (1970) 3-36; W. McDonald, 'The Tribunate of Cornelius', *CQ* 23 (1929) 196-208.]

57.1: *L. Cotta L. Torquato coss.*

L. Aurelius Cotta and L. Manlius Torquatus were consuls in 65.

57.1-2: *post annum quam superiores*

The speeches which we know were delivered in the previous year (i.e. 66) are the *de imperio Cn. Pompei*, the *pro Cluentio*, the *pro Fundanio*, the *pro Manilio*, and the *pro Mucio* (W.W. How, *Cicero: Select Letters* [Oxford, 1925] p. xiii). The implication here is that Asconius had commented on some at least of the speeches of the previous year; if so, those comments have been lost. On the question of what other speeches Asconius may have commented on, see Part I, Section One.

57.5: *fuerat quaestor Cn. Pompeii*

Cornelius probably served as quaestor under Pompeius in Spain, in which case that office must have been held by 71. Cf. 61.16-17.

57.7: *in eo magistratu ita se gessit ut iusto pertinacior videretur*

Asconius here seems to be assessing Cornelius as a disinterested reformer, but that was an opinion probably derived from the sorts of things which Cicero would naturally say in a defence speech in public in the political situation of 65, especially when Cicero would have in mind his forthcoming consular candidature. There are indications, however, that Cornelius, if not a Pompeian protégé, was at least sympathetic to Pompeius' interests. He had served under Pompeius; he shared his concern for good provincial government (57.10, 58.1-2); he protected the tribunate which Pompeius had restored from the attacks of the *pauci* who were political opponents of Pompeius; the disruption of Cornelius' first trial in 66 was caused by gangs thought to have been provided by Manilius, a Pompeian supporter; and Cornelius was alleged to have been behind Manilius' proposal regarding the distribution of freedmen (65.10ff.). It should be noted that the five *principes civitatis* listed as behind the prosecution (60.19-21, 79.20-23) were all known opponents

Pro Cornelio 215

of Pompeius; the consul Piso, with whom Cornelius had come into conflict, was also an opponent of Pompeius (see below on 58.18). For further discussion of Cornelius' connection with Pompeian interests, see A.M. Ward, *TAPA* 101 (1970) 554-6, and Griffin, pp. 208-10. McDonald, p. 199, sees Cornelius more as a champion of the *populares* against the domination of the senate by the *pauci*; in this context, note that Cicero characterises the *principes civitatis* as long-standing opponents of the tribunate (in Ascon. 78.18-22, 79.17-18; cf. R. Seager, in *Hommages à Renard* [Brussels, 1969] Vol. II, pp. 680-6).

57.8: *alienatus autem a senatu est ex hac causa*

Asconius' subsequent explanation of the reason for Cornelius' alienation from the senate raises the question of the order of events in Cornelius' tribunate. For McDonald, p. 203, following Münzer, *RE* 4 (1901) 1251, and now followed by Kumaniecki, pp. 3-5, the rejection of Cornelius' proposal *ne quis legatis exterarum nationum pecuniam expensam ferret* is not sufficient to explain why Cornelius retaliated by putting forward the proposal that no one should be granted an exemption from the laws except with the approval of the people. He sees a more logical nexus in Dio's account of the tribunate (36.38.1-40.2) between Cornelius' bribery proposal (which is not specifically mentioned in Asconius' introduction, but which he clearly knew about — see 74.21ff.) and the senate's tactics to defeat that proposal by instructing the consul, C. Calpurnius Piso, to draw up a counter-proposal on bribery and by granting him an exemption from the *leges Aelia et Fufia* so that he could present the proposal, now that the date for the elections had been announced. McDonald puts the proposal about loans to foreign envoys earlier in the year, and does not give a time for the law on praetorian edicts; he then suggests the following order of events for the bribery and *solutio* proposals:

(a) Cornelius proposed a law on bribery (Dio 36.38.4).

(b) The senate modified his proposal, and voted that a revised law should be drawn up and introduced before the elections; a *privilegium* was passed exempting the consul from the *leges Aelia et Fufia* (Dio 36.38.5-39.1).

(c) Cornelius was annoyed and retaliated by proposing a law *ne quis nisi per populum legibus solveretur*. The senate obstructed this measure through the tribune Globulus (58.3ff.; Dio 36.39.2-3).

(d) The attitude of obstruction by the senate resulted in a serious riot (58.14; Dio 36.39.4). This disorder occured immediately before the date set for the consular elections, and the senate's apprehension led to the first postponement of the elections.

(e) Soon after, and shortly before the new date set for the elections,

216   Commentary

Piso attempted to carry his *lex de ambitu*. *Divisores* broke up the assembly (75.24ff.), and the elections were postponed for a second time.

(f) The second attempt of Piso to carry the law was successful (76.1-2), and the elections were then held.

(g) Cornelius subsequently modified his *solutio* proposal, and it was passed without disturbance (58.24-59.4).

Recently, Griffin has argued in favour of Asconius' order of events (for the arguments, and the criticism of McDonald's views, see Griffin, pp. 196-203), which may be summarised as follows:

(a) Cornelius made his first proposal regarding loans to foreign envoys; this was rejected by the senate, who stated that the practice was already covered by a *senatus consultum* (57.8-16).

(b) Annoyed at this, Cornelius put his first *solutio* proposal at a *contio*, the proposal was vetoed by Globulus, and there was a riot against Piso when he objected to Cornelius' attempt to read the bill out despite Globulus' veto; Cornelius then disbanded the meeting (57.16-58.24; Dio. 36.39.2-4).

(c) Cornelius modified his *solutio* proposal, and it was passed (58.24-59.4; Dio 36.39.4).

(d) Cornelius put a proposal *ut praetores ex edictis suis perpetuis ius dicerent*, which was passed (59.7-9; Dio 36.40.1-2).

(e) Cornelius proposed *alias quoque complures leges*, most of which were vetoed (59.11-12). These presumably included the bribery proposal, which Asconius does not specify, but which he clearly knew about (74.24).

(f) Then came Piso's counter-proposal *de ambitu*, which modified Cornelius' proposal; the *divisores* broke up the meeting which was to vote on Piso's proposal. It was presented again at a subsequent meeting, to which Piso brought a stronger bodyguard, and this time passed (76.1-2).

Griffin's strongest argument against McDonald's order is that the logical nexus in Dio between Cornelius' first *solutio* proposal and the senate's tactics in blocking his bribery proposal by granting Piso a dispensation to present a counter-proposal on bribery is not as strong as McDonald thinks. For in Dio's account, Cornelius' first *solutio* proposal is linked with the senate's granting of office to anyone seeking it in a way not prescribed by law (36.39.2: μὴ ἐξεῖναι τοῖς βουλευταῖς μήτε ἀρχήν τινι ἔξω τῶν νόμων αἰτήσαντι διδόναι..; cf. 38.2, where the development of factions and cliques in regard to the elections, which had particularly

Pro Cornelio   217

developed at this time, now that the tribunate had been restored, is mentioned), and not with Piso's *privilegium*. For other objections to Dio's order, see Griffin, esp. p. 199. A further argument in favour of Asconius' order is that the speech of Cicero (as cleverly reconstructed by Kumaniecki, pp. 18ff.) has the laws in the order of *solutio* proposals, law on praetorian edicts, and bribery law (i.e. Asconius has followed Cicero's order).

57.9-10: *exterarum nationum legatis pecunia magna daretur*

Foreign nations, especially client kingdoms, were always clamouring to be recognised or to be supported against enemies, and they were chronically short of money and forced into borrowing, both to pay for the 'gifts' necessary to secure the senate's provision of these services and even to keep up with the accumulating interest they already owed. This provided an opportunity for wealthy *negotiatores* whose interest was traditionally in finance rather than in trade (even down to the time of Cornelius' tribunate); and individual senators also found financial activities lucrative. On this development, see E. Badian, *Roman Imperialism in the Late Republic*, 2nd edn. (Oxford, 1968) pp. 66-73. Some examples: around 100 Nicomedes III of Bithynia had masses of his subjects sold into slavery to discharge debts (Diod. 36.3); in 88 large sums of money were lent to Ptolemy Alexander I to enable him to collect a fleet and regain the Egyptian throne; and of course there were the loans secured by Ptolemy Auletes to bribe Romans to restore him to his throne. There were attempts to control loans to foreign nations, but they proved to be ineffective (or were circumvented). In 94 there was a *senatus consultum*, which apparently forbade the making of loans to foreigners (see below on 57.14-16); A. Gabinius proposed a law confirming the prohibition (it is not clear whether it was in his tribunate, praetorship or consulship; see below on 57.16, and cf. SB *Att.* 1.339); there was a *senatus consultum* in 60, arising out of negotiations with Sicyon, about which little is known but which seems to have denied recognition to debts incurred by free communities (Cic. *Att.* 1.19.9; see SB *Att.* 1.339). It is interesting to note (in view of Cornelius' concern with *privilegia*) that, despite these measures, senators were able to secure *privilegia* exempting them from the terms of the laws. The most glaring example is the exemption given to Brutus to make a loan to Cyprian Salamis and to extract interest at four times the usual rate (discussed in Badian, op. cit. pp. 84-5). Admittedly this example comes from a later period, but the same no doubt happened in Cornelius' day.

57.13-14: *s.c. quod ante annos... [L.] Domitio C. Caelio coss. factum erat*

There are gaps in the manuscripts here: in S, there are no figures after

Commentary

annos and no *praenomen* for Domitius; in P, the *praenomen* is written as *Cn.*, and in M. as *Gneo*. Most editors put the *praenomen* L. for Domitius (following Manutius), taking this as a reference to the consulship of L. Domitius Ahenobarbus and C. Coelius Caldus in 94. Consequently the figure *septem et XX* is usually given after *annos* (so KS, St, and G). The emendation *Coelio* (KS) is to be preferred to *Caelio*. It is normally Asconius' practice to name the consuls in the order in which they appear in official lists: in this instance, he has reversed the official order. Asconius is the only source to mention this decree, which may have been part of a wider administrative clean-up (Badian, *Athenaeum* 34 [1956] 104-23).

57.14-16: cum senatus . . . decrevisset ne quis Cretensibus pecuniam mutuam daret

Dio, fr. 111, mentions an embassy to Rome from the Cretans, which hoped to renew the old treaty and to secure favour in return for saving the quaestor (?) and his soldiers. The senate replied, however, by issuing an ultimatum; Dio adds (frag. 111.3) . . . καὶ προσυποπτεύσαντες τοὺς πρέσβεις ἐπιχειρήσειν τινάς, ὡς καὶ κωλύσαντες τὴν στρατείαν, διαφθεῖραι χρήμασιν, ἐψηφίσαντο ἐν τῇ βουλῇ μηδένα αὐτοῖς μηδὲν δανεῖσαι. Diodorus' account of the incident (40.1.1-3) separates the embassy (which in his account was received favourably) from the ultimatum (which was taken at the insistence of a Lentulus Spinther). The incident as described by Dio is dated by Boissevain to 70, which Griffin (pp. 197 n. 14 and 209) argues is preferable to Mommsen's date of 69 (*Staatsrecht*, 3³.1154 n. 2), on the grounds that Cicero expected (*Verr*. 2.2.76) that war would be declared against the Cretans in the next year (i.e. 69), presumably because he thought they would not comply with the ultimatum. But the ultimatum at least makes better sense if dated to 69: for part of the ultimatum as described by Dio was that a consul was to be sent out against the Cretans to see that they obeyed the terms of the demand, and a Cretan command was created in 69 for one of the consuls (eventually being taken by Q. Caecilius Metellus). Cicero's expectation may have nothing to do with the embassy and ultimatum: following the defeat of M. Antonius and the continuing menance of the pirates, it was clear that a new command would probably be created. The date of the embassy depends whether it was closely associated with the ultimatum (Dio) or was some time earlier than it (Diodorus).

57.16: pecuniam mutuam

Apparently, part of the decree relating to the Cretans was that no one should lend money to them, and this clause was taken from the earlier decree of 94. The strife of the 80's and the squalid record of misgovernment in the 70's had, in Cornelius' view, made the decree of 94 a dead letter, but the senate denied this. The proposal of Cornelius may not have been entirely dropped, however; a *lex Gabinia* is attested as operative in the 50's to forbid legal action to recover loans on interest to provincials (Cic. *Att.* 5.21.12, 6.2.7). Gabinius was tribune in the same year as Cornelius, and he was more likely to propose such a law during his tribunate than his praetorship or consulship. So, although Cornelius had initiated the discussion of the proposal, it may have eventually been passed in Gabinius' name (cf. the suggestion at 64.10-11 that Manilius got the law on freedmen's voting rights from Cornelius).

58.1-3: *exhauriri provincias usuris . . . darent*

As Griffin points out (p. 209 n. 123), Clark's reading here is 'eccentric, being unrelated to the problem Cornelius was considering as revealed in Dio frag. 111, and grammatically faulty'. Stangl's reading (partly derived from Mommsen) makes better sense: *exhauriri provincias usuris propter id unum, ut haberent legati unde praesentia munera darent*. Rau, p. 120, suggests: *exhauriri provincias usuris; providendum ne haberent legati unde praesentem pecuniam dividerent*.

58.12: *potentissimi quique ex senatu*

Presumably including, if not comprising, the five *principes civitatis* listed by Asconius later (60.19-21, 79.20-24). Cf. 58.11 (where they are called *pauculi*), 59.6 (*optimates* and *pauci*), 61.8 (*clarissimi cives*), 61.13 (*principes*), and 61.20 (*principes civitatis*). It would seem that Cornelius was engaged more in a struggle with these men over the powers of the restored tribunate and their attempts to exercise political control than anything else (cf. 61.13), but it should be noted that they were political opponents of Pompeius, and Cornelius may therefore have been working in his interests (cf. above on 57.7).

58.13: *P. Servilius Globulus*

His role is interesting, for although he was found to veto the first form of Cornelius' *solutio* proposal in 67, he gave his support to Cornelius at the trial in 65 (61.15-16). Asconius is the only source to mention Globulus' veto; it was clearly an important piece of information, for the charge against Cornelius revolved around his non-acceptance of the tribunician veto.

58.17-18: *tum Cornelius ipse codicem recitavit*

A tribune might impose a veto on a bill by forbidding the crier to read it out; but what if an equally sacrosanct fellow-tribune proceeded to read out the bill himself? The most famous example of a bill being vetoed during its reading was in the tribunate of Cato in 62 when he snatched the bill from

220   *Commentary*

the herald's hand; when the proposer of the bill, Metellus Nepos, also a tribune, proceeded to recite the bill from memory, another tribune, Q. Minucius Thermus, put his hand over Nepos' mouth (Plut. *Cat. Min.* 28; Dio 37.43.2). One of the charges of the prosecution against Cornelius was that he had read out the law himself (Quint. 4.4.8, 10.5.13; cf. Cic. *Corn.* frag. 5 P, *Vat.* 5, and Ascon. 59.22ff.). The question to be settled was whether Cornelius' action actually contravened an enacted law, or was simply contrary to *mos maiorum*. Asconius' account of Piso's reaction (58.18-20) suggests the latter, and the prosecution's chain of interpretation (see below on 61.5-7) implies that they were dealing with the spirit of the law, rather than the letter. Mommsen, *Staatsrecht*, 3.391 n. 4, says that it was forbidden in the late republic for a tribune to read out a bill himself: even if that were so, it does not follow that reading out a bill in person was an offence expressly listed in the *lex Cornelia de maiestate*, under which Cornelius was being tried (see below on 62.7ff.).

58.18: *C. Piso*

The consul of 67 seems to have been particularly hostile towards Pompeius. He opposed the legislation of A. Gabinius for the granting of an extraordinary command against Mediterranean piracy to Pompeius; even when the bill was passed, he did not give up resistance, for he sought to block Pompeius' levies and interfered with the equipment and recruitment of his fleets (Plut. *Pomp.* 27.1; Dio 36.37.2). When M. Lollius Palicanus sought to stand as a candidate for the consulship of 66, Piso refused to accept his candidature, despite a popular outcry (Val. Max. 3.8.3). Palicanus as tribune in 71 had agitated for the full restoration of tribunician powers in co-operation with Pompeius. On Piso's anti-Pompeian attitude, see E.S. Gruen, *Calif. Stud. Class. Ant.* 1 (1968) 156-9, and L. Hayne, *Class. Phil.* 69 (1974) 280. Piso's opposition to Cornelius might suggest that the latter was working in Pompeius' interests (cf. above on 57.7).

59.2: *nisi CC adfuissent*

Cornelius' requirement of a minimum attendance of two hundred senators for the granting of exemptions from the operation of the laws implies that attendance sometimes was much smaller (cf. Cic. *Q.f.* 2.10.1, 3.2.2); he says as much at 59.5 (*per paucos*). It was a heavy requirement. Sulla recruited a senate of 600, and legislated for the automatic entry of the twenty quaestors each year to maintain the numbers in the senate at that level. Actual attendance even at the most important meetings was never above 400 or so (Cic. *Att.* 1.14.5; App. *BC* 4.30), and Cicero regarded a turn-up of 'a full two hundred' including six consulars in December 57 just before the holidays as remarkably good (Cic. *Q.f.* 2.1.7). For the possibility that *frequens senatus* was a technical term for a meeting at which a stated minimum of senators was required, see J.P.V.D. Balsdon, *JRS* 47 (1957) 19-20.

59.3-4: *haec sine tumultu res acta est*

The fact that the altered form of Cornelius' *solutio* proposal was passed without disturbance suggests some sort of compromise. The majority of the senate must have been prepared to accept the altered form; as Asconius points out, even the *pauci* could not deny that it did favour the senate's authority. In his defence of Cornelius, Cicero was prepared to concede the prosecution's contention that Cornelius' original proposal had been bad, and he concentrated on Cornelius' willingness to alter a bad proposal into a good one which respected the senate's authority (Cic. *Corn.* I frags. 5, 20-27 P; Griffin, p. 199). For McDonald, p. 204, the compromise was 'that Cornelius consented to make his law against senatorial dispensations less severe on condition that the senate reinstate in its *consultum* on bribery the clause in respect of the *divisores*.' His view, of course, relies on the acceptance of Dio's order, but it has been suggested above (see on 57.8) that Asconius' order may be more acceptable. Further, it is not certain that the senate's *consultum* on bribery did restore the clause about the *divisores*: Cicero (frag. 41 P = 74.21-75.2) seems to suggest that the *lex Calpurnia* did not include penalties for the *divisores* (see Kumaniecki, p. 25, and Griffin, p. 197 n. 15). Why the *divisores* should have rioted against the *lex Calpurnia* when it was first put is a puzzle if there were no penalties prescribed in it for them; perhaps they would be opposed to any law which was likely to affect their role. For further discussion, see below on 74.22-23.

59.8-9: *ut praetores ex edictis suis perpetuis ius dicerent*

On entering office, a praetor published a list of model cases for which he would grant legal actions throughout his year of office; the list would often be taken over *in toto* from his predecessor. Before this law of Cornelius, the praetor's edict was merely a statement of intent by the praetor concerned, which he was morally but not legally bound to observe. On praetorian edicts, see W. Kunkel, *An Introduction to Roman Legal and Constitutional History*, 2nd edn., trans. J.M. Kelly (Oxford, 1973) pp. 91-4 and 211-2. Griffin, p. 209, sees this law of Cornelius as relating to provincial governors also (the term *praetor* often being used for them) and links it with Pompeius' concern for better provincial government; the suggestion, though attractive, cannot be treated as secure. That there was a need for such a law when the principle had long existed might suggest that there had been recent scandalous abuses.

59.11: *alias quoque complures leges*

Apart from the proposals already mentioned by Asconius, the only law we know is the bribery proposal described by Dio 36.38.4. Although Asconius nowhere specifically mentions this proposal, he clearly knew about it, for he preserves a fragment of Cicero relating to it (74.21ff.). For discussion of the order of the proposals, see above on 57.8.

59.15: *M'. Lepido L. Volcacio coss.*

M'. Aemilius Lepidus and L. Volcacius Tullus were consuls in 66.

59.17: *lege Cornelia de maiestate*

For discussion of this law, see below on 61.5-7.

59.18: *subscripsit Gaius*

The mss. all agree in giving the *praenomen* C. here, but Cic. *Cluent.* 100 suggests that the two brothers were named Publius and Lucius. See Badian, *Studies*, p. 248 (= *JRS* 46 [1956] 220). Nothing, however, is really gained by emendation; the difference rests solely between the letters C. and L., which may have been transmitted carelessly in either Cicero's or Asconius' text. When the trial was resumed in 65, only one Cominius is mentioned (60.14, 61.24, 62.16; cf. Cic. *Brut.* 271), but presumably both brothers were again involved.

59.18: *P. Cassius praetor*

Plausibly to be identified with the man later implicated in the Catilinarian conspiracy and with Cicero's competitor for the consulship of 63, L. Cassius Longinus (cf. *comm. pet.* 7, and Ascon. 82.7), in which case the *praenomen* should be L. (so *MRR* 2.152). Obviously the man was in charge of the *maiestas* court in 66.

59.18: *decimo die*

The usual interval fixed by the president of the court between the formal acceptance of a charge (*nominis receptio*) and the appearance of the defendant was ten days (Greenidge, *Legal Procedure*, pp. 466-7).

59.19: *non adfuisset*

In the case where the magistrate did not appear, the case was presumably deferred until the defendant was summoned again. Where the accuser failed to turn up, the charge was dismissed. When a defendant on a criminal charge failed to turn up on the appointed day before the *iudices*, the case went on to its legitimate end, a vote was taken and the penalty fixed by the law was imposed; mere interdiction of the absentee was not resorted to, except that, where a person was absent because he had gone into voluntary exile and had secured the *civitas* of another city, he could

Pro Cornelio 223

be interdicted without the formality of a condemnation. There were some instances where absence was excusable: absence on public business, the holding of office, the need to appear on the same day in another court, and illness. On all of this, see Greenidge, *Legal Procedure*, pp. 461-3 and 473-4.

59.21-22: *notis operarum ducibus*

The phrase is used by Cicero in a passage (= frag. 17 P) on which Asconius does not comment, but which should presumably be located in the context of Cicero's description of the assault on the Cominii. It is in the mid-60's that we first hear of armed gangs of professional ruffians. Manilius' band of freedmen and slaves in 67 was collected together because of their interest in improved voting rights for freedmen, but it may have included a stiffening of professionals such as he used to disturb the trial described at 60.11-12 (where Asconius uses the same term, *operarum duces*). Sallust's account of the attempt to rescue Lentulus from custody in 64 shows a similar combination (*Cat.* 50.1): discontented free and slave members of the proletariate, and *duces multitudinum* who were mercenary ruffians. P. Autronius, the displaced consul for 65, formed a band from gladiators and runaway slaves (Cic. *Sull.* 15 and 68). The hired gangs at first were made up of professionals (i.e. gladiators) but later they were made up of slaves, freedmen and urban poor, with a core of professionals who trained the gang into the semblance of an army. On the development of the gangs, see Lintott, *Violence*, pp. 74-85.

60.2: *in scalas*

Scalae normally means 'ladder' or 'stairs', but here it must have the idea of 'closet' or 'cupboard'. Cicero made some reference to these incidents in the speech (frags. 13, 14 and 15 P); one of these fragments is quoted in the scholia on Juv. *sat.* 7.118, and that helps to elucidate the meaning of *scalae*. For the scholia say that it means 'upstairs apartments inhabited by impoverished advocates' or 'stalls, closets for advocates' books and other apparatus'. The meaning 'cupboard' is also suggested by the use of the word in Cic. *Phil.* 2.21 (cf. 2.49, *Mil.* 40), where he describes the occasion when in 53 M. Antonius was pursuing Clodius in the forum and would have killed him *nisi se ille in scalas tabernae librariae coniecisset*. On the date of this latter incident, see J. Linderski and A. Kaminska-Linderski, *Phoenix* 28 (1974) 216-7. On the meaning of *scalae* as *armaria advocatum*, see G. Puccioni, *RFIC* 95 (1967) 180-5.

60.10-14: *cum primum apparu[isset] Manilius . . . esset damnatus*

At the end of 66, after the expiry of Manilius' tribunician term but before the end of the year, Manilius was brought before Cicero, who was praetor in charge of the extortion court that year, on a charge of *res repetundae* (Cic. *Corn.* in Ascon. 62.15; Plut. *Cic.* 9.4-6; Dio 36.44.1-2). Plutarch says the charge was *peculatus* (κλόπη), but Cicero makes it clear (*Corn.* in Ascon. 62.15, *Cluent.* 94 and 147) that during his praetorship he presided over the extortion court, and his colleague, C. Orchivius, presided over the embezzlement court. The charge against Manilius was probably instigated by the optimates in retaliation for his tribunician actions, but it is not easy to see why a charge of extortion should have been brought against him (for a discussion of this, see E.J. Phillips, *Latomus* 29 [1970] 597). When brought before Cicero, Manilius asked for the customary ten-day postponement of his trial; knowing that this would put the trial into the next year, he probably hoped that Cicero, no longer president of the court, would undertake to defend him, in view of the support Cicero had given to his bill on Pompeius' Mithridatic command and to Pompeius' interests in general. But Cicero, thinking ahead to his candidature for the consulship and not wishing to offend the optimates by defending Manilius, but at the same time not wanting to alienate Pompeian support, refused Manilius' request and allowed him a postponement of only one day (meaning that the trial would come up before Cicero, prior to the expiry of his praetorship: on the date of Manilius' first appearance, see Phillips, art. cit. 597-600). The Roman people were annoyed at Cicero's apparent abandonment of Manilius, and before the trial began two tribunes summoned Cicero to appear at a public assembly and attacked his action; Cicero explained that he had granted only a one-day postponement because he had wanted Manilius to be tried before himself rather than some other, perhaps less friendly, praetor; the people, accepting the explanation apparently, simply requested him to defend Manilius, and Cicero agreed (implying that he now granted a longer postponement until such time as he would be free to defend Manilius). At the same time, he delivered a vigorous harangue against the oligarchs and those who were jealous of Pompeius (Plut. *Cic.* 9.6; cf. Dio 36.44.2). By his undertaking of the defence of Manilius Cicero had placed himself firmly in the Pompeian camp, and he gained by it (cf. *comm. pet.* 51). This does not mean he alienated the majority of the senate, but simply the same narrow group whom he opposed in defending Cornelius (Ward, *TAPA* 101 [1970] 547-8; cf. Phillips, art. cit. 599-600, and Stockton, *Cicero: a Political Biography*, p. 62).

Dio says that rioting prevented the court from being convened, but Asconius' account here suggests that the proceedings were disrupted only after the trial had begun (60.10ff.: *cum primum apparuisset ... deinde ... ambo consules ... praesidebant ei iudicio*, where *ei iudicio* must refer back to *iudicium* two lines earlier). After the interruption, the proceedings were resumed under the watchful eyes of the consuls. Schol. Bob. 119.4ff. says that L. Domitius Ahenobarbus counteracted Manilius' attempts to disrupt his trial for *maiestas*; on the basis of this statement

Pro Cornelio 225

some have argued that Manilius was charged with extortion in 66 and a new charge of *maiestas* in 65 (e.g. Münzer, *RE* 14 (1930) 1134; *MRR* 2.153; Seager, *Historia* 13 [1964] 345 n. 30, repeated in *Pompey: a Political Biography* [London, 1979] p. 58; Gruen, *Last Generation*, p. 262; J.T. Ramsey, *Phoenix* 34 [1980] 323-36). For a discussion of this view, see Ward, art. cit. 548-9, and Phillips, art. cit. 603-5, both of whom reject that there was a change in the charge. It should be noted that Asconius connects Ahenobarbus' activities not with a trial of Manilius but with his law on freedmen (see above on 45.11). It is easy to see how Schol. Bob. could have been mistaken over the charge; confusion with the actions and trial of Cornelius could explain it. Cicero (*Cluent.* 116) says that many persons had been acquitted of treason whose penalty, after they had been found guilty of extortion, was assessed under the heading of treason (for an interpretation of this passage, see M.I. Henderson,*JRS* 41 [1951] 76-8; contra, A.N. Sherwin-White, *JRS* 42 [1952] 43-55); and R.A. Bauman, *The Crimen Maiestatis in the Roman Republic and the Augustan Principate* (Johannesburg, 1967) pp. 27-30 and 85-7, has pointed out that acts which could have been the subject of a charge of treason were often attacked through a more concrete charge such as extortion which was easier to prove. The question to some extent hinges on the year of C. Attius Celsus' praetorship and the court over which he presided (see below on 65.8).

It is not clear whether, when the trial was resumed, Cicero continued with the defence of Manilius: the disturbance of the trial would have given him grave reservations (cf. his later comments on it at 66.2-6) and he would have been worried about the political effect of his association with those responsible for the disturbances, if Asconius' identification (66.7) is correct. The wording of *comm. pet.* 51 may be significant: it speaks of *Cornelio defendendo*, but only of *Manili causa recipienda*. A refusal by Cicero to continue the defence would also help to explain why Manilius decided not to appear when the court reconvened. He was condemned in his absence (accepting Stangl's reading *absensque* at 60.13, instead of *atque* of M, P^2 and Clark). On this question, see Ward, art. cit. 552-3. There is a fragment of a speech by Cicero *pro Manilio* preserved in Nonius, which Phillips, art. cit. 606, says belonged to the *contio* at which Cicero explained his actions in late 66, but which Ward, art. cit. 552 n. 27, assigns to the first hearing of the trial which was disrupted; it does not help to solve the problem whether Cicero continued in his defence of Manilius. There is a possible reference in Cic. *leg. ag.* 2.49 to the popular demand two years earlier that Cicero defend Manilius when he ceased to be praetor (B. Rawson, *Class. Phil.* 66 [1971] 26-9; cf. T.N. Mitchell, *Cicero: the Ascending Years* [New Haven, 1979] p. 157, and Ramsey, art. cit. 324 n. 5).

Note the parallels (especially the use of *operarum duces*) between the disruption of Cornelius' first trial in 66 and the disruption of a trial in 65. It could just be that the very corrupt passage at 60.9ff. deals not with the disruption of a renewed trial of Manilius, but attempted disruption of the trial of Cornelius, i.e. Manilius was interrupting Cornelius' trial with his mobs, and the consuls intervened to allow the trial of Cornelius to proceed, with the warning that if he did not put in an appearance he would be condemned in absence. If that is what the corrupt passage deals with, we have no evidence at all that Manilius' trial was ever resumed (which is the view of, e.g., TP, 1.174; M. Gelzer, *Cicero: ein biographischer Versuch* [Wiesbaden, 1969] pp. 60 and 65; Stockton, op. cit. p. 71; contra, Seager, op. cit. p. 57 n. 5).

60.13: *praesidebant*

This does not mean that the consuls supplanted the praetor as president of the court (so Ward, art. cit. 549 n. 15). The regular word for presiding over a court is *exercere* (cf. 29.8 and 62.5; Cic. *Att.* 7.9.4, *Brut.* 304, *fin.* 2.54), whereas the verb here, *praesidere*, means 'to protect' (cf. Cic. *Mil.* 101). This is relevant to the question of C. Attius Celsus' praetorship, and whether the charge against Manilius was altered from extortion to treason (see below on 65.8). If the consuls of this year were authorised by the senate to 'keep watch' over a trial disturbed by the activities of Manilius, this might be the explanation of the award of a body-guard to them, which is usually associated with the so-called 'first' Catilinarian conspiracy (further on this, see below on 66.2ff., and B.A. Marshall, *Class. Phil.* 72 [1977] 318-20). For the armed protection of a court by a consul, cf. Pompeius' action in regard to Ahenobarbus' request for protection in the trial of Milo (40.9-11).

60.20-21: *Q. Hortensius, Q. Catulus, Q. Metellus Pius, M. Lucullus, Mam. Lepidus*

Q. Hortensius Hortalus (cos. 69) and Q. Lutatius Catulus (cos. 78), brothers-in-law (Hortensius being married to Catulus' sister) and both known as staunch optimates, had opposed the bill of Cornelius' colleague in the tribunate, A. Gabinius, granting Pompeius an extensive command against the pirates and the bill of the tribune of the following year, C. Manilius, giving Pompeius command of the war against Mithridates (references in *MRR* 2.144-5 and 153). Q. Caecilius Metellus Pius (cos. 80) had been joined by Pompeius in the war against Sertorius, but this had led to political opposition between them (Badian, *FC*, pp. 278-83; contra, Gruen, *AJP* 92 [1971] 1-16, and B. Twyman, *ANRW* 1.1 [1972] 834). For Lucullus, one of the mss. (P) has the *praenomen* L., but that it should be M. seems confirmed by 79.20; the emendation *M. et L.*, based on Val. Max. 8.5.4, should be rejected (see G.V. Sumner, *JRS* 54 [1964] 41), because of the list of the five men at 79.20-22 and because at this time L. Licinius Lucullus was still in the East. M. Terentius Varro Lucullus (cos.

Pro Cornelio 227

73), brother of the Mithridatic commander, shared his brother's opposition to Pompeius: they were linked with the Metelli, being the sons of a Caecilia Metella, and with the Aurelii Cottae (Badian, *Studies*, pp. 36ff.; *FC*, pp. 280-1), and both were prosecuted by Pompeius' supporter and *adfinis*, C. Memmius, during his tribunate in 66 (on Memmius' association with Pompeius through marriage connection to the house of Sulla, see above on 28.18ff.; Gruen, *Historia* 18 [1969] 76-7; E. Courtney, *Philologus* 105 [1961] 152 and 156). For Lepidus, two of the mss. (S and M) have the *praenomen* L., but no one of that name is known for this period, and the third has M.; Manutius emended the latter to *M'*., making it a reference to the consul of 66 (accepted by Griffin, p. 213). The problem with this emendation is that the consul of 66 appeared as an *advocatus* for Cornelius at the first abortive attempt to bring him to trial, and he can only be placed in the ranks of the opposition if he had changed his stance (though persons involved could change their mind — witness the action of Globulus). Sumner, art. cit. 41-7, suggests the emendation *Mam.* (a similar emendation of *M.* to *Mam.* has to be made at 81.6), arguing that the consul of 66 was not of sufficient standing to be placed in the same company as the other four, and making it a reference to Mam. Aemilius Lepidus Livianus (cos. 77). This man is not known as an opponent of Pompeius (his possible nomination as *princeps senatus* by the pro-Pompeian censors of 70 [Val. Max. 7.7.6] would argue against it), but the man linked with M. Lucullus is described as *inimicus tribuniciae potestatis* (79.20, cf. 81.1ff.), suggesting a *clarissimus vir* from the period 78 to 70 when there was resistance to agitation for the restoration of tribunician powers (whereas the consul of 66 had actually supported the tribune Cornelius); and he may have had Sullan connections (like the other four in the list). The list of *principes* is similar to the group who supported Archias when he was prosecuted in 62 (Cic. *Arch.* 6) and to the group ranged against Clodius in the Bona Dea scandal.

61.3: *ad crimen imminutae maiestatis tribuniciae pertinere*

There can have been no such thing as 'tribunician majesty' in a law of Sulla, in view of his attitude to the tribunate: 'majesty' attached to the Roman people. There is a difficulty with this whole phrase: Orelli proposed *potestatis* for *maiestatis*, but one must then ask whether it was an express crime 'to diminish tribunician power'. The relevant passages of Quintilian imply that it was not: 'C. Cornelius diminished majesty, for as tribune he read the text of a bill himself' (4.4.8), and 'Would majesty be violated if a magistrate read his own bill to the people?' (10.5.13). It would seem, then, that the charge of the prosecution that Cornelius had diminished tribunician power (cf. 61.6-7) is a link in the chain of interpretation, and not a crime specified in Sulla's law. The *tribuniciae* would best be deleted here, as an intrusion based on *tribuniciam potestatem* at 61.7.

61.5-7: *non poterat negare . . . tribuniciam potestatem*

Cornelius' action had been witnessed by the five *principes civitatis* and thousands of others, and the defence could not deny its occurrence. After 70, when the limitations placed on the tribunate by Sulla were finally lifted, even the oligarchic leaders in the senate were committed to a defence of the negative powers of the office (e.g. the right of Trebellius to obstruct Gabinius [see below on 72.10] and of Globulus to obstruct Cornelius were held to be essential to republican order). The process of argument used by the *principes* might be reconstructed as follows: to read the text of a bill in the face of a colleague's veto is to destroy intercession; to destroy intercession is to diminish tribunician power; to diminish tribunician power is to diminish the majesty of the Roman people. By claiming to be defending a popular institution, they tried to show that Cornelius' action fell within the spirit of Sulla's law on *maiestas*, if not the strict letter (see below on 62.7-10). Cicero attacked the chain of interpretation at each link. Cornelius had not read the text to override Globulus' intercession but to refresh his memory (cf. Cic. *Vat.* 5; a speciously plausible defence in view of the practice in the ancient world of reading aloud, even to oneself); absence of seditious intent was shown by his immediate dismissal of the assembly (ibid.; Ascon. 58.23-24), though he did that only after the consul had been threatened; even if intercession was rejected at the reading of the bill, there were other opportunities for intercession before voting commenced (71.2ff.). The sincerity of the defence of tribunician power by the *principes* is questioned (76.5ff., 78.18-22, 79.17-18). Tribunician power was not affected, Cicero argues. He did not hesitate to deal with the wider question of principle — was the tribunician power of veto an absolute? The episode in which Gabinius overrode the intercession of Trebellius (71-72) was right, claimed Cicero. He was endorsing the *popularis* theory of the tribunate expressed by Ti. Gracchus (Plut. *Ti. Gracch.* 15; cf. Cic. *part. or.* 105, and Stockton, op. cit. p. 57). For discussion of the interpretation of the law in this case, see Bauman, op. cit. pp. 71-5; Griffin, p. 202 with n. 55; Gruen, *Last Generation*, p. 264 n. 12. For a general discussion of tribunician intercession, see C. Meier, *Mus. Hel.* 25 (1968) 86-100.

61.8-9: *dignitatem clarissimorum civium contra quos dicebat non violaret*

Asconius' implication that Cicero managed to avoid trouble is incorrect. In a letter of late July 65 (*Att.* 1.2.2), Cicero wrote to Atticus: 'I need you here soon; there is a strong feeling abroad that your noble friends will oppose my candidacy for the consulship.' A reading of the speech does not make clear that Cicero acted with restraint: although there are occasions where he speaks respectfully of the men behind the prosecution (see below on 63.8-9), there are other instances where he is highly critical of their credibility and sincerity (see below on 73.2-3 and 5-6).

61.17-18: *apud duas [decurias] . . . et ex tertia*

Following the law of L. Aurelius Cotta in 70, the jury panels were divided between the *ordines* (see below on 67.11-12); it was not until 59 by the law of Q. Fufius Calenus that the votes of each order were tabulated separately (see above on 28.25). Asconius seems to know how each of the divisions voted, though it may be only surmise on his part (cf. below on 89.18-19). The clear majority for acquittal shows the widespread sympathy for Cornelius' programme.

61.23-24: *exstat oratio Comini accusatoris*

Malcovati, *ORF*^{2}, pp. 440-1. The speech seems to have been extant in Tacitus' day (Tac. *dial* 39.5). For an attempted reconstruction of Cominius' speech, see Kumaniecki, esp. pp. 9-10. On Cominius' ability as an orator, see Cic. *Brut.* 271; the two brothers had undertaken the prosecution of Staienus (Cic. *Cluent.* 100-102), in the aftermath of the trial of Oppianicus in 74.

62.4: *in duas orationes*

Although the defence lasted four days (Plin. *ep.* 1.20.8), Cicero published his speeches in condensed form. Cornelius Nepos (*HRR* 2.34 = *Cic.* frag. 2) says that the published version was almost word for word identical with the speech as delivered; that cannot be so if the defence lasted four days and only two speeches were published. Kumaniecki, pp. 10-33, has attempted a reconstruction of both speeches, and argued that the second speech is really drawn from that part of Cicero's defence where he rebutted the prosecution's witnesses and from the peroration. On the outstanding quality and tremendous effect of the speech, see Quint. 8.3.3.

62.5: *iudicium id exercuit Q. Gallius praetor*

Q. Gallius had been plebeian aedile in 67 (88.5-9; *MRR* 2.144), and was praetor in charge of the treason court in 65. For the question of the presidency of the court at Manilius' resumed trial, see below on 65.8.

62.7-10: *utrum certae aliquae res . . . quod accusator proponit*

Asconius' authorship of this passage is not accepted; whoever wrote these lines, however, seems to have had access to the whole text of the *pro Cornelio*. From the description of the first question under consideration, it seems clear that the prosecution's charge against Cornelius, that he had read out the text of a bill himself when a colleague had imposed his veto by forbidding the herald to read it out, was not an offence expressly listed in Sulla's law on *maiestas*. The defence pointed out that it was not (cf. 61.5-7), while the prosecution argued, by its chain of interpretation, that it was against the general spirit of the law (hence they wanted 'a free interpretation of the law'). The jury would have to decide which line to take: if it adopted the free interpretation, it would still have to determine whether Cornelius intended to diminish tribunician power, and whether that constituted a diminishing of the majesty of the Roman people (the second and third issues).

62.15-16: *postulatur apud me praetorem primum de pecuniis repetundis*

This is taken to be a reference to Manilius who was first brought before Cicero as praetor in charge of the extortion court in 66, just before the end of Cicero's term of office (see above on 60.10-14). On the evidence of Schol. Bob. 119.16-17, Manilius' accuser was Cn. Minucius, but that evidence says the charge was treason, so he may have been the accuser only after the charge against Manilius was changed (if that is in fact what happened). Cominius was not present as *accusator*; he was only there to see how things would go.

62.17: *homines faeneos*

The appearance of 'men of straw' adds further weight to the idea that the trial of Manilius never really got off the ground.

63.8-9: *nam Metellus et postulaverat Curionem et destiterat*

As Asconius goes on to explain, Q. Caecilius Metellus Nepos (cos. 57), at the request of his father on his death bed, had undertaken a prosecution of C. Scribonius Curio (cos. 76), in retaliation for a prosecution which Curio had launched against his father (63.19-21). The prosecution of Nepos the elder by Curio took place probably in the early 90's (97 is suggested by Malcovati, *ORF*[2], p. 298, and Gruen, *Politics and Courts*, p. 308), for Curio is said to have been a young man at the time (Apul. *Apol.* 66), and nothing is heard of Nepos following his consulship in 98. As Curio was a protégé of the Metelli, the charge may have been the result of a private quarrel, and not part of the factional rivalries evident in other court cases in the 90's (though there was not always a clear distinction between the two). On the case, see Gruen, *Historia* 15 (1966) 42. Of the prosecution of Curio by Nepos the younger, we know little. There is some evidence that the case was begun in 70; it ought to have taken place close to the death of the elder Nepos, but there is no reason to suppose that he did not survive until about 70, even though we do not hear anything of him after his consulship. Ps.-Ascon. 207.18-20 (on Cic. *Verr.* 1.6, which deals with the delaying tactics of the defence in the case of Verres in 70 by which another prosecutor was given two days less than Cicero to collect evidence so that his case could be put on before Verres') lists two pairs of antagonists — Rupilius and Oppius (though uncertain who was

Pro Cornelio

prosecutor and who defendant), and Nepos and Curio. Schol. Gronov. 331 and 332 has an Oppius, a former governor of Achaea, as the accused and Dasianus (?) or Piso as the prosecutor. On the identification of Oppius, see *MRR* 2.111 (somewhat confused). Pseudo-Asconius' second pair would make sense: the Metelli were actively involved in defending Verres, and Nepos may well have helped by launching this delaying prosecution; Curio had recently been governor of Macedonia following his consulship in 76, and prosecution for provincial extortion in Achaea (supervised by the governor of Macedonia) would have been a reasonable charge to bring; the charge was easily abandoned when it turned out that Cicero defeated the ploy by collecting his evidence in a short period of time; the charge would be no threat to Curio's connection with the Metelli (cf., e.g., his pleasure at the election results for 69: Cic. *Verr.* 1.19), as the case was a ploy. For further discussion of the possibility that this is the case referred to by Asconius, see Marshall, *Philologus* 121 (1977) 83-9; contra, T. Zielinksi, ibid. 52 (1893) 256-7.

Note how Cicero covers up the deal which Nepos and Curio made (63.9-11): this complimentary reference by Cicero to a Metellus might have been designed not to alienate too much Metellus Pius who was assisting the prosecution (Kumaniecki, pp. 13-4; for other complimentary references to the Metelli, cf. ibid. 20ff.).

63.13-14: *plures Quinti Metelli*

There were alive at the time of Cornelius' trial four Caecilii Metelli with the *praenomen* Quintus. Q. Caecilius Metellus Pius, consul of 80 as a colleague of Sulla, and subsequently commander against Sertorius in Spain (79-71), was one of the five *principes* named by Asconius as promoting the prosecution; he had also been pontifex maximus since 81. Q. Caecilius Metellus Creticus was consul in 69 (cousin of the consul of 68) and subsequently commander against the pirates in Crete (hence the additional *cognomen*), coming into conflict there with Pompeius. The other two were Q. Caecilius Metellus Nepos (cos. 57) and Q. Caecilius Metellus Celer (cos. 60): both had seen service as *legati* under Pompeius, with whom they were linked by his marriage to their half-sister Mucia, but following his divorce of her at the end of 62, they joined the opposition, Celer most noticeably in his consulship by opposing proposals made on behalf of Pompeius (references in *MRR* 2.183) and Nepos by his opposition to the coalition of Pompeius, Crassus and Caesar in 59 (Cic. *Att.* 2.12.2) and by his support of Clodius' anti-Pompeian activities in 57 (Cic. *Sest.* 89; Dio 39.6.3-8.2). Celer and Nepos were the sons of another Q. Caecilius Metellus Nepos (cos. 98). The Mucia who was married to Pompeius c. 80 is described by Cicero as their *soror* (*fam.* 5.2.6); she was the daughter of a Mucius Scaevola, presumably the consul of 95, and is described by Asconius as Mucia Tertia (see above on 19.18-19). This all

232 Commentary

suggests that the mother of Nepos and Celer and of Mucia had been married to both Nepos the elder and Scaevola, but the order of the marriages is not clear. J. Carcopino, *Sylla ou la monarchie manquée* (Paris, 1931) p. 191, suggests that the mother was married to Nepos first and Scaevola second. Celer must have been born at the latest by 102, in view of the date of his consulship, and Nepos the younger by 99; they were older than Mucia, which could suggest that they were the offspring of their mother's first marriage. The absence of mention of Nepos the elder following his consulship in 98 could suggest death and the availability of his wife for remarriage in the early 90's (though divorce is just as possible). On the other hand, for Mucia to have been of marriageable age by 80, she must have been born by the mid-90's, and as she was the third daughter, the marriage of her mother to Scaevola must have existed for some time before then, so the marriage to Scaevola may have preceded rather than followed that to Nepos (Gruen, *Historia* 15 [1966] 42 n. 61). In the end, we should admit that we do not know the answer, since *soror* can also mean 'cousin'. For further discussion of the relationship, see Gelzer, *Caesar: Politician and Statesman*, 6th edn., trans. P. Needham (Oxford, 1968) p. 66 n. 6; T.P. Wiseman, *CQ* 21 (1971) 180-2; D.R. Shackleton Bailey, *AJAH* 2 (1977) 148-50 (who adds a third marriage for the mother of Celer, Nepos, and Mucia — to Ap. Claudius Pulcher, cos. 99, since Nepos is referred to as *frater* [i.e. 'first cousin'] of Ap. and P. Claudius Pulcher in Cic. *Att.* 4.3.4 and *dom.* 7); and T.W. Hillard, *PBSR* 50 (1982) 36.

63.17-18: *patrem Q. Metellum Nepotem . . . qui consul fuit cum T. Didio*

The father of Nepos and Celer had been consul in 98 with T. Didius (*MRR* 2.4); they were responsible for the law requiring three *nundinae* between the promulgation of a proposal and the vote on it.

63.24: *Curio assertorem ei comparavit*

The claim that a person treated as a slave was really a free man was dealt with under the procedure of the *legis actio sacramento in rem*. The person held as a slave could not himself initiate or act in the proceedings, but any citizen could act as the *adsertor in libertatem*, summon the apparent master before the magistrate, and make the claim that the supposed slave was free. By a provision of the Twelve Tables, the person who was the object of the proceedings would remain in *de facto* freedom while they were going on. On this procedure, see A. Watson, *Rome of the XII Tables: Persons and Property* (Princeton, 1975) pp. 95 and 125-33.

64.8: *in Curionem calumniam iuravit*

On the oath against *calumnia*, see above on 29.4.

Pro Cornelio 233

64.8-9: *cum hoc autem Metello postea Cicero simultates gessit*

This refers to Nepos' attacks on Cicero at the very end of 63, soon after Nepos had entered office as tribune, and in the following year in regard to Cicero's action in putting the Catilinarian conspirators to death (references in *MRR* 2.174). Cf. the stiff exchange of letters between Metellus Celer and Cicero on this topic (*fam.* 5.1 and 2).

64.11: *de libertinorum suffragiis*

On the issue of voting rights for freedmen, see above on 52.18-19.

64.17: *P. Sulpicium in tribunatu hanc eandem legem tulisse*

In his tribunate in 88, P. Sulpicius introduced four bills, including one enrolling the new Italian citizens (resulting from the recent war with the allies) and freedmen in all the tribes (App. *BC* 1.55-56; Liv. *per.* 77; cf. Vell. Pat. 2.18.5-6), and another to transfer the Mithridatic command from Sulla to Marius. For the view that Sulpicius did not have the *cognomen* Rufus, see H.B. Mattingly, *Athenaeum* 53 (1975) 264-6.

64.21: *ab initiis bonarum actionum ad perditas progressus esset*

For the sentiment, see the collection of sources in Greenidge and Clay^2, pp. 160-2, esp. Cic. *har. resp.* 43 and Vell. Pat. 2.18.5-6. For Sulpicius' volte-face, see above on 25.6-8.

64.23: *Sulpicius consulum armis iure oppressus esse visus est*

Mitchell, op. cit. p. 69 with n. 31, suggests that the tense of *visus est* here shows Asconius is not reporting his own opinion, but how Sulpicius' action was viewed at the time, and that the suppression of Sulpicius by the arms of the consuls was seen as a legitimate act (cf. App. *BC* 1.57, and Meier, *Res Publica Amissa* [Wiesbaden, 1966] p. 224). This hostile tradition about Sulpicius no doubt owes a lot to Sulla's memoirs (cf. A.W. Lintott, *CQ* 21 [1971] 442-3 and 452-3).

65.3-5: *celeritatem actionis significat . . . legem eandem Compitalibus pertulit*

The 'same law' presumably refers to the one Cicero had already dealt with (64.11ff.), relating to the distribution of freedmen in all the tribes; the law was hastily carried (45.11-19) and promptly annulled (*s.c. damnata* — 65.17). According to Dio (36.42.3-4), Manilius, afraid because the people were annoyed, at first ascribed the idea to Crassus and some others, but then paid court to Pompeius' interests by proposing to transfer the Mithridatic command to him. The law was passed on the Compitalia, the date of which varied (see above on 7.18), but which in 66 seem to have been held on the last day of the year (Dio 36.42.2). As tribunes entered office on 10th December, Manilius must only just have met the requirement of the *lex Caecilia Didia* that three *nundinae* must be observed between promulgation of and voting on a law (for a discussion of this law in relation to the meaning of *trinum nundinum*, see Lintott, *CQ* n.s. 15 [1965] 281-2, and A.K. Michels, *The Calendar of the Roman Republic* [Princeton, 1967] pp. 46 and 205). At this point in the speech, Cicero seems to be rejecting the prosecution's argument that Cornelius was really responsible for Manilius' bill about the freedmen's votes (cf. frag. 10 P = Ascon. 64.11-16) because the bill was ready so early in Manilius' tribunate (on this point of reconstruction, see Kumaniecki, pp. 15-6). On the violent opposition of L. Domitius Ahenobarbus to Manilius' proposal, see above on 45.11.

65.8: *C. Attium Celsum significat*

Since Cicero refers to him by office and not by name, it would seem that he was in office when the *pro Cornelio* was delivered, and that Cicero is suggesting he was acting in an official capacity. This would further suggest that Celsus' connection with the case was as president of the court by which Manilius was being tried (Phillips, art. cit. 604; cf. Gruen, *Last Generation*, p. 262 n. 7). As Q. Gallius was in charge of the *maiestas* court in 65, it would follow (if the above suggestions are right) that the charge against Manilius remained extortion, and was not changed to treason, and that Celsus was praetor in charge of the extortion court in 65. It is, of course, possible that there had been a change of presidents in the course of the year and that Celsus had been in charge of the treason court first, followed by Gallius, and it is possible therefore that the charge against Manilius had been changed. It has already been shown (see above on 60.13) that the consuls did not supplant the president after the interruption of Manilius' trial, and so that cannot be used to suggest that the charge was changed. On the other hand, Ward, art. cit. 549, argues that all we know is that Celsus was a praetor when he made his request to Cicero, and that the request might have been made in 66 when Manilius was first brought before Cicero (i.e. Celsus was praetor in 66). On Celsus' origins, see R. Syme, *Historia* 13 (1964) 113, and Wiseman, *New Men*, p. 216.

66.2: *magnis hominibus*

Gruen, *Class. Phil.* 64 (1969) 20-4, questions Asconius' identification of these 'important men' as Catilina and Piso, on the grounds that Cicero would not have used this phrase to describe men such as them; he accepts that Catilina and Piso took part in the disruption of Manilius' trial, but looks for more important figures behind them. Along with P.A. Brunt, *CR* n.s. 7 (1957) 193-5, he rejects the common view that Crassus was behind

Catilina (at least) and Piso at this time, and looks for a connection between Catilina and Q. Lutatius Catulus (cf. C.E. Stevens, *Latomus* 22 [1963] 398-435). Ward, art. cit. 550-1, reverts to the older view that Crassus was behind Catilina, pointing out his connection with Piso in 65 (Sall. *Cat.* 19.1-2). Phillips, *Rhein. Mus.* 116 (1973) 353-7, argues that Asconius' identification of the *magni homines* is acceptable. On Catilina's reputation as a disrupter of trials, see below on 86.24-25.

66.7: *L. Catilinam et Cn. Pisonem videtur significare*

The mention of these two in connection with the disturbances at Manilius' trial has been taken by some to suggest that the disturbances should be identified with the so-called 'first' Catilinarian conspiracy: Seager, *Historia* 13 (1964) 338-47; Gruen, *Class. Phil.* 64 (1969) 22-4; Phillips, *Latomus* 29 (1970) 601 and 606. The dates normally connected with Catilina and a conspiracy (the end of December 66 and 5th February 65) would make sense if associated respectively with Manilius' appearance before Cicero and the disrupted trial. Further, the story that a body-guard was voted to the consuls of 65 for protection against an alleged conspiracy (Dio 36.44.4) might well have arisen out of the appearance of the consuls at the senate's direction to keep an eye on Manilius' disrupted trial (see above on 60.13)

66.8-10: *Catilina... se ostendisset*

On Catilina's trial and consular candidature, see below on 85.10ff. and 89.6ff.

66.12-13: *Cn. quoque Piso, adulescens potens et turbulentus*

On Piso's association with Catilina, see Cic. *in tog. cand.* in Ascon. 92.11-14 and 93.11-14. On his subsequent appointment to Spain and death there, see below on 92.20-25. On the grounds of Crassus' association with Piso, reinforced by their known opposition to Pompeius, Crassus is thought to have been behind the 'first' Catilinarian conspiracy; on this question, see below on 83.2 and 22. Val. Max. 6.2.4 records the prosecution of a Manilius Crispus by a young man, Cn. Piso; the Manilius was shielded by his backer Pompeius, and the prosecutor turned his invective upon Pompeius himself. In view of Piso's hostility to Pompeius, Gruen has identified this young prosecutor with the quaestor of 65 and the Manilius Crispus with the tribune of 66 and placed the trial in 69 or 68 (*Calif. Stud. Class. Ant.* 1 (1968) 160-2; cf. Ward, art. cit. 550 n. 17); Asconius' description of Piso may well fit the young man in the incident described by Valerius Maximus. Piso's opposition to Pompeius raises a difficulty (made even more difficult if he had previously prosecuted Manilius) — why did he co-operate in disturbing the trial of Manilius, Pompeius' protégé, in 65? Catilina too, for that matter, for he was not a

Pompeian, being prosecuted by L. Lucceius, a Pompeian supporter, in 65 (but cf. below on 91.12). The answer may lie in the fact that Piso had changed his stance or that one should not see politics in this period as rigidly pro and anti-Pompeian (Phillips, *Rhein. Mus.* 116 [1973] 355-6).

66.15ff.

Kumaniecki, pp. 18-19, argues that the following fragments (up to the passage about Scipio Africanus at 69.14ff.) were designed to show that laws introduced by eminent persons, even consuls, often turned out to be bad and were repealed or altered. The examples were introduced to combat the prosecution's argument that Cornelius had proposed a bad law: Victorin. *de defin.* 29.5 St (= frag. 5 P) specifies three charges made by Cominius — *quod malam legem tulit, quod legendo codicem intercessionem sustulit, quod seditionem fecit.*

66.19: *hic est Cotta de quo iam saepe diximus*

He has already been mentioned at 14.19ff., and he is mentioned again in the following passage and at 78.23-25.

66.19-20: *magnus orator habitus . . . et C. Caesari*

On his reputation as an orator, see Cic. *Brut.* 183 (where he and P. Sulpicius are said to have ranked in first place among the orators of their generation), and for a discussion of his style, see ibid. 202, *or.* 106, *de or.* 2.98, 3.31. He left nothing in writing (Cic. *or.* 132, cf. *Brut.* 206-207); the occasions of his speeches are listed in *ORF*[2], pp. 288-91. The description *compar P. Sulpicio* is used at 14.20-21, but here C. Caesar has been added; because of that Kiessling and Schoell have supplied *aequalibus* for the lacuna, but that is unwarranted since Cicero says that Cotta and Sulpicius were slightly younger than Caesar (*Brut.* 182) and Cotta and Sulpicius themselves were almost the same age (*de or.* 3.31).

66.21: *videntur autem in rebus parvis fuisse leges illae*

In drawing his conclusion that these abrogated laws must have dealt with unimportant matters (because he can find no mention of them in other sources), Asconius overlooks one of these 'unimportant' laws which is mentioned in the very next passage on which he comments — the *lex de iudiciis privatis.* There is the suggestion of another law dealing with censorial leases and authorising the consuls to undertake the letting of contracts instead of the censors (Cic. *Verr.* 2.3.18-19; cf. Ps.-Ascon. 251.23-25; G. Rotondi, *Leges publicae populi Romani* [Milan, 1912] p. 365); Broughton, *MRR* 2.96, says this law too was abrogated in the following year. Cotta also concluded a treaty with King Hiempsal (Cic. *leg. agr.* 2.58).

Pro Cornelio 237

66.23-24: *apud Sallustium . . . apud Livium . . . apud Fenestellam*

The reference to this law of Cotta comes in Sall. *hist.* 2.49, 3.48.8 M; for Livy we do not have a reference (probably book 93); for Fenestella, cf. Peter, *HRR* 2.85. This is the only reference to Sallust as a source (elsewhere he is mentioned in connection with the trial of Milo during his tribunate); Livy is mentioned in one other place (77.4-5, where he is called *Livius noster*); and Fenestella is mentioned at 5.9, 31.14-15, 85.13-14 and 86.15-18.

67.1: *in consulatu [tulit invita] nobilitate*

The mss. reading is *in contione . . . nobilitate*, the gap being five letters in S, seven in P, and twelve in M. Madvig suggests *consulatu* to go with Manutius' *tulit invita* for the lacuna; Kiessling and Schoell, Clark and Giarrantano follow them. Stangl suggests *non consentiente* for *in contione*. The sense is clear: the nobility opposed the agitation for tribunician reform which had begun with Cn. Sicinius, tribune in 76, and continued until all bars were removed by Pompeius and Crassus in 70. For the unwillingness of the nobility, cf. Cic. in Ascon. 78.18-22. It is not clear whether Cotta himself belonged to the conservative nobility and proposed this measure to placate popular agitation, or whether he sided with the popular demand: it hinges, to some extent, on the interpretation of Sallust's description of him as *ex factione media* (*hist.* 3.48.8 M). For discussion and bibliography on this question, see Marshall, *Rhein. Mus.* 118 (1975) 142ff.

67.2-3: *ut eis [qui tr. pl.] fuissent alios quoque magistratus [capere liceret]*

Cf. 78.23-25 and App. *BC* 1.100. Among the restrictions which Sulla placed on the tribunate six years before, holders of that office were prevented from seeking further offices. For the other restrictions placed on the tribunate by Sulla, see the references in *MRR* 2.75; there is some debate whether the tribunes' power of initiating legislation was taken away (see D.H. Kelly in *Auckland Classical Essays* [Auckland and Oxford, 1970] pp. 133-42). The tribune Q. Opimius is said to have supported Cotta's law (Ps.-Ascon. 255.11-13); that may have had something to do with his condemnation in the following year for using his veto contrary to the Cornelian law (Cic. *Verr.* 2.1.155-157; Schol. Gronov. 341.9; H.W. Benario, *Historia* 22 [1973] 70).

67.11-12: *L. Cotta . . . tribunos aerarios*

The law was passed, probably in September or October 70 (Cic. *Verr.* 2.5.178, cf. 1.31), by L. Aurelius Cotta when he was praetor. Although on occasion the sources loosely speak of the juries being divided between

238 Commentary

senators and equites (e.g. Cic. *Font.* 36, *Cluent.* 121 and 130; Vell. Pat. 2.32.3; Liv. *per.* 97 says the courts were handed over to the equites), it is clear that they were to be divided between these three orders (cf. Cic. *Att.* 1.16.3). There are some who see the law as connected with the trial of Verres and with a factional struggle between Pompeius and the Metelli (e.g. Badian, *FC*, pp. 282-4; Ward, *Latomus* 29 [1970] 67-71). Others see the prosecution of Verres as having little effect on the situation that had led to agitation for reform of the courts (which had begun in 74), and say that the trial cannot be used to reconstruct the attitude of factions (e.g. Gruen, *AJP* 92 [1971] 1-16; cf. Brunt, *JRS* 58 [1968] 231). Pompeius had indicated his intention to pay attention to corruption in the law-courts at a public meeting in 71 (Cic. *Verr.* 1.45; Schol. Gronov. 328.29-30); it is odd that nothing was done till late in the next year, and that action was then taken by a praetor, not the consul (Pompeius being one of the consuls of 70). According to Plut. *Pomp.* 22.3, Pompeius in the end merely 'allowed' (περιεῖδεν) the reform; this need not mean that he had no interest in it (Stockton, *Historia* 22 [1973] 217-8; contra, A.N. Sherwin-White, *JRS* 46 [1956] 7-8). There is debate over the definition of the *tribuni aerarii*: see above on 17.6-7.

67.13: *adeptique sunt omnes consulatum*

Gaius was consul in 75, Marcus in 74, and Lucius in 65. Seager, *Hommages à Renard*, Vol. II, pp. 680-6, suggests that L. Cotta's slow progress to the consulship (he was eligible for 67, and only got it by default for 65) was due to his alignment with the Pompeian reform cause and retaliatory blocking by the opponents of that cause (i.e. the *principes civitatis* who were behind Cornelius' prosecution).

67.20: *L. Licinium Crassum oratorem*

Regarded as the leading orator of his day; for an assessment of his rhetorical skill, see Cic. *Brut.* 143-148. He is made the principal interlocutor in Cicero's *de oratore*. For a list of the speeches he is known to have delivered, see *ORF*^{2}, pp. 240-59, and for discussion of some of his cases, see Gruen, *Politics and Courts*, pp. 107-8, 127-30, 133-4, 158-9, 193-203, 208-13. On the marriage connection between Crassus and Scaevola, see above on 14.24-25.

67.20-21: *Q. Mucium Scaevolam . . . iuris consultum*

Scaevola was pontifex maximus from c. 89 to 82, obtaining an office which had been held by his father (130-c.115) and by his uncle, P. Licinius Crassus Dives Mucianus (132-130). On his oratorical ability and legal knowledge especially, see Cic. *Brut.* 145-148, 155 and 163; Vell. Pat. 2.9.1. Cicero's summing up of the comparison between Crassus and Scaevola is that Crassus was *eloquentium iuris peritissimus*, and Scaevola *iuris peritorum eloquentissimus* (*Brut.* 145). Only two cases in

Pro Cornelio 239

which he was involved are known: *pro M. Coponio adversum M'. Curium* (ibid. 145 and 194ff.), and *pro Rutilio* in 92 (ibid. 115, *de or.* 1.229). He published the first systematic treatise, supposedly in eighteen books, on civil law (Pomp. *Dig.* 1.2.2.41: *ius civile primus constituit generatim in libros decem et octo redigendo*); on this legal treatise, see Watson, *Law Making in the Later Roman Republic* (Oxford, 1974) pp. 143-58. His *liber singularis* ὅρων (*definitionum*) was the earliest work excerpted in Justinian's *Digest* (Kübler, *RE* 16 [1935] 442-5). The defence of Rutilius, who had been a legate of Scaevola during his governorship of Asia and who took over as acting governor when Scaevola left (see above on 15.5-6), shows another link with C. Aurelius Cotta (just mentioned by Cicero): Rutilius' sister was married to Cotta's father, and Cotta was one of Rutilius' defence counsel.

67.22-23: *hi enim legem eam . . . in consulatu tulerunt*

The verb *redigere* has been restored here and in the first line of the lemma from 68.3-4 and Schol. Bob. 129.19 (on Cic. *Sest.* 30). The law was not an expulsion order (cf. Cic. *off.* 3.47); it struck from the lists allies who had illegally usurped Roman citizenship and set up a *quaestio* to investigate dubious cases (Badian, *FC*, p. 297; cf. R.W. Husband, *Class. Phil.* 11 [1916] 321-4; E. Gabba, *Athenaeum* 31 [1953] 260-7), though the practical effect may have been that some were expelled by the *quaestio* set up under the terms of the law (Badian, *Historia* 18 [1969] 489-90). The law was sponsored by both consuls of 95, who had some connections with the Metellan group, and behind the measure stood the advice of M. Aemilius Scaurus, the *princeps senatus* and leader of the Metelli (Cic. *de or.* 2.257); this suggests that the Metellan group was opposed to granting concessions to the Italian allies and that the law was part of the factional struggle between them and the friends of Marius (Badian, *Historia* 6 [1957] 318-44; cf. Gruen, *Politics and Courts*, pp. 202-3, and Sherwin-White, *The Roman Citizenship*, 2nd edn. [Oxford, 1973] p. 140). In this context, note that one of the first persons to be brought before the newly-established *quaestio* was T. Matrinius, who had been enfranchised by Marius under the terms of Saturninus' colony bill of 100; note too that in 92 Crassus, in his censorship with Cn. Domitius Ahenobarbus, published a joint edict expelling Latin rhetors from Rome (references in *MRR* 2.17), a further indication of his attitude towards the Italians. The question of a factional struggle is complicated by the fact that Crassus' daughter Licinia was married (or betrothed) to Marius' son about this time (placed after the *lex Licinia Mucia* by Badian, art. cit. 329, but in 96 or 95 by Gruen, *Historia* 15 [1966] 43) and that Crassus apparently offered to defend Matrinius (Cic. *Balb.* 49); cf. Brunt, *JRS* 55 (1965) 106-7.

68.1: *summa cupiditate civitatis*

Sherwin-White, op. cit. pp. 135ff., argues that the allies' main complaint was against inequality of privilege and that they desired the citizenship, not for its political advantage in the narrow sense, but as a guarantee of equality. Brunt,*JRS* 55 (1965) 101-6, stresses that it was the vote that the allies (or rather the leading men in the allied states who would be most able to exercise it) really wanted (cf. above on 22.5-6) because of the possibilities it presented for striking political bargains and exerting influence. Gabba's view, *Athenaeum* 32 (1959) 239-44, is that the Italian gentry wanted the vote in order to secure control over Roman external policy and so to advance their economic interests.

68.2: *magna pars eorum pro civibus Romanis se gereret*

The *lex Licinia Mucia* did not physically expel aliens, but dealt with the unlawful arrogation of citizenship. Just how these persons were illicitly registered as citizens is debated: Badian, *Historia* 6 (1957) 333, sees masses of Italians registered as citizens by the censors of 97-6, who were friends of Marius, and the *lex Licinia Mucia* as a reaction by the opposing faction in the very next year. Sherwin-White, op. cit. p. 140 n. 2, and Brunt, art. cit. 106-7, disagree, the former saying that censorial registration was not a valid form of enfranchisement and the latter that the process had been more gradual. It is difficult to determine the numbers involved as no census figures for 97-6 survive; an anecdote (Diod. 37.13.1) speaks of 10,000 of those facing disfranchisement at the hands of the censors of 92 when the *lex Licinia Mucia* would have its full effect, being led to Rome with concealed weapons.

68.4-5: *principum Italicorum populorum*

Badian, *FC*, p. 213, sees these as men of a class like Marius, who on becoming citizens would at once be *equites Romani*, and as the ones who were accepted on the lists of Roman citizens, 'with remarkable laxity', by the censors of 97-6. Brunt, art. cit. 92, disagrees: it is unlikely that many Italians of rank and note had acquired the citizenship surreptitiously (cf. Sherwin-White, op. cit. p. 140 n. 2). What alienated the *principes* was the intransigence which the law displayed. Brunt points out that it was these men, the *domi nobiles*, who would take the lead in Italian aspirations (cf. Liv. *per.* 71: *in consiliis principum*).

68.5: *vel maxima causa belli Italici*

In making the *lex Licinia Mucia* perhaps the most important cause of the Italian war, Asconius may be overstating the case; there is no doubt it was an important proximate cause, but it was only one link in the chain of events which had frustrated the Italians in their quest for the citizenship, and the events of M. Livius Drusus' tribunate in 91 are likely to have been more important immediate causes. Brunt, art. cit. 92, accepts that it was the chief cause and suggests that the delay of over three years before the revolt broke out was due to the realisation by the Italian leaders that they needed time to prepare, and to their attempts at persuasion to avoid the final recourse of rebellion. For other ancient views on the causes, see the sources in Greenidge and Clay[2], pp. 138-9.

68.6: *post triennium*

Asconius has miscalculated here, for the Italian war broke out in 91, four years after the passage of the *lex Licinia Mucia*.

68.7: *quattuor omnino genera sunt*

Cic. *rep.* 3.33 (in Lact. *inst. div.* 6.8.6-9) lists four verbs — *obrogare, derogare, abrogare* and *solvere*; *Att.* 3.23.3 has the first three. Asconius deals only with three of the four types mentioned by Cicero, and it seems likely that the fourth category not dealt with was *abrogatio* (the annulment of the Livian laws being presumably the example of *solutio*). At 68.19 two of the mss. have *quartum* (and the third has *quantum*); either the word should be emended to *alterum*, or the whole passage should be moved to follow the third category. No help is gained from the order of the verbs in the two passages of Cicero referred to above, as it is different in both passages.

68.12: *Q. Caecilius Metellus Numidicus, M. Iunius Silanus*

Consuls in 109: Metellus was given command of the war against Jugurtha in Numidia, and Silanus campaigned against the Cimbri.

68.13-14: *bello Cimbrico quod diu prave simul et infeliciter administratum est*

Asconius is making a general comment on the whole war, not just providing a reason why Silanus was able to secure the repeal of certain laws. For a summary of the poor conduct of the campaigns against the Cimbri by senatorial commanders and their subsequent prosecutions, see Gruen, *Politics and Courts*, pp. 150-1 and 160-5.

68.15-16: *Iunius male rem adversus Cimbros gessit*

Silanus was sent to Gaul (where the Romans had been operating only since 125) during his consulship in 109, and he stayed on as proconsul in 108; at some time in that period, when the senate rejected a request from the Celtic tribes that they be allowed to settle on the frontiers, Silanus was defeated somewhere in the valley of the Rhone. Liv. *per.* 65 places the Celtic request after the battle, Flor. 1.38.4 before. Subsequently in 104 he was brought to trial by a tribune of that year, Cn. Domitius Ahenobarbus, for his failure (see below on 80.20ff.).

242   *Commentary*

68.16-18: *plures leges . . . quibus militiae stipendia minuebantur, abrogavit*

We do not know what these laws were, nor when they were passed; they may have been Gracchan (Rotondi, op. cit. p. 324; Brunt, *Italian Manpower*, p. 401 n. 4: 'C. Gracchus' military law [Plut. *C. Gr.* 5.1; Diod. 34/5.25.5] may have revived the proposal ascribed to his brother [Plut. *Ti. Gr.* 16] of limiting military service.'). Their existence testifies to the dislike of conscription so evident in the second century, and their repeal acknowledges that Silanus must have had a strong case. Fear of the Celts must have been the case, and there must have been no other way to raise the troops whom it was felt Rome needed; cf. the proclamation by P. Rutilius Rufus (cos. 105) following the defeat at Arausio that men under thirty-five should not leave Italy (Gran. Licin. 21 B).

68.22: *illis consulibus*

L. Marcius Philippus and Sex. Iulius Caesar, mentioned in the lemma, were consuls in 91.

68.22-69.1: *leges Livias quas . . . M. Livius Drusus tribunus plebis tulerit*

The programme of M. Livius Drusus in his tribunate in 91 included the following proposals: 1. a *lex frumentaria*; 2. a *lex agraria*, involving both colonial foundations and viritane grants; 3. a *lex iudiciaria*, by which three hundred equites were to be enrolled in the senate and the enlarged body would provide the jurors for criminal trials (a brief bibliography to the controversy over the nature of this bill is found in Gruen, *Historia* 15 [1966] 61 n. 180; cf. Weinrib, *Historia* 19 [1970] 414-43); 4. an additional clause to the preceding, or perhaps a separate bill, to set up a *quaestio* to make equites liable to charges of corruption to secure an unjust conviction (Gruen, *Politics and Courts*, p. 209); 5. a *lex nummaria* providing for the addition of one-eighth of bronze to the silver coinage; 6. a proposal to extend Roman citizenship to the Italian allies (references in Rotondi, op. cit. pp. 335-8). It is not clear which of these proposals were carried and subsequently annulled (see below on 69.5).

69.2-3: *senatus partes tuendas suscepisset et leges pro optimatibus tulisset*

There is almost unanimous agreement in the ancient sources that Drusus' initial proposals were designed to enhance the prestige and influence of the senatorial order, and especially of a particular group in the senate (whom Asconius calls optimates). His grain and land laws may well have been aimed at getting the populace on side, so as to secure support for his judicial proposal: the example of his father, the anti-Gracchan tribune of

Pro Cornelio 243

122, provided him with a lesson in how to manipulate popular legislation to secure a reform programme. The proposal to incorporate three hundred equites into the senate was not designed to placate the equites, but it was more likely that it would alienate the rest, and the additional clause which made the equites liable to prosecution for bribery showed his true attitude to them. Drusus had links with prominent members of the aristocracy: he had once been married to Servilia, the daughter of Q. Servilius Caepio, who had proposed the law restoring senators to control of (or a share in) the jury-courts for extortion in his consulship in 106. His sister Livia was married to another Caepio, the son of this consul (for the reason for the split between Drusus and this Caepio, see above on 21.23-24); the Servilii Caepiones had links with the Metelli, who were now headed by M. Aemilius Scaurus, the *princeps senatus* (on the links, see Badian, *Studies*, pp. 37ff.). Drusus' aunt Livia was married to P. Rutilius Rufus, whose condemnation by an equestrian jury in 92 was the scandal which provided the personal motivation for Drusus' tribunate and led the group supporting him to press for judicial reform. His advisers, especially for the judiciary law, included Scaurus and L. Crassus; Crassus had offered to defend Rutilius at his trial, but the latter permitted only Scaevola and his nephew C. Aurelius Cotta to speak. Scaevola had shared most of his offices with Crassus (see above on 14.24) and his sister was married to Crassus; the Aurelii Cottae can be linked to the faction, for Rutilius' sister was married to M. Aurelius Cotta, and their three sons eventually reached the consulship (see above on 67.13), and one of them, Gaius, was a close friend of Drusus. This whole group was anxious for judiciary reform, because equestrian control of the courts was proving a bottleneck for senatorial politics: Scaurus himself provided a recent instance of this, for in 92 or early 91 he was indicted for *repetundae* by Caepio, who had been inspired by the conviction of Rutilius, but he turned the tables on Caepio by bringing a counter-charge against him (see above on 21.18ff.). Both were acquitted.

69.3-4: *postea eo licentiae est progressus ut nullum in his morem servaret*

According to App. *BC* 1.35, Drusus' proposal to enfranchise the Italians was the central aim of his tribunate, the other measures being designed to win the support of various groups; according to Vell. Pat. 2.4.1, it was an afterthought, aimed at securing support to overcome opposition to his judiciary reform and at gaining *gloria* for resolving a burning issue. But the other members of the group are not likely to have supported this proposal: Scaurus, Crassus and Scaevola had recently made clear their attitude to the Italian franchise (see above on 67.22-23), but in the face of attacks on the faction in the senate by the consul Philippus they decided to maintain a united front. Crassus used the occasion of a denunciation of the senate by Philippus as a body with whom the consul could no longer carry on the business of the state, to deliver one of his most brilliant orations. Cicero's story of a long consultation by members of the faction (*de or.* 1.24-26) before Crassus agreed to deliver the speech on Drusus' behalf suggests that they were unhappy with his proposal for Italian franchise and that Crassus' speech did not deal with that matter; rather it seems to have dealt with the dignity of the senatorial order and may have had as its background the judiciary reform. The result of Crassus' speech was a vote of censure on Philippus, and retention, for the moment, of Drusus' programme; but within a week Crassus had died, and Philippus, taking advantage of divisions and tensions, succeeded in having Drusus' laws invalidated. Drusus continued to press for his proposals, but was soon after murdered in the forum by an unknown agent; there was no enquiry into the circumstances of his death. Asconius' view, therefore, of the reason for Drusus' failure is not quite accurate: it is true that he did not have the full support of his associates on the franchise question, but they did not entirely abandon him (see E.J. Weinrib, *Historia* 19 [1970] 435-43).

69.4: *Philippus cos. qui ei inimicus erat*

Philippus was not so much opposed to Drusus personally as to the group which supported him; there was an occasion when Drusus and Philippus engaged in a scuffle which produced a bleeding nose for the consul but the incident was a manifestation of the opposition to Drusus' programme. There is no need to think that Philippus opposed Drusus' legislation on principle; he may not have wanted to see credit secured by a rival senatorial faction. There is no reason to think that he opposed reform of the courts, for in the wake of 92 he too had been threatened with prosecution (Flor. 2.5.5; cf. Badian, *FC*, p. 217). Caepio, the former brother-in-law of Drusus, joined Philippus in opposing Drusus, who at one stage threatened to hurl him from the Tarpeian rock; this typical punishment proposed by a tribune suggests that Caepio was in office (praetor?) that year also (cf. *MRR* 2.24 n. 5). The opposition took advantage of the outrage of the equites, the distaste of conservative senators for an addition of 300 new men to the senate, suspicion of Drusus' demagoguery, and the anger of some Italians (especially Etruscans and Umbrians) at Drusus' agrarian and colonial law which threatened the confiscation of Italian land, to get the senate to invalidate the laws (see Gruen, *Politics and Courts*, pp. 210-3).

69.5: *ut leges eius omnes uno s.c. tollerentur*

Philippus at first failed to get the senate to invalidate Drusus' laws, because of Crassus' speech. After Crassus' death and just before Drusus' murder, Philippus succeeded in getting the senate to conduct an examination into the validity of Drusus' laws (App. *BC* 1.36 speaks of a δοκιμασία; cf. Badian, *FC*, p. 219), and they were declared invalid. Of the proposals of Drusus, it is likely that all (except the last, dealing with the Italian franchise) had passed into law, and it was all of them which were declared invalid. There is general agreement that the agrarian and colonial law and the judiciary law had passed (e.g. Rotondi, op. cit. pp. 335-7; Badian, *FC*, p. 217).

69.6: *contra auspicia esse latas*

Cic. *dom.* 41 says that the laws were declared invalid because they were passed contrary to the *lex Caecilia Didia*; Asconius says that they were passed in defiance of the auspices; while Livy (*per.* 71) and Florus (2.5.9) emphasise that they were carried *per vim*. Some have suggested, because of Cicero's reference to the *lex Caecilia Didia*, that Drusus' laws were declared invalid because they had been passed *per saturam*; that law did not deal solely with that particular irregularity (E.G. Hardy, *CR* 27 [1913] 262; R. Thomsen, *C. & M.* 5 [1942] 30-1). Cicero's reference is made in the context of one of that law's other provisions, the requirement of three *nundinae* between promulgation and vote on a proposal, and it may have been that irregularity which was the basis for invalidating Drusus' laws. Lintott, *Violence*, pp. 140-1, thinks that the *lex Caecilia Didia* confirmed the *leges Aelia et Fufia* and therefore included coverage of procedure in regard to omens (hence Asconius' reason, coupled with the reference of Cicero, may be correct).

69.10: *cui derogaretur*

Derogatio refers to changes made to an existing law by amending or cancelling some provisions in that law. It is not clear from Asconius' comment just what provisions in the *lex Calpurnia* were amended; in view of the mention of *pecuniaria poena*, it may have been in this area that the amendment was made, for there was considerable pressure for a tightening up of bribery laws in the middle 60's (Cic. *Mur.* 46-47). On the other hand, the amendment may have related to some technical point where it had become evident that the law was ill-defined: cf. Cic. *Mur.* 67 where a clarification of the *lex Calpurnia* had to be made by senatorial decree (note!); on the *s.c.*, see below on 83.6-7. Further, the imperfect may have a conative force: there were other attempts to propose bribery laws, particularly to stiffen penalties, in this period (though cf. the use of the imperfect at 68.11), but they failed, since Cicero's *pro Murena* shows that the *lex Calpurnia* was in force until Cicero's own bribery law, passed in his consulship in 63. A.W. Zumpt, *Criminalrecht*, 2.2.249-50, regards the *lex Fabia* as the outcome of the *s.c.* mentioned here, but if a new law was passed it would be an instance of *obrogatio*, not *derogatio*. The *lex Fabia* restricted the number of attendants permitted to accompany a candidate (Cic. *Mur.* 71), but there is no evidence as to the date and proposer of the law; the number of attendants was an area which had to be clarified in the senatorial decree mentioned in Cic. *Mur*. 67. On the date of the *lex Fabia*, see *MRR* 2.164 n. 4.

69.11: *lex haec Calpurnia de ambitu erat*

As Asconius goes on to say, this law, proposed by the consul Piso, was passed two years earlier (67). It was put forward, at the request of the senate, as a counter-proposal to that put forward by Cornelius, and is an instance of the conflict between the consul and the tribune in that year: on the conflict, see above on 57.8. Although according to Dio 36.38.4 the senate instructed the consuls to frame the counter-proposal, the law on bribery is known only under the name of Calpurnius (L. Hayne, *Class. Phil.* 69 [1974] 282).

69.12-13: *praeter alias poenas pecuniaria quoque poena erat adiecta*

Under the Sullan law on bribery, a candidate found guilty of illegal canvassing was prevented from standing for that office for ten years (Schol. Bob. 78.35-37); the *lex Calpurnia* excluded convicted candidates from office altogether, expelled them from the senate, and subjected them to a fine (Dio 36.38.1). It is not clear whether bribery agents (*divisores*) were subject to penalties under the *lex Calpurnia* (see below on 74.22-23); as Cic. *Mur.* 47 speaks of a heavier penalty being demanded in 63 against the plebs, it follows that the *lex Calpurnia* was directed against persons other than senatorial offenders. The pressure for an increase in penalties for bribery probably reflected a growing fierceness in electoral competition which may have resulted from the tightening up of the requirements for office by Sulla and his increase in the ratio of quaestors to higher magistrates, the eligibility of ex-tribunes for higher office, and the attempts of men expelled from the senate in 70 to regain their rank by holding office again; the pressure was not decreased by the scandals of 66 when the two consuls-elect were found guilty under the *lex Calpurnia*. For an account of the bribery proposals in the 60's, see Gruen, *Last Generation*, pp. 212-24.

69.19-20: *secundo consulatu Scipionis post septimum annum quam Carthaginensibus bello secundo*

P. Cornelius Scipio Africanus was consul for the second time (following the first in 205) in 194, with Ti. Sempronius Longus as his colleague. Peace was concluded with the Carthaginians in the Second Punic War in 201.

69.21: *Antias tradidit*

Valerius Antias is mentioned as a source in one other place — 13.8.

Antias' version differs from that of Cicero: the former believes that the allocation of reserved seats for senators was made at the Roman Games, while Cicero believes it was at the Megalesian Games (*har. resp.* 24, discussed subsequently by Asconius: the lemma at 69.14ff. gives no indication of which games). Livy's version, which presumably followed that of Antias, believes that the allocation was made at the Roman Games (34.44.5, 54.4). Both sets of games are known to have been conducted by the curule aediles of that year, A. (or C.) Atilius Serranus and L. Scribonius Libo. Livy's version (like Antias') stresses that the aediles set seats aside for the senators on the instructions of the censors, Sex. Aelius Paetus and C. Cornelius Cethegus, but adds the information that Scipio as *auctor eius rei* repented of the suggestion (34.54.8). As Scipio was nominated *princeps senatus* for the second time by these censors (Liv. 34.44.4), it is clear that he was politically associated and so in a position to influence their actions.

69.21-22: *ludis Romanis*

These games were associated with the worship of Jupiter and were connected with the Ides of September, the great festival day of that god, marking the *dies natalis* of the Capitoline temple and the day of the *epulum Jovis*. In the fourth century the games lasted three days, until Camillus added a fourth (Liv. 6.42.12; Plut. *Cam.* 42.6), and on the motion of M. Antonius a fifth day was added (19th September) in honour of Caesar (Cic. *Phil.* 2.110). Yet Cicero seems to imply that the games were longer than four days in his time and began before the Ides of September (*Verr.* 1.31). W.W. Fowler, *The Roman Festivals of the Period of the Republic* (London, 1899) pp. 216-7, says they developed out of votive games, which show the connection between the festival of Jupiter and the ceremony of driving a nail into the wall of the cella Iovis. This may explain why votive games appear in one of the versions (70.12). At a time when elections were held later in the year, the *ludi Romani* provided entertainment for voters who came to Rome for the *comitia*, just as the *ludi Apollinares* did at a later period when the elections were held in July (Taylor, *Historia* 17 [1968] 190).

69.22: *Atilius Serranus*

Manutius adds the *praenomen* C., making it refer to the praetor of 185; others suggest the *praenomen* should be A., referring to the praetor of 192 (which in point of time seems the better choice). See *MRR* 1.346 n. 2.

70.2ff.: *in ea autem ... videtur significare*

The passage which Asconius quotes comes from *har. resp.* 24. Asconius is somewhat splitting hairs in saying that there is a difference in 'allowing' and 'being the author'; in both passages Cicero stresses the role of Scipio (ignoring, apparently, the role of the curule aediles and censors). As Asconius himself recognises (70.11-12), the aediles were responsible for conducting the games, and the consul can only have been responsible for suggesting the idea of separate seats to them, and this is all that Cicero is implying in both passages.

70.7: *Matris Magnae*

The passage of Cicero is incorrectly quoted here, for the phrase following *templum* should be *in ipso Matris Magnae conspectu Megalesibus fieri* etc. This indicates clearly that Cicero thought the reservation of seats was made at the Megalesian Games. A more important point of difference between the two passages which Asconius might have discussed is the question of which games. On the confusion between the various versions, see Wiseman, *Phoenix* 27 (1973) 195.

70.10-13: *et collega eius . . . Scipio et Longus coss. fecerint*

Something has apparently dropped out at the end of the quotation. As we have here apparently a third version of when the seats were reserved (at some votive games conducted by the consuls), which disagrees with the version accepted by Asconius, Kiessling and Schoell, following Madvig, suggest *Fenestella quoque a Scipione Africano II cos. et collega eius* etc. That is attractive because of the possibility of parablepsis, and because of Asconius' frequent disagreement with Fenestella.

70.11: *Megalesium*

The worship of the Phrygian Magna Mater was introduced into Rome in 204 as a result of a Sibylline oracle which said that the enemy would not be driven out of Italy till the worship of this goddess was introduced (Liv. 29.10.4-8, 14.1-14; Ov. *Fast.* 4.259); with the co-operation of Attalus of Pergamum, a sacred stone was brought from Phrygia and placed in the temple of Victory on 4th April, which became the festival day of the goddess. Thirteen years later, on 10th April, a temple was dedicated, and the games eventually lasted from 4th to 10th April (*CIL* 1^2.314). On the Megalesia, see Fowler, op. cit. pp. 69-71.

70.13ff.: *non praeterire autem*

Asconius is right to attempt to see some difference in Cicero's presentation of material depending on his audience. But the logic of his analysis of the passage from the *pro Cornelio* is hard to follow: Scipio's repentance at having reserved seats for senators is not likely to elevate the prestige of the senate — rather it is likely to be an attack on that body for being unworthy of its privileges (this latter point being more likely in a *popularis causa*). Similarly the logic of the analysis of the passage from

Pro Cornelio

the *de haruspicum responsis* is faulty, for the senate would have been flattered whether Cicero said Scipio was the initiator of the grant or had actually made it himself. The context in that speech is designed to draw attention to the contrast between the sort of people who attended the Megalesian Games normally, and those who attended the games when conducted by Clodius.

71.2-3: *quot loca . . . intercessions sint*

The lemma which Asconius goes on to quote contains a list of the stages in the procedure of a legislative assembly at which a veto could be interposed (for a discussion of them, see Meier, *Mus. Hel.* 25 [1968] 86-100). The passage of Cicero has a number of lacunae, but it is clear that a veto could be interposed up until the actual voting was commenced, even at the time when the people were moving into their tribal positions (Mommsen, *Staatsrecht*, 1^3.285; Taylor, *Roman Voting Assemblies* [Ann Arbor, 1966] p. 75 with n. 37). Cicero is obviously talking about procedures at legislative meetings of the tribal assembly (for further discussion of procedures, see U. Hall, *Historia* 13 [1964] 267ff.; Taylor, op. cit. pp. 74-8).

71.5-6: *quam diu . . . ferundi transferuntur*

Stangl's apparatus gives the various emendations and additions of Rau, Bücheler and Mommsen for the lacuna here. The general sense seems to be either that the non-voters were removed (i.e. those who had the right to vote were separated) or it refers to the movement of the people into their tribal groups in preparation for determining their vote (cf. the addition of Mommsen *summovetur populus* at 71.7 below). This latter sense is suggested by Asconius' comment at 71.14-15. It seems clear that there is no particular order observed by Cicero in his list, for this particular stage which he puts first (whichever of the two ideas it conveys) would presumably have come later in the process than the stages which he goes on to list.

71.6-7: *id est . . . lex*

Kiessling and Schoell's conjecture for the lacuna is *dum recitatur*, which makes good sense. One of the charges against Cornelius was that he had read out the bill himself when a veto had been interposed by forbidding the herald to read it out: see above on 58.17-18.

71.7: *dum [summovetur populus]*

On the basis of Liv. 25.3.16 (*testibus datis tribuni populum submoverunt sitellaque lata est ut sortirentur ubi Latini suffragium ferrent.*), Mommsen has supplied *summovetur populus* here. One objection to this

250 *Commentary*

suggested addition is that it seems to repeat the idea of *transferuntur* (i.e. the idea of people moving into their tribal groups), and another is that it is based on the existence of some sort of sequence in Cicero's list (which, it has been suggested above, does not exist).

71.7-8: *dum sitella defertur*

Following the recitation of the law and the issue of the instruction *discedite*, the urn for the lot was brought in (Cic. *leg*. 3.11: *lex recitata est; discedere et tabellam iubebo dari.*). For a description of *sitellae* and discussion of the methods of using them, see Taylor, op. cit. pp. 71-3. The lot was used for two purposes: to determine the choice of tribe in which the citizens of Latin colonies who happened to be present were to vote, and to select the order in which the tribes were to vote. One of the ways to stop the voting was by the theft of the *sitella* (Plut. *Ti. Gracch*. 11.1).

71.8: *dum aequantur sortes*

The lots are usually referred to as *sortes*, but the word *pila* is also used (*Tabula Hebana* 23), especially for the lots used in the selection of jurors (Ascon. 39.18-20; cf. Prop. 4.11.19-20). On the process of *aequatio*, see above on 39.19-20.

71.14-15: *sed in suam quisque tribum discedat in qua est suffragium laturus*

After the instruction *discedite*, the people moved into their tribal groups in order to cast their votes. For the way in which the tribes were physically organised for the actual voting, see the discussion in Hall, *Historia* 13 (1964) 292-3; Taylor, op. cit. pp. 39-54; and E.S. Staveley, *Greek and Roman Voting and Elections* (London, 1972) pp. 159-60. On the question whether the tribes voted simultaneously or successively at legislative assemblies, see below on 72.18.

72.8: *de ea lege [Gabini] Ciceronem nunc dicere*

Gabinius, who proposed the law to establish the command against the pirates, was tribune in the same year as Cornelius. In this passage, Cicero is drawing a contrast between the actions of the two tribunes: he had been unable to deny that Cornelius had read out the bill, so Cicero tried to play that down by saying that he touched the *codex* (Quint. 5.13.25) and later that Cornelius had merely read out the bill to refresh his memory (Cic. *Vat*. 5). The list of instances when a veto could be imposed, given in the preceding fragment, was also related to playing down Cornelius' reading of the bill, because Cicero wished to demonstrate that the point at which a veto could be imposed was not fixed and that Cornelius had not yet given the order to proceed to the vote (cf. 71.12), but rather disbanded the

Pro Cornelio 251

assembly before a vote was taken (58.23-24). This presumably was intended to show that he would not have entirely neglected the veto (cf. Kumaniecki, p. 22). In contrast, Gabinius went much further (though the veto in the end was withdrawn); despite the veto, Cicero does not condemn the violent action of Gabinius, for his action was carried out in the interest of the state. One may suspect that Cicero was justifying his own support of Manilius' bill to transfer the Mithridatic command to Pompeius, while condemning Manilius' violence (cf. 65.11-15). It illustrates the responsible *popularis* line Cicero was taking at this time (Stockton, op. cit. p. 57; cf. above on 61.5-7).

72.10: *L. autem Trebellius*

Trebellius, also tribune in 67, interposed his veto on the Gabinian law. As Asconius goes on to relate (cf. Dio 36.30.1-2), the vote on the Gabinian law was postponed, until a new motion to deprive Trebellius of his office was heard; seventeen tribes voted for his deposition, and as the eighteenth was about to vote, Trebellius withdrew his veto. He was joined in his opposition to Gabinius' law by one of the other tribunes, L. Roscius Otho (Plut. *Pomp*. 25.6; Dio 36.24.4, 30.3-4). From Dio's account it would seem that Roscius also tried to interpose a veto, but was cowed by the treatment of Trebellius; all he could do was hold up two fingers, indicating that he thought two men should be appointed to the command. In view of Roscius' later connection with Crassus (he served as an officer in the Parthian campaign: Plut. *Crass*. 31.2), Gruen, *Last Generation*, p. 187, suggests that Roscius, and presumably Trebellius, were acting for Crassus in opposing the Gabinian law, but there is no evidence that Crassus did oppose the granting of commands to Pompeius in 67 and 66.

72.11: *nam senatui promiserat*

This is the only source where it is said that Trebellius swore to die rather than allow the passage of the Gabinian law; as it turned out, he did not keep his oath. Dio 36.24.1-2 says that the senate as a body was opposed to granting the pirate command to Pompeius, but Plut. *Pomp*. 25.3 says more correctly that the most important and influential members were opposed to it. Among those known to have opposed the bill are Catulus, Hortensius (Cic. *imp. Cn. Pomp.* 52), and the consul for the year, Piso (Plut. *Pomp*. 25.4, 27.1-2; Dio 36.24.3, 37.2); Catulus and Piso were known opponents of Pompeius (for Piso's anti-Pompeian activities in 67, see above on 58.18). Plut. *Pomp* 25.4 says that Caesar was the only prominent senator who did not oppose the law, but there must have been others (cf. the list of consulars who supported the Manilian law in Cic. *imp. Cn. Pomp.* 68).

72.14: *Ti. Gracchus tribunus M. Octavio collegae*

For the references to Ti. Gracchus' deposition of Octavius, see *MRR*

252   *Commentary*

1.493. The important difference between the two instances is that, after seventeen tribes had voted for Octavius' deposition, Tiberius asked him to withdraw his veto; when he refused, the vote of the eighteenth tribe determined his removal from office.

72.18: *post quam X et VII tribus rogationem acceperunt*

These two instances show that the tribes voted successively, or at least the tribes' decisions were reported successively (so Hall, art. cit. 275-8; Taylor, op. cit. p. 77), against the view of Mommsen, *Staatsrecht*, 3.1.397, and others, that voting was simultaneous. Whether this was true at all periods of the republic is not clear; it seems there was a change to simultaneous voting in electoral meetings of the *comitia tributa* in the late republic (Hall, art. cit. 290-7). It also seems clear that, although a decision could be reached by the eighteenth tribe, the votes of all thirty-five tribes were taken (Hall, art. cit. 284-6; Taylor, op. cit. p. 78; contra, Staveley, op. cit. pp. 181-2).

73.2-3: *isti defensores iudiciorum*

At this point, Cicero is attempting to show that Cornelius' law was not bad but useful (hence the comment about Gabinius' bill), and that the amended version of the proposal was not directed against the authority of the senate, but rather reinforced its authority (cf. 59.4-5; Arus. *GL* 7.466 = frag. 33 P: *nihil senatui detraxisse Cornelium*). To demonstrate the usefulness, he refers to the recent case of Faustus Sulla: a small group of nobles whom Cicero ironically calls 'defenders of the courts' would have been able to prevent Faustus Sulla from being brought before a court (because they were previously able to control senatorial decisions on *privilegia* [cf. 58.10-11, 59.5-7]) if it had not been for the existence of this law, requiring a quorum of 200 senators for decisions on *privilegia*. Obviously a decision had been made recently rejecting a *privilegium* for him, for he was brought before a court in 66 (Cic. *Cluent.* 94), but the case was dropped (see below on 73.6-7). There had apparently been frequent attempts to bring Faustus Sulla to court, led by the tribunes (it was a tribune who laid the charge in 66), but they had been resisted by this small group of nobles. They are probably to be identified with the five *principes civitatis* who were the backbone of the prosecution of Cornelius (see above on 58.12) and most of whom were Sullan connections. Cicero is here alluding to their hypocritical stance: in Cornelius' trial, they claimed to be defending the courts and their security, yet in the case of Faustus Sulla they wished to prevent the judicial processes, and he goes on in the next fragment to provide another instance where the nobility suspended the functioning of the courts. Cicero's choice of Faustus Sulla's case as an instance where the conservative aristocrats tried to hinder the courts by a favourable *privilegium* is not a good one perhaps, since his case was dropped by the courts anyway.

73.5-6: *causam longe aliter praetor in contione defendi*

Cicero expressed the view, at a public meeting in 66 when he was praetor, before the case of Faustus Sulla came to court, that it should be deferred to a more opportune time, since there was a good deal of popular excitement at the time which might prejudice the jury's decision. Kumaniecki, p.22, argues that this was a convenient compromise for Cicero, since he would not have wanted to alienate popular feeling by opposing the tribunician agitation against Sulla, nor to have created ill-will among the powerful men backing Faustus Sulla by supporting the moves to have him impeached. That Cicero did not wish to alienate the small group of nobles may be doubted: his ironic reference to them as 'defenders of the courts', his attacks on their sincerity (76.5ff., 78.18-22, 79.17-19), indeed his defence of Cornelius when they were on the opposite side (though he speaks of them with respect: see above on 63.8-9), suggests the reverse. Fragments preserved by the grammarian Arusianus Messius indicate the firmness of his opposition (= frags. 11-13 P): 'If you place this man's fortunes at the disposal of the hatred of a few . . . '; 'You would allow to be handed over to a cruel and wretched tyranny'; 'How assiduous you ought to be in the pursuit of freedom'. For difficulties which this stance created for Cicero, see above on 61.8-9. Cicero's opposition to the narrow clique was not suicidal, since he retained his connection with Pompeian supporters (such as those who supported the Manilian law).

73.6-7: *quod idem iudices postea statuerunt*

Faustus Sulla's case was heard before C. Orchivius (praetor in 66 and in charge of the court *de peculatu*) on a charge *de pecuniis residuis*; the jurors decided to do what Cicero had earlier proposed — to defer the case, because they thought that, with a tribune as the prosecutor, the matter could not be determined without prejudice (Cic. *Cluent.* 94, cf. *leg. ag.* 1.12). Another case in the same year may be connected: M. Lucullus was prosecuted by C. Memmius, a tribune in that year, presumably on a charge of maladministration of funds during the Sullan régime (Plut. *Luc.* 37.1). The connection is discussed by Gruen, *Athenaeum* 49 (1971) 56-8.

73.9: *defuerat superioribus temporibus in aerario pecunia*

The most recent occasion on which the treasury was short of money was in 75-74 (Sall. *hist.* 2.47.6-7, 98.2 and 7-10 M); these financial difficulties persisted until 70, for a proposal to grant land allotments to the Spanish veterans was deferred because of a lack of funds (Dio 38.5.2; Marshall, *Antichthon* 6 [1972] 43-52). Brunt, *Italian Manpower*, p. 379 n. 1, gives the reason as the great numbers of men in the army at that period. Earlier than this, there was an economic crisis due to a collapse of credit in 88 following Mithridates' activities in Asia (Cic. *imp. Cn. Pomp.* 19). To

254 Commentary

judge from Cicero's comments in the speech on the Manilian law (§ § 14ff.), there was not a shortage in the treasury in 66, only the fear of a drop in revenue because of renewed activity by Mithridates. It would seem, then, that the prosecution of Faustus Sulla was not motivated by economic, but rather political, considerations (Kumaniecki, p. 22). One of the clauses in Rullus' agrarian proposal in 63 provided for reclaiming for public use money gained from booty by generals (or their heirs): Cic. *leg. ag.* 1.12.

73.13: *Cornelium Faustum dictatoris filium*

Faustus Cornelius Sulla was the son of Sulla by his marriage to Metella, the daughter of the consul of 119: on Faustus' connection with the children of Sulla's other marriages, see above on 20.7. His name is written oddly here (a copyist's mistake in the exemplar?): elsewhere it is written as Faustus Cornelius (28.13) or as Faustus Sulla (20.7, 34.17).

73.15: *sumpserat pecunias ex vectigalibus et ex aerario*

There is no evidence by which one can arrive at an estimate of Sulla's property, and so the inheritance which his son received: Pliny merely remarks that he died the richest man in Rome (*NH* 33.134). Some items of relevance are known: when Sulla needed funds for the Mithridatic War in 88, some 9000 pounds of gold had to be taken from the property of the temples (App. *Mith.* 22), because the treasury had been completely bankrupted by the Social War. In the East, because he received no support from home, Sulla exacted whatever he needed, e.g. by robbing the temples of Delphi, Olympia and Epidaurus (Plut. *Sull.* 12). Of the 20,000 talents in indemnities which he imposed on the Asiatic cities at the end of the Mithridatic war (App. *Mith.* 62; Plut. *Sull.* 25.4), he deposited only about one-fifth (15,000 pounds of gold and 115,000 pounds of silver: Plin. *NH* 33.16) in the treasury, and even this he drew upon whenever he needed it. To pay expenses and reward himself and his supporters, he instituted confiscations on a vast scale and used the state treasury as his own purse, appropriating whatever he needed to keep it replenished. When he resigned, he must have kept much of it for himself (though we cannot calculate how much he had expended); we do not know what was left in the treasury, but it cannot have been much for it was chronically short of funds in the decade after Sulla's death. Further on this, see T. Frank, *An Economic Survey of Ancient Rome*, Vol. I (New Jersey, 1933) pp. 231-2; C.T. Barlow, *AJP* 101 (1980) 211.

73.16: *res saepe erat agitata, saepe omissa*

There is no evidence of any attempt prior to 66 to recover public money from Faustus Sulla, apart from this comment by Asconius. There was apparently another attempt in 63 to subject Faustus to an investigation, if

Pro Cornelio

we can believe Cicero (*leg. agr.* 1.12): he again refers to the decision of the court in 66 not to proceed against Faustus. On the technicalities of the charge, see I. Shatzman, *Historia* 21 (1972) 196.

73.17: *gratiam Sullanarum partium*

The small group of nobles which had previously manipulated *privilegia* is to be identified as that led by the five *principes*: they might fairly be called a 'Sullan party', since most of them had some connection with the dictator. The first in the list, Hortensius, was married to Catulus' sister; he was a friend from youth of L. Lucullus, brother of the fourth man on the list (Plut. *Luc.* 1.5); that a L. Hortensius served under Sulla in the East may constitute a link. Catulus, second on the list, had Sullan links: his father had perished at the hands of the Marians in 87, and he secured his revenge with the Sullan victory (Luc. 2.173-174); Sulla may have supported his election to the consulship of 78 (Badian, *Studies*, p. 232). Metellus Pius was even more closely linked to Sulla: he was one of the first to join Sulla when he returned from the East; Sulla had earlier married his cousin Metella, daughter of the consul of 119; and he became Sulla's colleague in the consulship of 80. M. Lucullus was the younger brother of L. Lucullus: they were cousins of Sulla's wife Metella and of Metellus Pius; they had both served under Sulla; Lucius was highly regarded by Sulla, who in his will preferred him to Pompeius as guardian of his son. If the last man on the list is to be identified as Mam. Aemilius Lepidus (see above on 60.20-21), a Sullan connection can be found: he suffered a *repulsa*, most likely at the consular elections in 79 (Sall. *hist.* 1.86 M), when Sulla had been displeased at the election of M. Lepidus, and this suggests that Sulla had supported Mam. Lepidus (Badian, *Studies*, p. 232; cf. p. 217 for evidence of his earlier service under Sulla).

73.25: *bello Italico*

On the outbreak of the Social War, see above on 68.5.

73.26: *cum multi Varia lege inique damnarentur*

The following are the known cases:

1. M. Aemilius Scaurus (see above on 22.8ff.). His was the first case, but the outcome is not clear: Gruen, *JRS* 55 (1965) 62-4, and Seager, *Historia* 16 (1967) 42, argue that he was acquitted, but Badian, *Historia* 18 (1969) 467-8, thinks that the case may have been abandoned by the prosecution (though it is clear at least that he was not convicted).

2. C. Aurelius Cotta (see Gruen, art. cit. 64). A verdict of condemnation was obvious, and he withdrew into exile before the case was closed, returning to Rome after Sulla's victory in 82.

3. L. Calpurnius Bestia (see Gruen, art. cit. 64-5). He withdrew into exile before the case even came into court (App. *BC* 1.37).

4. Q. Pompeius Rufus (see Gruen, art. cit. 65). Acquittal is implied by the fact that he stood for the consulship in the year following his trial.

5. L. Memmius. Gruen, art. cit. 66-7, identifies him with a L. Mummius Achaicus who is said by App. *BC* 1.37 to have been condemned and exiled; Badian, art. cit. 469, rejects this and retains Memmius as a separate defendant (on the grounds of Asconius' comment that many were convicted under this law). Cic. *Brut.* 304, the only direct reference to Memmius' trial, does not state whether he was acquitted or convicted. There is a problem in identifying which L. Memmius is being referred to: see Wiseman, *CQ* 17 (1967) 164-7; contra, Gruen, loc. cit.

6. L. Mummius Achaicus. If he is to be regarded as a separate identity, he was convicted.

7. M. Antonius. It is not clear whether he was tried in the first phase of the operation of the Varian commission or the second (Badian, art. cit. 457-8; cf. Gruen, art. cit. 67-8). It seems, however, that he was acquitted, for he was sent on a mission to Metellus Pius in 87 (Gran. Licinian. 19 F = Greenidge and Clay^2, p. 173). Cic. *Brut.* 304 notes that in 90 Antonius 'was away'; this should not necessarily be taken to imply exile and therefore condemnation.

8. Q. Varius Severus Hybrida. He was condemned under his own law, in what is regarded as the second phase in the operation of the law.

9. Cn. Pompeius Strabo (or Cn. Pomponius). The outcome is not recorded. For the problems associated with this case, see below on 79.5. His case too fell into the second phase.

It is generally agreed that 'prosecutions under the *lex Varia* illustrate the unscrupulous use of the courts for political ends' (Gruen, art. cit. 60, accepted by Badian, art. cit. 451). No matter what the scope of the *crimen Varianum* (see next comment), persons whose actions would indicate that they could not be guilty of the charge were brought to trial under it, because the court provided a convenient vehicle for their political rivals to attack them. Hence Asconius says that many were unjustly convicted (cf. App. *BC* 1.37). The 'many' may be an exaggeration, for in the first phase about which he is commenting (i.e. the cases which led to the suspension of all the courts, or of the Varian commission, the other courts having already been suspended: on this, see below on 74.1-3) we know only of three convictions (or four if Mummius and Memmius are separated and both regarded as convictions). The persons attacked in the first phase

Pro Cornelio 257

illustrate the political motivation: the first five persons on the above list can be linked with what may be called for convenience the Metellan group (see above on 69.2-3; on their Metellan links, see Gruen, art. cit. passim) which had supported some of the measures of Livius Drusus (though not necessarily his proposal for Italian enfranchisement: see above on 69.3-4). The opponents of Drusus (e.g. Q. Servilius Caepio, who initiated the prosecution of Scaurus, and L. Marcius Philippus, who gave vehement evidence against Rufus and Memmius), taking advantage of equestrian anger at the attempt to take away their control of the courts and focusing public attention on the dissatisfaction with the nobility over the rejection of citizenship for the allies (cf. 22.5-6), used the Varian commission to attack Drusus' supporters. But the Metellan group can hardly be accused of sympathising with the Italians, when two of its members were responsible for the *lex Licinia Mucia* (see above on 67.22-23), when another had been partly responsible for the censorial edict of 92 expelling Latin rhetors, and when Scaurus had expressed such contempt for non-Romans, unless one accepts a volte-face by the group (as does Badian, *Historia* 11 [1962] 223-5). Yet no doubt their opponents took advantage of their connection with Drusus to suggest they were sympathetic to Italian franchise (Gruen, art. cit. 62).

73.27: *quasi id bellum illis auctoribus conflatum esset*

This judgment not only 'exposes the flimsiness of the circumstantial evidence used' (Gruen, art. cit. 62) and suggests that the opponents of the Metellan group had been able to involve the group in Drusus' proposal for Italian enfranchisement (when they probably had not supported it); it also helps to re-inforce the argument that the *lex Varia* established not a general court *de maiestate* (so Gruen, art. cit. 59-60) but a *quaestio extraordinaria* (so Seager, *Historia* 16 [1967] 37-40) whose scope was to investigate those *quorum ope consiliove socii contra populum Romanum arma sumpsissent* (22.7-8; cf. 22.10-11, 16-17; App. *BC* 1.37; Val. Max. 8.6.4). On the question of the scope of the *lex Varia*, cf. above on 22.7-8.

73.27-74.1: *crebraeque defectiones Italicorum nuntiarentur*

The *lex Iulia* of late 90 produced the effect which Asconius mentions here: it granted citizenship to those who had remained loyal to their alliance with Rome (App. *BC* 1.49), hence *defectiones* should not be applied to them, but perhaps only to those who had taken up arms and had voluntarily laid them down again (Vell. Pat. 2.16.4; cf. Brunt, *JRS* 55 [1965] 95 and 107). At any rate the passage of the law produced an atmosphere in which it was no longer feasible to use the Social War as grounds for attacking political enemies, and which assisted the agitation for its suspension.

74.1-3: *nanctus iustitii occasionem senatus decrevit ne iudicia ... exercerentur*

There is a conflict in our evidence here. Cic. *Brut.* 304-305 says that in 90 the other courts had been interrupted by the Social War but that the Varian court was still sitting. Asconius here tells us that during the war the senate decreed the suspension of the courts because many were being unjustly condemned under the Varian law; this ought to mean that all the courts were suspended at the same time, and that at a time when the Varian court was already in existence and included among them. The solution seems to be a compromise: the other courts were suspended first (soon after the outbreak of the war, which would be the most likely time) and the Varian court later. There is a possibility that the Varian court was not suspended at all (Seager, *Historia* 16 [1967] 39; Badian, *Historia* 18 [1969] 452-3, but cf. 462). In any case Asconius has been guilty of some misunderstanding about the suspension of the other courts and of the Varian court (Badian, ibid. 460).

The implication of 79.9 is that the courts were functioning again before the passing of the *lex Plautia* sometime in 89. The suspension of the courts may provide the reason for the introduction of the *lex Varia* in the first place: Varius could not proceed through the normal courts, since they were no longer in action, and so he introduced his own law (Badian, ibid. 450). The suspension might also explain why he was prosecuted under his own law, even though he should not have been considered guilty of sympathy with the Italians as sponsor of the law in the first place. His opponents may have pursued him under his own law either because it was the only one which had continued in operation (Seager, art. cit. 39) or because it was revived when the other courts remained closed (Badian, art. cit. 462: this hinges on the date of Varius' trial — see below on 79.5). In either case, Varius' prosecution does not imply that his law was a general one dealing with treason just because he was prosecuted under it; the flimsiness of pretext has been shown in other cases.

74.2: *tumultus Italicus*

In such an emergency, all privileges and exemptions were suspended: on the arrangements, see e.g. *lex Coloniae Genetivae Iuliae*, or *lex Ursonensis* (*FIRA*[2] no. 21) ch. 62, and Sherwin-White, *The Roman Citizenship*, pp. 82-3. As Rome was short of commanders for the Social War, the praetors could not be kept at Rome employed in non-military affairs (Badian, art. cit. 460). This further suggests that the courts were suspended at the outbreak of the war; it is not likely to have been a controversial measure (see next comment). As the *lex Varia* was passed after the outbreak of the war, and as its very purpose was to enquire about those who had sympathised with the allies, it clearly must have continued to operate during the war, and that adds to the argument that it was

Pro Cornelio

suspended (if at all) after the other courts, and not at the same time (as Asconius implies).

74.3-4: *quod decretum eorum in contionibus populi saepe agitatum erat*

As Asconius gives the reason for the senate's decision for the suspension of the 'courts' that many were being condemned unjustly under the Varian law, it can only have been the suspension of that court which can have caused debate at public meetings (Bauman, *Crimen Maiestatis*, pp. 63-4; Badian, art. cit. 452); and in view of the obvious political manipulation of the court in its first phase, there could well have been agitation for an end to the witch-hunt. There is not likely to have been much agitation about the suspension of the other courts, in view of the crisis which Rome was facing. Asconius seems to have misunderstood the reasons for the suspension of the courts, and to have run them together: the other courts were suspended because of the *tumultus Italicus*, while the Varian court was later suspended because of agitation resulting from unjust decisions.

74.5: *C. [Curio pater]*

The name is missing in the mss., but can easily be supplied from *Curionis adulescentis* in the next line. The identification is accepted by Griffin, p. 213 n. 166, and Kumaniecki, p. 23 n. 38, but Badian, art. cit. 453-4, rejects Asconius' identification here.

74.6: *Curionis adulescentis*

Despite earlier opposition to both Pompeius and Caesar, he secured a tribunate for 50 at a supplementary election and to the surprise of senatorial conservatives initiated a programme of *popularis* reform and began to defend Caesar's position against those who wished to remove him from the Gallic command. It was Curio who moved the motion in July or August 50 that both Pompeius and Caesar should disarm, which was carried in the senate by 370 votes to 22. After attacking Caesar's opponents on the last day of his tribunate, he hastened to join Caesar, urging him to prepare for war without delay (App. *BC* 2.31-32; Dio 40.66.5); he was subsequently sent to Rome with a message that Caesar was still willing to resign his command if other commanders did likewise, but this was ignored, and Curio joined M. Antonius and C. Cassius and others in fleeing to Caesar's camp. For an account of Curio's political activity in 50 and early 49, see W.K. Lacey, *Historia* 10 (1961) 318-29, and Gruen, *Last Generation*, pp. 470-90. In the civil war he won Sicily for Caesar in April 49, and from there crossed to Africa where he died fighting.

74.9: *C. Volcacium*

Cicero has moved on from attempting to show that Cornelius' law regarding *privilegia* was not a bad one, to suggesting that his law concerning praetor's edicts was also useful: this is shown in the next two lemmata which Asconius quotes. In the first, an unfair judgment of Cn. Cornelius Dolabella in the case of C. Volcacius is mentioned. We know nothing of the details: presumably it occurred in the praetorship of Dolabella in 81. Kumaniecki, p. 24, conjectures that this Volcacius may have been the father of L. Volcacius Tullus, cos. 66; in that case it would be easy to see why Cicero mentioned the case, since the consul of 66 had shown a favourable attitude to Cornelius when the charge was first laid against him in 66 (see above, 60.2).

74.11: *duo fuerunt eo tempore [Cn.] Dolabellae*

On the careful distinction between the two Dolabellae, see above on 26.15, and for details of the two trials, see above on 26.16-18.

74.16: *P. Scipioni*

Kumaniecki, p. 24, very plausibly believes that Cicero deliberately chose this example, for this young man was adopted by Q. Metellus Pius, one of the principal witnesses for the prosecution. The date of the adoption is not known, but as Metellus Pius died a year or two after the trial, it is reasonable to assume that the adoption was at least contemplated in 65. On adoption he took the name Q. Caecilius Metellus Pius Scipio Nasica; he was the last son of the Scipionic family, and eventually became the father-in-law of Pompeius, joining him in the consulship of 52 (cf. above on 31.9). For other complimentary references to the Metelli, see above on 63.8-9. L. Cornelius Sisenna, praetor in 78, had apparently varied his edict to decide that the property of Cn. Cornelius (otherwise unknown) should not pass to the young Scipio. On this case, see Lintott, *CQ* 27 (1977) 184-6. Cicero had obviously referred to other examples of unscrupulous praetors, as the *illorum* at 74.13 shows.

74.19: *L. Sisennam*

L. Cornelius Sisenna was *praetor urbanus et peregrinus* in 78 (*CIL* 1^2.2.589) when the case referred to by Cicero must have been heard. Of the rest of his career we know only that he supported Verres in 70 and that he served as a legate under Pompeius in 67, dying during that year (App. *Mith.* 95; Dio 36.18-19). His history of Rome, in at least twelve books (and not the twenty-three of frag. 132: A.H. McDonald, *OCD*[2], p. 994), covered the Social War and the Sullan civil war, from 90 to at least 83 and perhaps to the death of Sulla, after a brief *archaeologia* at the beginning; the fragments are collected in Peter, *HRR* 1.276-95. Cicero regarded him

Pro Cornelio 261

as the best Roman historian to date (*Brut.* 228, *leg.* 1.7), and Sallust regarded his account of Sulla as the best and most careful (*Iug.* 95.2). Badian, *Athenaeum* 42 (1964) 422ff., developed in *Studies*, pp. 212-4, argues that his account of Sulla presented the case of those who had stayed at home 'waiting for Sulla'. Further on Sisenna, see Niese *RE* 4 (1901) 1512-3, s.v. 'Cornelius' no. 374, and E. Rawson, *CQ* 29 (1979) 327-346.

74.22-23: *nisi poena accessisset in divisores*

In his introduction to the speech, Asconius does not specifically mention Cornelius' bribery proposal (presumably including it among the *alias complures leges* at 59.11), but it is clear from his preservation of this fragment of Cicero that he knew of the law. Cornelius' proposal presumably included penalties for the *divisores*, but the consul for 67 was instructed to draw up a modified bribery proposal to counter that of Cornelius; it was this proposal which was eventually carried (see 75.24ff.) and which was still in operation at the time of Cornelius' trial. For the connection between Cornelius' proposal and Piso's counter-proposal, see above on 57.8. It is not certain whether Piso's law included penalities for *divisores*: McDonald, p. 204, argues that it did (cf. Staveley, op. cit. p. 204; Gruen, *Last Generation*, pp. 214-5; and above on 59.3-4), but this passage of Cicero seems to suggest that penalties for *divisores* were not included in the *lex Calpurnia* (and that is why it proved to be ineffective), and hence the people pressed for Cornelius' proposal (Kumaniecki, p. 25; Griffin, p. 197 n. 15; Seager, *Pompey*, p. 30, thinks popular pressure forced Piso to water down his proposal). If there were no penalties for *divisores* in the *lex Calpurnia*, it is difficult to see why they caused a riot when that bill was first put to the vote (75.26-27); perhaps they would have opposed any law which dealt with bribery. On *divisores*, see Nicolet, *L'ordre équestre*, 1.603-4 and 2.911, 997 and 1068-9.

75.7: *P. Sullam et [P.] Autronium significat*

The two successful candidates at the consular elections held in 66, P. Cornelius Sulla and P. Autronius Paetus, were accused of electoral malpractice and found guilty, and so prevented from taking up office (references in *MRR* 2.157). Supplementary elections were held, and two new consuls elected, L. Aurelius Cotta and L. Manlius Torquatus; Catilina attempted to stand at the supplementary elections. Sulla and Autronius were subsequently thought to have been involved in the so-called 'first' Catilinarian conspiracy, the victims of which were supposed to be the consuls elected to take their place.

75.7-8: *alterum L. Cotta, alterum L. Torquatus*

L. Aurelius Cotta and L. Manlius Torquatus were unsuccessful at the ordinary elections and, as often happened, initiated prosecutions against the successful candidates for electoral malpractice; following the success of the prosecutions, Cotta and Torquatus were subsequently successful at the supplementary consular elections. On the increasingly common practice of launching prosecutions for bribery against successful candidates by unsuccessful ones, see Gruen, *Last Generation*, pp. 272 and 301. What needs to be stressed is the uniqueness of the condemnation of two consuls-elect, made all the more startling by the number of cases which failed. Cotta was one of the prosecutors, but Asconius has made a mistake in saying that Torquatus also joined in the prosecution; it was the son of Torquatus who actually undertook the prosecution, as Cic. *Sull.* 49-50 and *fin.* 2.62 show (Badian, *Studies*, p. 248; McDermott, *Hermes* 97 [1969] 242 n. 2; E.W. Gray, *Antichthon* 13 [1979] 64-5). The mistake has been accepted by some (e.g. *MRR* 2.157), but it does seem preferable to accept the evidence of a contemporary speaking to an audience who knew the men than the scholiast (to paraphrase Badian's argument). It is not a serious mistake, since Asconius is probably speaking loosely of the fact that father and son would have felt the same about the prosecution (cf. Taylor, *Party Politics in the Age of Caesar*, p. 114; Gruen, *Last Generation*, pp. 272-3). But it is a careless mistake when it is remembered that Asconius had access to Cicero's *commentarii* (87.11) and when he may even have written a commentary on the *pro Sulla* (see Part I, pp. 7 and 12-3). Perhaps Asconius relied on his memory, and this mistake illustrates the difficulty of doing that.

75.11-12: *Philerotem servum*

In this part of the speech, obviously connected with the passing of the *lex Calpurnia*, Cicero seems to be attempting to answer the prosecution's charge that Cornelius had something to do with provoking the disturbances associated with the vote on the *lex Calpurnia* (Kumaniecki, pp. 25-6). There is a fragment of the speech, recorded in Victorinus and usually placed immediately before the fragment in Asconius here (frags. 44 and 45 P), which claims there was not the least suspicion attaching to Cornelius in this respect (*hinc intellegitis nulla tenuissima suspicione describi aut significare Cornelium*). We do not know who Phileros was or what role he played in Calpurnius' proposal: presumably the prosecution claimed that a slave Phileros had something to do with the opposition to Calpurnius' proposal and that the slave belonged to Cornelius, hoping to cast suspicion on him, and it was this claim that Cicero attempted to refute by the arguments preserved in Asconius.

75.17: *collegia et s.c. et pluribus legibus sunt sublata*

In the year following Cornelius' trial, the *collegia* were suppressed by senatorial decree (see above on 7.9-11), the reason being that they had

Pro Cornelio 263

been formed *adversus rem publicam* (cf. the phrase *malo publico* at 75.16 here). *Collegia* were allowed again under a law of Clodius passed early in his tribunate in 58 (8.22-23). It is not clear what Asconius means by *plures leges*: J. Linderski, in M.N. Andreev et al., *Gesellschaft und Recht im Griechisch-Römischen Altertum* (Berlin, 1968) pp. 96-101, believes that the phrase refers to measures ranging from 64 to Asconius' own time. In the republican period there were several moves to control organisations: in 56 a senatorial decree was passed that political clubs should be broken up (Cic. *Q.f.* 2.3.5), the sponsor being apparently Q. Hortensius (Linderski, *PP* 16 [1961] 304-11); in 55 came Crassus' law, declaring illegal some of the activities of the *sodalitates*, clubs organised within tribes and employed for arranging and distributing bribes (on the connection between these two measures, see Gruen, *Last Generation*, pp. 228-31, and cf. Linderski, *Hermes* 89 [1961] 106-19); there was a clause in the *lex Iulia de vi publica* about membership of a *collegium* (*Dig.* 47.22.2; Lintott, *Violence*, p. 123).

75.19: *fabrorum fictorumque*

The mss. read *lictorum* for the second group; Manutius conjectures *fictorum* (based on Plin. *NH* 35.159). These were two of the older type of guilds, composed of men practising the same craft or trade, which might have a local basis as well. Because of their long existence and respectability (some traced their organisation back to Numa Pompilius: Plut. *Numa* 17.3), they were not suspect like some of the more recently formed clubs, which were being used for political purposes. The trade-guilds were only one of the several types of *collegia*; their main purpose was to foster friendliness and social activities among their members. Most *collegia* had some religious connection: they might adopt a patron deity, not necessarily connected with the trade but perhaps only of general or local prominence (e.g. *collegium fabrum Veneris*: *CIL* 3.1981), or they might hold their meetings in temples, or their club-house might bear the name of a divinity (e.g. *ILS* 7218). On the *collegia* in general, see S. Accame, *Bull. Mus. Imp. Rom.* 13 (1942) 13-48; Lintott, *Violence*, pp. 78-83; S. Treggiari, *Roman Freedmen during the Late Republic* (Oxford, 1969) pp. 168-77.

75.25: *legem ... graviorem*

On the penalties under the *lex Calpurnia*, see above on 69.12-13: the penalties were stiffer than any previous bribery legislation, and the law gained a reputation for severity (Cic. *Mur.* 46: *erat enim severissime scripta Calpurnia*).

75.26ff.

For the attitude of the *divisores* to Piso's bribery proposal, see above on

57.8, 59.3-4 and 74.22-23. After being driven from the forum, Piso returned with a larger band (Dio 36.39.1 says the senate voted the consuls a body-guard to protect them against the opposition to the bribery law), and posing as the wronged champion of reform and calling on all patriotic citizens he secured the passage of the bill. Cicero tries to turn the situation to his client's advantage by claiming that Cornelius' activities led to the consul's calling on those who were interested in the well-being of the state to pass a law which was in the interests of the state.

76.7-8: *qui restituerunt eam potestatem*

Having dealt with the usefulness to the state of Cornelius' activities as tribune, Cicero turns to a general consideration of the tribunician power itself (Kumaniecki, p. 26, calls it the third part of the speech). Manilius' actions had brought discredit on the recently restored tribunician power, though at least one of his proposals was useful to the state (see above, 65.11-15, and cf. Cicero's attitude to Gabinius' tribunate at 72.1ff.). The persons responsible for the restoration of the tribunician power were Pompeius and Crassus in their consulship in 70 (references in *MRR* 2.126); Asconius goes on to say that of these two Crassus was present in court as a *iudex* (he was also censor that year) and Pompeius was absent on the Mithridatic campaign. McDermott, *Class. Phil.* 72 (1977) 49-52, has argued that Pompeius alone was responsible for the law, and that Crassus is only being flattered by Cicero here; but cf. below on 81.5. Cicero's mention of Pompeius may have been to gain sympathy for Cornelius who is known to have had some connection with Pompeius (on the strength of the link, see above on 57.7). There is a fragment of the speech preserved in Quintilian (= frag. 47 P, placed by Kumaniecki after this fragment, but before by others) in which Cicero turns aside from his discussion of the tribunician power to praise of Pompeius. He probably also intended to justify the restoration of the tribunician power, by saying it had the backing of powerful men like Pompeius and Crassus who were not, however, in a position to defend their action.

76.17: *Mons Sacer*

In the oldest versions, the plebs seceded to the Aventine on the first and second occasion (Liv. 2.32.2-3, quoting Piso as a source, and 3.51.10; cf. Diod. Sic. 12.24 and Sall. *Iug.* 31.17). But the whole position of the tribunate was safeguarded by *leges sacratae* (cf. above, 76.15), and it was natural to connect their origin with the Mons Sacer (App. *BC* 1.1), and so there was a development of the tradition which had both the secessions take place on the two hills (see Cic. *rep.* 2.58 and 63). This was later improved by allotting the first secession to the Mons Sacer and the second to the Aventine, and this became the standard version (Cic. *Brut.* 54, *Corn.* in Ascon. 76.17 and 77.20; Liv. 3.51.10, but cf. 52.1 and 54.9-10).

For discussion of the development of the tradition, see R.M. Ogilvie, *A Commentary on Livy, Books 1-5* (Oxford, 1965) pp. 311 and 489. On the problems in general associated with the establishment of the tribunate, see R.T. Ridley, *Latomus* 27 (1968) 535-40.

76.20: *tr. pl.*

Two of the mss. (P and M) include the number ten before *tribuni plebis* here. This is a mistake, obviously resulting from a copyist's knowledge that later there were ten tribunes. On the basis that Asconius is aware of the tradition that originally there were five tribunes, Rau, p. 140, has conjectured that the figure should be five, but in view of Asconius' insistence that Cicero's figure was two, perhaps we should read *duo* here, or nothing at all (following ms. S).

76.20: *comitiis curiatis*

The annalistic tradition had developed the view that the tribunes were elected by the *comitia curiata* (Dion. Hal. 9.41; Cic. *rep.* 2.5) until the formal recognition of the *concilium plebis* as the *comitia tributa* by the *lex Publilia* of 471 and the right of that body to elect tribunes (Liv. 2.58.1). The association of the election of tribunes with the *comitia curiata* may have been an attempt to find a respectable origin for the institution, but the revolutionary nature of the tribunate makes it necessary to reject the tradition that the *comitia curiata*, organised by family and birth, was used to elect the tribunes; they must have originally been chosen at some unofficial assembly of the plebs (Ogilvie, *Commentary*, p. 381).

76.23: *post XVI annos*

Asconius accepts the tradition followed by Cicero that the creation of the tribunate is to be dated to 494 (that is, in the consulship of A. Verginius Tricostus and T. Veturius Cicurinus: see 76.28, where both names have had to be corrected in Asconius' text). There is another view, based on Diod.11.68.8 (τότε πρώτως κατεστάθησαν δήμαρχοι τέτταρες; cf. Liv. 2.58.1), that the tribunate was created in 471: for this view, see J. Lengle, *RE* 6A (1937) 2455. Ogilvie rejects this view on the grounds that Diodorus was emphasising the fact that this was the first time four tribunes were elected, and that Diodorus' account of 494 is missing (*Commentary*, pp. 309 and 382). The most recent discussion of the date for the origin of the tribunate is by R. Urban, *Historia* 22 (1973) 761-4, who concludes that it is not possible to decide between 494 and 471. Asconius' mathematics are inaccurate here: normally he counts exclusively (e.g. 5.20, 64.19), but here he is either counting inclusively or else he has loosely followed Cicero's more accurate *anno XVI* (76.13). If he has made a mistake, it is ironic that he credits Cicero with an accurate calculation (76.26-27).

76.24: *leges sacratas*

Cf. Dion. Hal. 6.89.3; Liv. 2.33.3. 'The *lex sacrata* which later historians rationalized into a law passed by the *comitia curiata* recognizing the sacrosanctity of the tribunes was in reality the oath by which the plebeians banded themselves as an individual body and dedicated to the goals of self-help and hostility to the patricians', the sort of oath creating a sworn confederacy noticeable in the social and military history of the Osco-Sabellian races (Ogilvie, *Commentary*, p. 313; J. Bleicken, *Lex Publica: Gesetz und Recht in der römischen Republik* [Berlin, 1975] pp. 88-90). Asconius' reason that such laws could not be *restituta* in 494, but only *constituta*, is that the plebs did not have tribunes until then (and presumably no one to put motions until then); it is probable that laws could not even be *constituta* until 471, when the first moves were made to incorporate the tribunes and the *concilium plebis* (as the *comitia tributa*) into the constitution (see next comment).

77.1: *non duo tr. pl. ... sed quinque*

There is a variety of opinions on the original number of tribunes, and on the development of the number; Asconius has tried to preserve these various opinions, and nominates a number of his sources. Livy's view (2.33.2-3) is that two were created, and that they appointed three colleagues; he preserves another version which states that only two were created. The other version may have derived from the annalist Piso (cos. 133), but Livy may have got the version through Valerius Antias (see Ogilvie, *Commentary*, pp. 381-2). Dion. Hal. 6.89.1 has a similar view to Livy, though he gives different names (see below on 77.6-7). There may have been confusion of these various versions with the events of 471 when the *comitia tributa* was established: in 2.58.1, Livy specifically mentions Piso as a source and says that according to him the number of tribunes was increased by three in 471, as if there had originally been only two. Diod. Sic. 11.68.9 states that in 471 four tribunes were elected for the first time, but we do not have his account of 494 (see above on 76.23); as the main reform of 471 was the creation of a tribal assembly, and as the four urban tribes were the most politically significant at that time, it follows that the number four is to be connected with the four urban tribes and that the number of tribunes was raised from two to four in 471 (Ogilvie, *Commentary*, p. 382). Later antiquarians tried to explain the historical number of ten tribunes by connecting it with the five Servian classes (cf. Liv. 3.30.7); part of that explanation was to suppose that the original number was five, or that it was increased to five in 471 (see next comment).

77.2: *singulos ex singulis classibus*

Ogilvie, *Commentary*, p. 311, argues that the number of five tribunes was

Pro Cornelio 267

a post-Gracchan supplement (through the annalist Piso) which aimed at bringing the number of tribunes into relation with the number of classes at a time 'when the Servian constitution was the subject of tendentious interpretation [and] antiquarians were at pains to conceal the radical nature of the tribunate' (ibid. p. 382).

77.4-5: *Tuditanus et Pomponius Atticus, Livius quoque noster*

C. Sempronius Tuditanus (cos. 129) was a jurist and historian; one of his works was the *libri magistratuum* in at least thirteen books, presumably the source of Asconius' information here. The fragments of his works are in Peter, *HRR* 1.143-7. This is the only reference Asconius makes to him. Atticus wrote a number of historical works (Nep. *Att.* 18.1-4), all now lost, including the *liber annalis* (cf. above on 13.18), a chrohological table of world, and especially Roman, history which became a standard work and which included lists of magistrates (Nep. loc. cit.), hence most likely the work used here. Livy's view has not been given the right emphasis here: it is that two tribunes were created and that they co-opted another three (cf. 77.5-6). It is only a variant version recorded by Livy which stresses that there were only two tribunes created originally.

77.6-7: *nomina duorum*

Asconius may be quoting only Tuditanus for the names here, and not the common tradition, for Livy gives a different list, as does Dionysius of Halicarnassus, our only other extant source for the names (and his list may come from Pomponius Atticus). Liv. 2.33.2 gives C. Licinius and L. Albin(i)us, with *Sicinius quidam* as one of their co-opted colleagues (cf. 2.32.2). The substitution of Licinius for Sicinius points to the work of C. Licinius Macer, whom Livy may have used as a source for the secession of the plebs; it is significant that Macer was a friend of a Sicinius (Cn. or L.) at a time when there was strong agitation over tribunician rights during their tribunates in 73 and 76 respectively. Dion. Hal. 6.89.1 lists the first two tribunes as L. Iunius Brutus and C. Sicinius Vellutus (or Bellutus), with the three co-opted colleagues as P. and C. Licinius and C. Viscellius Ruga (there are variant readings for the *gentilicium* and *cognomen*); he must therefore have been following a tradition 'much influenced by the late democratic prestige of the Iunii Bruti, a prestige due in part to Atticus' researches into the family and in part to the activities of the tyrannicides' (Ogilvie, *Commentary*, p. 311). Atticus wrote an account of the family of the Iunii Bruti at the request of M. Brutus (Nep. *Att.* 18.3); if he was responsible for the tradition followed by Dionysius of Halicarnassus for the names of the first two tribunes, he is not being followed by Asconius (though he has just been mentioned as a source). Dionysius' account varies in other ways: there is a ten-man delegation to negotiate with the plebeians, and the person responsible for settling affairs is M'. Valerius

(6.43.4), not Menenius Agrippa (Liv. 2.32.8-12). Cf. the *elogium* of M'. Valerius set up in the forum Augusti (*CIL* 1². pp. 189ff. = *Inscr. Ital.* 13.3.78); the strongly Valerian bias suggests the use of Valerius Antias.

77.9-10: *secundam constitutionem tribunorum et decemvirorum finitum imperium*

These events occurred in 449 (Livy. 3.50-54).

77.15-16: *Appium Claudium . . . L. Verginium*

For the account of Appius Claudius' abuse of his power as one of the decemvirs to seduce the daughter of L. Verginius, see Liv. 3.40-49; it was the immediate incident which supposedly provoked the second secession. For an analysis of the developmment of the story, see Ogilvie, *Commentary*, pp. 476-8.

77.20: *in Aventino*

For a discussion of the conflict in the tradition over the locality of the first and second secessions, see above on 76.17. In this speech Cicero has followed the version which puts the first secession on the Mons Sacer, and the second on the Aventine.

77.21: *in Capitolium*

In Livy's version (2.54.10-15) the election of the tribunes took place on the Aventine and the other measures conceded by the senate were enacted in the Flaminian meadows.

77.22: *decem tr. pl.*

It is not clear whether this is the first time that ten tribunes were elected. Liv. 3.30.7, dealing with 457, suggests that that was the year in which the number of tribunes was increased to ten. A possible source for this confusion is that the consul of 449, M. Horatius (Barbatus), who initiated several democratic reforms, had the same name as the consul of 457, M. (or C.) Horatius (Pulvillus), and the increase in the tribunate was associated with the wrong consulship (Ogilvie, *Commentary*, p. 446; cf. *MRR* 1.27 n. 1). 449 is perhaps a more acceptable date if the plebeians insisted on a number corresponding to the decemvirate which was removed then (W.G. Maddox, *The Roman Tribunate 287-133 B.C.* [diss., Sydney, 1970] p. 3). Dio (in Zon. 7.15) dates the increase to 471, but the increase then was smaller (see above on 77.1).

77.25: *omnes consulares*

On the three-man embassy, see Liv. 3.50.15; the names agree, except that the mss. of Asconius have P. Tarpeius, and Livy has Sp. C. Iulius was consul in 482; Sulpicius is given the *praenomen* P. by both Livy and Asconius, but as the only consular known is Ser. Sulpicius (cos. 461) it is he who is intended (*MRR* 1.50 n. 2); Sp. Tarpeius was consul in 454.

77.25-26: *pontifex max. fuit M. Papirius*

In Livy's account (3.54.5, cf. 11), the pontifex maximus who conducted the tribunician elections was Q. Furius. Elsewhere in Livy, this man's *praenomen* is given as C. (e.g. 4.12.1, 22.7, 31.1), but Q. seems to be confirmed by Diod. 12.35.1 (Ogilvie, *Commentary*, p. 551; contra, *MRR* 1.55 n. 1). Livy and Asconius give Papirius Crassus' *praenomen* as M., but Diodorus gives Μάνιος. These two men were colleagues in the consulship of 441; some event must have been recorded for that year which indicated that one of the consuls was pontifex maximus, without specifying which one, and this has led to the confusion. Ogilvie, *Commentary*, pp. 494-5, questions that the pontifex maximus presided over the elections; he may have been there to perform some ceremony of auspication to mark the recognition of the tribunate.

78.1: *Porciam*

Cic. *rep* 2.54 indicates that there were three *leges Porciae*, but the authors and dates cannot be identified with certainty. They all dealt with the *ius provocationis*, extending it to Roman citizens in Italy and the provinces (Cic. *Verr*. 2.5.163; Gell. 10.3.13), and regulated corporal punishment of citizens (Cic. *Rab. post.* 8 and 12; Sall. *Cat.* 51.21; Liv. 10.9.4). The authorship of one of the laws is usually attributed to P. Porcius Laeca, either in his tribunate in 199 or his praetorship in 195; coinage issued by two of his descendants celebrates a measure dealing with *provocatio* (Crawford, *RRC*, 1. 293 and 313-4). Another is possibly to be associated with the elder Cato who is said to have delivered a recommendation on this matter (Festus, p. 266, 29 L = ORF^2, fr. 117). The third is even less certain: Rotondi, op. cit. p. 269, suggests L. Porcius Licinus, cos. 184. One of the Porcian laws had the effect of allowing condemned persons the alternative of exile (Sall. *Cat.* 51.40). On the *leges Porciae*, see Rotondi, op. cit. pp. 268-9; A.H. McDonald, *JRS* 34 (1944) 19-20; *MRR* 1.327, 2.472; Lintott, *ANRW* 1.2 (1972) 249-53.

78.5: *lex Cassia*

The *lex Cassia tabellaria*, proposed by a tribune of 137, L. Cassius Longinus Ravilla, and strongly supported by Scipio Aemilianus, extended the use of secret ballot to all *iudicia populi*, except those for *perduellio* (Cic. *Brut.* 97, cf. *Sest.* 103; Schol. Bob. 135.4-5; Ps.-Ascon. 216.20-21). The use of the ballot at electoral assemblies had already been provided for by the *lex Gabinia* of two years earlier; it was extended to legislative assemblies in 130 by the *lex Papiria*. A coin issued in 63 (Crawford, *RRC*, 1 440) by L. Cassius Longinus, has on the reverse V[TI ROGAS], suggesting a link with voting on legislation, but it seems to allude to the law of 113 which set up a commission to try three Vestals, presided over by L. Cassius Longinus Ravilla (see above on 46.3-4). Two other coins showing on the reverse a voting urn and tablet inscribed A[BSOLVO] C[ONDEMNO], issued by Q. Cassius Longinus in 55, while showing links with the *lex tabellaria*, also deal with the trial of the Vestals in 113 (Crawford, *RRC*, 1. 452).

78.6: *paulo ante*

Obviously a passage of Cicero not preserved or commented upon in Asconius. In this part of the speech, Cicero has picked up an earlier theme, dealing with the usefulness of some tribunician legislation (cf. above on 73.2-3).

78.9-10: *L. Cassius L. f. Longinus tribunus plebis*

Tribune in 104, as a colleague of Cn. Domitius Ahenobarbus and L. Marcius Philippus.

78.10: *plures leges*

The only one known to have been proposed by Cassius is the one referred to here. Asconius may have in mind the laws passed by his colleagues in the tribunate.

78.11: *ad minuendam nobilitatis potentiam*

Cassius' law, which was aimed at Q. Servilius Caepio particularly (see next comment), was one of a series of laws aimed at senatorial commanders in the last decade of the second century who had acted ineptly or had failed, not only against the northmen but also with regard to Jugurtha. The laws took advantage of popular dissatisfaction with these commanders, but factional rivalry played a part also (see next comment). Cassius' colleague, Ahenobarbus, accused M. Silanus (cos. 109) of beginning the war with the Cimbri illegally, but failed to convict him (see below on 80.18ff.); he accused M. Aemilius Scaurus of improper celebrations of sacred rites, but failed to secure a conviction (see above on 21.3ff.); he deprived the *nobiles* of their privilege of co-opting new members to the priestly colleges by a law making appointment to the colleges subject to an election by seventeen of the tribes. Another colleague, Philippus, attempted to gain popular favour by proposing an agrarian law (Cic. *off.* 2.73).

78.14: *simultates cum Q. Servilio*

Q. Servilius Caepio had been consul two years before Cassius' tribunate,

Pro Cornelio 271

as Asconius says (106); during his consulship he proposed a law restoring senators to juries for the *quaestio de repetundis* (see below on 79.8-9), exclusively according to one view (Tac. *ann.* 12.60), along with the equites according to another (Livy in Obsequens 41); during command in Gaul he captured the sacred treasure at Tolosa. As proconsul in Gaul in 105 he refused to co-operate with the consul, Cn. Mallius, and brought about the disastrous defeat at Arausio, for which he was deprived of his *imperium* (Liv. *per.* 67; Gran. Licin. 11 F; Dio frag. 91; Bauman, *Rhein. Mus.* 111 [1968] 48-9). By the law of Cassius he was expelled from the senate in 104; in the same year the people instituted a special court to investigate the disappearance of the treasure captured at Tolosa, and Caepio was one of those accused before it (the outcome is not clear: he may have been acquitted, or the penalty may simply have been a fine). In 103 he was accused of treason by a tribune, C. Norbanus, for the loss of his army at Arausio, under the law passed by another tribune of the year, Saturninus, and went into exile after conviction. The Servilii Caepiones had connections with the Caecilii Metelli: e.g. M. Scaurus, the virtual head of the Metellan family, was one of the chief supporters of Caepio (Cic. *de or.* 2.197), and Caepio's daughter was married to Livius Drusus, while Caepio's son married Drusus' sister (cf. the links at the end of the next decade discussed at 69.2-3). It is noticeable that some of the tribunician attacks in 104 were directed at Metellan connections: Cassius' law was aimed at Caepio, and Ahenobarbus confronted Scaurus, while Philippus was, later at least, an opponent of the Metelli. Factional rivalry, therefore, seems to have played a part in Cassius' law (Gruen, *Politics and Courts*, p. 163).

78.20: *inimicissimi C. Cottae*

Cicero may have been distorting the attitude of the *nobiles* towards Cotta's law regarding the tribunate. Cotta is described as *ex factione media* in Sall. *hist.* 3.48.8 M, which can be taken to mean 'from the heart of the nobility', and may suggest that the conservative nobility was prepared to compromise with the popular agitation for the restoration of tribunician powers. As Cicero made his comment in defence of a 'popular' tribune, it suited his purpose to claim that the conservative nobles would have opposed such a move as Cotta's and been hostile to him. See Marshall, *Rhein. Mus.* 118 (1975) esp. 143-4, and cf. above on 67.1.

78.29: *Aurelia lege*

For the *lex Aurelia iudiciaria*, see above on 67.11-12.

78.30-79.1: *L. Roscius Otho biennio ante*

He was tribune in 67 and therefore a colleague of, among others, Cornelius and Gabinius; he had joined Trebellius in opposing Gabinius'

272   Commentary

proposal for Pompeius' pirate command, but had been quickly quietened (see above on 72.10). As a new man (Wiseman, *New Men*, no. 359), his sponsoring of legislation to favour the equestrian order was no doubt designed to assist his candidature for future office (he reached the praetorship, probably in 63). To the same end, he may have formed connections with Crassus (Gruen, *Last Generation*, p. 187), for two Roscii later served among Crassus' officers in the Parthian campaign.

79.1-2: *equitibus Romanis XIIII ordines spectandi gratia darentur*

On the basis of Cic. *Mur.* 40 (*equestri ordini restituit non solum dignitatem* . . . ; cf. Vell. Pat. 2.32.3), some have argued that the equites had a previous right to reserved seats, and that this had been taken away, perhaps by Sulla (e.g. H. Hill. *The Roman Middle Class in the Republican Period* [Oxford, 1952] p. 160; Badian, *Publicans and Sinners* [Oxford, 1972] p. 95). Other sources, however, stress Otho's innovation (Juv. *sat.* 3.159; Plut. *Cic.* 13.2); Wiseman, *Historia* 19 (1970) 72 and 80, sees the measure as an attempt to restore the *dignitas* of the real equestrian order (hence Cicero's phrase) in contrast to the increasing influence of those with the equestrian census who claimed to be equites. To support this, he suggests that there must have been some point in the reservation of fourteen rows: a calculation based on a reconstruction of Pompeius' theatre indicates sufficient space for the 1800 *equites equo publico* (ibid. 72; contra, Badian, op. cit. pp. 84 and 144 n. 9). Though Cicero says here (cf. *Mur.* 40) that Otho's measure had the support of the people, in 63 he was hissed by the audience at the theatre (Plut. *Cic.* 13.3); this might suggest popular dissatisfaction with the privilege (Gruen, *Last Generation*, p. 438; cf. Cic. *Att.* 2.19.3, and Wiseman, *PBSR* 42 [1974] 15-7) or an antipathy towards new men (Wiseman, *New Men*, p. 7 n. 4).

79.3: *cum primum*

Balsdon, *PBSR* 14 (1938) 101 (cf. *JRS* 55 [1965] 230), argues that this does not mean 'when for the first time' but rather 'as soon as' (accepted by Badian, *Historia* 18 [1969] 465-6; cf. Seager *Historia* 16 [1967] 39 n. 13). The passage cannot confidently be used, therefore, to suggest that mixed juries could not have existed before 89, nor does Cicero's statement (*Verr.* 1.38) that equites sat on the juries *annos prope quinquaginta continuos* (i.e. the period from C. Gracchus to Sulla) necessarily imply that they sat alone on the juries, and so it is not incompatible with the earlier existence of mixed juries. Hence, for example, Caepio's law is more likely to have allowed for mixed juries; the Livian evidence suggests this, while it is Tacitus, obviously giving a brief general survey, who says Caepio's law returned control of the courts to the senate (Balsdon, art. cit. 103-5; Gruen, *Politics and Courts*, p. 158; cf.

above on 78.14). The juries established by the *lex Varia* were composed of equites until the *lex Plotia* was passed.

79.5: *Cn. Pompeium*

There are a number of problems associated with accepting the name Cn. Pompeius here. One is the date of the *lex Plotia*: the tribunate of M. Plautius Silvanus is usually placed in 89, and Asconius' remark that the law was passed in the consulship of Pompeius Strabo and Cato makes a tribunate in 89 more probable (so Gruen, *JRS* 55 [1965] 69 n. 126), but Badian, *Studies*, pp. 76-7, says that the evidence is not conclusive for Plautius' tribunate and it could be either 89 or 88, with the *lex Plotia* being passed in December 89 at the beginning of a tribunate for 88. The second is that Cn. Pompeius (the reference must be to Strabo) had been chiefly responsible for Roman successes against the Italian allies, and can hardly have been prosecuted under the *lex Varia*, which was aimed at those sympathetic to the Italian cause (though the court was being used for political purposes — even Varius himself was to be tried and convicted under his own law). The third is that Pompeius, being consul in 89, was immune from prosecution that year; the usual answer to that is that his trial took place in the next year (so Gruen, art. cit. 69; Seager, *Historia* 16 [1967] 39-40), but if that was the case and if the *lex Plotia* was passed in 89, that would leave a gap between the passing of the law and Pompeius' trial, whereas Cicero's words imply that the two were close together. There is a further complication: Pompeius was proconsul in 88, and in that position was also immune from prosecution (Bauman, *Crimen Maiestatis*, p. 68 n. 2). A fourth problem is the relationship of the trial of Varius and that of Pompeius: Varius' trial took place early in 89 (soon after he lost his tribunician immunity) and he was convicted. If his trial took place before the *lex Plotia* was passed, we have to assume that he was condemned by the same sort of jury which had convicted some of his political opponents the year before and was made up of equites who would have supported the passage of Varius' law. A fifth problem is that Cicero, in what was a published speech, describes the man prosecuted under the new arrangements as *dis ac nobilitati perinvisum*; in a speech defending a man who had served under Pompeius, it is hardly likely that Cicero would refer to Pompeius' father in this way (Badian, *Historia* 18 [1969] 473-4, followed by Seager, *Pompey*, p. 59 n. 24). Gruen's answer to the second problem is to say that after 90 sympathy with the Italians was no longer used as a reason for prosecution, and that Strabo was simply prosecuted for *maiestas* on the grounds of his complicity in the murder of Pompeius Rufus, cos. 88, and his refusal to hand over his army (art. cit. 70-1), but that would leave an even longer gap between the passing of the *lex Plotia* and Strabo's trial. Gruen's answer to the fourth problem is that a moderate reaction had set in against the misuse of judicial processes in 90 (ibid. 68); this is criticised by Badian, *Historia* 18 (1969) 467-70, on the grounds that it is only the trial of Varius which can be used to argue for a change of attitude. Badian's solution is to read *Cn. Pomponium* for *Cn. Pompeium* (ibid. 474-5), and this seems to be a satisfactory solution to all the problems; the correction was first put forward by Pighius, and has been tentatively accepted, e.g., by Gray (Greenidge and Clay[2], p. 151), Bauman (op. cit. p. 68 n. 2), and Nicolet (*L'ordre équestre*, 1.572). The correction clearly avoids the second and third problem; it allows the trial to take place in 89 (Cn. Pomponius was a colleague of Varius in the tribunate in 90, and would not be immune from prosecution in 89), and helps to confirm that the *lex Plotia* was passed in that year; it allows the trials of Varius and Pomponius to come close together and so explain Varius' conviction (i.e. he was convicted by a jury composed under the new arrangements); Varius and Pomponius appear to have co-operated during their tribunate, for Cic. *Brut.* 305 says that the two *habitabant in rostris*, and so the epithet *nobilitati perinvisum* would be applicable to Pomponius. The scribal change is minimal: in one of the two instances where the name Pomponius occurs in Asconius (77.4), two of the mss. (S and M) have *Pompeius*, though the name is that of the familiar Pomponius Atticus, so it is easy to see that the better known Pompeius could mistakenly have been written for the lesser known Pomponius, especially with *Cn. Pompeio Strabone* following so closely (79.7).

79.8: *secundo anno*

Not strictly accurate, since the war had broken out in 91 and Asconius is talking about the events of 89, i.e. the third year of the war. For another miscalculation about the start of the Social War, see above on 68.6.

79.8-9: *cum equester ordo in iudiciis dominaretur*

This seems to suggest that the courts had resumed operations following their suspension due to the Social War (so Seager, *Historia* 16 [1967] 39; cf. above on 74.1-3). The last known law dealing with the composition of the courts (apart from the law of Livius Drusus which was repealed) was the *lex Servilia Glauciae*, passed some time before 100, which revoked the law of Caepio and gave the courts back to the equites. Asconius may be referring only to equestrian domination of the juries under the *lex Varia*, but he could have in mind the general view that the equites had controlled the courts since Glaucia's law (cf. above on 79.3) and that they had begun to abuse their position towards the end of the 90's (witness the condemnation of P. Rutilius Rufus). On the composition of the juries, see Gruen, *Politics and Courts*, pp. 159 and 166, and Griffin, *CQ* 23 (1973) 108-21.

79.9: *legem tulit*

This passage of Cicero with Asconius' comment is our only evidence for

Pro Cornelio 275

the existence of this law. There is some dispute over its scope: some believe it to have been a general judiciary law, altering the composition of all the juries (e.g. Gruen, *Politics and Courts*, p. 221; cf. Balsdon, *PBSR* 14 [1938] 101), but Griffin, art. cit. 111-2 and 120, believes that the *lex Plotia* affected only the composition of the juries established by the *lex Varia*. Nor is it clear how long the *lex Plotia* remained in operation: it may have lasted until Sulla's law of 81, or it may have been repealed within a year (for a summary of views on this question, see Hill, *The Roman Middle Class*, pp. 137-8; Nicolet, *L'ordre équestre*, 1.571).

79.9-10: *adiuvantibus nobilibus*

The *lex Plotia* was not simply part of a struggle in these years between the senate and the equites for control of the jury-courts, nor was it an attack on the equites for misconduct in the Varian trials in 90 (Gruen, *JRS* 55 [1965] 68-9; cf. Badian, *Historia* 18 [1969] 470 and 475). The aim was to restore senatorial influence in the courts. As it was passed early in 89, it is possible to connect it with the action of the praetor, A. Sempronius Asellio, in favouring debtors against creditors and his murder by the enraged money-lenders at a religious ceremony (Liv. *per.* 24; Val. Max. 9.7.4; App. *BC* 1.54); the *nobiles* may have taken advantage of the discredit which fell on the equites for this murder to change the composition of the courts (Badian, *FC*, p. 227 n. 4, elaborated in art. cit. 475-81; Gruen, art. cit. 69, accepted more definitely in *Politics and Courts*, p. 221). The arrangements for compiling the list of jurymen would have favoured the senatorial class (see next comment).

79.11-12: *tribus singulae ex suo numero quinos denos*

For the *album iudicum* each tribe was to select fifteen jurors regardless of their status, and this meant, according to Asconius (79.14), that some men came *ex plebe*. This may have been 'a calculated piece of democratic machinery' (Badian, *Historia* 18 [1969] 475-6), designed by the traditional leaders to gain the support of the plebs; cf. their concern to secure popular approval for the suspension of the courts during the Social War (74.3-4). However, 'the control of voting power in the tribes would be drawn overwhelmingly from the senatorial order' (Gruen, *JRS* 55 [1965] 69; cf. Badian, art. cit. 470). Badian also suggests that the men *ex plebe* may possibly have been just below equestrian status, like the *tribuni aerarii* of the *lex Aurelia* of 70.

79.15: *PRO CORNELIO [II]*

The heading *pro Cornelio* is included in two of the mss. (S and P) but omitted in the third (M). *Secunda oro* has been added in the margin of P, presumably on the basis of 62.4 and 79.23. See the apparatus in 62 St.

276 Commentary

79.18: *inimici tribuniciae potestatis*

There are indications that one of the two men referred to here, M. Terentius Varro Lucullus (cos. 73), was opposed to tribunician power. He was consul in the year that C. Licinius Macer was tribune, and Macer was active in agitating for the restoration of the tribunician powers. Macer's derogatory comments on a grain law proposed by Lucullus and his colleague (Sall. *hist.* 3.48.19 M) suggest conflict between the consul and the tribune; moreover, Lucullus' brother, consul in the preceding year, had checked the agitation of L. Quinctius, a tribune of that year, for the restoration of the tribunician powers (ibid. 3.48.11 M; Plut. *Luc.* 5.4). The attitude of the other man towards the tribunate depends on his identification: that he was one of the *principes civitatis*, and *inimicus tribuniciae potestatis*, suggests a consul from the period of the 70's and points to Mam. Aemilius Lepidus Livianus (cos. 77), though he is not known to have opposed the tribunate, nor to have been an opponent of Pompeius, like the other four listed here. On the problem of his identification, see above on 60.20-21.

79.19: *adsentatores eorum atque adseculae*

On the strength of Cicero's criticism of the *principes civitatis*, see above on 73.5-6, and cf. Asconius' judgment at 61.8-9.

79.20: *M. Lepidum significat*

The mss. all have *M.* for the *praenomen*. Manutius emended it to *M'.*, making it a reference to the consul of 66; it may need to be emended to *Mam.* For the identification, see above on 60.20-21.

79.21-22: *testimonium dixerunt*

J. Humbert, *Contribution à l'étude de sources d'Asconius* (Paris, 1925) pp. 79ff., has shown that Asconius has misunderstood the nature of the second speech, taking it to be part of the speech for the defence, whereas it was a literary adaptation of the interrogation of the witnesses, following the speeches of the prosecution and the defence (cf. Kumaniecki, p. 30). The incidence of interrogatives in the few fragments of the speech preserved by Asconius suggests its nature, as well as the listing of the principal witnesses in his comment on the first fragment. Asconius' misunderstanding of the nature of the speech has 'misled him into believing that most of the witnesses were questioned before Cicero spoke' (Griffin, p. 202), whereas they must not have been questioned until after Cicero had delivered his opening speech (cf. 79.23-24; *et duo qui nondum dixerant*), the second speech being a summary of that interrogation. That Catulus was questioned is indicated by the following two fragments; he may have been questioned before Lucullus and Lepidus, since

Pro Cornelio

Asconius says the third fragment was located twenty lines earlier than the second fragment (80.5-6), which seems to follow straight on from the first.

79.25: *avunculus tuus*

The reference is to Cn. Domitius Ahenobarbus, the uncle of Q. Lutatius Catulus (cf. 80.16: *idem Domitius*). Catulus' father (cos. 102) had married (first, presumably) a Domitia, the sister of Ahenobarbus; he subsequently married Servilia, the sister of Caepio (cos. 106), and a daughter of that marriage, Lutatia, later married Q. Hortensius Hortalus. On these connections, see Badian, *Studies*, pp. 37-8, 218 and 232-3.

80.2: *potentissimorum hominum*

Cicero's choice of Domitius Ahenobarbus' tribunate is most apt: it demonstrated a conflict between a man using popular dissatisfaction and a clique bound together by their Metellan connections (in fact, one might also call them the next generation of the Metellan faction). Cicero elsewhere uses similar phrases to describe Cornelius' opponents (e.g. 58.12).

80.2-3: *conlegiis eripuit cooptandorum sacerdotum potestatem*

Scaurus had refused to co-opt Ahenobarbus into one of the priestly colleges to fill the vacancy left by the death of his father; Ahenobarbus retaliated by bringing Scaurus before the people on a charge related to some religious misdemeanours, during his tribunate (see above on 21.1ff.). He also passed a law in that year allowing for appointment of new members of the priestly colleges to be made by a popular vote of seventeen of the tribes (Cic. *leg. ag.* 2.18-19; for the procedure, see SB *Q.f.* 233-4), securing his own election in the process, and actually becoming pontifex maximus (*MRR* 1.565).

80.4: *hoc egere enarratione*

Asconius' attempt at assisting the forgetful reader is really not much help, for the passage he goes on to quote does not indicate who the man was who took away the colleges' right of co-option; rather it explains who the nephew of this man was (i.e. Q. Catulus).

80.18-19: *Domitius tr. pl.*

The evidence here, that Ahenobarbus was tribune five years after Silanus' consulship, and at 81.7-8, that he was tribune in the consulship of Marius (for the second time) and C. Fimbria, points to the holding of the office in 104. Vell. Pat. 2.12.3, however, says that it was in Marius' third consulship (i.e. 103) that Ahenobarbus carried his law about election to the priestly colleges. G. Niccolini, *I fasti dei tribuni della plebe* (Milan, 1934) p. 19, followed by *MRR* 1.562 and 565, prefers Asconius' date, but Sumner, *Orators*, pp. 97-100, argues at length for 103 (for the part of the argument based on Ahenobarbus' rejection from one of the priestly colleges, see above on 21.4-5). Part of his argument is based on the suggestion that Ahenobarbus replaced L. Caecilius Metellus Delmaticus in 103 both as pontiff and pontifex maximus, using the sequence of events described in Liv. *per.* 67 to suggest a date in the second half of 103 for Ahenobarbus' election as pontifex maximus, since according to Sumner this election is reported after Marius' election to the consulship for 102. But this is not true, for the summary of Livy mentions Marius' election to his second, third and fourth consulships, and then Ahenobarbus' election, so it could have taken place in any one of those years. Moreover, we have no evidence for the year of Delmaticus' death; we know of it only because Ahenobarbus was elected to take his place — he could quite easily have died in 104, creating the vacancy which Ahenobarbus was elected to fill. Further, Ahenobarbus' law regarding election to the priestly colleges had nothing to do with election for the position of pontifex maximus, which was an elective position long before that law (Taylor, *Class. Phil.* 37 [1942] 421-4), so the two elections need not be connected. Finally, why assume that Velleius is right in his date (in what is clearly a summary), and Asconius wrong (when he is explaining a detail)?

80.20-21: *Domitius eum apud populum accusavit*

As consul and proconsul, Silanus' military operations in Gaul led to a serious defeat at the hands of the Cimbri (see above on 68.15-16); he was defeated despite the success of his proposal abrogating laws which had reduced military conscription (see above on 68.16-18). Although other commanders who had been unsuccessful against the northmen were put on trial, Silanus escaped indictment for four years. In 104, however, following Caepio's disastrous defeat at Arausio, Ahenobarbus took the opportunity to take up the old criticism of Silanus: he brought him before the people on a charge of having waged war on the Cimbri without authority (80.21-22). The outcome of the trial was a comfortable acquittal for Silanus, with only two of the thirty-five tribes voting for condemnation (80.24-25). On the trial, see Gruen, *Politics and Courts*, p. 174, and Bauman, *Crimen Maiestatis*, p. 38. It is not necessary to assume that Silanus was shielded by his powerful Metellan associates; the outcome suggests that there was no real case against him.

80.21-22: *criminabatur rem cum Cimbris iniussu populi gessisse*

A case involving Ahenobarbus and Silanus, mentioned in Cic. *div. in Caec.* 67 and *Verr.* 2.2.118, is usually identified with the trial mentioned by Asconius (so Giarratano, n. ad. loc.; *MRR* 1.559; Gruen, loc. cit.); that case was brought on because of injuries to a family friend,

Pro Cornelio

Aegritomarius, who came from Transalpine Gaul. The case occurred *nuper* in relation to the process against Verres. Perhaps the case mentioned by Cicero is a different one, part of a continuing *inimicitia* between these two men. Perhaps the references are to the same case; the charge of failure against the Cimbri was the main one, but it involved also general accusations of maladministration, of which the injuries to Aegritomarius were an instance (brought in perhaps because Ahenobarbus realised he did not have much of a case for the main charge). It is significant that the injured party came from the area where Silanus had exercised his command. For further discussion, see Marshall, *AJP* 98 (1977) 419-23.

80.22: *principium fuisse calamitatum*

It is a little unfair to suggest that Silanus' defeat 'had helped considerably to precipitate the crisis in the north' (Gruen, op. cit. p. 174). The consul of 113, Cn. Papirius Carbo, who had been sent to head the Cimbri off when they first appeared on the borders of Italy, suffered a defeat in a battle near Noreia. It is true that Silanus suffered the first in a successive series of defeats following the re-appearance of the northmen (who in 113 had moved off westwards).

80.23: *ac de eo tabellam quoque edidit*

It would have been normal procedure in judicial assemblies by this time for the voters to have been provided with a single tablet on which were inscribed two letters (either L D, or A C: see above on 28.25); they then simply crossed out the letter which did not represent their verdict (Staveley, op. cit. p. 160). If this was normal procedure, there seems to be no point in Asconius' bothering to mention the publication of a *tabella*, unless there was something unusual about it. One explanation (Marshall, *LCM* 2 [1977] 11-12) is that Ahenobarbus tried to 'fix' the outcome of the trial by issuing a voting tablet marked for only one sort of verdict. Cf. the famous example of P. Clodius who in 61 issued voting tablets for a legislative assembly without the letter U (which signified an affirmative vote) in an attempt to secure the rejection of a bill (Cic. *Att.* 1.14.5). One objection to this explanation is the use of the singular, where we would have expected the plural (cf. Cic. *Cluent.* 184, *Sull.* 42). Another explanation is that it means Ahenobarbus published a deposition about Silanus (cf. Tac. *dial.* 36.7, where the singular is used). A third possibility is that *tabellam dare* is the same as the phrase *ex tabella pronuntiare* or *recitare*; a magistrate when he delivered the verdict read it out from a written record, using the proper form of words (the *periculum*: cf. Cic. *Verr.* 2.3.183 — *tabulae publicae periculaque magistratuum*). On the procedure, see Suet. *Claud.* 15.3; Mommsen, *Strafrecht*, p. 447 nn. 4 and 5. Given that there must be something unusual about Asconius' mention of Ahenobarbus' action, this explanation would suggest that Ahenobarbus prepared his written verdict beforehand and read it out as an indication of how he wanted the tribes to vote, presumably before the vote was taken (since in the end the tribes did not vote the way he wanted).

81.3: *contemptissimum nomen electum*

M. Terpolius was tribune in 77, according to Asconius (81.5-6: twelve years before the trial of Cornelius in the consulship of D. Iunius Brutus and Mam. Aemilius Lepidus Livianus). Our only reference to his tribunate is this fragment of Cicero and Asconius' comment on it. His name does not readily spring to mind as one who had been active in agitation for a restoration of the tribunician power and therefore despised by the *nobiles*: the agitation is usually taken to have begun with Sicinius (tr. pl. 76), followed by L. Quinctius in 74, C. Licinius Macer in 73, and M. Lollius Palicanus in 71. Cicero's comment here is ironic, just as the complimentary tone of the earlier passage comparing Ahenobarbus' tribunate is ironic (80.7ff. = frag. 5 P): Terpolius is chosen precisely because he did nothing at all and because he was not of the slightest account.

81.5: *restitutam a Cn. Pompeio*

On the basis of this passage, and Cic. *Verr.* 1.44, *leg.* 3.22, Vell. Pat. 2.30.4, Plut. *Pomp.* 22.3, and Ps. Ascon. 220.14-5, some have argued that Pompeius alone proposed the law for the restoration of the tribunician powers (e.g. A. Garzetti, *Athenaeum* n.s. 20 [1942] 15; McDermott, *Class. Phil.* 72 [1977] 49-52). But other sources include Crassus (Sall. *Cat.* 38.1; Liv. *per.* 97; Ps. Ascon. 189.8-9), and it is reasonable to assume he helped to propose the law (Marshall, *Crassus: a Political Biography* [Amsterdam, 1976] pp. 53-4).

81.6: *Mam. Lepido*

All three mss. have *M.* for the *praenomen*, but it is clear that it has to be emended to *Mam.*

81.7: *ante II de XL annos*

Asconius' clear statement that Domitius was tribune in the consulship of Marius (for the second time) and C. Fimbria, and earlier that it was five years after the consulship of M. Silanus (80.18), points to the year 104. In that case Asconius has made another error in calculation, for he should have written thirty-nine, not thirty-eight, years before (or forty if he were counting inclusively, though his usual practice in phrases like this [cf. above, e.g., 64.19 and 81.6.] is to count exclusively).

81.9: *magno numero sententiarum*

That the votes cast by the three *ordines* were not separately tabulated until 59, see above on 28.25. Until then, at least the margin of votes must have been known.

THE COMMENTARY ON THE SPEECH *IN TOGA CANDIDA*

82.1: *L. Caesare C. Figulo coss.*

L. Iulius Caesar and C. Marcius Figulus were consuls in 64. The latter may be the Thermus mentioned in Cic. *Att.* 1.1.2 (SB *Att.* 1.292).

82.4: *sex competitores*

In *Att.* 1.1.1, written in July 65, Cicero lists as certain competitors four of those listed by Asconius (Galba, Antonius and Cornificius, and Catilina, if he is acquitted); the two others who are not mentioned by Cicero are L. Cassius Longinus (cf. *comm. pet.* 7) and C. Licinius Sacerdos. Cicero also mentions as possible but not certain competitors four whom Asconius does not list: M. Caesoninus and C. Aquillius Gallus (whom he did not expect finally to stand) and T. Aufidius and M. Lollius Palicanus (whose chances he did not rate very highly). The discrepancy between Asconius' list and that of Cicero could be taken to suggest that Asconius did not use the letters as a source (see Part I, pp. 47-50).

82.5: *P. Sulpicium Galbam*

The date of Galba's offices are not certain: his aedileship may have been 71 or 69 (see *MRR* 2.136 n. 4); he must have been praetor by 66 to be standing for the consulship of 63. He was co-opted as a pontiff between 73 and 69 (L.R. Taylor, *AJP* 63 [1942] 385-412; *MRR* 2.137 n. 11), and is last heard of as a pontiff in 57 (Cic. *har. resp* 12), though he may have been the praetorian Galba killed in 47 by mutinous soldiers in Rome (Plut. *Caes.* 51.1; cf. App. *BC* 2.92-93; SB *Att.* 1.289). He was a patrician of good character (Cic. *Mur.* 17; cf. below, 82.12), but lacking in energy (*comm. pet.* 7: *sine nervis*).

82.5: *L. Sergium Catilinam*

Catilina had served as a legate under Sulla in 82, and held a praetorship in 68, which he followed with a governorship of Africa in 67-66. On his return from Africa he attempted to stand at the consular elections in 66 but his candidature was rejected. In 65 he was charged with extortion and the jury's decision at that trial that 'it was night-time at noon' (Cic. *Att.* 1.1.1) cleared the way for his candidature in 64.

82.6: *duos nobiles*

Asconius seems here to be using the strict definition of *nobilis*, a man whose forebears had attained the consulship, and not the looser meaning (Cic. *Mur.* 17) which allowed nobility to the descendants of senators who had reached praetorian rank or of equestrians who had not entered the senate at all (J. Hellegouarc'h, *Le vocabulaire latin des relations et des partis politiques sous la république* [Paris, 1972] pp. 472ff.). Asconius distinguishes between the sons of consulars and the sons of men who were recent entrants to the senate. On the definition of nobility, see M. Gelzer, *The Roman Nobility*, trans. R. Seager (Oxford, 1969) pp. 27-40.

82.6: *C. Antonium*

C. Antonius, called Hybrida, was the younger son of the orator, M. Antonius. He had been prefect in charge of cavalry in Greece under Sulla (see below on 84.13-14) and had profited from the Sullan proscriptions; he was expelled from the senate in 70 (see below on 84.20-25), presumably having held a quaestorship before that date and entering the senate under Sulla's law admitting quaestors to that body. He may have held a tribunate in 68, which would have restored him to membership of the senate (see below on 84.20-21); at any rate he would certainly have regained senatorial status by the holding of the praetorship in 66 (see below, 85.21ff. and 92.26ff.).

82.7: *M. Antoni oratoris*

See above on 25.14.

82.7: *L. Cassium Longinum*

Longinus came from a family with a number of consulships, and it was this which gave him hopes of a consulship. Though not mentioned as a competitor by Cicero, he is listed as a candidate along with Galba in *comm. pet.* 7. He had presumably been a *monetalis* c. 78-76 (Crawford, *RRC*, 1.403), and hence his filiation would be Q.f.; the choice of Liber and Libera as coin types suggests allusion to the *lex Cassia tabellaria* (cf. above on 78.5 for coins issued by other members of the family referring to that law). He was praetor in 66, in charge of the *maiestas* court; for his part in assisting the defence at the first attempt of the Cominii to bring a charge against C. Cornelius, see above on 59.18ff. For Longinus' character and subsequent activity, see below on 82.13ff., and for the details of his career, see F. Münzer, *RE* 3 (1899) 1738-9.

82.9: *Q. Cornificium*

Asconius' comment suggests that, although Cornificius and Sacerdos were not the first from their families to enter the senate, they both came from families which had only recently gained entry. T.P. Wiseman, *CQ* 14 (1964) 123 (cf. *New Men*, pp. 227 and 237) puts both fathers as senators c. 100 (?). The Cornificii came from Lanuvium (R. Syme, *Historia* 4 [1955] 61). This man had been tribune of the people in 69 (Cic.

Verr. 1.30) and praetor in 67 or 66; he was a *praetorius* in 63 (Sall. *Cat.* 47.4; App. *BC* 2.5; cf. Cic. *fam.* 12.28.2), being assigned as guardian of one of the arrested Catilinarian conspirators. That action, and his characterisation as *sobrius ac sanctus* (82.12), suggests that he was 'a respectable, sturdy optimate' (SB *Att.* 1.290). Cicero did not think much of his chances at the consular elections (*Att.* 1.1.1); that would probably be due to the newness of his family. Cornificius became well-off (ibid. 12.17) and is last heard of in 61 (ibid. 1.13.3).

82.9: *C. Licinium Sacerdotem*

The father of this man was presumably the first senator in the family; Cic. *Cluent.* 134 mentions an eques C. Licinius Sacerdos in 142. The man referred to by Asconius was *praetor urbanus* in 75 (Cic. *Verr.* 2.1.130) and subsequently propraetor in Sicily in 74, the immediate predecessor of Verres. He had recently served as a legate under Metellus Creticus (Cic. *Planc.* 27). Asconius comments (82.13) that he was not known for any impropriety.

82.10-11: *in petitione patrem amisit*

On the evidence of Cic. *Att.* 1.6.2, Cicero's father died in 68. In view of Asconius' statement that he died in 64, objections have been raised to the evidence of Cicero's letter (for some of the objections and answers to them, see TP, 1.132-3, and SB *Att.* 1.281-2) and changes to the wording of the letter have been suggested (e.g. Madvig, pp. 70-1, would emend *decessit* to *discesserat*, on the ground that the tone of the letter is too joyful to be about the death of Cicero's father). The choice lies between convicting Asconius of error, or changing the reading in Cicero: both Tyrrell and Purser and Shackleton Bailey believe the passage of Asconius is unsound (another error). Harrison's suggestion that Asconius wrote *omisit* finds some favour with Tyrrell and Purser (loc. cit.): 'it may have been customary in the *professio* to give the father's name with one's own' and 'Cicero may have excited comment by omitting this customary formality.' And Asconius' mention of him playing down his father's name may have been prompted by his preceding comment (*equestri erat loco natus*). R.S. Stewart, *TAPA* 93 (1962) 469 n. 17, gives an explanation for Asconius' error: there is a chronological disorder in the first eleven letters to Atticus in the collection as we have it, and while the first two letters are mainly concerned with Cicero's consular candidature and were written in July 65, the next nine belong to 68-66 but bear no dates, so that a reader's first assumption would be that the Kalends of December mentioned in 1.6.2 were those of 65. Stewart concludes: 'It would be perverse any longer to maintain the view that . . . Asconius had not seen the *Epistulae ad Atticum* in their edited form.' As Shackleton Bailey, however, points out (SB *Att.* 1.68), 'Asconius' error does not show that he himself had seen the letters (still less, of course, that they had been published when he wrote). He may have got this piece of misinformation at second hand.' On the question whether Asconius did use Cicero's letters, see Part I, pp. 47-50, and cf. below on 85.16ff.

82.13-16: *Cassius quamvis stolidus . . . fuisse auctorem*

On the evidence of Cicero, he was one of the ringleaders of the Catilinarian conspiracy. He was principally involved in the negotiations with the Gallic envoys to secure assistance for the conspiracy (Cic. *Cat.* 3.9, *Sull.* 36-39), and he was to supervise the arson in Rome (*Cat.* 3.14, 4.13, *Sull.* 53), which is probably the point of Asconius' reference to *cruentissimae sententiae.* Cf. also *Cat.* 3.25, and Sall. *Cat.* 17.3, 50.4. Cicero mentions the corpulence of Cassius (*Cat.* 3.16): does Asconius have that in mind when he calls Cassius *stolidus*? Cicero earlier had a more favourable opinion of Cassius (*Cluent.* 107) for his vote in the trial of Oppianicus in 74 (even if the opinion was exaggerated for his present purpose).

82.14-15: *post paucos menses*

Asconius is wrong in suggesting that the Catilinarian conspiracy began a few months after the consular elections (i.e. in late 64). Cf. the similar mistake of Sallust (*Cat.* 17.1) who dates the formation of the conspiracy to June 64 (before the consular elections). The conspiracy was not formed until after the failure of Catilina (for the third time) to secure a consulship at the elections in 63.

83.1: *infamis eorum vita*

In the case of Antonius, presumably a reference to the heavy debts and licentiousness which had led to his expulsion from the senate in 70 (see below on 84.20ff.), and in the case of Catilina to the affair of the Vestal virgin, Fabia (see below on 91.19ff.), to the way in which he married Aurelia Orestilla (Sall. *Cat.* 15.2-5; cf. below on 91.28), to his activities during the Sullan proscriptions, and to his misgovernment of Africa. Cf. the general picture of Catilina in Cic. *Cael.* 10-14, and of both in *comm. pet.* 8-10.

83.2: *coierant enim ambo*

Though unethical, the practice of two or more candidates pooling their resources for an electoral effort was not illegal (U. Hall, *Historia* 13 [1964] 301; contra, Mommsen, *Strafrecht*, pp. 872ff.; Taylor, *Party Politics in the Age of Caesar* [Berkeley, 1949] pp. 64 and 68). Well known instances of candidates combining in the Ciceronian period were Pompeius and Crassus in 71 (Plut. *Pomp.* 22.1), Verres' supporters in 70,

Caesar and Lucceius in 60 (Cic. *Att.* 1.17.11; Suet. *Iul* 19.1), and Memmius and Domitius Calvinus in 54 (Cic. *Q.f.* 2.14.1). There are also instances where candidates combined to attempt to secure the defeat of a common rival (e.g. M. Porcius Cato at the censorial elections in 184: Liv. 39.41.1-4); part of the aim of Catilina and Antonius in forming their combination was to keep Cicero out (cf. below, 83.19-20). *Coitio* frequently found expression in some sort of electoral bribery, and for this reason the suggestion of collusion was prominent in the prosecutions of the Ciceronian period, because in a bribery charge it was likely to prejudice a jury, and it would have been easier to substantiate a charge of collusion than electoral corruption (Taylor, loc. cit.; E.S. Staveley, *Greek and Roman Voting and Elections* [London, 1972] pp. 205-6). In general on *coitiones* in this period, see C. Meier, *Res Publica Amissa* (Wiesbaden, 1966) pp. 178ff.

83.3-4: *adiutoribus usi firmissimis M. Crasso et C. Caesare*

P.A. Brunt, *CR* n.s. 7 (1957) 195, has questioned the commonly held view of Crassus' and Caesar's support of Catilina: it is 'an article of faith with all the books [that Crassus and Caesar were supporting the candidature of Catilina and Antonius], but it rests, apart from inferences and conjectural interpretations of the political situation, only on two passages of Asconius (83.2 and 21), of which the second is explicitly and both are probably derived from Cicero's secret memoir', which was blatantly hostile to Crassus and Caesar and not published till after Cicero's death (see below on 83.22). Cicero himself, in intimate letters and even when he was most hostile to these two, never alludes to their support of Catilina and Antonius against his own candidature (cf. Gruen, *Last Generation*, p. 138). However, there is no reason why Cicero should have invented (as opposed to exaggerated) in secret memoirs for posthumous publication, and the argument from silence in his letters is not strong. It is a plausible conjecture that Crassus in particular would want to back candidates for the consulship at that stage.

83.4: *contra solos*

The fragments of the speech preserved by Asconius deal almost exclusively with Catilina and Antonius, who were in any case the strongest of his rivals (having the support of Crassus); the results of the voting show their relative importance (Cicero topped the poll, Antonius was second, and Catilina third). One might compare the space devoted to Catilina and Antonius in *comm. pet.* 8-10 and 28 (if that document is a genuine piece of advice to Cicero), with that given to the other rivals in §7. Compare too the advice in §52: 'See that your competitors are smeared with an evil reputation, which fits their character, for crime, vice or bribery.' Two of the mss. (P and S) actually have as part of the title of the speech *contra C. Antonium et L. Catilinam competitores*.

83.6-7: *in dies licentia ambitus augeretur*

The action of the censors of 70 in striking a large number off the list of senators had created even more intense competition in the electoral struggles, as the ousted men turned to more desperate methods in their attempts to get back into office; as a result there was agitation for stronger controls on electoral malpractice (for a discussion, see Gruen, *Last Generation*, pp. 212ff.; cf. Wiseman, *JRS* 59 [1969] 66-7). Sulla had included a law on *ambitus* in his legislation, which prohibited a candidate found guilty of electoral malpractice from standing as a candidate again for ten years. It was not until 67 that another law was passed, the *lex Calpurnia* (see above on 57.8 for the conflict over the passing of this law), which, although it provided for stricter penalties (69.12-13, cf. 74.22-23), failed to act as a deterrent since in the very next year the two successful consular candidates were found guilty of *ambitus* and deprived of their designated office (75.7-9). In 65 there was a *senatus consultum* which authorised an amendment to the *lex Calpurnia* (69.10), possibly tightening its provisions (Gruen, loc. cit. p. 217, cf. p. 456 n. 27). It is a little unfair of Asconius to suggest that the activities of Catilina and Antonius were responsible for the senatorial proposal; while Antonius had been anxious to get back into the senate by holding office, and while there might have been some immediate concern at the financial power of their backers, there had been this continuing pressure for bribery legislation in the 60's.

83.9: *Q. Mucius Orestinus tr. pl. intercesserat*

The only known office for Orestinus is his tribunate in 64. He may have interposed his veto because of personal connection with Catilina: the latter was married to an Aurelia Orestilla (Sall. *Cat.* 15.2), and her name might suggest a family link with Orestinus. The tribune delivered a verbal attack on Catilina's rival, Cicero, and used his veto against a bill which might have been considered an *ad hominem* measure directed at Catilina and Antonius; this might suggest at least alignment with their cause (cf. 86.1). E.T. Salmon, *AJP* 56 (1935) 308, takes Orestinus' veto to have been imposed at the instigation of Crassus, which makes sense if the latter was supporting Catilina and Antonius and if the bill was directed against them. Further on Orestinus, see below on 86.4ff. and 88.18-19.

83.18: *aut C. Caesaris aut M. Crassi domum*

Innuendo on the part of Cicero, and supposition on the part of Asconius. No matter whose house was involved, the money could have come only from Crassus and not Caesar (who was busy accumulating debts: just prior to his departure for his propraetorship in Spain in 61 he owed a total of twenty-five million denarii according to App. *BC* 2.8, and Crassus lent him five million to stave off his most demanding creditors [Plut. *Crass.* 7.6, *Caes.* 11.1; Suet. *Iul.* 18]). Crassus had a lot of experience in using his money to place people under an obligation (Plut. *Crass.* 3.1, 7.1-9; cf. Sall. *Cat.* 48.3-9). Crassus may have preferred to do his negotiating in someone else's house; his own had a reputation as *castissima* (Cic. *Cael.* 9, cf. *fam.* 5.8.2; Suet. *Iul.* 50.1; Plut. *Cic.* 25.2; cf. Wiseman, *CQ* n.s. 18 [1968] 297-8).

83.22: *expositione consiliorum suorum*

This *expositio* is usually identified with Cicero's secret memoirs (E. Schwarz, *Hermes* 32 [1897] 557-9, in Brunt, art. cit. 193); that seems to be confirmed by Dio's title for the secret memoirs, περὶ τῶν ἑαυτοῦ βουλευμάτων (39.10.3), which is parallel to the title given by Asconius. Cicero thought about beginning these memoirs in 59 (*Att.* 2.6.2: *itaque ἀνέκδοτα a nobis quae tibi uni legamus, Theopompio genere aut etiam asperiore multo pangentur. neque aliud iam quicquam* πολιτεύομαι *nisi odisse improbos*); they were still unfinished in late 44 (ibid. 14.17.6, cf. 16.11.3). Dio says that Cicero left instructions to his son that the memoirs were not to be published until after his death; he also says that in this book Cicero made many denunciations against Crassus and Caesar (39.10.3). According to Asconius (see next comment), Cicero alleged that Crassus was the author of the so-called 'first' Catilinarian conspiracy; Plut. *Crass.* 13.2-4 says that, in a certain speech published after the death of both men, Cicero clearly inculpated Crassus and Caesar in the Catilinarian conspiracy of 63, stressing that this was a changed attitude adopted by Cicero later. It is not clear what Plutarch means by the death of both men — Crassus and Caesar, or Crassus and Cicero, but whatever he means, it looks like the same point which Dio made, that the statements of Cicero were not published until after his death, and so Plutarch's 'certain speech' should probably be identified with the secret memoirs. On the evidence of Asconius and Plutarch the one certain comment Cicero made in the secret memoirs was to inculpate Crassus and Caesar in the Catilinarian conspiracies, and that comment would be consistent with the sort of denunciations said by Dio to be contained in the memoirs. On the likelihood that the various versions of Cicero's treatise on his consulship made the same sorts of denunciations, and further on the memoirs, see B.A. Marshall, *Latomus* 33 (1974) 806-8.

83.22-25: *eius quoque coniurationis... M. Crassum auctorem fuisse*

As well as falling into the error of interpreting Cicero's statements in the light of what subsequently happened (i.e. he knew how Catilina eventually turned out), Asconius has read into Cicero's statements the later changed attitude of hostility to Caesar and especially Crassus, manifest in the secret memoirs (which the *arguit* shows he was using here): on Asconius' misunderstanding of this hostile attitude, see Brunt, art. cit. 193-5, and on the development of Cicero's hostile attitude to Crassus, see Marshall, art. cit. 804ff. There is no indication that at this point in the speech Cicero referred to the alleged plot of 66-65, or to Crassus' and Caesar's involvement in it; while they were alive, he never dared to make such allegations publicly. At most in the speech he could only hint darkly at their involvement in a plan for *caedes optimatum* (cf. 92.11-14, and the *mali cives* of 93.10-14). That so-called 'first' Catilinarian conspiracy is now largely regarded as a fabrication: see, e.g., M. Frisch, *C. & M.* 9 (1947) 10-35; R. Seager, *Historia* 13 (1964) 338-47; E.S. Gruen, *Class. Phil.* 64 (1969) 20-4. That it may be identified with the disturbances connected with the trial of Manilius at the end of 66, see above on 66.7. The development of the tradition about the 'first' conspiracy shows that from 59 on writers were concerned with directing scandal against Crassus and Caesar (M. I. Henderson, *JRS* 40 [1950] 13-4; Seager, art. cit. 341 and 345-6); Suetonius' version (*Iul.* 9) that Crassus was to be made dictator and Caesar his *magister equitum* demonstrates the ultimate in that development, but the nature of Suetonius' sources for the version shows it up as a fiction. Cicero may even have helped in the development of this hostile tradition (cf. the letter to Axius in Suet. *Iul.* 9), or at least accepted it, incorporating it in his secret memoirs.

83.23: *ante annum*

Seager, art. cit. 339, argues that it is impossible that a plot should be described as *facta* in 65 (the year before this speech was delivered; the same phrase is used at 92.17), if it had been hatched in 66 for execution on 1st January 65 (the Sallustian version). He thinks that Asconius, and presumably Cicero, are talking only about a plot for 5th February, and that the plot for 1st January had not yet become part of the myth. But that is all asking too much of the precision of Asconius' chronology, which is often suspect. Cf. below on 92.17.

84.5: *nominatim etiam postea*

Stangl, n. ad. loc., thinks that the list of victims was given in connection with the fragments quoted at 90.16-24. The list given by Asconius differs from that in *comm. pet.* 9-10; common to both are Q. Caecilius, L. Tanusius (though *comm. pet.* uses the plural Tanusii; the text of Asconius is corrected here on the basis of the mention of Tanusii in the *comm. pet.*) and M. Marius (Gratidianus); Asconius alone mentions M. Volumnius, and the *comm.pet* alone refers to Titinii and Nannii. On the relevance of this difference to the question of the authenticity of the *comm. pet.*, see C. Nicolet and S. Demougin, *ANRW* 1.3 (1973) 257-62.

84.6: *Q. Caecilium*

Tyrrell and Purser, 1.159, identify this man as the Q. Caecilius Metellus Celer mentioned as an orator in Cic. *Brut.* 305. In *comm. pet.* 9 the man killed by Catilina is said to have been the husband of Catilina's sister, an eques who belonged to no party, most honest and peaceable both by nature and because of his age at that time. The orator of *Brut.* 305 is usually taken to be the tribune of 90 (*MRR* 2.26; Sumner, *Orators*, pp. 132f.), so he ought not to be identified with the Q. Caecilius of *comm. pet.* 9 (who was only an eques; cf. Nicolet, *REL* 50 [1972] 171). Moreover, it is unlikely that a member of the family of the Caecilii Metelli would have been on the Sullan proscription list; so Tyrrell and Purser's identification ought to be rejected. It is true that we hear no more of this man following his tribunate in 90 (and with his family connection he ought to have reached high office — unless there were not enough consulships for the prolific Metelli!), but that ought not to suggest a violent end to his career; natural death could be a sufficient explanation. Henderson, *JRS* 40 (1950) 10, argues that the author of the *comm. pet.* has confused Catilina and Clodius, and given the former the latter's brother-in-law, and that this mistake shows the *comm. pet* to be a later forgery (contra, Balsdon, *CQ* n.s. 13 [1963] 246-7; J.S. Richardson, *Historia* 20 [1971] 438 n. 18).

84.6: *M. Volumnium*

It is not clear what this man's background was. There are several senators with the name Volumnius at the end of the second and in the first centuries:

1. C. Volumnius C.f. Men., senator in 129 (mentioned in *s.c. de agro Pergameno*: *MRR* 2.498).
2. L. Volumnius L.f. Ani., member of the *consilium* of Cn. Pompeius Strabo (N. Criniti, *L'epigrafe di Asculum di Gn. Pompeio Strabone* [Milan, 1970] 113).
3. L. Volumnius, friend and correspondent of Cicero in 51-50 (*fam.* 7.32.1; cf. Varro *RR* 2.4.11); it is conjectural whether he was a descendant of the consul of 307 (Badian, *Historia* 12 [1963] 142, says he was not).
4. L. Vol. L.f. Strabo, *monetalis* c. 81 (Wiseman, *New Men*, p. 283; perhaps a Volumnius, according to Badian, loc. cit.).
5. C. or T. Volumnius, friend of M. Terentius Varro Lucullus, killed after Philippi in 42 (Val. Max. 4.7.4: *ortus equestri loco*, implying that he had risen to senatorial status; cf. Nicolet and Demougin, art. cit. 259).

There is also a P. Volumnius recorded as a jury-man at the trial of Cluentius in 66 (Cic. *Cluent.* 198), but after the *lex Aurelia* of 70 jury

290   Commentary

service did not imply senatorial status; however, he may be identifiable with the minor pontiff of Macrob. 3.13.11 (Taylor, *AJP* 63 [1942] 388-9). There is also mention of a wealthy Roman knight, P. Volumnius Eutrapelus, with whom Cicero corresponded (*fam*. 7.32 and 33, cf. 9.26.1 and 15.8.1, *Phil*. 13.3); he was *praefectus fabrum* for M. Antonius (Nep. *Att.* 12.4), and on friendly terms with Atticus (ibid. 9.4, 10.2). It is not possible to say whether Catilina's victim came from a minor senatorial family, or from an equestrian background (cf. Nicolet and Demougin, loc. cit.; Gruen, *Last Generation*, p. 195 n. 124).

84.6: *L. Tanusium*

For the emendation of the mss. reading *Tantasium*, see above on 84.5. *Comm. pet.* 9 says this man was an eques (cf. 89.20). Nicolet and Demougin, art. cit. 260, suggest he can be perhaps connected with two persons:

1. L. Tanusius, the historian cited by Plutarch, Seneca, Strabo and Appian. They do not, however, mention that he should be identified with Tanusius Geminus, cited as a source by Suetonius (*Iul.* 9); he must have been alive into the 60's for he was a source for the 'first' Catilinarian conspiracy. Münzer, *RE* 4A (1932) 2231-2, s.v. 'Tanusius' no. 2, would argue that he was a senator because of his detailed knowledge of senate proceedings (cf. Wiseman, *New Men*, p. 264). He cannot have been Catilina's victim (since he was still alive in the 60's), but the victim was perhaps a relative of the historian.
2. There is a Tanusia who was married to T. Vinius; her husband was proscribed in 43, but she saved him with the help of a slave (Dio 47.7.4; Suet. *Aug.* 27.2; App. *BC* 4.187). Perhaps it was her father who was Catilina's victim.

84.7: *M. etiam Mari Gratidiani summe popularis hominis*

For Gratidianus' popularity, cf. the comment of Cicero at 87.17. He gained his popularity during his first praetorship by anticipating a joint-declaration agreed upon by his colleagues in the praetorship and supported by the tribunes and by issuing alone an edict establishing an office to test and eliminate debased coinage which had been issued under a law of M. Livius Drusus in 91 (Cic. *off*. 3.80-81; Plin. *NH* 33.46 and 132, 34.27; Crawford, *RRC*, 2.616).

84.8: *bis praetor fuit*

The date of 87 for Gratidianus' tribunate is based on reasonably secure inferences (*MRR* 2.52 n. 2; cf. B.R. Katz, *L'Antiquité Classique* 44 [1975] 113). The date of his first praetorship is either 86 or 85 (*MRR* 2.59

In Toga Candida

n. 1), with a preference for the latter in view of the likely tribunate in 87. Cic. *off.* 3.81, in explaining his behaviour in his first praetorship, says that he had set his sights on the consulship; on the basis of this and Val. Max. 9.2.1 which says Marius was *praetor* when murdered in 82, Sumner, *Orators*, p. 119, conjectures that Gratidianus had hoped for the consulship of 82, but when this was pre-empted by the illegal election of Marius the younger he received a second praetorship as a consolation prize. However, Firm. Mat. *math.* 1.7.31 calls Gratidianus *praetorius vir* at the time of his death, and this is taken by some to date his second praetorship to 84 or 83 (*MRR* 2.59 n. 1). This period was so irregular that certainty about the dates of the two praetorships is unattainable on the present evidence.

84.8-9: *caput abscisum per urbem sua manu Catilina tulerat*

There seem to be two versions of the death of Gratidianus. The Ciceronian version is that the head of Gratidianus was cut off by Catilina, carried through the city from the Janiculum to the temple of Apollo and delivered to Sulla, full of life and breath (cf. Plut. *Sull.* 32.2). The other version seems to start with Sallust; in it Gratidianus is cruelly tortured before dying, with atrocities to various parts of the body; there is nothing about his head being cut off, and there is no mention of Catilina as the executioner, and the execution is said to have taken place before the tomb of Catulus (Sall. *hist.* 1.44 M; Liv. *per.* 88; Val. Max. 9.2.1; Luc. 2.160-173; Flor. 2.9.26). The two versions were subsequently combined (*comm. pet.* 10; Sen. *de ira* 3.18.1-2; Firm. Mat. *math.* 1.7.31; Oros. 5.21.7-8).

The question should be asked whether Catilina really did murder Gratidianus (cf. E.S. Beesly, *Catilina, Clodius and Tiberius* [London, 1878] pp. 20-2, who answers in the negative). Some arguments, admittedly from silence, can be put forward to support the belief that Catilina did not murder Gratidianus and that Cicero made the story up. First, since Gratidianus was a relative of Cicero, he could hardly have thought of collaborating with Catilina in 65 with an eye to securing him as a running-mate at the consular elections the next year, if Catilina had murdered a relative of his. Second, Cicero never mentions the story again (except for the oblique references at *Att.* 1.16.9 and *Pis.* 95 to the two unjust acquittals of Catilina), not even in the *First Catilinarian*, when he was scratching around for evidence of Catilina's criminal nature. The only speech in which Cicero made the claim was the *in toga candida*: as a candidate for the consulship Cicero followed the sort of advice given in *comm. pet.* 52 (even if he did not actually receive that document) to rake up as much prejudice as possible against his two main rival candidates, Catilina and Antonius. He knew at the time that a prosecution was being prepared against Catilina for murders carried out during the Sullan

292 *Commentary*

proscriptions; the case was actually heard a few months after the delivery of the *in toga candida*. The prosecutor was L. Lucceius, and he conducted a malicious case, raking up all sorts of scandal. Perhaps Cicero borrowed some of the details from the impending prosecution as they suited the purpose of his speech; it is not inconceivable that Cicero and Lucceius, who were personal acquaintances, collaborated to fabricate the story. Third, it is significant to note that it is only in the Ciceronian version that Catilina is made the executioner of Gratidianus; there is no mention of his role in the Sallustian version (yet Sallust would have had no desire to whitewash Catilina).

Another question to be asked is whether Catilina was related to Gratidianus. In a comment on Luc. 2.173, the Berne Scholiast says that Catilina was married to Gratidianus' sister at the time of his murder. *Comm. pet.* 9 says that Catilina murdered with his own hands the husband of his sister and gives his name as Q. Caecilius (cf. above on 84.6), and Plutarch (*Sull.* 32.2, *Cic.* 10.2) says that he killed his ἀδελφός, persuaded Sulla to put his name on the proscription list to justify the murder retrospectively, and in return for the favour killed Gratidianus. In both of these accounts, the murder of the relative is a separate act and they go on to list the death of Gratidianus as another atrocity committed by Catilina. It would appear that the Berne Scholiast has confused the two separate executions by Catilina and run them together, making Catilina a relative of Gratidianus. It seems preferable to accept that Catilina had only two wives (see below on 91.28), and that a Gratidia was not one of them.

84.10-11: *Gratidianus arta necessitudine Ciceroni coniunctus*

The leading families of Cicero's native town, Arpinum, were the Tullii and the Gratidii, with whom the Marii were intermarried. C. Marius' sister, Maria, was married to M. Gratidius, whose sister married M. Tullius Cicero, grandfather of Cicero. The son of the first marriage was adopted by his uncle (the brother of the great general, M. Marius) and became known as M. Marius Gratidianus. For further details and stemma, see T.F. Carney, *A Biography of C. Marius* (Proceedings of the African Classical Associations, Supplement No. 1, 1961) pp. 8-9 and 77. Cicero's grandfather had persistently opposed the introduction of the secret ballot in Arpinum, a move which was being promoted by his brother-in-law, M. Gratidius (Cic. *leg.* 3.36; I. Shatzman, *Ancient Society* 5 [1974] 216-7 [wrongly saying it was Cicero's father]); note that the move was being made at about the same time as Marius' law in regard to the ballot, passed in his tribunate in 119 (Carney, loc. cit.). On Cicero's connection with Gratidianus, and the concept of *necessitudo* in general, see R.J. Rowland, *Class. Journ.* 65 (1969) 193-8; note that a M. Gratidius served as a legate under Cicero's brother when he was governor of Asia (Cic. *Q.f.* 1.1.10, *Flacc.* 49).

In Toga Candida 293

84.13-14: *spoliaverat nactus de exercitu Sullano equitum turmas*

Asconius is our only source for the information that Antonius carried out depredations while prefect of cavalry in Greece; the date would be 84 or earlier (*MRR* 2.61-2), since he was serving under Sulla. Gelzer, *Caesar: Politician and Statesman*, 6th edn., trans. P. Needham (Oxford, 1968) p. 23, says he was a *legatus*.

84.14-15: *eduxerunt Antonium in ius ad M. Lucullum praetorem*

M. Terentius Varro Lucullus was *praetor peregrinus* in 76, and the case of Antonius' depredations was heard before him (cf. *comm. pet.* 8; Plut. *Caes.* 4.1). There was considerable delay between the offence and the trial, but such delays were not unknown (e.g. M. Iunius Silanus was tried in 104 on a charge of *perduellio* for defeats sustained in Gaul as proconsul five years earlier: see above on 80.20-21). Plutarch's version gives Antonius the *praenomen* Publius and has Lucullus as praetor of Macedonia (Μακεδονίας στρατηγός — probably a confusion with his later command following his consulship in 73). If Lucullus was *praetor peregrinus*, as Asconius says, this must have been a civil case, or else 'Lucullus (exceptionally) acted as *praetor repetundarum*' (Gelzer, op. cit. p. 23); that it was only a civil case seems indicated by the fact that it involved litigation by one Greek (Cic. in Ascon. 84.2; *comm. pet.* 9), whereas *repetundae* cases usually involved complaints by a number of provincials. W. W. Buckland, *JRS* 27 (1937) 43, argues on the other hand that it was not a civil case, since it was heard before the praetor (whereas civil suits went before a *iudex* or *arbiter*, or often, where *peregrini* were concerned, before *recuperatores*); he thinks that Lucullus had accepted the *nomen* for a *quaestio* when the tribunes intervened.

84.16: *[C. Caesar]*

On the basis of Plut. *Caes* 4.1, Caesar's name is usually added here following the suggestion of Manutius. An additional argument is Asconius' comment *de quo paulo ante mentionem fecimus*, referring presumably to 83.4 and/or 83.18.

84.19: *appellavit tribunos*

'A party who felt himself to be unfairly treated used to appeal at once . . . to a tribune of the people (or to the whole college of tribunes); and intercession was granted after an investigation of the facts in the course of which the jurisdictional magistrate also had an opportunity of setting forth the grounds for his decision. It only had the effect of quashing the decree: the decree became void, but no one could compel the magistrate to set a new one in its place. This could only be accomplished by trying one's luck with another competent magistrate; in particular, on

294 Commentary

the expiry of the official year, with the successor of the magistrate who had been unsuccessfully approached' (W. Kunkel, *An Introduction to Roman Legal and Constitutional History*, 2nd edn., trans. J.M. Kelly [Oxford, 1973] p. 91).

84.20: *aequo iure uti non posset*

Cf. the lemma of Cicero (*in sua civitate cum peregrino negavit se iudicio aequo certare posse*), and *comm. pet.* 8 (*se Romae iudicio aequo cum homine Graeco certare non posse*). Plut. *Caes.* 4.1, because he says that the case took place in Greece, infers that Antonius' claim was that he could not have a fair trial in Greece against Greeks.

84.20-21: *Gellius et Lentulus censores sexennio*

L. Gellius Publicola and Cn. Cornelius Lentulus Clodianus were censors in 70, and removed in all sixty-four senators (references in *MRR* 2.126-7). Under the *lex Atinia* which made tribunes members of the senate (Gell. 14.8.2; G. Rotondi, *Leges publicae populi romani* [Milan, 1912] pp. 330-1; R. Develin, *CQ* 28 [1978] 141-4), Antonius may have regained senatorial status by holding a tribunate in 68 (depending on the date of the *lex Antonia de Termessibus*: Taylor, *Class. Phil.* 36 [1941] 121; *MRR* 2.141 n. 8).

84.24-25: *bonaque sua in potestate non habeat*

As a third reason for their expulsion of Antonius, the censors had noted that he was virtually bankrupt through debt. This may mean that he did not have the property qualification for membership of the senate, though it is not clear whether there was a formal minimum census for senators under the republic; Augustus made it one million (or 1,200,000) HS, but here he may have been institutionalising rather than innovating (cf. Nicolet, *JRS* 66 [1976] 27). Cf. Cicero's statement at 87.26-27: by 64 Antonius' lands had been partly awarded to creditors by the civil process of *saltum addictio*. Henderson, *JRS* 40 (1950) 10-1, has argued that *comm. pet.* 8 has misunderstood this process to be *proscriptio bonorum* (which virtually amounts to death or exile), confusing it with the known exile following his condemnation at a trial for misgovernment in 59, and therefore that the *comm. pet.* is a later forgery; the argument is refuted by Balsdon, *CQ* n.s. 13 (1963) 247, who shows that *proscriptio bonorum* could mean an enforced sale of property (e.g. Cic. *Quinct.* 56, *Flacc.* 74; cf. above on 54.20-21).

85.4-5: *legati Afri . . . questi sunt*

Cf. 89.7-8.

In Toga Candida 295

85.11-12: *accusatus est repetundarum*

Asconius clearly dates the prosecution to 65 (in the year before this speech was delivered and in the consulship of L. Manlius Torquatus and L. Aurelius Cotta). That date is confirmed by Cic. *Att.* 1.1.1 (written shortly before 17th July 65 and mentioning that Catilina's trial is still to come up) and 1.2.1 (written shortly after the preceding letter and mentioning that Cicero was thinking of defending Catilina), and *Cael.* 10 (which dates the trial to the year after Cicero's praetorship in 66). Elsewhere Asconius contradicts this dating: at 89.11 (*quaerebatur repetundarum*) he gives as the reason for L. Volcacius Tullus' rejection of Catilina's candidature at the consular elections in 66 the fact that Catilina was under a charge of extortion (unless the phrase should be taken to mean that he was merely under threat of a prosecution because of the complaints made by the African envoys and that he had not yet been formally charged), and at 66.8-9 (*illo tempore erat reus repetundarum*) Asconius says that at the time of the disturbance to Manilius' trial (i.e. the end of 66) he was actually a defendant on a charge of extortion. Cf. Sall. *Cat.* 18.3 who says that Catilina was prevented from standing at the consular elections in 66 because he was *pecuniarum repetundarum reus*. That the initial indictment had come in 66 is accepted, e.g., by Gruen, *Last Generation*, p. 271; that it was merely threatened in 66 is proposed, e.g., by D.L. Stockton, *Cicero: a Political Biography* (Oxford, 1971) p. 74; cf. Sumner, *Phoenix* 19 (1965) 228. Tyrrell's solution was to postulate two trials to fit the evidence — one for extortion in 66 immediately after Catilina's return from Africa (which was used as the reason for the rejection of his candidature) and another in 65 on a charge of misappropriating public money (*The Correspondence of Cicero*, 2nd edn. [London, 1885] 1.147). This runs counter to Cicero's later statements (*Att.* 1.16.9, *Pis.* 95) that Catilina was acquitted twice (i.e. at the extortion trial in 65 and at the trial *inter sicarios* in 64). It seems preferable to accept the evidence of Cicero for one trial, instituted by Clodius for extortion in 65. If the charge had not been formally laid in 66, that has repercussions for the question of the rejection of Catilina's candidature at the consular elections in that year: see below on 89.11-12.

85.12: *a P. Clodio adulescente*

For Clodius' part in the trial and the extent of his collusion, see above on 9.14-15, and cf. below, 87.13-15 and 92.8-10. For the voting of the jurors in the trial, see 89.18-19. Gruen, *Last Generation*, p. 271, repeating the view put forward in *Athenaeum* 49 (1971) 59-62, argues that collusion by Clodius is an unnecessary hypothesis: in 73 Clodius had initiated his public career by launching a prosecution of the Vestal Fabia for *incestum*, and Catilina was implicated in this charge, and hence Gruen argues that the prosecution of Catilina for extortion in 65 was part of a continuing

296   Commentary

inimicitia between Clodius and him, and that Clodius is therefore not likely to have been collusive in that trial. But that argument ignores the point that collaboration about *reiectio iudicum* (Cic. *Att.* 1.2.1; Ascon. 87.14) was very important.

85.13: *ut Fenestella tradit*

On Asconius' use of Fenestella as a source, and in particular on his disagreements with him, see Part I, pp. 53-5.

85.16ff.

The burden of Asconius' argument on this and the next two pages against the statement of Fenestella that Cicero defended Catilina is three-fold:

1. Cicero makes no mention of the fact in the speech *in toga candida*, nor does Asconius know of the existence of any speech of Cicero on Catilina's behalf, though *commentarii* or *principia* of Cicero's speeches existed (87.10-12).
2. One would have expected Cicero to mention this *beneficium* to Catilina (if it existed), since it would have helped to create ill-feeling towards a competitor because of his ingratitude, and since Cicero mentions *beneficia* in the case of two other opponents (Antonius and Orestinus).
3. If he had defended Catilina, he would not have mentioned the trial so disparagingly so often, nor would he have been so critical of Catilina.

All of this is acceptable, but Fenestella could have been answered so simply by reference to Cicero's letters. That raises the whole question whether there was a collection of letters available in Asconius' time and whether he consulted them (see Part I, pp. 47-50). The conclusion must be that Asconius' silence can prove nothing about the publication date; a collection of letters existed, but for some puzzling reason (known only to himself) Asconius did not refer to them. Perhaps he relied on getting his information at second hand from sources such as Tiro's biography (though elsewhere he consults primary material, like the *acta diurna*) or perhaps, as he admits on other occasions, his research had not been completed. Before being too critical of Asconius for not consulting the letters (presuming they were available in some form), one should realise the difficulty of checking references in ancient *volumina* and the problems involved in consulting a work if one did not have a copy of it oneself (the latter would be a particular problem for Asconius if the letters had not yet been published but existed only in various collections).

85.19-20: *eum ex ultimo loco praeturae candidatum ad tertium pervenisse*

'An already elected candidate [i.e. one who had already secured ½ + 1 of the available votes] was in a strong position to ensure that votes which would otherwise be cast for him were cast for a political associate instead' (Staveley, *Voting and Elections*, p. 184). This is how Staveley interprets the lemma of Cicero on which Asconius is commenting; a similar view is held by Hall, *Historia* 13 (1964) 288-90 and 296, in her comments on the passage, but she says there are other possible interpretations. The *collatio centurianum* in the next lemma of Cicero suggests that not just the man with ½ + 1 of the votes but all the candidates remaining would engage in some dealing.

85.28: *Q. enim Mucius tr. pl. intercedebat*

See above on 83.9. Asconius comments (86.1) that Orestinus seems to have been acting on Catilina's behalf, and that would suggest his alignment with the cause of Catilina and Antonius. The bribery proposal must eventually have been shelved, as the *lex Calpurnia* continued to be the operative law on bribery till replaced by the *lex Tullia* of the next year.

86.4-5: *hesterno die me esse dignum consulatu negabas*

In interposing his veto on a bribery proposal, Orestinus delivered a verbal assault on Cicero, and Cicero's speech *in toga candida* in reply was a denunciation of Catilina and Antonius (see above on 83.4). Part of Orestinus' attack was to claim that Cicero was unworthy of the highest office; Catilina and Antonius replied to Cicero's speech by attacking his newness (93.24-94.1). Cf. Catilina's jibe in 63, *inquilinus civis* (Sall. *Cat.* 31.7, cf. 23.5-6 and 35.3; App. *BC* 2.2; cf. Cic. *Sull.* 22), and C. Calpurnius Piso's comments on the unsuitability of M. Lollius Palicanus for the consulship when rejecting his candidature in 67 (Val. Max. 3.8.3). For further comments on the attitude towards unworthy candidates for high office, see Wiseman, *New Men*, pp. 103-4.

86.17: *de causa Muci*

As the lemma shows, Orestinus was indicted on a charge of theft by L. Calenus, and he had secured the assistance of Cicero as his defence counsel. Asconius is our only evidence for this trial; no date is known, but it cannot have been later than 65, since Orestinus was tribune in 64 and Cicero remarks on the ingratitude shown by him in that year for the earlier assistance. Proceedings came to an end when Orestinus made an agreement with the prosecutor (86.12-13). Gruen, *Last Generation*, p. 529, suggests that the prosecutor was presumably a Fufius Calenus, related to the tribune of 61 and praetor of 59 (see above on 44.21), and perhaps to be identified with the L. Calenus who testified against Verres (Cic. *Verr.* 2.2.23; Wiseman, *New Men*, p. 232).

86.23: *stupris se omnibus ac flagitiis contaminavit*

Cf. above on 83.1; Sall. *Cat.* 14-16; and *comm. pet.* 9-10.

86.24-25: *leges quaestiones iudicia violavit*

On Catilina's disturbance of the courts, see above on 66.2ff. Cicero was personally involved, since Manilius, whose trial was disturbed, first appeared before him as praetor at the end of 66.

87.1-2: *equites Romanos*

Cicero here lumps the two *ordines* of equites and *tribuni aerarii* together; they had apparently voted for Catilina's acquittal, while the senators had voted for condemnation (see below on 89.18-19). For a similar use of *equites Romani* for both equites and *tribuni aerarii* on jury-panels, see *Cluent.* 121, *Font.* 36, *Flacc.* 4, *Rab. Post.* 14; elsewhere Cicero mentions the three orders (*Att.* 1.16.3, *Q.f.* 2.4.6, 15.3). Cf. above on 17.6-7 and 67.11-12.

87.3: *Q. Metellum Pium*

It is likely that Metellus Pius had played a leading part in the senatorial discussion of Catilina's activities as governor of Africa and subsequent censure (following complaints by the provincials: 85.3-6, 89.7-8), and in promoting the prosecution of Catilina, hence Cicero singles him out for comment here. The Metellan family had connections with Africa: Metellus Pius' father had the command against Jugurtha and acquired the *cognomen* Numidicus, and Metellus Pius withdrew to Africa during the *Cinnanum tempus*, emerging to join Sulla in 83 (details of his position in Africa in Badian, *Studies*, pp. 221, 224 and 229).

87.11: *commentarii Ciceronis causarum*

Orators' *commentarii* could be either prepared notes for a speech (Cic. *Brut.* 164, 301; Sen. *contr.* 3 pr. 6) or the outline of a speech written up after delivery with a view to publication (it is clear that many *commentarii* were published: Quint. 3.8.48 and 67, 4.1.69); they could range from very elaborate, almost word-for-word preparation to just a bare outline (Sen. loc. cit.). Tiro collected and edited Cicero's *commentarii*, indeed condensed them, according to Quint. 10.7.30-31 (which suggests they were full notes). Further on *commentarii*, see von Premerstein, *RE* 4 (1901) 727.

87.12: *principium*

Quint. 4.1.1 says that the *principium* is the same as the *exordium*, though later (§ 42) he divides the *exordium* into *principium* (designed to secure good-will and attention) and *insinuatio* (used especially where the case is not strong; cf. Cic. *inv.* 1.20). Cf. Cic. *de or.* 1.121, and Juv. *sat.* 6.245. Asconius' comment suggests that Cicero's introductions were collected and published.

87.14: *praevaricatus*

See above on 9.15 for the extent of Clodius' collusion.

87.14: *reiectio iudicum*

It is noteworthy that Asconius makes no reference to Cic. *Att.* 1.2.1, where Cicero says that part of his reason for thinking of defending Catilina at the extortion trial in 65 was that *iudices habemus quos volumus, summa accusatoris voluntate*. That is relevant to the question whether Asconius had access to Cicero's letters. Cicero must have withdrawn from the defence at the last minute, since the rejection of the jurors had taken place (as the present tense of the verb shows and as the first person is used: SB *Att.* 1.67). In the courts following the Sullan reorganisation, each side had the right of rejecting a limited number of jurors: according to Cicero, non-senators could reject only three, and while it is not stated how many senators could reject, Verres is known to have turned down six (*Verr.* 2.2.77). After the *lex Aurelia* of 70, when the juries were larger, it is likely that provision was made for a larger number of rejections (Jones, *Criminal Courts*, p. 69).

87.19: *paulo ante*

For the murder of Gratidianus, see above on 84.8-9.

87.25: *manifestum est C. Verrem significari*

It is not clear to us that C. Verres is being referred to from the lemma quoted by Asconius. Perhaps in the last sentence there is reference to Cicero's defence of the injuries done to the Sicilians in his prosecution of Verres, but the first sentence would make more sense if it were a reference to Catilina rather than to any insults from Verres in an incident that took place six years earlier. The lemma does occur in the context of bitter criticism of his rival candidate Catilina, and the latter is known to have hurled insults at Cicero (cf. the jibe *inquilinus civis* recorded in Sall. *Cat.* 31.7, and the insults of Orestinus referred to at 86.3-5). Still it must be conceded that Asconius had the whole of the speech in front of him, and the lemma could have occurred in the context of a reference to C. Verres.

87.27: *pastores*

Presumably slave-herdsmen: the growth of *latifundia*, especially in the south of Italy (see Brunt, *Italian Manpower*, ch. XX passim, though he stresses that the large holdings were not solely devoted to grazing but were given over to other produce as well), where the land was more suited to grazing, had only been possible because of the availability of large numbers of slaves. Maltreatment of the slave-herdsmen had been the occasion for a number of outbreaks of violence: one rebellion in 185 had been quickly suppressed (Liv. 39.29), and the majority of the slaves in Spartacus' rebellion were herdsmen (Plut. *Crass.* 9.3; App. *BC* 1.116). On this point see Brunt, op. cit. pp. 551-2; G.P. Verbrugghe, *Historia* 24 (1975) 198-9. For other examples of the attempt to use herdsmen for violent activities, cf. Caes. *BC* 1.24.2, 3.21.4 (Milo, on instructions from Caelius in 48, attempted to recruit herdsmen from the district of Thurii for the civil war). Part of the reason for their usefulness in such activities was that they needed to be armed already to protect their flocks against animals and brigands.

87.29: *C. Antonium*

It must at least have been plausible that Antonius was in a position to do what Cicero alleged, but it does seem hard to believe that Antonius intended, still more avowed openly, to raise a *bellum fugitivorum*.

88.5: *Q. Gallium, quem postea reum ambitus defendit*

The trial of Q. Gallius on a charge brought by M. Calidius (see above on 20.17) provides the basis for a major argument for or against the authenticity of the *comm. pet.* Asconius clearly dates Cicero's defence of Gallius, praetor in 65 (see above, 62.5), after the delivery of the *in toga candida* (unless the *postea* expresses a relationship to the sale of the troop of gladiators: cf. Henderson, *JRS* 40 [1950] 11), whereas *comm. pet.* 19 suggests that he had already undertaken the defence of Gallius (*nam hoc biennio* [66-64 presumably] *quattuor sodalitates hominum ad ambitionem gratiosissimorum tibi obligasti, C. Fundani, Q. Galli, C. Corneli, C. Orchivi: horum in causis ad te deferendis quid tibi eorum sodales receperint et confirmarint scio*). Henderson, loc. cit., argues that there are two pieces of information in Asconius here: (a) the identification of the person referred to in the lemma, and (b) the date of the trial of Gallius. She says that (a) is wrong, that Cicero must have been referring to another, but that Asconius was speaking cautiously enough about that. A further argument is that, if we accept the date of the *comm. pet.* for the trial and Asconius' identification, we would have to suppose that Cicero was here denouncing Gallius for the very crime on which he had just defended him. But because (a) is wrong, it does not follow that (b) is wrong: Henderson argues that it is highly unlikely that Asconius would get the date of a speech wrong, for he is careful in dating them (see 1.1-2, 18.1-4, 30.1-2, 57.1-2, 82.1-2; cf. Gell. 15.28.4 for his correction of Fenestella's mistaken date for the *pro Sex. Roscio*). So, Henderson concludes, the author of the *comm. pet.* has made a slip, and this belies the authenticity of the document. Her argument perhaps accepts too much accuracy on the part of Asconius; it is one thing to date a speech on which he is commenting in the opening lines (as is the case with the datings listed above), and he presumably found these dates in the *commentarii* of the speeches prepared by Tiro which he may have had in front of him when writing his comments, while it is another thing to remember the date of a speech mentioned in passing. There is one way to rescue the authenticity of the *comm. pet.*: the charge of *ambitus* brought against Gallius was presumably connected with his candidature for the praetorship (i.e. the gladiatorial display) which he stood for in 66; he would have been exempt from prosecution during office in 65, but a charge could well have been foreshadowed as early as 66 and Gallius could have negotiated to have Cicero as his defence counsel before the case came on (Balsdon, *CQ* 13 [1963] 248-9, followed now at length by J.T. Ramsey, *Historia* 29 [1980] 402-21). The wording of *comm. pet.* 19 is capable of such an interpretation, so in the end this passage fails to be decisive against the authenticity of the *comm. pet.*

88.7-8: *bestias non habuerat, dedit gladiatorium [munus]*

During his aedileship in 67 (*MRR* 2.144) Gallius had not followed the fairly common practice of putting on games. He made up for this by putting on a gladiatorial display when a candidate for the praetorship in 66; as often, this display was put on in memory of his father (for some examples, see B.A. Marshall and R.J. Baker, *Historia* 24 [1975] 227-8 n. 31, and cf. above on 30.8-9). Later putting on a gladiatorial display in memory of someone, provided it was *ex testamento*, was a way around the *lex Tullia de ambitu* (see above on 31.6-7).

88.15: *legem Calpurniam*

See above on 57.8, 69.11 and 74.22-23.

88.18: *de quibus iam diximus*

See above on 75.7.

88.18-19: *cognomen . . . fuit Orestinus*

According to Münzer, *RE* 16 (1935) 423-4, s.v. 'Mucius' no. 12, the *cognomen* shows that Orestinus was connected with the family of L. Aurelius Orestes (cos. 157), whose son was consul in 103; the name of Catilina's wife, Aurelia Orestilla (Sall. *Cat.* 15.2), connects her with this family (Seager, *Pompey: a Political Biography* [Oxford, 1979] p. 62, makes her the sister of the tribune Orestinus). Hence there may have been a personal connection between Catilina and Orestinus, which re-inforced their political alignment at this time (Stockton, op. cit. p. 120 n. 29; Gruen, *Last Generation*, pp. 183 n. 74 and 218 n. 36; Marshall, *RFIC* 105 [1977] 151-4; cf. above on 83.9).

88.24-25: *praedonem . . . significavimus*

Cf. above on 84.13-14.

88.26: *gladiatorem*

As a Sullan agent, Antonius would have profited from the Sullan proscriptions. For the use of *gladiator* in this derogatory way, see below on 93.18.

88.27: *quadrigarium*

Cf. below, 93.5-6, where the comment is also made that certain *nobiles homines* took part in these chariot races.

88.28: *cum Sulla post victoriam circenses faceret*

The *ludi Victoriae Sullanae* were established in 82, to commemorate the victory at the Colline Gate which gave Sulla control of Rome (Vell. Pat. 2.27.6; cf. Cic. *Verr.* 1.31, and Ps.-Ascon. 217.20); the games lasted from 26th October to 1st November, and are mentioned in five sets of fasti (see *CIL* 1^2.1.p.333). Cf. below, 93.4-5. The great feast which Sulla gave later and in which he consecrated a tenth of his property to Hercules (Plut. *Sull.* 35.1) emphasised the military nature of his position; for Sulla's association with the cult of Hercules, see B. Rawson, *Antichthon* 4 (1970) 31.

89.6: *paulo ante diximus*

See above, 85.3ff.

89.7: *petiturus consulatum*

It is not clear whether Catilina tried to stand at the normal elections or at the supplementary election held after the conviction for bribery of the two men successful at the normal elections (P. Cornelius Sulla and P. Autronius Paetus). After describing the conviction and disqualification of these two men, Sallust goes on to say (*Cat.* 18.2-3) that 'a little later' (*post paulo*) Catilina was prevented from standing; this could be taken to mean that he put himself forward at the supplementary election (so A. Garzetti, *Athenaeum* 20 [1942] 24-5; Sumner, *Phoenix* 19 [1965] 226). On the

In Toga Candida 303

basis of Sallust's further point, that Catilina was prevented from standing because he had not made his *professio* within the required period (*intra legitumos dies*), Stockton, op. cit. p. 74 n. 19, accepts that Catilina was a candidate at the supplementary election and suggests that a nice legal point was involved, on which the presiding magistrate took advice: 'not having given due notice of candidature for the first election Catilina could not now be admitted to the second.' Mello's argument (*PP* 18 [1963] 37-9) that the phrase used by Cicero and Asconius (*professus petere consulatum*) indicates candidature at a normal election is a little thin; the procedure at both elections would presumably have been the same.

89.10: *consilium publicum*

In addition to the rejection of Catilina's candidature, there had recently been another case of rejection, when C. Calpurnius Piso (cos. 67) had rejected M. Lollius Palicanus' candidature at the consular elections of the previous year (Val. Max. 3.8.3; cf. Cic. *Att.* 1.1.1). In both cases, party political reasons can be suspected: Piso was a vehement *inimicus* of Pompeius (see above on 58.18), while Palicanus as tribune in 71 had strongly supported Pompeius' platform for his consulship in 70, and so it appears that Piso was trying to prevent a Pompeian candidate from standing. Catilina was suspected of having been put up by Crassus, and there were some leading senators who would not like to have seen Crassus' candidate successful, thus securing a favourable consul in the year he would be censor. There are some who suggest that Catilina had Pompeian leanings, based on his co-operation with Pompeian supporters like Manilius (e.g. Seager, *Historia* 13 [1964] 344-5; Phillips, *Rhein. Mus.* 116 [1973] 355-6; contra, Gruen, *Class. Phil.* 64 [1969] 23-4). That in turn might suggest that part at least of Volcacius Tullus' *consilium* was made up of the same group of optimate senators who supported the prosecution of Cornelius; cf. Cicero's description of them as *principes civitatis* (above, 89.3, cf. 60.19 and 61.20). Note that one of the group was Q. Caecilius Metellus Pius, and he had taken a leading part in the complaints made about Catilina's governorship of Africa (above, 87.3); note, however, that another member of that group was Q. Catulus, and he was known as a friend and patron of Catilina (Sall. *Cat.* 35.1ff.). There is also the consideration that the situation in 66 broke new ground: two consuls-elect had just been unseated for bribery, and a new candidate had put himself forward at the supplementary election. This unique situation alone may explain why Volcacius Tullus sought the advice of a *consilium*. On the consul's *consilium*, see Mommsen, *Staatsrecht*, 1^3.311, and J.A. Crook, *Consilium Principis* (Cambridge, 1955) pp. 6-7.

89.11-12: *nam quaerebatur repetundarum*

The usual reason for the rejection of Catilina's candidature by Volcacius

Tullus, given by both Asconius and Sallust, is that he was facing a charge of extortion; Sallust gives the additional reason that he had not made his *professio* within the required period. It is not clear whether Catilina had been formally charged at the time of the elections: see above on 85. 11-12. A person under a charge (or under threat of a charge) was not legally barred from candidature; if Catilina were so barred, Volcacius Tullus would not have found it necessary to consult his *consilium* before rejecting his candidature, for the legal situation would have been perfectly clear. It is better to assume that Catilina had not been formally charged at the time of the elections in 66, and in that case it is easy to see why special action on the part of the consul was necessary to reject his candidature: Volcacius Tullus, the consul presiding over the elections, simply exercised his prerogative of not accepting Catilina's *professio*, the quite legitimate exercise of consular *imperium* (D.C. Earl, *Historia* 14 [1965] 331; cf. Staveley, *Voting and Elections*, p. 210 with n. 408). Cicero stresses in the lemma on which Asconius is commenting that Volcacius Tullus used his prerogative as electoral officer to reject Catilina's candidature after seeking advice. In the consultations mention was no doubt made of Catilina's activities in his governorship and the possibility of an impeachment, and these were probably put forward as the 'official' reasons for the decision not to accept his candidature (obviously the party political reasons, if there were any, could not be stressed), and that may explain how involvement in a trial came to be part of the account of the reasons for the rejection of his candidature.

Sallust's additional reason that Catilina had not made his *professio* within the legal period needs closer examination. There would seem to be reasonable agreement that at this time *professio* was obligatory and that it had to be made within a specified period (Earl, art. cit. 329-30; Staveley, op. cit. pp. 146-8), but that it was not required in person until 63 (while presence at the actual election had been required since the second century; contra, Balsdon, *JRS* 52 [1962] 140-1, and A.E. Astin, *Historia* 11 [1962] 252-5). Now, Asconius seems to be talking about Catilina's presentation of himself as a candidate to the presiding magistrate and Volcacius Tullus' consideration as if procedure was being followed in the normal way, assuming that the procedure for nomination was the same, whether Catilina was standing at the ordinary elections in 66 or at the supplementary ones (note that in 51 Caelius was allowed to nominate at a supplementary tribunician election, though he had not nominated for the original election: see Cael. in Cic. *fam.* 8.4.2, and cf. above on 89.7). If normal procedure was being followed, Sallust's phrase *intra legitumos dies* makes no sense, for Asconius' account suggests that Catilina observed all the procedures for making a *professio*. It is true that a man could persist with candidature though his nomination had not been accepted, or that a man who was legally disqualified from standing or who had not even been nominated could in fact receive a majority of votes in an

In Toga Candida 305

election, but it is also true that the presiding magistrate, by virtue of his *imperium*, could declare that he would not return a candidate after he had expressed an intention to stand or that he would refuse to put a candidate's name to the vote or that he would take no notice of votes cast in favour of a particular person when announcing the results of an election (Earl, art. cit. 329-30 and 331 n. 28; Staveley, op. cit. pp. 148 with n. 266 and 210). In view of the presiding magistrate's powers and the requirements of *professio* mentioned above, there would have been little point in Catilina's nominating as a candidate outside the required period, for he would have realised that he would have had no chance of success. Hence Asconius' account suggesting that he made his *professio* in the proper way seems preferable, and Sallust's additional reason should be rejected; it was perhaps inserted by the author in view of later laws connected with electoral procedure, such as the *lex Pompeia* of 52 and Caesar's candidature for a second consulship *in absentia* (matters which would have been more strikingly familiar to Sallust as a politician active in that later period).

89.18-19: *senatorum urna damnaret, equitum et tribunorum absolveret*

Asconius mentions only two *urnae*, putting together the equites and *tribuni aerarii* as one group, as Cicero frequently does (see above on 87.1-2). Separate tabulation of the voting by the three orders was not introduced until 59 (see above on 28.25), but here Asconius seems to imply that separate voting was in existence as early as 65; he has been 'guilty of a laxity of expression' (C. Macdonald, *CR* 7 [1957] 198), and has surmised the voting pattern from the internal evidence of the speech. He knew that the senate was hostile to Catilina (85.1-6) and hence inferred that the senatorial jurors voted against Catilina. But the inference is based on what is most likely a misunderstanding by Asconius of the point of Cicero's reference in the lemma; Cicero is probably referring to the senate's reaction to the complaints laid by the African envoys, not to senatorial votes at Catilina's trial. Having misunderstood, Asconius assumes an attitude on the part of the non-senatorial voters, and expresses the verdict in language appropriate to the separate voting of later trials. It cannot be argued that at Catilina's trial the voting was open and so it could have been known how the various *ordines* voted. Under the *lex Cornelia* of Sulla the defendant, or perhaps either party, could request that the voting be open, and the order of voting was determined by lot (Cic. *Cluent.* 55 and 75), but Cicero speaks of this as no longer being the rule in 66, and it had presumably been abolished by the *lex Aurelia* of 70 (Jones, *Criminal Courts*, p. 73).

89.21: *equester ordo pro Cinnanis partibus contra Sullam*

It is too glib to say that the equites in general supported the Cinnan régime,

306   *Commentary*

but it is true to say that Marius and his supporters had wide equestrian connections (witness the special courts and the struggle over the control of the courts in the last decade of the second century); how else, too, are we to explain the vengeance exacted by Sulla after his victory in the civil war? For the attitude, cf. Cicero's description of the Cinnan period as *equester splendor* (*Rosc. Amer.* 140) and his view of Sulla's attitude to the equestrian order (e.g. *Cluent.* 151: ... *pro illo odio, quod habuit in equestrem ordinem,* ...), and see Badian, *Publicans and Sinners* (Oxford, 1972) p. 94, and R.T. Ridley, *Wein. Stud.* n.f. 9 (1975) 88-90.

89.24: *erant interfecti*

According to App. *BC* 1.95, 1600 equites were put on the proscription list (compared with forty senators initially, and the addition of other senators later); Flor. 2.9.25 says that a total of 2000 men from the senate and the equestrian order were proscribed.

90.1: *Mari Gratidiani*

On the murder of Gratidianus, see above on 84.8-9.

90.7: *aedes Apollinis in Palatio*

For the references to the building of this temple, see Lugli, *Fontes ad topographiam veteris urbis Romae pertinentes* (Rome, 1962) Vol. 8, liber XIX, pp. 57ff., and Platner-Ashby, pp. 16-9. It was built on ground that had been struck by lightning and for that reason vowed as public property by Octavianus in 36 B.C. during his campaign against Sex. Pompeius (Dio 49.15.5); it was dedicated in 28 B.C. (and so not as many years after Cicero's death as Asconius' *multis annis* [90.9] would imply). Its festival date was 9th October (*CIL* 1^2.1.p. 331), and it was dedicated to celebrate the naval victory at Actium (cf. below, 90.10-11), which was credited to the intervention of Apollo (Verg. *Aen.* 8.704-706); hence among the epithets of the god worshipped here are *navalis* (Prop. 4.1.3) and *Actius* or *Actiacus* (ibid. 4.6.67; Ov. *Met.* 13.715). For Octavianus' regard for the god Apollo as his protector, see Taylor, *The Divinity of the Roman Emperor* (Middletown, 1931) pp. 118-20 and 139-40. There is dispute over the specific site of the temple: see, e.g., O.L. Richmond, *JRS* 4 (1914) 193-266, *CQ* 8 (1958) 180-4; contra, J.H. Bishop, *CQ* 6 (1956) 187-92, 11 (1961) 127-8.

90.11: *illam*

The only temple of Apollo in existence at the time of Gratidianus' murder was this one outside the porta Carmentalis (cf. Liv. 27.37.11) on the site of the later theatre of Marcellus. It is elsewhere described as *in pratis Flaminiis* (Liv. 3.63.7), near the theatre of Marcellus (Aug. *RG* 21.2), and near the Capitol (Dio frag. 50.1). It had been vowed in 433 because of a plague which had raged in Rome, and was dedicated in 431 by the consul Cn. Iulius (Liv. 4.25.3, 29.7). In his version of the death of Gratidianus, Plut. *Sull.* 32.2 has Catilina deliver the head to Sulla, who was sitting in the forum, and wash his hands in the holy water of the temple of Apollo nearby. For further details of this temple, see Platner-Ashby, pp. 15-6.

90.25: *L. Luscius*

All that we know of this man is what is found in Asconius here: he was a former centurion of Sulla who became a rich man as a consequence of his Sullan activities. The reference at Dio 37.10.2 to a man (unnamed) who was condemned *inter sicarios* by the court set up in 64 is usually taken to be to Luscius. Asconius says there were three victims, Dio many; that probably means that only three murders were included in the formal indictment, but that others were mentioned by the prosecutors. If we can believe Sallust's comment that *gregarii milites* were added to the senate by Sulla (*Cat.* 37.6), it is possible that this man, with his military rank and wealth (many times the equestrian census), was admitted to the senate. On the sort of men added to the senate by Sulla, see R. Syme, *PBSR* 14 (1938) 22ff.; E. Gabba, *Athenaeum* 29 (1951) 262ff.; J.R. Hawthorn, *G. & R.* 9 (1962) 53-60.

91.1-2: *L. quoque Bellienus*

Again we are mainly indebted to Asconius for information on this man, that he was the uncle of Catilina, that he was the executioner of Lucretius Ofella (Dio 37.10.2 and Plut. *Sull.* 33.4 do not name the latter's executioner), and that he was condemned by the same court as L. Luscius.

91.2: *damnatus erat*

The court by which these men were condemned was specially set up in 64 to investigate murders during the Sullan proscriptions; it is generally believed that Caesar served as *iudex quaestionis* for these trials (Suet. *Iul.* 11.1; Gelzer, *Caesar*, p. 42 n. 7). Ex-aediles, as Caesar was in 64, were often chosen as *quaesitores*, especially when there was a shortage of praetors (Greenidge, *Legal Procedure*, p. 432; Jones *Criminal Courts*, pp. 58-9); for a list of known ex-aediles who served as court-presidents, see ibid. p. 128 nn. 86-87. Gruen, *Last Generation*, pp. 76-7 n. 124, and Seager, *Historia* 13 (1964) 347 n. 43, argue that Caesar was merely prosecutor in some of the trials heard by this court (on the basis of Cic. *Lig.* 12, Dio 37.10.3, and Schol. Gronov. 293.31-32).

91.3: *Lucretium Ofellam*

Q. Lucretius Ofella, a former Marian (Vell. Pat. 2.27.6), had gone over to

Sulla's side and been put in charge of the siege of Marius the younger in Praeneste (Liv. *per.* 88; Plut. *Sull.* 29.8; App. *BC* 1.88, 93-94). Ofella wished to stand for the consulship, though he was still only of equestrian status and had held none of the minor magistracies, and when he persisted despite Sulla's instruction not to, Sulla had him executed (Liv. *per.* 89; Plut. *Sull.* 33.4; App. *BC* 1.101; Dio 37.10.2). The incident is usually dated to 82 (cf. 91.5: *Sullae tunc dictatoris*). That the *cognomen* should be Afella, see Badian, *JRS* 57 (1967) 227-8.

91.7: *imperatori ac dictatori paruisse*

The *lex Valeria*, proposed by the *interrex* of 82, L. Valerius Flaccus, gave the force of law to all of Sulla's previous acts (Cic. *leg. ag.* 3.5), and the *lex Cornelia de proscriptione*, which formalised the proscriptions, provided that the proscribed might be killed with impunity (Cic. *Rosc. Am.* 125-126). The defendants clearly pleaded not guilty on the grounds of these laws. It is questionable whether prosecutions for the executions were legally admissible, but the *iudex quaestionis* obviously decided that they were. The political climate was favourable: cf. the enquiries into the properties of Faustus Sulla and M. Lucullus in 66 (above on 73.16), and Cato's stringent investigation of bounties paid to Sullan agents during his quaestorship in 64 (Plut. *Cat. Min.* 17.5-7).

91.10: *paucos post menses*

Asconius says that Catilina was not made a *reus* until after he had suffered defeat in the consular elections (91.10-12), and that he underwent the trial on the charge *inter sicarios* a few months after the delivery of the speech. The lemma of Cicero, however, on which Asconius is commenting implies that Catilina had already been charged (unless it is wishful thinking on Cicero's part that Catilina would be hauled up before the court which had recently condemned other Sullan assassins). The lemma before that (90.16-18, especially *potes in defensione tua dicere*) also implies that Catilina was going to have to defend himself and therefore that he had already been charged. It is reasonable to assume that, as the special court *inter sicarios* had already begun hearing cases before the elections (e.g. Luscius and Bellienus), Catilina's case had been put on the list. It would be consistent with the statements of Cicero and the comments of Asconius to suggest that Catilina was charged before the consular elections but that the case was not actually heard until after the elections. It follows from this that a person facing a charge was not necessarily excluded from standing for office; cf. the comments above on 89.11-12 concerning Catilina's candidature in 66. For similar examples of candidates allowed to stand though facing a charge, cf. the case of Scaurus in 54 (above, 19.11f.) and of Clodius in 57 (Cic. *Att.* 4.3.3-5, *Q.f.* 2.1.1-3; Dio 39.7.3-4). For further discussion of the timing of Catilina's trial, see Marshall, *Scripta Classical Israelica* 3 (1976/7) 127-9.

91.12-13: *L. Lucceius... quoque petiit*

The description *paratus eruditusque* indicates that this man was the historian (whom Cicero approached to write a complimentary account of his consulship: *fam.* 5.12). He had been *praetor urbanus* in 67 (Dio 36.41.1, accepting the emendation Λουκκήιος for Λούκουλλος), and he is taken to have been a connection of Pompeius, on the basis of Cic. *fam.* 13.41 and 42 (though the date is disputed: McDermott, *Hermes* 97 [1969] 233-46, who also takes the letters to concern L. Lucceius M.f., and not the historian L. Lucceius Q.f.). Assuming he was a connection of Pompeius, some see his prosecution as indicating a breach between Catilina and the adherents of Pompeius, with whom Catilina had earlier co-operated (e.g. Seager, *Historia* 13 [1964] 344 and 347 n. 43); others deny that there was ever any connection and see Lucceius' prosecution as a Pompeian attack on Catilina's associates who were *inimici* of Pompeius (e.g. Gruen, *Class. Phil.* 64 [1969] 23-4). Yet again, it could be argued that he acted on behalf of the optimates (i.e. the same group who had prevented Catilina's candidature two years earlier); he was prepared later to join with the optimate candidate Bibulus for the consular elections of 60, if he did not secure a *coitio* with Caesar (Cic. *Att.* 1.17.11). From this letter we know that Lucceius was thinking about running with Caesar at the consular elections held in 60, and according to Suet. *Iul.* 19.1 he did agree to combine with Caesar and provide financial backing for their joint-candidature (for his role in the formation of the coalition between Pompeius, Crassus and Caesar, see G.R. Stanton and B.A. Marshall, *Historia* 24 [1975] 215-8). McDermott, art. cit. 241-3, argues that the man who sought the consulship was L. Lucceius M.f., and not the historian who prosecuted Catilina, and he has therefore to claim that Asconius' comment about the prosecutor of Catilina who later sought the consulship is an error. Part of his argument is that the honest historian would not have been capable of the chicanery associated with Caesar's electoral candidature, but he seems to have overlooked the fact that the honest historian was capable of the most scandalous muck-raking in his prosecution of Catilina (below, 91.27ff.). While McDermott lists other examples of error in Asconius' work, he fails to show that he was wrong in this detail: see SB, *Fam.* 1.319.

91.19: *Fabia virgo Vestalis causam incesti dixerat*

The trial took place in 73 (Cic. *Cat.* 3.9); the case of Crassus and the Vestal Licinia (Plut. *Crass.* 1.2) is most likely to be associated with it (Münzer, *RA*, p. 96 n.). The prosecutor of Fabia was Clodius, while the young M. Cato intervened and forced the prosecutor to withdraw (Plut. *Cat. Min.* 19.3); Q. Catulus was influential on Catilina's behalf (Sall. *Cat.* 35.1). Further details in Gruen, *Athenaeum* 49 (1971) 60-1.

310   Commentary

91.19-20: *cum ei Catilina obiceretur*

It is not clear whether Catilina was formally charged along with Fabia. Oros. 6.3.1 states explicitly that he was and that he was acquitted with the help of Catulus. There are some problems: in *Att.* 1.16.9 and *Pis.* 95, Cicero says that Catilina was twice acquitted, and the two trials to which he refers must be the trial for extortion in 65 and for murder in 64 (so SB *Att.* 1.319; cf. Gruen, art. cit. 61 n. 28). T.J. Cadoux (in a private communication) counters by saying that Cicero was deliberately limiting himself to unjust acquittals, the only sort relevant to his purposes, and that Catilina's 'acquittal' in 73 was just (or at least Cicero had to say so in public: cf. *etiam cum culpa nulla subesset* in the lemma), because if it was unjust he would imply that Fabia, his wife's relative, was guilty. Shackleton Bailey reports the view that Cicero chose to ignore the prosecution of Catilina in 73 because Fabia was related to his wife, but argues himself that Catilina was not prosecuted; to the argument based on Cicero's comment that Catilina was twice acquitted, he adds that in *Cat.* 3.9 and *Brut.* 236 Cicero speaks only of the trial and acquittal of the virgins (note the plural, which suggest the case of Licinia should be associated), and that in *Cat.* 15.1 Sallust merely numbers an anonymous Vestal among Catilina's *multa nefanda stupra*. He further argues that in the account of the case of Licinia and Crassus, Plutarch says only that Licinia was prosecuted (*Crass.* 1.2: καὶ δίκην ἔφυγεν ἡ Λικκινία Πλωτίου τινὸς διώκοντος). However, as Cadoux points out, Shackleton Bailey has missed that a little later Plutarch writes that Crassus ὑπὸ τῶν δικαστῶν ἀφείθη; the history of trials of Vestals for incest shows that their paramours, if identified, were always prosecuted with them.

91.21: *soror erat Terentiae*

Plut. *Cat. Min.* 19.3 also calls Fabia ἀδέλφη of Terentia. It is usually taken that she was a half-sister (e.g. Münzer, *RE* 6 [1909] 1885, s.v. 'Fabius' no. 172), but we do not know the precise relationship — it could be simply 'cousin'.

91.28: *duxisse uxorem*

This was the second (or possibly the third) of Catilina's marriages. Cic. *Cat.* 1.14 refers anonymously to Catilina's murder of a former wife and the taking of a new wife, and Sall. *Cat.* 15.2 (cf. Val. Max. 9.1.9 and App. *BC* 2.2) refers to Catilina's murder of his stepson to clear the way for his marriage to Aurelia Orestilla. Though they differ on the victim of the murder, Cicero and Sallust seem to be referring to the same event; we should combine the two accounts to say that Catilina's new wife was Aurelia Orestilla who replaced a former unknown wife. The Berne Scholiast on Luc. 2.173 says that Catilina was married to Gratidia, the

In Toga Candida 311

sister of one of his victims in the Sullan proscriptions, M. Marius Gratidianus. The scholiast is tentatively accepted by Syme, *Sallust* (Berkeley and Los Angeles, 1964) pp. 84-6, who suggests that Catilina had therefore three wives: Gratidia would have been his first, being promptly discarded after the death of her brother; the anonymous former wife of Cic. *Cat*. 1.14 would have been his second, and Aurelia Orestilla his third. But it is likely that the Berne Scholiast is wrong, having run together the account of Catilina's murder of his sister's husband and the murder of Gratidianus (see above on 84.8-9). A further argument against accepting this marriage is that it is never mentioned by Cicero (or explained away), yet it would have created a family connection with Catilina, since Cicero's own family was connected with the Gratidii through his grandfather's marriage to a Gratidia. The fact that Aurelia Orestilla was a relative of Mucius Orestinus (see above on 88.18-19) and that the latter was working in Catilina's interests in 64 might suggest that the marriage had taken place in the mid-60's (Marshall, *RFIC* 105 [1977] 151-4).

92.2: *in orationibus quas in eum scripsit*

We have no other evidence of Lucceius' oratorical activity; he was more successful as a historian than as a prosecutor. McDermott, art. cit. 242, suggests that Lucceius composed pamphlets for distribution, containing material against Catilina which he had not used at the trial, but there is no reason to suppose that they were not normal published versions of the speeches delivered in court.

92.2-3: *nomina harum mulierum nondum inveni*

Syme, *Sallust*, p. 85, says that Asconius despaired too soon; although the name of the woman with whom Catilina committed adultery is beyond recovery, the allusion to the daughter/wife is clearly to Aurelia Orestilla (cf. McDermott, art. cit. 242-3). Plutarch partly preserves the scandalous charge, alleging Catilina's incest with his daughter but not mentioning marriage (*Cic*. 10.2).

92.8: *dictum est iam saepius*

See 9.17-18, 66.8-11, 85-89.

92.15: *quos nominat intellegitis*

The mss. reading *nominat* is preferable here, rather than *non nominet* suggested by Kiessling and Schoell and followed by later editors. That emendation is based on Cicero's *ne quem alium nominem*, but it would be unusual for Asconius not to explain such an obscure allusion. The opening sentence of his comment is meant to anticipate the explanation of the persons actually mentioned in the lemma — Cn. Piso (clearly nominated) and Catilina (whom Cicero is addressing, as *conatum tuum* shows). On this point, see Brunt, *CR* n.s. 7 (1957) 193-4.

92.15: *opinio*

What follows here is Asconius' inference: he is, unfortunately, writing at a time when the myth about the 'first' Catilinarian conspiracy had developed (cf. above on 83.22 for his use of Cicero's secret memoirs). It is difficult to disentangle precisely what Cicero thought took place, up to the time he delivered this speech (mid-64), and to remove later additions to the myth. There is some indication that Asconius used Sallust here (see below on 92.19-20), but even so there are disagreements between them; and it should be remembered that Sallust too was writing when the myth had developed. On Asconius's use of *opinio*, see Part I, p. 60.

92.16: *adulescentem perditum*

For a similar description of his character, cf. 66.13 and Sall. *Cat.* 18.4.

92.17: *ad caedem senatus*

Similar phrases are used in other passages: in the lemma (92.13-14: *caedem optimatum*), Cic. *Mur.* 81 (*consilium senatus interficiendi*), Cic. *Cat.* 1.15 (*principes civitatis*), Sall. *Cat.* 18.7 (*plerique senatores*). Liv. *per.* 101 knows only of a plot to assassinate the consuls, presumably the first of the plots said by Sall. *Cat.* 18.5 to have been planned for lst January (for him the murder of senators is added only to the second plot planned for 5th February); at *Cat.* 1.15, Cicero adds the *principes civitatis* to the consuls as intended victims in the plot of 1st January, but that claim was made after the delivery of the *in toga candida* when Cicero had begun to embroider the myth. Cicero's *caedem optimatum* is typical hyperbole (Gruen, *Class. Phil.* 64 [1969] 21); the 'conspiracy' of Catilina and Piso should probably be connected with disturbances to the trial of Manilius (see above on 66.7).

92.17: *ante annum*

See above on 83.23 for the argument that Asconius (and Cicero) can be talking only about a plot hatched in 65 (i.e. the one planned for 5th February) and that the plot for lst January had not yet become part of the myth. At *Mur.* 81, Cicero describes a plot, which is shown by its instigators (Catilina and Piso) and its objects (the murder of senators) to be identical with the plot mentioned in the lemma here; Cicero says that a *triennium* had elapsed between the inception of the plot and the trial of Murena in 63, and that is compatible with (but will not confirm) the date suggested by Asconius for that plot. That in turn tends to confirm that up

In Toga Candida 313

until the trial of Murena the plot of 1st January had not yet been added to the myth (Seager, *Historia* 13 [1964] 339 and 342). For another attempt to dissociate what Catilina and Piso were doing from the demonstration against the incoming consuls on 1st January, see Gruen, art. cit. 21-2.

92.19-20: *prius quam parati essent coniuratis signum dedisset Catilina*

This is the reason given by Sall. *Cat.* 18.8 for the failure of the plot on 5th February. C.E. Stevens, *Latomus* 22 (1963) 406, says that Asconius was using Sallust here, but if he was, why does he contradict Sallust in regard to other events connected with Catilina at the time (e.g. the reason for the rejection of his candidature in 66: see above on 89.11-12)? Seager, art. cit. 339 n. 10, on the other hand, thinks that Asconius and Sallust found the date independently: 'the possibility must be reckoned with that Asconius observed this similarity (the purpose of the plot and reason for its failure) and took his date from Sallust (and hence dated it to 65), but the fact that he does not repeat the precise date offered by the historian militates strongly against this.'

92.21: *in Hispaniam missus a senatu*

Part of the supposed 'conspiracy' was to send Piso to take possession of the two Spanish provinces (Sall. *Cat.* 18.5); despite the failure of the 'plot', Piso was sent as *quaestor pro praetore* of Nearer Spain *ex senatus sententia* through the agency of Crassus (Sall. *Cat.* 19.1; cf. Suet. *Iul.* 9.3). The usual interpretation of this action is that Crassus was attempting to establish through Piso a *point d'appui* against the time of Pompeius' return, because he had something to fear from the great general. This interpretation is based on the assumption that Crassus was involved in the 'first conspiracy', but that may be part of the later myth (see above on 83.22-25). The sending of Piso to Spain was a quite separate incident, and may have no connection with the 'conspiracy' at all (see next comment). Seager, art. cit. 346, says no extravagant theory is needed to explain Crassus' action: he had a *clientela* in Spain (Badian, *FC*, pp. 266-7 and 316), which Piso may have undertaken to revive and strengthen. Piso's family too had long been connected with the province.

92.22: *per honorem legationis*

Asconius' terminology is incorrect here: Piso was not sent as a *legatus*, but as *quaestor pro praetore (CIL* 1^2.2.749 = *ILS* 875). For a similar mistake, see Schol. Bob. 133.19, where Cato is called *legatus* for his mission to Cyprus in 58, when he was *pro quaestore pro praetore*. Perhaps the commentators have both slipped into imperial terminology, where *legatus* would describe a governor. Piso's appointment was extraordinary in the strict sense, but there are other examples of a quaestor being sent out as *quaestor pro praetore*: see W. Jashemski, *The Origins and History of the Proconsular and Propraetorian Imperium to 27 B. C.* (Chicago, 1950) pp. 78-80 and 153 (Marcellinus), 86-7 and 155 (Scaurus), 58 and 131 (Antistius), 58 and 129 (Annius), 156 (Cassius). It may have been that the governor designated for Nearer Spain had died and there was no other replacement, so Piso was sent (Seager, art. cit. 346). Balsdon, *JRS* 52 (1962) 134-5, agrees that there was nothing startling or sinister in the appointment at all, and so says that another element in the 'first conspiracy' breaks down (contra, Gruen, *Calif. Stud. Class. Ant.* 1 [1968] 160 n. 15). Stockton, *Cicero*, p. 76, objects to the argument that Piso's appointment was not really extraordinary, saying that none of the scant parallels is cogent; it cannot have been entirely coincidental that Crassus' influence is stressed by Sallust, that the lot was not used for the appointment, and that Piso was murdered in Spain, with the suspicion that Pompeius' friends were responsible.

92.24-25: *a Cn. Pompeii clientibus Pompeio non invito*

Piso's cruelty and insolence seems to have been what provoked the Spaniards to assassinate him (Dio 36.44.5; cf. 92.23). Sall. *Cat.* 19.4-5 records the view that Piso was killed by long-standing Spanish clients of Pompeius with his approval; while not committing himself to a decision on its truth, Sallust does discount the explanation that simple cruelty and injustice were the cause of Piso's murder, pointing out that the Spaniards had put up with a good deal of that from earlier governors. It is hardly credible that Pompeius himself, far away in the East, could have ordered Piso's murder, but his clients were widespread in Spain and there were clients of the Calpurnii and Licinii Crassi as well (Badian, *FC*, pp. 266-7, 312, 316, 318); it is reasonable to assume that Crassus and Piso had hoped to expand their Spanish *clientelae* at the expense of Pompeius, and that this rivalry played a part in Piso's removal (Gruen, art. cit. 160; Phillips, *Rhein. Mus.* 116 [1973] 355-6). The comment may be evidence of Asconius' borrowing from Sallust (see Part I, p. 53).

93.5-6: *alios quosdam nobiles homines*

Cf. 88.28-29, where Asconius calls them *honesti homines*. It was considered undignified for men of such rank to compete in games.

93.7: *vectigales quadrigas*

Cf. Cic. *Phil.* 2.62: *tum Antonius existimavit se . . . equos vectigales Sergio mimo tradere*. The *equi vectigales* of Cicero, or *quadrigas vectigales* of Asconius, are the *curules equi* of Liv. 24.18.10; cf. Festus *verb. signif.* 3, s.v. *curules equi vectigales*. That contracts for the supply of race-horses which ran in the public games is meant by these terms, as well as the provision of horses and chariots for religious processions, is shown by Dio 55.10.5 who tells us that Augustus extended to the new games in honour of Mars the privilege which already existed for the *ludi Romani* and the *ludi Apollinares* 'that even senators might contract for the supply of horses for the races.' The point of Cicero's reference to Antonius' action is that the latter gave the contract to a low-class actor, whereas previously such contracts had been undertaken by senators or eminent knights (no doubt more for popularity than profit).

93.9: *Boculus*

Cicero comments earlier (88.21-22) that Antonius was victorious in the chariot races at Sulla's games; the point of his reference to Boculus in the lemma here is that Antonius was not prepared to concede first place in the race to this well known driver, but went all out to win himself.

93.10: *malis civibus*

Brunt, *CR* 7 (1957) 194-5, argues that Asconius' comments here lend no support to the view that Crassus and Caesar are meant, and that there is no allusion here to their complicity in the 'plot' of 66-5; he suggests rather that Asconius understood Cicero to be speaking of the *grex Catilinae*. However, Asconius did know of the later development of the fiction about the 'first' Catilinarian conspiracy (to which Cicero himself contributed — see above on 83.22-25) and of the *opinio* that Catilina and Piso had joined in a plot to murder senators (92.15-20); Crassus was said to have helped to secure Piso's appointment to Spain (Sall. *Cat.* 19.1), and Caesar to have been involved with Piso in nefarious plots (Suet. *Iul.* 9). In view of these latter traditions, Asconius might well have thought that Crassus and Caesar were the *mali cives* who were promoting Catilina and Antonius (he says as much at 83.3-4) and who had promoted Piso (though Crassus alone is mentioned as helping to secure his governorship of Spain, and Asconius mentions only Crassus as secretly behind the 'plot' of 66-5). In the end, one cannot tell whom Cicero meant; as so often, he may have been deliberately imprecise.

93.12-13: *nervos incidere civium Romanorum*

Brunt, art. cit. 194, conjectures that this 'refers to some (otherwise unattested) damage to the interests of citizens in the province (cf. the cases of Verres and Gabinius).'

93.15: *Hispaniensem pugiunculum*

An obvious reference to Piso's governorship of Spain. Brunt, art. cit. 194, pushes Cicero's colourful language too far in suggesting that Cicero has in mind a distinctive action on the part of Piso (as a feeble instrument of the 'bad citizens' which the diminutive implies) and that it was not connected with the 'plot' of 66-5.

93.18: *Licinium gladiatorem*

It is very difficult to make even a guess at the identity of this man, particularly in view of the very corrupt phrase which follows. The *gladiatorem* is probably not to be taken literally, but in the sense found in Cic. *Quinct.* 29, *Rosc. Am.* 8, 17, 118, *Mur.* 83, *Phil.* 7.17. If that is so, and if the corrupt phrase means 'subjected Catilina to a trial on a capital charge', we are not much better off, since we know of only two trials (for *incestum* in 73, and for extortion in 65). For the latter Clodius was the prosecutor; for the former Clodius was originally the prosecutor until scared off by M. Cato (Plut. *Cat. Min.* 19.3), so Licinius may have taken up that prosecution. However, there may have been other attempted prosecutions of Catilina, or Licinius may have assisted in the two prosecutions we know of.

93.18-20: *immisisse capillum Catilinae* †*iudic. qua Q. ve Curium*

Two of the mss. have *capillum* (P and M), the other (S) has *lapillum*. Clark would read *submisisse capillum Catilinae iudicio, itemque Q. Curium*, taking *submisisse* from Plin. *ep.* 7.27.14. Madvig already rejected this sort of interpretation and proposed instead of *capillum* a name like *C. Attilium* for a man who had once been a juror at a trial of Catilina. Rau, pp. 147-8, suggests *in se immissum esse et cupidum Catilinae iudicem Q. Curium*. Kiessling and Schoell, preceded by Bücheler, propose *inmisisse lapillum Catilinae iudicio quasi alterum Q. Curium*, using *lapillum* in the sense of 'a vote' (cf. Ov. *Met.* 15.41-42). This reading seems to make good sense: the tone of Cicero's statement is derogatory, and Cicero regarded Catilina's acquittal at his trial for extortion in the previous year (an event he could well be alluding to here) as unjust (*Att.* 1.16.9, *Pis.* 95). He may be referring to two corrupt jurymen, for Curius' reputation was not good.

93.19-20: *Q. Curium hominem quaestorium*

Usually identified with the Catilinarian conspirator, who was expelled from the senate, probably by the censors of 70 (Sall. *Cat.* 23.1; App. *BC* 2.3): so Giarratano, n. ad loc., and *MRR* 2.122. A further identification is made by some with a Q. Curius who was praetor by 67, but there are problems about identifying this man (see *MRR* 2.149 n. l; cf. *Suppl.* 22). Knowledge of him is based on the reading *Curium* in Cic. *Att.* 1.1.2, which is taken to refer to a candidate for the consulship of 64 (hence praetor by 67); SB *Att.* 1.292-3, following Boot and Constans, rejects the reading *Curium* in favour of another reading *Turium*, taking the latter as a reference to L. Turius who almost made the consulship (Cic. *Brut.* 237).

Münzer, *RE* 4 (1901) 1839-40, s.v. 'Curius' nos. 1 and 7, while accepting the reading *Curium* in Cicero's letter, rejects the identification of this candidate for the consulship with the Catilinarian conspirator, on the grounds that an ex-quaestor expelled from the senate in 70 would hardly have had time to become eligible for a consulship in 64 (cf. Mommsen, *Staatsrecht*, 1³.522 n. 3, and Syme, *Class. Phil.* 50 [1955] 134). Clark, taking the reference in the lemma here to be to the candidate for the consulship, emends *quaestorium* to *quaestuosum*, presumably on the grounds that the man must have been of more than quaestorian rank at the time this speech was delivered (if he had been a candidate for the consulship the year before). Sallust describes the Catilinarian conspirator as belonging to the senatorial order at the time the conspiracy was formed (*Cat.* 17.3; cf. *comm. pet.* 10). It seems preferable to have only one Q. Curius, who had regained senatorial status (as Sallust indicates) by holding the quaestorship (as the lemma here indicates), and to read *Turium* at Cic. *Att.* 1.1.2. For further discussion of the identification of Q. Curius, see Marshall, *L'Antiquité Classique* 47 (1978) 207-9.

93.21: *notissimus . . . aleator*

An activity which would be in line with the criminal and immoral character attributed to the Catilinarian conspirator, which had led to his expulsion from the senate (Sall. *Cat.* 23.1; App. *BC* 2.3).

93.21-22: *damnatusque postea est*

The date of the conviction is not known (except that it must have come after the delivery of Cicero's speech), nor is the charge. Curius turned informer against his fellow-conspirators in 63 (Sall. *Cat.* 26.3, 28.2) and subsequently tried to implicate Caesar in a list laid before the senate, but the latter appealed to the senatorial records which showed that, on Cicero's own admission, he had warned the consul about the plot; Curius was deprived of the bounty he had been earlier awarded by the senate (Suet. *Iul.* 17). Turning state's evidence presumably provided immunity against charges related to the conspiracy, and so Curius' condemnation probably came after 63, but if his condemnation did not involve exile, a date of 64 for his trial is a possibility (Gruen, *Last Generation*, p. 526).

93.22: *hendecasyllabus Calvi elegans*

Frag. 1 in Morel (p. 84). Mueller emends the mss. *talus* or *calus* to *talos*.

93.25: *responderunt*

Manutius emended the mss. pluperfect. For the replies of Catilina and Antonius, see Quint. 9.3.94; App. *BC* 2.2; Schol. Bob. 80.13-14 (on *Sull.* 22). The latter two sources refer to Cicero's newness and non-

Roman origin. Asconius regards the replies as fictitious (cf. Syme, *Fondation Hardt Entretiens* 18 [1971] 6).

93.25-94.1: *invecti in novitatem eius*

For the attacks on Cicero's newness, and hence his unworthiness for the consulship, cf. above on 86.4-5.

94.2-3: *obtrectatoribus*

Schol. Bob. 80.14 includes Clodius with Catilina and Antonius as criticising Cicero's *novitas* at this time.

94.4: *omnium consensu*

Cicero was returned at the top of the poll with Antonius securing the other consulship (Sall. *Cat.* 24.1; Plut. *Cic.* 11.2.)

94.5: *patris nomen*

C. Antonius was a son of the famous orator, M. Antonius (cos. 99), and brother of M. Antonius (pr. 74) who received an extraordinary command against pirates from 73-71. Cicero's competitor thus had strong family claims to office. He might also have received some help from L. Iulius Caesar, the current consul, who had ties with the Antonii.

BIBLIOGRAPHY

[Only those items which have been used more than once, or which are of particular significance have been listed here.]

Astin, A.E.   *'Professio* in the Abortive Election of 184 B.C.', *Historia* 11 (1962) 252-255.

———   *Scipio Aemilianus* (Oxford, 1976).

Babcock, C.   'The Early Career of Fulvia', *AJP* 86 (1965) 1-32.

Badian, E.   'Q. Mucius Scaevola and the Province of Asia', *Athenaeum* 34 (1956) 104-123.

———   'Caepio and Norbanus', *Historia* 6 (1957) 318-346.

———   *Foreign Clientelae (264-70 B.C.)* (Oxford, 1958).

———   'Forschungsbericht: From the Gracchi to Sulla (1940-1959)', *Historia* 11 (1962) 197-245.

———   *Studies in Greek and Roman History* (Oxford, 1964)

———   'Sulla's Augurate', *Arethusa* 1 (1968) 26-46.

———   *Roman Imperialism in the Late Republic*, 2nd edn. (Oxford, 1968).

———   'Quaestiones Variae', *Historia* 18 (1969) 447-491.

———   'Cicero and the Commission of 146 B.C.', in *Hommages à Marcel Renard*, ed. J. Bibauw (Brussels, 1969) Vol. I, pp. 54-65.

———   *Publicans and Sinners* (Oxford, 1972).

———   'Marius' Villas: the Testimony of the Slave and the Knave', *JRS* 63 (1973) 121-132.

Balsdon, J.P.V.D.   'Q. Mucius Scaevola and *ornatio provinciae*', *CR* 51 (1937) 8-10.

———   'The History of the Extortion Court at Rome, 123-70 B.C.', *PBSR* 14 (1938) 98-114.

———   'Consular Provinces under the Late Republic', *JRS* 29 (1939) 57-72.

———   'Roman History, 58-56 B.C.: Three Ciceronian Problems', *JRS* 47 (1957) 15-20.

320 Bibliography

	'*Auctoritas, Dignitas, Otium*', *CQ* n.s. 10 (1960) 43-50.
	'Roman History, 65-50 B.C.: Five Problems', *JRS* 52 (1962) 134-141.
	'The *Commentariolum Petitionis*', *CQ* n.s. 13 (1963) 242-250.
Barlow, C.T.	'The Roman Government and the Roman Economy, 92-80 B.C.', *AJP* 101 (1980) 202-219.
Bauman, R.A.	*The Crimen Maiestatis in the Roman Republic and Augustan Principate* (Johannesburg, 1967).
Benario, H.W.	'Asconiana', *Historia* 22 (1973) 64-71.
Best, E.E.	'Literacy and Roman Voting', *Historia* 23 (1974) 428-438.
Bloch, G.	'M. Aemilius Scaurus: Etude sur l'histoire des partis au VIIe siècle de Rome', in *Mélanges d'histoire ancienne* 25 (Paris, 1909) 1-80.
Broughton, T.R.S.	*The Magistrates of the Roman Republic*, 2 vols (New York, 1951-2).
Brunt, P.A.	'Three Passages from Asconius', *CR* n.s. 7 (1957) 193-195.
	'Italian Aims at the Time of the Social War', *JRS* 55 (1965) 90-109.
	''Amicitia' in the Late Roman Republic', *PCPS* n.s. 11 (1965) 1-20.
	Italian Manpower 225 B.C.—A.D.14 (Oxford, 1971).
Buckland, W.W.	'Civil Proceedings against Ex-Magistrates in the Republic', *JRS* 27 (1927) 37-47.
Bücheler, F.	'Coniectanea', *Rhein. Mus.* 34 (1879) 341-356.
Carcopino, J.	*Les secrets de la correspondance de Cicéron* (Paris, 1974).
Carney, T.F.	*A Biography of Marius* (Assen, 1961).
Chapman, C.M.	'Cicero and P. Sulpicius Rufus (Tr. Pl. 88 B.C.)', *Acta Classica* 22 (1979) 62-71.
Ciaceri, E.	*Cicerone e i suoi tempi* (Milan, 1930).

Clark, A.C.	*The Descent of Manuscripts* (Oxford, 1918).
——	Review of Humbert's two books, *CR* 41 (1927) 74-76.
Clarke, M.L.	*Higher Education in the Roman World* (London, 1971).
Cody, J.M.	'The Use of *Libero-Damno* and *Absolvo-Condemno* in the Judicial Proceedings of the Late Republic', *Class. Phil.* 68 (1973) 205-207.
Conole, P.	'Allied Disaffection and the Revolt of Fregellae', *Antichthon* 15 (1981) 129-140.
Courtney, E.	'The Prosecution of Scaurus in 54 B.C.', *Philologus* 105 (1961) 151-156.
Crawford, M.H.	*Roman Republican Coinage*, 2 vols (Cambridge, 1974).
Criniti, N.	*L'epigrafe di Asculum di Gn. Pompeo Strabone* (Milan, 1970).
Dahlmann, H.	'M. Terentius Varro (Antiqu.)', *RE Suppl.* 6 (1935) 1243-1246.
Degrassi, A. (ed.)	*Inscriptiones Italiae*, Vol. XIII, Fasc. 1 (Fasti Consulares et Triumphales) (Rome, 1947).
Douglas, A.E. (ed.)	*M. Tulli Ciceronis Brutus* (Oxford, 1966).
Earl, D.C.	'Appian *B.C.* I, 14 and "Professio"', *Historia* 14 (1965) 325-332.
——	'The Early Career of Sallust', *Historia* 15 (1966) 302-311.
Ewins, U.	'The Early Colonisation of Cisalpine Gaul', *PBSR* 20 (1952) 54-71.
——	'The Enfranchisement of Cisalpine Gaul', *PBSR* 23 (1955) 73-98.
Feger, R.	'T. Pomponius Atticus, III. Schriften', *RE Suppl.* 8 (1956) 520-523.
Flambard, J.-M.	'Notes sur l'histoire du texte d'Asconius à l'époque moderne', *MEFRA* 88 (1976) 375-396.
——	'Clodius, les collèges, la plèbe et les esclaves: reserches sur la politique populaire au milieu du Ier siècle', *MEFRA* 89 (1977) 115-156.

Fowler, W.W.	*The Roman Festivals of the Period of the Republic* (London, 1899).
Fraccaro, P.	'Scauriana', *Rend. Acc. Lincei*, ser. 5, 20 (1911) 169-196.
Frank, T.	*An Economic Survey of Ancient Rome*, Vol. I (New Jersey, 1933).
Frederiksen, M.W.	'Caesar, Cicero and the Problem of Debt', *JRS* 56 (1966) 128-141.
Frier, B.W.	'Augural Symbolism in Sulla's Invasion of 83', *ANSMusN* 13 (1967) 111-118.
———	'Sulla's Priesthood', *Arethusa* 2 (1969) 187-199.
Frisch, H.	'The First Catilinarian Conspiracy: a Study in Historical Conjecture', *C. & M.* 9 (1947) 10-36.
Gabba, E.	'Politica e cultura in Roma agli inizi del I secolo a.C.', *Athenaeum* 31 (1953) 259-272.
———	'Le origini della guerra sociale e la vita politica romana dopo l'89 a.C.', *Athenaeum* 32 (1954) 41-114 and 293-345.
———	'Il ceto equestre e il senato di Silla', *Athenaeum* 34 (1956) 124-138.
Garzetti, A.	'M. Licinio Crasso: l'uomo e il politico', *Athenaeum* 20 (1942) 12-40, 22-23 (1944-5), 1-62.
Geer, R.M.	'M. Aemilius Scaurus (Suetonius *Nero* ii.1 and Asconius on Cicero *pro Scauro* 1)', *Class. Phil.* 24 (1929) 292-294.
Geiger, J.	'The Last Servilii Caepiones of the Republic', *Anc. Soc.* 4 (1973) 143-156.
Gelzer, M.	*Caesar: Politician and Statesman*, 6th edn., trans. P. Needham (Oxford, 1968).
———	*Cicero: ein biographischer Versuch* (Wiesbaden, 1969).
———	*The Roman Nobility*, trans. R. Seager (Oxford, 1969).
Giarratano, C.	'Due codici di Asconio Pediano, il Forteguerriano e il Madrileno', *SIFC* 14 (1906) 195-205.
Gordon, P.W.G.	*Two Renaissance Book Hunters: The Letters of*

	Poggius Bracciolini to Nicolaus de Niccolis (New York and London, 1974).
Greenidge, A.H.J.	*The Legal Procedure of Cicero's Time* (London, 1901).
Griffin, M.T.	'The 'leges iudiciariae' of the pre-Sullan Era', *CQ* n.s. 23 (1973) 108-126.
———	'The Tribune C. Cornelius', *JRS* 63 (1973) 196-213.
Gruen, E.S.	'The Political Allegiance of P. Mucius Scaevola', *Athenaeum* 43 (1965) 321-332.
———	'The Lex Varia', *JRS* 55 (1965) 59-73.
———	'The Dolabellae and Sulla', *AJP* 87 (1966) 385-399.
———	'Cicero and Licinius Calvus', *HSCP* 71 (1966) 215-233.
———	'Political Prosecutions in the 90's B.C.', *Historia* 15 (1966) 32-64.
———	'P. Clodius: Instrument or Independent Agent?', *Phoenix* 20 (1966) 120-130.
———	'Pompey and the Pisones', *Calif. Stud. Class. Ant.* 1 (1968) 155-170.
———	'M. Antonius and the Trial of the Vestal Virgins', *Rhein. Mus.* 111 (1968) 59-63.
———	*Roman Politics and the Criminal Courts, 149-78 B.C.* (Cambridge, Mass., 1968).
———	'Notes on the 'First Catilinarian Conspiracy'', *Class. Phil.* 64 (1969) 20-24.
———	'Pompey, the Roman Aristocracy, and the Conference of Luca', *Historia* 18 (1969) 71-108.
———	'The Consular Elections for 53 B.C.', in *Hommages à Marcel Renard*, ed. J. Bibauw (Brussels, 1969) Vol. II, pp. 311-321.
———	'Pompey, Metellus Pius, and the Trials of 70-69 B.C.: the Perils of Schematism', *AJP* 92 (1971) 1-16.
———	'Some Criminal Trials of the Late Republic: Political

	and Prosopographical Problems', *Athenaeum* 49 (1971) 54-69.
	The Last Generation of the Roman Republic (Berkeley and Los Angeles, 1974).
Gwynn, A.	*Roman Education* (Oxford, 1926).
Hall, U.	'Voting Procedure in Roman Assemblies', *Historia* 13 (1964) 267-306.
Hardy, E.G.	'Consular Provinces between 67 and 52 B.C.', *CR* 31 (1917) 11-15.
Haury, A.	'Philotime et la vente des biens de Milon', *REL* 34 (1956) 179-190.
Hayne, L.	'The Politics of M'. Glabrio, cos. 67', *Class. Phil.* 69 (1974) 280-282.
	'M. Lepidus and his Wife', *Latomus* 33 (1974) 76-79.
Hellegouarc'h, J.	*Le vocabulaire latin des relations et des partis politiques sous la république* (Paris, 1972).
Henderson, M.I.	'De Commentariolo Petitionis', *JRS* 40 (1950) 8-21.
	Review of H.H. Scullard, Roman Politics 220-150 B.C., *JRS* 42 (1952) 114-116.
	'The Establishment of the 'equester ordo'', *JRS* 53 (1963) 61-72.
Hill, H.	*The Roman Middle Class in the Republican Period* (Oxford, 1952).
Hillard, T.W.	'The Sisters of Clodius Again', *Latomus* 32 (1973) 505-514.
Hirzel, R.	'Ein Symposium des Asconius', *Rhein. Mus.* 43 (1888) 314-317.
Humbert, J.	*Les plaidoyers écrits et les plaidoiries réelles de Cicéron* (Paris, 1925).
	Contribution à l'étude des sources d'Asconius dans ses relations des débats judiciares (Paris, 1925).
John, C.	'Die Enstehungsgeschichte der catilinarischen Verschwörung', *Jahrb. Cl. Phil.*, suppl. 8 (1876) 703-819.

Jones, A.H.M.	*The Criminal Courts of the Roman Republic and Principate*, ed. J.A. Crook (Oxford, 1972).
Katz, B.R.	'The First Fruits of Sulla's March', *L'Antiquité Classique* 44 (1975) 100-125.
———	'Caesar Strabo's Struggle for the Consulship — and More', *Rhein. Mus.* 120 (1977) 45-63.
Kornemann, E.	'Coloniae', *RE* 4 (1901) 513-522.
Kumaniecki, K.	'De oratione Tulliana in toga candida habita', in *Atti dello I congresso internazionale di studi Ciceroniani* (Rome, 1961) Vol. I, pp. 157-166.
———	'Les discours égarés de Cicéron pro Cornelio', *Med. Kon. Vlaam. Acad. Belg.* 32 (1970) 3-36.
Kunkel, W.	*An Introduction to Roman Legal and Constitutional History*, 2nd edn., trans. J.M. Kelly (Oxford, 1973).
Laurand, L.	*Etudes sur le style des discours de Cicéron*, 2nd edn. (Paris, 1925).
Lengle, J.	'Tribunus', *RE* 6A (1937) 2454-2490.
Lepage, Y.G.	'Cicéron devant le mort de Tullia d'après sa correspondance', *LEC* 44 (1976) 245-258.
Lichtenfeldt, C.	*De Q. Asconii Pediani fontibus ac fide* (Breslau, 1888).
Linderski, J.	'Three Trials in 54 B.C.: Sufenas, Cato, Procilius and Cicero 'Ad Atticum', 4.15.4', in *Studi in onore di Edoardo Volterra* (Milan, 1969) Vol. II, pp. 281-302.
———	'The Aedileship of Favonius, Curio the Younger and Cicero's Election to the Augurate', *HSCP* 76 (1972) 181-200.
———	'The Mother of Livia Augusta and the Aufidii Lurcones of the Republic', *Historia* 23 (1974) 463-480.
Linderski, J. &	Kaminska-Linderski, A. 'The Quaestorship of M. Antonius', *Phoenix* 28 (1974) 213-223.
Lintott, A.W.	'P. Clodius Pulcher — Felix Catilina', *G. & R.* 14 (1967) 157-169.
———	'*Nundinae* and the Chronology of the Late Roman

Republic', *CQ* n.s. 18 (1968) 189-194.

—— *Violence in Republican Rome* (Oxford, 1968).

—— 'Cicero and Milo', *JRS* 64 (1974) 62-78.

—— 'The leges de repetundis and associate measures under the Republic', *Zeitschrift der Savigny-Stiftung (Röm. Abt.)* 98 (1982) 162-212.

Macdonald, C.   'The Lex Fufia of 59 B.C.', *CR* n.s. 7 (1957) 198.

Madvig, J.N.   *De Q. Asconii Pediani et aliorum veterum interpretum in Ciceronis orationes commentariis disputatio critica* (Copenhagen, 1828).

Malcovati, E.   *Orationum Romanorum Fragmenta Liberae Rei Publicae*, 2nd edn. (Turin, 1955).

Mare, A.C. de la   *The Handwriting of Italian Humanists*, Vol. I, fasc. 1 (Oxford, 1973).

Marrou, H.I.   *A History of Education in Antiquity*, 3rd edn., trans. G. Lamb (London, 1971).

Marshall, B.A.   'Apuleius *Apologia* 20', *AJP* 95 (1974) 62-66.

—— 'Pompeius' Temple of Hercules', *Antichthon* 8 (1974) 80-84.

—— 'Cicero and Sallust on Crassus and Catiline', *Latomus* 33 (1974) 804-813.

—— 'The Date of Delivery of Cicero's *in Pisonem*', *CQ* n.s. 25 (1975) 88-93.

—— 'Appositio', *Glotta* 53 (1975) 292-293.

—— 'Q. Cicero, Hortensius and the lex Aurelia', *Rhein. Mus.* 118 (1975) 136-152.

—— 'The Date of Q. Mucius Scaevola's Governorship of Asia', *Athenaeum* 54 (1976) 117-130.

—— *Crassus: a Political Biography* (Amsterdam, 1976).

—— 'Some Crassi in Cicero's *pro Scauro*', *Latomus* 35 (1976) 91-96.

—— 'Catilina: Court Cases and Consular Candidature', *Scripta Classical Israelica* 3 (1976/7) 127-137.

—— 'Two Court Cases in the Late Second Century B.C.', *AJP* 98 (1977) 417-423.

——	'The Vote of a Body-Guard for the Consuls of 65', *Class. Phil.* 72 (1977) 318-320.
——	'Another Rigged Voting Tablet?', *Liverpool Classical Monthly* 2 (1977) 11-12.
——	'The Case of Metellus Nepos v. Curio', *Philologus* 121 (1977) 83-89.
——	'The Date of Catilina's Marriage to Aurelia Orestilla', *RFIC* 105 (1977) 151-154.
——	'Q. Curius, homo quaestorius', *L'Antiquité Classique* 47 (1978) 207-209.
McDermott, W.C.	'De Lucceiis', *Hermes* 97 (1969) 233-246.
——	'The Sisters of P. Clodius', *Phoenix* 24(1970) 39-47.
——	'In Ligarianam', *TAPA* 101 (1970) 317-347.
——	'Q. Cicero', *Historia* 20 (1971) 702-717.
——	'M. Cicero and M. Tiro', *Historia* 21 (1972) 259-286.
——	'Cicero's Publication of his Consular Orations', *Philologus* 116 (1972) 277-284.
——	'*Lex de tribunicia potestate* (70 B.C.)', *Class. Phil.* 72 (1977) 49-52.
McDonald, W.	'The Tribunate of Cornelius', *CQ* 23 (1929) 196-208.
Meier, C.	*Res Publica Amissa* (Wiesbaden, 1966).
——	'Die loca intercessionis bei Rogationen', *Museum Helveticum* 25 (1968) 86-100.
Mello, M.	'Sallustio e le elezione consolari del 66 a.C.', *PP* 18 (1963) 36-54.
Michels, A.K.	*The Calendar of the Roman Republic* (Princeton, 1967).
Mitchell, J.F.	'The Torquati', *Historia* 15 (1966) 23-31.
Mitchell, T.N.	'The *Volte-Face* of P. Sulpicius Rufus in 88 B.C.', *Class. Phil.* 70 (1975) 197-204.
——	*Cicero: the Ascending Years* (New Haven, 1979).
Mommsen, T.	*Römische Forschungen*, 2 vols (Berlin, 1864-79).

328 Bibliography

	Römisches Staatsrecht, 3 vols (Leipzig, 1887).
	Römisches Strafrecht (Leipzig, 1899).
Münzer, F.	*De gente Valeria* (diss., Berlin, 1891).
	'Cassius' no. 64, *RE* 3 (1899) 1738-1739.
	'Cornelius' no. 18, *RE* 4 (1901) 1252-1255.
	'Cornelius' no. 205, *RE* 4 (1901) 1375.
	'Cornelius' no. 342, *RE* 4 (1901) 1487-1488.
	'Curius' nos. 1 and 7, *RE* 4 (1901) 1839 and 1840.
	'Domitius' no. 11, *RE* 5 (1905) 1316-1318.
	'Lucilius' no. 25, *RE* 13 (1927) 1642-1645.
	'Mucius' no. 12, *RE* 16 (1935) 423-424.
	'Munatius' no. 32, *RE* 16 (1935) 551-553.
	'Novius' nos. 7 and 12, *RE* 17 (1937) 1216 and 1218.
	'Rutilius' no. 30, *RE* 1A (1920) 1268.
	'Seius' no. 4, *RE* 2A (1923) 1121-1122.
	Römische Adelsparteien und Adelsfamilien (Stuttgart, 1920).
Nardo, D.	*Il 'commentariolum petitionis': la propaganda elettorale nella 'ars' di Quinto Cicerone* (Padua, 1920).
Niccolini, G.	*I fasti dei tribuni della plebe* (Milan, 1934).
Nicolet, C.	*L'ordre équestre à l'époque républicaine (312-43 av. J.-C)*, 2 vols (Paris, 1966-74).
	'Arpinum, Aemilius Scaurus et les Tullii Cicerones', *REL* 45 (1967) 276-304.
	'Amicissimi Catilinae (à propos du Commentariolum Petitionis)', *REL* 50 (1972) 163-186.
	Les noms des chevaliers victimes de Catilina dans le *Commentariolum Petitionis*', in *Mélanges d'histoire ancienne offerts à William Seston* (Paris, 1974).
	Le métier de citoyen dans la Rome républicaine (Paris, 1976).

Nicolet, C. & Demougin, S. 'Le 'Commentariolum Petitionis' de Quintus Cicéron. Etat de la question et étude prosopographique', *ANRW* 1.3 (1973) 239-277.

Nisbet, R.G.M. 'The *Commentariolum Petitionis*. Some Arguments against Authenticity', *JRS* 51 (1961) 84-87.

―――― *Cicero: in L. Calpurnium Pisonem Oratio* (Oxford, 1961).

Ogilvie, R.M. *A Commentary on Livy Books 1-5* (Oxford, 1965).

Petersen, H. 'The Numeral Praenomina of the Romans', *TAPA* 93 (1962) 347-354.

Phillips, E.J. 'Cicero and the Prosecution of C. Manilius', *Latomus* 29 (1970) 595-607.

―――― 'Asconius' *magni homines*', *Rhein. Mus.* 116 (1973) 353-357.

―――― 'Catiline's Conspiracy', *Historia* 25 (1976) 441 - 448.

Platner, S.B. *A Topographical Dictionary of Ancient Rome,* rev. T. Ashby (Oxford, 1929).

Puccioni, G. *M. Tulli Ciceronis orationum deperditarum fragmenta*, 2nd edn. (Milan, 1972).

―――― 'Recupero semantico di un vocabulo latino, scalae', *RFIC* 95 (1967) 180-185.

Ramsey, J.T. 'Studies in Asconius (diss. summary)', *HSCP* 80 (1976) 311-313.

―――― 'A Reconstruction of Q. Gallius' Trial for *Ambitus*: One Less Reason for Doubting the Authenticity of the *Commentariolum Petitionis*', *Historia* 29 (1980) 402-421.

―――― 'The Prosecution of C. Manilius in 66 B.C. and Cicero's *Pro Manilio*', *Phoenix* 34 (1980) 323-336.

Rau, S.J.E. *Variarum lectionum liber ad Ciceronis orationes pertinens* (Leiden, 1834).

Richardson, J.S. 'The 'Commentariolum Petitionis'', *Historia* 20 (1971) 436-442.

Rinkes, S.H. 'De Q. Asconii Pediani in Ciceronis orationes commentariis emendandis', *Mnemosyne* 10 (1861) 199-225.

Rotondi, G.	*Leges publicae populi romani* (Milan, 1912).
Rowland, R.J.	'Cicero's *Necessarii*', *Class. Journ.* 65 (1969) 193-198.
Ruebel, J.S.	'The Trial of Milo: a Chronological Study', *TAPA* 109 (1979) 231-249.
Salmon, E.T.	'Catiline, Crassus and Caesar', *AJP* 56 (1935) 302-316.
———	*Roman Colonization under the Republic* (London, 1969).
Seager, R.	'The First Catilinarian Conspiracy', *Historia* 13 (1964) 338-347.
———	'Clodius, Pompey and the Exile of Cicero', *Latomus* 24 (1965) 519-531.
———	'Lex Varia de Maiestate', *Historia* 16 (1967) 37-43.
———	'The Tribunate of Cornelius: Some Ramifications', in *Hommages à Marcel Renard*, ed. J. Bibauw (Brussels, 1969) Vol. I, pp. 680-686.
———	'*Factio*: Some Observations', *JRS* 62 (1972) 53-58.
———	'Iusta Catilinae', *Historia* 22 (1973) 240-248.
———	*Pompey: a Political Biography* (Oxford, 1979).
Setaioli, A.	'On the Date of Publication of Cicero's Letters to Atticus', *Symbolae Osloenses* 51 (1971) 105-120.
Settle, J.N.	'The Trial of Milo and the Other *Pro Milone*', *TAPA* 94 (1963) 268-280.
Shackleton Bailey, D.R.	'Sex Clodius — Sex. Cloelius', *CQ* n.s. 10 (1960) 41-42.
———	*Cicero's Letters to Atticus*, 7 vols (Cambridge, 1965-70).
———	*Cicero* (London, 1971).
———	'The Prosecution of Roman Magistrates-Elect', *Phoenix* 24 (1970) 162-165.
———	'*Mumpsimus-Sumpsimus*', *Ciceroniana* n.s. 1 (1973) 3-9.

	Cicero: Epistulae ad Familiares, 2 vols (Cambridge, 1977).
	'Brothers or Cousins?', *AJAH* 2 (1977) 148-150.
Shatzman, I.	'Scaurus, Marius and the Metelli: a Prosopographical-Factional Case', *Anc. Soc.* 5 (1974) 197-222.
	Senatorial Wealth and Roman Politics (Collection Latomus, 142) (Brussels, 1975).
Sherwin-White, A.N.	'Violence in Roman Politics', *JRS* 46 (1956) 1-9.
	The Roman Citizenship, 2nd edn. (Oxford, 1973).
Stangl, T.	'Asconiana', *Philologus* 69 (1910) 489-550.
Staveley, E.S.	*Greek and Roman Voting and Elections* (London, 1972).
Stein, A.	'Pupius' no. 10, *RE* 23, 2 (1959) 1987-1993.
Stevens, C.E.	'The 'Plotting' of B.C. 66/65', *Latomus* 22 (1963) 398-435.
Stewart, R.S.	'The Chronological Order of Cicero's Earliest Letters to Atticus', *TAPA* 93 (1962) 459-470.
Stockton, D.L.	*Cicero: a Political Biography* (Oxford, 1971).
	'The First Consulship of Pompey', *Historia* 22 (1973) 205-218.
Stone, A.M.	'*Pro Milone*: Cicero's Second Thoughts', *Antichthon* 14 (1980) 88-111.
Sumner, G.V.	'Manius or Mamercus?', *JRS* 54 (1964) 41-48.
	'Asconius and the Acta', *Hermes* 93 (1965) 134-136.
	'The Consular Elections of 66 B.C.', *Phoenix* 19 (1965) 226-231.
	The Orators in Cicero's Brutus: *Prosopography and Chronology* (Toronto, 1973).
Syme, R.	Review of E. Clift, Latin Pseudepigraphia, *JRS* 37 (1947) 202.
	Review of T.R.S. Broughton, The Magistrates of the Roman Republic, *Class. Phil.* 40 (1955) 127-138.
	'Missing Senators', *Historia* 4 (1955) 52-71.

332 Bibliography

	'Some Pisones in Tacitus', *JRS* 46 (1956) 17-21.
	Sallust (Berkeley and Los Angeles, 1964).
	'Senators, Tribes and Towns', *Historia* 13 (1964) 105-125.
Taylor, L.R.	'Caesar's Early Career', *Class. Phil.* 36 (1941) 113-132.
	'Caesar's Colleagues in the Pontifical College', *AJP* 63 (1942) 385-412.
	'The Election of the *pontifex maximus* in the Late Republic', *Class. Phil.* 37 (1942) 421-424.
	'On the Chronology of Cicero's Letters of 56-55 B.C.', *Class. Phil.* 44 (1949) 217-221.
	Party Politics in the Age of Caesar (Berkeley and Los Angeles, 1949).
	The Voting Districts of the Roman Republic (Rome, 1960).
	Roman Voting Assemblies from the Hannibalic War to the Dictatorship of Caesar (Ann Arbor, 1966).
Tibiletti, G.	'La politica delle colonie e citta latine nella Guerra Sociale', *Rend. Ist. Lomb.* 86 (1953) 45-63.
Treggiari, S.	*Roman Freedmen during the Late Republic* (Oxford, 1969).
Twyman, B.	'The Metelli, Pompeius and Prosopography', *ANRW* 1.1 (1972) 816-874.
Tyrrell, R.Y. & Purser, L.C. (ed.) *The Correspondence of M. Tullius Cicero*, 3rd edn., 7 vols (London, 1904).	
Urban, R.	'Zur Entstehung der Volkstribunates', *Historia* 22 (1973) 761-764.
Volkmann, H.	'Valerius' no. 98, *RE* 7A, 2 (1948) 2313-2340.
Walbank, F.W.	*A Historical Commentary on Polybius*, 3 vols (Oxford 1957-79).
Walsh, P.G.	*Livy: his Historical Aims and Methods* (Cambridge, 1961).
Ward, A.M.	'Cicero and Pompey in 75 and 70', *Latomus* 29 (1970) 58-71.

—— 'Politics in the Trials of Manilius and Cornelius', *TAPA* 101 (1970) 547-556.

—— *Marcus Crassus and the Late Roman Republic* (Columbia and London, 1977).

Watson, A. *Law Making in the Later Roman Republic* (Oxford, 1974).

Weinrib, E.J. 'The Prosecution of Roman Magistrates', *Phoenix* 22 (1968) 32-56.

—— 'The Prosecution of Magistrates-Designate', *Phoenix* 25 (1971) 145-150.

Whitehorne, J.E.G. 'Sallust and Fausta', *Class. World* 68 (1975) 425-430.

Willems, P. *Le Sénat de la République Romaine* (Louvain, 1885, repr. 1975).

Wiseman, T.P. 'Teidia's Husband', *Latomus* 22 (1963) 87-90.

—— 'The Potteries of Vibienus and Rufrenus at Arretium', *Mnemosyne* 16 (1963) 275-283.

—— 'Some Republican Senators and their Tribes', *CQ* n.s. 14 (1964) 122-133.

—— 'The Mother of Livia Augusta', *Historia* 14 (1963) 333-334.

—— 'The Ambitions of Q. Cicero', *JRS* 56 (1966) 108-115.

—— 'Lucius Memmius and his Family', *CQ* n.s. 17 (1967) 164-167.

—— 'Two Friends of Clodius in Cicero's Letters', *CQ* n.s. 18 (1968) 297-302.

—— 'Pulcher Claudius', *HSCP* 74 (1970) 207-221.

—— 'Celer and Nepos', *CQ* n.s. 21 (1971) 180-182.

—— *New Men in the Roman Senate 139 B.C. — 14 A.D.* (Oxford, 1971).

Wissowa, G. 'Compitalia', *RE* 4 (1901) 791-792.

—— *Religion und Kultur der Römer* (Munich, 1912).

Zetzel, J.E.G. '*Emendavi ad Tironem*: Some Notes on Scholarship in the Second Century A.D.', *HSCP* 77 (1973) 225-243.

INDICES

I. NAMES AND PLACES

Accius, 17
M'. Acilius (IIIvir 218), 65, 87
M'. Acilius Glabrio (cos. 67), 126, 150-1
M'. Acilius Glabrio (son of cos. 67), 150
Actium, 306
Aegritomarius, 279
L. Aelius Lamia, 8, 99
Sex. Aelius Paetus (cos. 198), 247
C. Aelius Staienus (qu. 77), 229
Aemilia (Vestal c. 113), 196-7
Aemilia (wife of Pompeius), 126-7, 150-1
L. Aemilius Buca, 151
M'. Aemilius Lepidus (cos. 66), 72, 169, 192, 222, 227, 276
M. Aemilius Lepidus (cos. 78), 122, 151, 153, 155, 255
M. Aemilius Lepidus (cos. 46 etc.), 72, 169, 177-8, 181, 192
Paullus Aemilius Lepidus (cos. suff. 34), 192
Mam. Aemilius Lepidus Livianus (cos. 77), 72, 227, 255, 276, 280
L. Aemilius (Lepidus) Paullus (cos. 50), 151, 155, 169
M. Aemilius Lepidus Porcina (cos. 137), 131, 197
L. Aemilius Paullus (cos. 182, 168), 50, 100
M. Aemilius Philemon (slave of Lepidus), 181-2
M. Aemilius Scaurus (cos. 115), 58, 68, 72, 119-158 passim, 239, 243, 255-7, 271, 277
M. Aemilius Scaurus (pr. 56), 18, 40, 48, 57, 59, 119-158 passim, 168, 173-4, 213, 308, 314
Agrigentum, 107
Alba Longa, 188
L. Albinius Paterculus (tr. pl. 493), 74, 267
T. Albucius (pr. c. 105), 18
Alfidia (mother of Livia), 212
M. Alfidius, 212
Alsium, 165
M. Annius (pr. before 218), 65, 87
M. Annius (qu. pro pr. 119), 314
P. Annius, 146
T. Annius (father of Milo), 64, 170, 205

T. Annius Milo Papianus (pr. 55), 11, 17, 32, 40, 46, 51, 53, 57, 59, 69, 116, 121, 128-9, 152, 154, 159-213 passim, 226, 237, 300
Antiochus III Magnus, 105-6
Antiochus IV Epiphanes, 105
P. Antistius (tr. pl. 88), 144
C. Antistius Vetus (cos. suff. 30), 314
M. Antonius (cos. 99), 54, 60, 109, 114, 141-3, 146, 197, 256, 282, 318
M. Antonius (pr. 74), 218, 318
M. Antonius (cos. 44 etc.), 58, 167, 175, 189, 223, 247, 259, 290
C. Antonius Hybrida (cos. 63), 12-3, 42, 44, 281-318 passim
Apollo, 306
Cn. Aponius, 211
L. Appuleius Saturninus (tr. pl. 104 etc.), 46, 134, 147, 209, 239, 271
M'. Aquillius (cos. 129), 141-2
C. Aquillius Gallus (pr. 66), 281
Arausio, 134, 242, 271, 278
Archias, 227
Aricia, 165
Aristonicus, 142-3
Arpinum, 292
Asculum, 197
C. Asinius Pollio (cos. 40), 58, 121, 160
C. Ateius Capito (tr. pl. 55), 185
L. Ateius Capito (pr. ?), 185
Athens, 185
A. Atilius Serranus (cos. 170), 106, 247
C. Atilius Serranus (pr. 185), 247
Sex. Atilius Serranus Gavianus (tr. pl. 57), 9, 100
Attalus I Soter, 248
C. Attius Celsus (pr. 65?), 225-6, 234
Attus Navius, 169
T. Aufidius (pr. 67?), 281
M. Aufidius Lurco (tr. pl. 61), 212
Aulus Gellius, 11, 35, 37-8, 59
Aurelia Orestilla (wife of Catilina), 32, 45, 284, 286, 301-2, 310-1
C. Aurelius Cotta (cos. 75), 6-7, 19, 43-4, 50, 51-2, 53, 73, 108-9, 145, 148, 236-9, 243, 255, 271
L. Aurelius Cotta (cos. 65), 43, 115, 214, 237-8, 261-2, 295
M. Aurelius Cotta (father of coss. 75, 74, 65), 239, 243

M. Aurelius Cotta (cos. 74), 73, 92, 238
L. Aurelius Orestes (cos. 157), 301
P. Autronius Paetus (cos. des. 65), 200, 223, 246, 261, 286, 302-3
Q. Axius, 288

basilica Aemilia, 169
basilica Porcia, 169
Bauli, 213
L. Bellienus, 307-8
L. Betutius Barrus, 197
Birria (slave of Milo), 166
Boculus, 315
Bona Dea, 73, 113, 165, 168, 189, 202, 204, 227
Bovillae, 46, 57, 163-5, 188, 205

Caecilia Metella (mother of Luculli), 227
Caecilia Metella (wife of Scaurus and Sulla), 120, 126-7, 254-5
Q. Caecilius (victim of Catilina), 288-9, 292, 311
Q. Caecilius Metellus Celer (tr. pl. 90), 289
Q. Caecilius Metellus Celer (cos. 60), 40, 95-6, 126, 147, 231-3
Q. Caecilius Metellus Creticus (cos. 69), 113, 218, 231, 283
L. Caecilius Metellus Delmaticus (cos. 119), 120, 131-2, 149-50, 197, 254-5, 278
L. Caecilius Metellus Diadematus (cos. 117), 149
Q. Caecilius Metellus Macedonicus (cos. 143), 154
Q. Caecilius Metellus Nepos (cos. 98), 126, 230-3
Q. Caecilius Metellus Nepos (cos. 57), 7-8, 13, 93, 95, 126, 150, 152-5, 200, 220, 230-3
Q. Caecilius Metellus Numidicus (cos. 109), 241, 298
Q. Caecilius Metellus Pius (cos. 80), 151, 153, 161, 226, 231, 255, 256, 260, 298, 303
Q. Caecilius Metellus Pius Scipio Nasica (cos. 52), 160-3, 164-5, 171, 175, 184, 212-3, 260
L. Caecilius Rufus (pr. 57), 200
C. Caecina Largus (cos. A.D. 42), 27, 28-9, 148
M. Caelius Rufus (pr. 48), 56, 92, 163, 171, 173, 194, 208, 212-3, 300, 304
Caere, 163
C. Caesennius Philo, 212

M. Caesoninus (pr. by 66), 281
M. Calidius (pr. 57), 128, 152, 300
L. Calpurnius Bestia (cos. 111), 14, 256
L. Calpurnius Bestia (tr. pl. 62), 13
M. Calpurnius Bibulus (cos. 59), 176, 309
C. Calpurnius Piso (cos. 67), 41, 53, 114, 215-7, 220, 246, 251, 261, 264, 297, 303
Cn. Calpurnius Piso (qu. pro pr. 65-4), 45, 53, 60, 67, 75, 76, 234-6, 312-6
L. Calpurnius Piso Caesoninus (cos. 58), 8, 9, 47, 60, 70, 71, 83-114 passim, 150, 153, 155
C. Calpurnius Piso Frugi (qu. 58), 65, 85, 91-2
L. Calpurnius Piso Frugi (cos. 133), 266-7
Calventius (grandfather of cos. 58), 66, 91, 93
campus Martius, 170
Capitol, 180, 200, 268, 307
Capua, 70, 99
Carneades, 106
C. Cassius Longinus (cos. 96), 129
C. Cassius Longinus (pr. 44), 210, 259, 314
L. Cassius Longinus (tr. pl. 104), 129, 270-1
L. Cassius Longinus (pr. 66), 64, 222, 270, 281-2, 284
L. Cassius Longinus (tr. pl. 44), 210
Q. Cassius Longinus (tr. pl. 49), 270
L. Cassius Longinus Ravilla (cos. 127), 195-6, 269-70
C. Causinius Schola (friend of Clodius), 165, 188, 201-2
Ap. Claudius (Xvir 451), 268
M. Claudius Marcellus (cos. 222 etc.), 101-2, 107
M. Claudius Marcellus (cos. 196), 102
M. Claudius Marcellus (cos. 166 etc.), 72, 101-2
M. Claudius Marcellus (cos. 51), 128, 152, 174
Ti. Claudius Nero (pr. 42), 92
Ap. Claudius Pulcher (cos. 143), 196
Ap. Claudius Pulcher (cos. 99), 232
Ap. Claudius Pulcher (cos. 54), 8, 14, 17-8, 54, 92, 100, 119, 124, 146-7, 152, 155-6, 172, 174, 183, 206, 211, 232
Ap. Claudius Pulcher (son of pr. 56), 172, 184-5, 206, 208
C. Claudius Pulcher (cos. 92), 54, 114
C. Claudius Pulcher (pr. 56), 124, 146-7, 172-3

Q. Claudius Quadrigarius, 103
clivus Capitolinus, 170
C. Clodius (companion of Clodius), 165, 188
P. Clodius Pulcher (tr. pl. 58), 8, 10, 12-3, 16, 40, 42, 46, 47, 57, 70, 71, 72, 73, 76, 96-9, 113, 116, 121, 126, 128-9, 146-7, 148, 151-6, 159-213 passim, 223, 227, 232, 249, 263, 279, 289, 295-6, 299, 308, 309, 316, 318
Sex. Cloelius, 95, 168-9, 197-8, 211, 213
A. Cluentius, 289
C. Coelius Caldus (cos. 94), 217-8
M. Coelius Vinicianus (tr. pl. 53), 176
collegia 94-6, 167 262-3
C. (or L.) Cominius, 222-3, 229-30, 236, 282
P. Cominius, 41, 64, 222-3, 229-30, 236, 282
Compitalia, 233-4
Considius (quaesitor 52), 186, 208, 210
C. Considius Longus (pr. 58?), 210
M. Considius Nonianus (pr. 54?), 210
Cornelia (daughter of Sulla), 168, 212-3
Cornelia (wife of Crassus and Pompeius), 161-3
Cornelia (wife of Lepidus), 72, 192
Cornelia (wife of Lepidus' son), 192
Cornelia (wife of Paullus Lepidus), 192
C. Cornelius, 260
C. Cornelius (tr. pl. 67), 41, 52-3, 153, 213-264 passim, 282
L. Cornelius Balbus (cos. suff. 40), 190
C. Cornelius Cethegus (cos. 197), 247
L. Cornelius Cinna (cos. 87-4), 140-1, 154, 298, 305-6
Cn. Cornelius Dolabella (associate of Saturninus), 147
Cn. Cornelius Dolabella (cos. 81), 147-8, 260
Cn. Cornelius Dolabella (pr. 81), 121, 135, 147-8, 260
Cn. Cornelius Lentulus Clodianus (cos. 72), 294
P. Cornelius (Lentulus) Dolabella (cos. suff. 44), 65, 92-3
P. Cornelius Lentulus Marcellinus (qu. pro pr. 74?), 314
L. Cornelius Lentulus Niger (pr. by 61), 63, 129, 151, 156
L. (or P.) Cornelius Lentulus Niger (son of above), 63, 151, 156-7
P. Cornelius Lentulus Spinther (cos. 57), 121, 130
P. Cornelius Lentulus Sura (pr. 63), 223

Cornelius Nepos, 11, 49-50, 58, 82-3
Cn. Cornelius Scipio (IIIvir 218), 65
P. Cornelius Scipio Aemilianus (cos. 149, 134), 101, 196, 269
P. Cornelius Scipio Africanus (cos. 205, 194), 46, 54, 246-9
L. Cornelius Scipio Asiagenes (cos. 83), 130
L. Cornelius Scipio Asiaticus (cos. 190), 107
P. Cornelius Scipio Asina (cos. 221), 65, 87-8
P. Cornelius Scipio Nasica (pr. c. 93), 160
P. Cornelius Scipio Nasica Serapio (cos. 138), 143
L. Cornelius Sisenna (pr. 78), 103, 260-1
Faustus Cornelius Sulla (qu. 54), 127, 151, 154, 169, 174, 252-5, 308
P. Cornelius Sulla (cos. des. 65), 155, 200, 206, 246, 261, 286, 302-3
L. Cornelius Sulla Felix (dict. 82-79?), 19, 120, 127, 130, 145, 147, 151, 152, 168, 169, 202, 212, 220, 227, 228, 231, 233, 237, 246, 255, 260-1, 272, 281-2, 286, 291-3, 298, 302, 306-8, 315
L. Cornificius (cos. 35), 181, 185, 208
P. Cornificius, 180-1
Q. Cornificius (pr. 67 or 66), 181, 281-3
Q. Cornificius (pr. c. 45), 181
Cosa, 89
Cremona, 85-9
curia Hostilia, 169, 177-8, 180, 191, 198
Q. Curius (qu. 71?), 316-7

Damio, 198
P. Decius (pr. 115), 118
Delphi, 254
Demetrius, 106
T. Didius (cos. 98), 232
Domitia (wife of Catulus), 277
Cn. Domitius Ahenobarbus (cos. 96), 58, 65, 109, 129-33, 239, 241, 270-1, 277-80
L. Domitius Ahenobarbus (cos. 94), 217-8
L. Domitius Ahenobarbus (cos. 54), 54, 64, 119, 124, 184, 186, 195, 224-5, 226, 234
Cn. Domitius Calvinus (cos. 53, 40), 122, 124, 128, 206, 285
Cn. Domitius Calvinus (son of above), 185, 206

Epidaurus, 254
Eudamus (slave of Milo), 166

Fabia (Vestal c. 73), 284, 295, 309-10
L. Fabius (quaesitor 52), 186, 208
Q. Fabius Maximus Verrucosus (cos. 233 etc.), 102
T. Fadius, 213
Faesulae, 47, 70, 202
C. Fannius (cos. 122), 117
Fausta (daughter of Sulla), 127, 152, 157, 165-6, 173, 183, 209
M. Favonius (pr. 49), 40, 186, 189, 206, 208
Fenestella, 4, 11, 34, 42, 47, 48, 53-5, 62, 76, 83, 114, 158, 160, 163, 237, 248, 296, 301
Fidenae, 90
C. Fidius, 211
T. Flacconius, 212
Flaminia (mother of P. Valerius Triarius), 127
Flaminian meadows, 268, 306
L. Flavius (pr. 58), 96, 198-9
C. Flavius Fimbria (cos. 104), 277, 280
C. Flavius Fimbria (leg. 86-5), 140, 146
P. Fonteius, 147
Fregellae, 50, 117
M. Fufius (or Fusius), 166
L. Fufius Calenus, 297-8
Q. Fufius Calenus (cos. 47), 9-10, 16, 157, 178, 193-4, 229, 297
L. Fulcinius, 210
Fulvia (wife of Clodius and Antonius), 167, 175, 189
Ser. Fulvius, 197
M. Fulvius Bambalio, 167
M. Fulvius Flaccus (cos. 125), 117
P. Fulvius Neratus, 185, 208
Q. Fulvius Nobilior (cos. 153), 101
Fundi, 123
M. Furius Camillus (dict. 396 etc.), 158, 247
Furius Crassipes (husband of Tullia), 57, 65, 92-3
C. (or Q.) Furius Pacilus Fusus (cos. 441), 269

A. Gabinius (cos. 58), 8, 52, 71, 99, 123, 128, 151, 152, 153, 157, 185, 199, 200, 206, 217-64 passim, 315
Galata (slave of Milo), 182
Q. Gallius (pr. 65), 69, 128, 229, 234, 300-1
L. Gellius Publicola (cos. 72), 294
Gratidia (wife of Catilina?), 292, 310-1
M. Gratidius (brother-in-law of Marius), 292

M. Gratidius (leg. 61-59), 292
Guarini of Verona, 1

Hercules, 302
C. Herennius (IIIvir 218), 65, 87
C. Herennius (tr. pl. 60), 96, 173
L. Herennius Balbus, 173
M. Horatius Barbatus (cos. 449), 268
M. (or C.) Horatius Pulvillus (cos. 457), 268
L. Hortensius (legate of Sulla), 255
Q. Hortensius Hortalus (cos. 69), 113, 128, 148, 150, 153, 174, 178, 193-4, 213, 226, 251, 255, 263
L. Hostilius Tubulus (pr. 142), 68, 139-40

Ilia (wife of Sulla), 168
Interamna, 165, 202
Cn. Iulius (cos. 431), 307
C. Iulius Caesar (cos. 59 etc.), 18, 44, 56-7, 58-9, 84-5, 100, 106-7, 122, 127, 147, 148, 151, 156, 168, 184, 187, 191, 210, 247, 259, 285-8, 293, 307, 309, 315, 317.
L. Iulius Caesar (cos. 90), 143, 146
L. Iulius Caesar (cos. 64), 94, 281, 318
L. Iulius Caesar (son of above), 122
Sex. Iulius Caesar (cos. 91), 242
C. Iulius Caesar Octavianus (Augustus), 49, 56, 86, 181, 191, 212, 294, 306, 315
C. Iulius Caesar Strabo Vopiscus (aed. 90), 18, 43-4, 143-6, 236
C. Iulius Hyginus, 75, 104-5
Iunia (wife of Lepidus), 192
D. Iunius Brutus (cos. 77), 211, 280
L. Iunius Brutus (tr. pl. 493), 267
M. Iunius Brutus (pr. 88), 125, 155
L. Iunius Brutus (tr. pl. 83), 155
M. Iunius Brutus (Q. Servilius Caepio) (pr. 44), 127, 174, 181, 190, 192, 217, 267
D. Iunius Silanus (cos. 62), 95, 127
M. Iunius Silanus (cos. 109), 129, 133, 157, 241-2, 270, 277-8, 293

Janiculum, 291
Jerome, 27, 30, 36, 76
John Corvinus of Arezzio, 1
Jugurtha, 118, 121, 125, 270, 298
Juno Sospes (or Sospita), 163-4

Labici, 90
C. Laelius (cos. 140), 196
Lanuvium, 53, 163-4, 181-2, 205, 282
Lavinium, 130, 132-3

Q. Lepta, 91, 93
Licinia (daughter of cos. 95), 160, 239
Licinia (Vestal c. 73), 196-7, 309-10
Licinius, 316
Licinius (sacrificulus), 182, 203
C. Licinius (tr. pl. 493?), 267
P. Licinius (tr. pl. 493?), 267
C. Licinius Calvus, 119, 121, 317
C. Licinius Crassus (tr. pl. 145), 196
L. Licinius Crassus (cos. 95), 108-12, 148, 160, 196-7, 238-9, 243-4
M. Licinius Crassus (cos. 70, 55), 44, 59, 67, 81, 92, 112, 115, 119, 121, 161, 184-5, 188, 192, 233, 235, 237, 251, 264, 272, 280, 284-8, 303, 309-10, 313-5
P. Licinius Crassus (cos. 97), 108, 140-1, 143, 146
P. Licinius Crassus (qu. 55), 161, 163
P. Licinius Crassus Dives Mucianus (cos. 131), 109, 142-3, 238
L. Licinius Lucullus (cos. 151), 101
L. Licinius Lucullus (cos. 74), 122, 153, 226-7, 255, 276
C. Licinius Macer (pr. 68?), 267, 276, 280
L. Licinius Murena (cos. 62), 164, 312-3
C. Licinius Sacerdos (eques), 283
C. Licinius Sacerdos (pr. 75), 281-3
Livia (sister of tr. pl. 91), 243, 271
Livia (wife of Augustus), 212
M. Livius Drusus (cos. 112), 242
M. Livius Drusus (tr. pl. 91), 7, 51, 73, 109, 134, 136-7, 144, 209, 240, 242-5, 257
Livy, 28, 50-1, 62
M. Lollius Palicanus (pr. by 69), 115, 220, 280, 281, 297, 303
Luca, 121, 152, 154-5, 201
L. Lucceius (pr. 67), 45, 236, 285, 292, 309, 311
C. Lucilius, 203
C. Lucilius Hirrus (tr. pl. 53), 176
Q. Lucretius Ofella (Afella), 307-8
ludi Apollinares, 72, 200, 247, 315
ludi Compitalicii, 40, 94-6
ludi Megalenses, 18, 40, 247-9
ludi plebeii, 18
ludi Romani, 72, 200, 247, 315
ludi Victoriae Sullanae, 302
L. Luscius (senator c. 81), 307-8
Lutatia (wife of Hortensius), 226, 255, 277
C. Lutatius Catulus (cos. 220), 65, 87-8
Q. Lutatius Catulus (cos. 102), 255, 277, 291

Q. Lutatius Catulus (cos. 78), 41, 115, 226, 235, 251, 255, 276-7, 303, 309-10

Magna Mater, 248
Cn. Mallius (cos. 105), 271
C. Mamilius Limetanus (tr. pl. 109), 118
C. Manilius (tr. pl. 66), 4, 6, 47, 52, 64, 73, 153, 184, 188, 195, 219-51 passim, 288, 295, 298, 303, 312
Q. Manilius Cumanus (tr. pl. 52), 163
C. Manlius (associate of Catilina), 70, 202
A. Manlius Torquatus (pr. c. 70), 185-6
L. Manlius Torquatus (cos. 65), 74, 100, 214, 261-2, 295
L. Manlius Torquatus (son of above), 74, 200, 206, 262
Marcia (Vestal c. 113), 196-7
Marcia (wife of Cato), 153-4
C. Marcius Figulus (cos. 64), 94, 281
L. Marcius Philippus (cos. 91), 98, 135, 154, 242-4, 257, 270-1
L. Marcius Philippus (cos. 56), 150, 154
Q. Marcius Rex (pr. 144), 196
Maria (sister of Marius), 292
C. Marius (cos. 107 etc.), 144-6, 233, 239-40, 277-8, 280, 292, 306
C. Marius (cos. 82), 239, 291, 308
L. Marius (tr. pl. 62), 123
L. Marius (?qu. 50), 63, 123, 155
M. Marius (pr. c. 102), 292
M. Marius Gratidianus (pr. 85, 83?), 42, 202, 288, 290-2, 299, 306-7
Masinissa, 101-2
Massilia, 208-9
C. Memmius (pr. 58), 122, 124, 127, 151, 154, 165, 212-3, 227, 253, 285
C. Memmius (tr. pl. 54), 155, 200
C. Memmius (son of pr. 58), 151, 155
C. Memmius (son of tr. pl. 54), 200
L. Memmius (tr. pl. 89?), 256-7
Menenius Agrippa, 268
C. Messius (aed. 55), 155
Cn. Minucius, 230
Q. Minucius Thermus (tr. pl. 62), 220
Mithridates, 122, 134-5, 144-5, 253-4
Mons Aventinus, 264, 268
Mons Sacer, 264, 268
monumentum Basili, 202
Mucia (wife of cos. 95), 109, 243
Mucia Tertia, 48, 93, 95, 126-7, 153, 231-2
Q. Mucius Orestinus (tr. pl. 64), 286, 296, 297, 299, 301-2, 311

Indices 339

P. Mucius Scaevola (cos. 133), 104, 109, 140, 149, 197, 238
Q. Mucius Scaevola (cos. 117), 161, 197
Q. Mucius Scaevola (cos. 95), 44, 109-12, 135, 231-2, 238-9, 243
L. Mummius Achaicus (son of cos. 146), 256
L. Munatius Plancus (cos. 42), 168
T. Munatius Plancus Bursa (tr. pl. 52), 47, 57, 64, 159-60, 163, 178, 183-4, 189, 191, 193-4, 203, 209-10, 213
Mutina, 152
Muttines, 107

Nicomedes III of Bithynia, 217
L. Ninnius Quadratus (tr. pl. 58), 95
Nola, 145
Nomentum, 163
C. Norbanus (tr. pl. 103), 271
Noreia, 279
L. Novius Niger (tr. pl. 58), 198
Numa Pompilius, 263
Q. Numerius Rufus (tr. pl. 57), 9

Ocriculum, 182, 205
Cn. Octavius (cos. 165), 148
Cn. Octavius (cos. 87), 141
M. Octavius (tr. pl. 133), 52, 251-2
Olympia, 254
L. Opimius (cos. 121), 50, 63, 117
Q. Opimius (tr. pl. 75), 19, 237
Oppius (propr. c. 73?), 230-1
C. Orchivius (pr. 66), 224, 253

M. Pacuvius (Claudus?), 123-4
Q. Pacuvius (Claudus?), 123-4
M. Papirius (Celer?), 199
Cn. Papirius Carbo (cos. 113), 279
M'. (or M.) Papirius Crassus (cos. 441), 269
C. (or P.) Papirius Maso (IIIvir 218), 65, 87-8
T. Papius, 205
L. Papius Celsus (monetalis c. 46), 205
Patavium, 26, 28, 33
Q. Patulcius, 208
C. Peducaeus, 152
Sex. Peducaeus (tr. pl. 113), 196
Penates, 130, 132-3
M. Perperna (cos. 130), 142
M. Perperna (cos. 92), 150, 153-4
Pharsalus, 185
Phileros (slave of Cornelius), 262
Philippi, 59, 289
Philodemus, 70, 114

Philotimus (freedman of Terentia), 208-9
Placentia, 46, 47, 50, 69, 85-9
Cn. Plancius (aed. 54), 210
P. Plautius Hypsaeus (pr. by 55), 160, 173, 176, 212
M. Plautius Silvanus (tr. pl. 89), 273
Pliny the Elder, 59
Poggio Bracciolini, 1
Pompeia (sister of Pompeius), 155
Pompeia (wife of Caesar), 168
Pompeia (daughter of Pompeius), 154
Sex. Pompeius (son of Pompeius), 306
Cn. Pompeius Magnus (cos. 70 etc.), 4, 6, 16, 18, 40, 41, 42, 48, 53, 54, 59, 81-2, 87, 91, 96, 100, 106-7, 113, 114, 115, 119-58 passim, 159-213 passim, 214-80 passim, 284
Q. Pompeius Rufus (cos. 88), 139, 145, 168, 256-7
Q. Pompeius Rufus (pr. 63), 212
Q. Pompeius Rufus (tr. pl. 52), 163-4, 173, 184, 191, 212-3
Cn. Pompeius Strabo (cos. 89), 18, 108, 145, 256, 273
Cn. Pomponius (tr. pl. 90), 256, 274
T. Pomponius Atticus, 106, 210, 211, 228, 267, 274, 290
C. Pomptinus (pr. 63), 123, 155
M. Popillius Laenas Curtianus, 152
Porcia (sister of Cato), 184
C. Porcius Cato (tr. pl. 56), 59, 98, 121, 152
L. Porcius Cato (cos. 89), 108, 273
M. Porcius Cato (cos. 195), 269, 285
M. Porcius Cato (Uticensis) (pr. 54), 40, 93, 97, 122-3, 127, 153-5, 157-8, 173-5, 184, 189, 205-6, 219-20, 308, 309, 313, 316
P. Porcius Laeca (pr. 195), 269
P. Porcius Licinus (cos. 184), 269
porta Carmentalis, 306
A. Postumius Albinus (cos. 99), 54, 114
Praeneste, 166, 209, 308
Ptolemy Alexander I, 217
Ptolemy Auletes, 121, 153-4, 176, 217
M. Pupius Piso Frugi Calpurnianus (cos. 61), 44, 57-8, 112-3

L. Quinctius (tr. pl. 74), 202, 276, 280
Quintilian, 26, 28, 33-8

Romulus, 158
L. Roscius Otho (tr. pl. 67), 251, 271-2
Rupilius, 230
Rutilia (sister of cos. 105), 239, 243

340 Indices

P. Rutilius Nudus (?qu. 74), 92, 99
P. Rutilius Rufus (cos. 105), 110-1, 124-5, 134-5, 239, 242-3, 274
C. Sallustius Crispus (tr. pl. 52), 15, 32, 34, 51-3, 62, 83, 123, 163-4, 178, 183, 184, 194
Ap. Saufeius, 209-10
C. Saufeius (qu. 99), 209
L. Saufeius, 210
M. Saufeius (associate of Milo), 57, 166, 186, 188, 209-10, 213
C. Scribonius Curio (pr. c. 121), 197
C. Scribonius Curio (cos. 76), 71, 230-2, 259
C. Scribonius Curio (tr. pl. 50), 162, 167, 213, 259
L. Scribonius Libo (pr. 192), 247
M. Seius, 211
Seleucus IV Philopator, 106
Sempronia (mother of Fulvia), 167, 189
A. Sempronius Asellio (pr. 89), 275
C. Sempronius Gracchus (tr. pl. 123-2), 14, 117, 272
Ti. Sempronius Gracchus (tr. pl. 133), 52, 109, 251-2
Ti. Sempronius Longus (cos. 194), 54, 246-8
C. Sempronius Tuditanus (cos. 129), 267
L. Sergius Catilina (pr. 68), 4, 12-3, 16, 32, 42, 44, 45, 47, 48, 53, 67, 70, 73, 93, 98-9, 113, 138, 202, 234-6, 281-318 passim
T. Sertius Gallus, 165
Q. Sertorius (pr. 83), 153, 226, 231
Servaeus (tr. pl. des. 50), 213
Servilia (wife of cos. 102), 277
Servilia (wife of Livius Drusus), 243, 271
Servilia (half-sister of Cato), 127, 151, 153, 155
Cn. Servilius Caepio (cos. 141), 140
Q. Servilius Caepio (cos. 106), 129, 134-7, 243, 270-1, 277-8
Q. Servilius Caepio (pr. c. 92), 58, 243-4, 257, 271
C. Servilius Geminus (pr. before 218), 87-8
C. Servilius Geminus (cos. 203), 65
C. Servilius Glaucia (pr. 100), 134-5
P. Servilius Globulus (tr. pl. 67), 215-6, 219, 227-8
P. Servilius Rullus (tr. pl. 63), 200
P. Servilius Vatia (son of cos. 79), 154-5
P. Servilius Vatia Isauricus (cos. 79), 84, 150, 152-5

P. Sestius (tr. pl. 57), 8, 119, 120, 213
Cn. (or L.) Sicinius (tr. pl. 76), 237, 267
C. Sicinius Vellutus (tr. pl. 493), 74, 267
Sicyon, 217
Silius Italicus, 26, 27, 33, 38
Statius Albius Oppianicus, 229, 284
P. Sulpicius (Rufus?) (tr. pl. 88), 43-4, 108-9, 144-5, 233, 236
Ser. Sulpicius Camerinus Cornutus (cos. 461), 269
P. Sulpicius Galba (pr. by 66), 281-2
Ser. Sulpicius Galba (pr. 54), 123
Ser. Sulpicius Rufus (cos. 51), 92, 139, 176-7
Syracuse, 101-2

Tanusia, 290
L. Tanusius (victim of Catilina), 290
L. Tanusius (eques), 288, 290
L. Tanusius Geminus, 290
Sp. (or P.) Tarpeius (cos. 454), 269
Tarquinium, 146
T. Tatius, 158
Sex. Teidius (qu. ?), 166-7
temple of Apollo, 27, 29, 291, 306-7
temple of Castor and Pollux, 149-50
temple of Concord, 200
temple of Honos et Virtus, 102
temple of Jupiter Capitolinus, 247
temple of Saturn, 188
temple of Venus Victrix, 81-2
temple of Victoria (Vica Pota), 105, 248
Terentia (wife of Cicero), 208-9, 310
M. Terentius Varro (pr. after 76), 211
M. Terentius Varro Gibba (tr. pl. 43), 211
M. Terentius Varro Lucullus (cos. 73), 17-8, 44, 105-7, 153, 211, 227, 253, 255, 276, 289, 293, 308
M. Terpolius (tr. pl. 77), 280
Tertulla (wife of Crassus), 192
theatre of Marcellus, 306
theatre of Pompeius, 81-2, 170, 180, 203, 272
Thurii, 300
Tibur, 168
Tigranes, 199
Tiro, 45, 49, 57-8, 82, 201, 296, 298, 301
Tolosa, 271
L. Trebellius (tr. pl. 67), 52, 228, 251, 271
tribuni aerarii, 116, 157, 238, 298, 305
Tullia (daughter of Cicero), 57, 65, 91-3
M. Tullius Cicero (grandfather of Cicero), 292, 311
M. Tullius Cicero (father of Cicero), 283

Indices

M. Tullius Cicero (son of Cicero), 287
Q. Tullius Cicero (pr. 62), 172, 292
L. Turius (pr. 67?), 316-7
Tusculum, 163, 167

Ulubrae, 181

Valeria (wife of Sulla), 152
C. Valerius, 210
Valerius Antias, 66, 103-4, 246-7, 266, 268
L. Valerius Flaccus (cos. 131), 143
L. Valerius Flaccus (cos. 100), 308
L. Valerius Flaccus (pr. 63), 154
M. Valerius Laevinus (cos. 210), 107
P. Valerius Leo, 173, 185, 206
M'. Valerius Maximus (dict. 494), 66, 102-3, 267-8
M. Valerius Messalla Niger (cos. 61), 129, 152-4
M. Valerius Messalla Rufus (cos. 53), 122, 128, 146, 178, 213
P. Valerius Nepos, 173
P. Valerius Publicola (cos. 509 etc.), 103-5, 108

C. Valerius Triarius (pr. 78), 122, 155
P. Valerius Triarius (son of above), 63, 122, 124, 126, 127
M. Valerius Volusus (cos. 505), 102-4
Q. Varius Severus Hybrida (tr. pl. 90), 58, 134, 137-8, 256-9, 273-4
P. Vatinius (cos. 47), 9, 119
Vergil, 30-1, 38
L. Verginius, 268
A. Verginius Tricostus (cos. 494), 265
C. Verres (pr. 74), 115, 124, 148, 230-1, 238, 260, 279, 283-4, 298, 299, 315
Vestal virgins, 51, 113, 149, 188, 196-7, 270, 310
L. Vettius, 151
T. Veturius Geminus Cicurinus (cos. 494), 65, 265
L. Veturius Varrus, 197
via sacra, 199
C. Vibienus (senator 52), 72, 167-8
T. Vinius, 290
C. Viscellius Ruga (tr. pl. 493), 267
C. Volcacius (father of cos. 66?), 260
L. Volcacius Tullus (cos. 66), 63, 150, 153, 222, 260, 295, 303-4
Volumnii, 289-90
M. Volumnius (victim of Catilina), 288-9

II. LAWS

Acilia repetundarum (122?), 18, 157-8, 187
Aelia et Fufia (c. 150), 97-8, 121, 215, 245
Aemilia frumentaria (78), 97
Antonia de Termessibus (68?), 294
Atinia de tribunis plebis (before 102), 294
Aurelia de iudiciis privatis (75), 236
Aurelia de tribunis plebis (75), 237, 271
Aurelia iudiciaria (70), 14, 42, 50, 51, 53, 184, 188, 229, 237-8, 271, 289, 299, 305

Caecilia Didia (98), 74, 232, 234, 245
Calpurnia de ambitu (67), 179, 206, 216-7, 221, 245-6, 261-4, 286, 297, 301
Cassiae, 18
Cassia tabellaria (137), 196, 269-70, 282
Cassia de senatu (104), 270-1
Cornelia de proscriptione (82), 308
Cornelia de tribunicia potestate (82), 237
Cornelia de ambitu (81), 206, 246, 286
Cornelia de maiestate (81), 220, 222, 227-8, 229-30
Cornelia de quaestoribus (81), 282

Cornelia de sicariis et veneficiis (81), 178, 186, 208
Cornelia iudiciaria (81), 275, 299, 305
Cornelia de edictis praetoriis (67), 216-7, 221, 260
Cornelia de privilegiis (67), 215-7, 220-1, 252, 260

Domitia de sacerdotiis (104), 131, 277-8

Fabia de numero sectatorum (67-63), 245-6
Fufia iudiciaria (59), 280, 305

Gabinia tabellaria (139), 269
Gabinia de bello piratico (67), 226, 250-2, 271-2
Gabinia de senatu legatis dando (67?), 217, 219

Iulia de civitate (90), 86, 143, 257
Iulia agraria Campana (59), 83
Iulia municipalis, 91
Iulia de vi publica, 181, 211, 263

Iulia iudiciaria (17?), 128
Iunia Licinia (62), 121

Licinia de sodaliciis (55), 119, 178, 185-6, 213, 263
Licinia Mucia de civibus redigundis (95), 12, 73, 137, 239-40, 257
Licinia Sextia de consule plebeio (367), 122
Livia agraria (91), 242, 244-5
Livia de civitate (91), 242
Livia frumentaria (91), 242
Livia iudiciaria (91), 242, 245, 274
Livia nummaria (91), 242, 290
Lutatia de vi (78?), 181, 210

Mamilia (109), 118
Manilia de imperio Cn. Pompei (66), 154, 224, 251, 253-4
Manilia de libertinis (66), 219, 225, 233-4
Maria tabellaria (119), 292

Papiria tabellaria (130), 270
Plautia (Plotia) iudiciaria (89), 258, 273-5
Plautia de vi (70?), 178, 180-1, 185-6, 201, 208, 210-1
Plotia agraria (70), 253
Pompeia de Transpadanis (89), 86
Pompeia iudiciaria (55), 116
Pompeia de ambitu (52), 178-80, 184, 186-7, 193-4, 206, 213

Pompeia de provinciis (52), 210
Pompeia de vi (52), 159-60, 163, 178-80, 184, 186-7, 193-4, 209
Pompeia Licinia de tribunicia potestate (70), 264, 280
Porciae, 60, 141, 269
Publilia de plebeiis magistratibus (471), 265

Rubria de colonia (122), 117

Sempronia de provinciis consularibus (123-2), 110
Sempronia frumentaria (123), 97
Sempronia militaris (123), 242
Servilia agraria (63), 254
Servilia Caepionis (106), 135, 271-2, 274
Servilia Glauciae (104 or 101), 135, 274

Terentia Cassia frumentaria (73), 97
Trebonia de provinciis consularibus (55), 185
Tullia de ambitu (63), 119, 179, 245, 297, 301

Valeria de Sulla dictatore (82), 308
Varia de maiestate (90), 74, 134, 137-8, 256-9, 273-5
Vatinia de provincia Caesaris (59), 84